THE
WORLD
THE
RAILWAYS
MADE

NICHOLAS FAITH
WITH AN INTRODUCTION FROM
CHRISTIAN WOLMAR

THE
WORLD
THE
RAILWAYS
MADE

Nicholas Faith is a distinguished British author and journalist. He was for many years a senior editor on the business pages of *The Sunday Times* and *The Economist* and was a regular contributor to the *Financial Times*.

Christian Wolmar is a journalist, author, politician and Britain's leading railway historian.

CONTENTS

FOREWORD

This book has the best title of any railway book I have encountered. It does precisely what it says on the cover. From start to finish, Nicholas Faith explains in great depth and with rigorous argument how the advent of the railways affected virtually every aspect of the way people lived.

The World the Railways Made is the antithesis of so many other railway books which focus on the railway as if the technology were their most important aspect. Of course the developments and changes in technology are important but the story of the railways is so much more than that, as demonstrated by almost every page of Faith's book.

Let's just set out a few societal changes covered in the book. Faith starts with the big picture, how railways helped to forge and unite nations. Vast nations like the United States, Canada or India, or even relatively smaller ones like Germany, did not exist until they were able to become federal states thanks to the connectivity that the railways afforded. The United States lived up to its name only when it became possible to travel across the continent. Russia managed to retain its hold over the distant lands of Siberia thanks to the construction of the Trans-Siberian railway.

They were, too, a democratising force. Here, though, as with many aspects of this account, the issue is more complex. On the one hand, the railways allowed people to travel and therefore to become more knowledgeable about their own – and indeed other – nations. By helping people form informal groupings which could meet to discuss anything from a common interest in butterflies to ways of changing the world, the railways empowered people. On the other hand, they could also be an instrument of repression. There were several early movements on the railways of troops sent to quell rebellions and restore order – the established order. The railways helped build these nations and glue them together permanently. But by creating the greater ability to travel, the railways also allowed the creation of forces that the authorities would find harder to control. It is inconceivable that the democratic forces which grew in strength throughout the 19th century were not, at least in part, due to the advent of the railways.

So was the growth of capitalism. Railways, as Faith points out, were by far 'the biggest projects undertaken since the time of the Romans'. This involved the gathering together of people on a scale of people which previously would only have been for bellicose purposes. Now it was the peaceful function of building railways across and between nations.

Technology to serve the railways developed far faster than otherwise would have happened. The huge requirement for bridges and tunnels, for example, led to rapid changes in the way these were constructed. Locomotives became more efficient almost every year, and signalling systems more sophisticated. The telegraph was an invention that was symbiotic with the railway and its spread was made far easier by allowing lines of poles to be sited alongside the railway tracks. The demand for steel from the railways stimulated the industry producing it.

There were numerous consequences resulting from the sheer scale of these enterprises. The impact on the wider economy did not end with the completion of the line. Quite the opposite. Railway companies quickly became the largest businesses in their respective countries. To cope with their investment needs, banks had to expand and find new sources of funding. In turn, the railway businesses, spread out over large areas, required new forms of management and even accounting. In short, the railways were the catalyst for the spread of the Industrial Revolution and its inventions.

Their very size meant they were able to change the nature of the cities they served by building big stations to show off their importance and the increasingly wide swathes of tracks sometimes required large scale demolition.

A whole host of industries were made possible by the transport opportunities that were created. Craft factories that may not have been viable previously could now prosper. Perishable goods, like fish, could be transported far further, enabling many more people to purchase them. Farmers were no longer dependent on their local market. Meat and milk could be refrigerated and transferred long distances.

The impact on warfare, too, was profound and long-lasting. The ability of the railways to supply armies meant that battles could be waged over a far wider area and lasted far longer. Wars became bloodier and the railways themselves became key battlegrounds.

All this and much more is covered extensively in this ground-breaking and comprehensive book. Faith shows conclusively that the railways were the most important invention of the 19th century if not, arguably, of any century. The book only lacks a chapter on what the railways did not change. It would have been a short one.

CHRISTIAN WOLMAR
London, September 2014

INTRODUCTION

The modern world began with the coming of the railways. They turned the known universe upside down. They made a greater and more immediate impact than any other mechanical or industrial innovation before or since. They were the first technical invention which affected everyone in any country where they were built – which, effectively, meant most of the world. They were the noisy, smoky, obtrusive heralds of a civilisation destined to be increasingly dominated by industrial innovations.

Because they were the first such intrusion, their effects, combined with the traumas that accompanied their arrival, were inevitably more profound – and more fascinating – than the influence of any subsequent invention. They provided the human frame, the human spirit, the human imagination, with the first and most shattering mechanically-induced shock they had ever experienced or are ever likely to experience.

The shock was both sudden and universal, far more so than that of the steamship, the railways' marine equivalent. Within fifty years after 1830, when the first regular passenger service came into operation, the railways redefined, transformed, expanded the limits of the civilised world. With the railways came the development of modern capitalism, of modern nations, the creation of new regions from the American Mid-West to Siberia, from Lake Victoria to the pampas of Argentina.

Their most obvious effect was on speed. Throughout recorded history, travel on land had never been faster than that of a galloping horse. The railway represented the first quantum leap. All subsequent inventions – the motor-car, the aeroplane – are merely continuing a revolution which began in 1830 with the steam locomotive.

Today, over a hundred and fifty years later, they retain their fascination. Mention them, and you are instantly surrounded by a crowd of 'railway bores', each anxious to contribute their special insight into some aspect, often highly recondite, of the subject. This fascination is not new. Tens of thousands of books have been written about railways, about the men who built them, about their locomotives and rolling stock, the trains themselves, the stations, the history, financing and construction and operation of individual lines, hundreds more on the romance of travel on trains old and new.

Unfortunately, most of these works are not remotely concerned with the effects of railways on society; they totally ignore anything outside the narrow world of the railways themselves. Until now, no-one has systematically turned the subject inside out, has looked out of the carriage window and analysed the world the railways created, the transformations they effected in every aspect of people's lives, economic, social, environmental. And because the emphasis has almost always been on specific railways, there has been no systematic world-wide comparison of the many themes that recur whenever any individual railway is examined.

When dealing with technological advances, authors have also largely ignored the social, economic and political climate which determined their spread and their success. In researching this book I have learnt to make the distinction between railways as passive forces, enabling changes to take place, but depending on other people's initiatives, and the rather fewer instances where they instigated change themselves.

Much of the existing literature, especially books about British railways, is marred by self-indulgence, the result of what the historian John Kellett calls:

> a personal urge to escape and . . . to make 'A Journey into Childhood'. The psychological roots of this . . . subjective form of nostalgia run extremely deep . . . no readers are more insatiable and compulsive than those who are seeking their

own past. The result, inevitably, is a mass of books to be wallowed in rather than read.

The imbalance and inadequacy of existing published treatment is obvious, and will be rectified only as the extraordinary spell which has been cast over the subject is broken, and contributions are made to railway history by writers whose main interests extend beyond the railways themselves and to whom the sights and sounds of the steam locomotive are not so overwhelmingly personal a memory.[1]

By contrast the best historians have always been fully aware of the railways' importance. Eric Hobsbawm grasped how:[2]

> the 100,000 railway locomotives, pulling their almost three quarters of a million carriages and wagons in long trains under banners of smoke . . . were part of the most dramatic innovation of the century, undreamt-of – unlike air travel – a century earlier . . . the railways collectively constituted the most massive effort of public building as yet undertaken by man. They employed more men than any other industrial undertakings. They reached into the centres of great cities, where their triumphal achievements were celebrated in equally triumphal and gigantic railway stations, and into the remotest stretches of the countryside where no other trace of 19th century civilisation penetrated.

A handful of authors, like Jack Simmons, Michael Robbins, Wolfgang Schievelbusch and Kellett himself have broken out of the spell of nostalgia; though not enough of them to provide any comprehensive coverage of most of the themes evoked in this book.

One of my hopes in writing it, therefore, is to encourage more historians to relate the railways' hardware, their lines, their locomotives, to the story of the countries through which they ran and the lives of the people involved. The unevenness of the existing literature has often forced me to bridge the gaps with guesses, all the while aware of my temerity in daring the crossing at all. But the subject is so vast that I can only behave like the railway itself, driving a rough and, I hope, more or less straight, path through the jungle, leaving the great majority of the 'railway country' untouched, awaiting the arrival of a later explorer.

I have attempted to analyse, to present in words and pictures the drama, the excitement, the universality, the sheer novelty of the railroad revolution. It was an upheaval which has all the charm, the inconsistencies, the waste, the tragedies, the dramas, the quirks and comedies, the sheer depth of interest of real life as interpreted by a great novelist – they were a truly Dickensian form of transport. Not surprisingly, imposing any sort of order onto such a narrative was a major task.

To do so I have had to impose a chronological limitation, for the railways' effects echoed for generations after they were first built. Industrially it often took up to half a century for their full impact to be felt, just as it is only now, forty years after the development of the first computer, that they have entered into people's everyday lives.

For reasons of simple manageability I have confined myself to the railways' first, 'primary' impact, and ignored their delayed, 'secondary' impact. Nevertheless the story is bound to sprawl, chronologically as well as geographically. In England the major lines had been built by 1852, but a century later the Chinese were only just embarking on their most ambitious programme of rail building, opening up regions the size of Europe in the subsequent couple of decades. In most cases, though, my story is confined to the railways' heroic age, the period between 1830 and World War I, before the world-wide spread of the internal combustion engine, the railways' great rival.

Even when I had devised the themes into which I hoped to group the railways' effects and the period I would explore, I was left with a major problem of arrangement. Railways have produced some splendid outbursts, magnificent poems and prose passages. Some are familiar, others less so, but I was anxious to include some of even the best-known ones, partly because of their inherent quality but also to present them in their true – and sometimes unexpected – context. Nevertheless they could not be included in the main body of the text without seriously interrupting the flow. Equally, many of the themes I explore are best illustrated with stories or individual pen portraits which, again, are too substantial to be included in the main text. So I have separated these passages, these stories, as separate features at the end of each chapter.

I believe that I have written this book at a particularly appropriate moment. It was in fact sparked off by a series I wrote for *The Economist* in 1985, entitled 'Return Train', which, somewhat to my surprise, established that virtually every country in the civilised world was investing heavily in railways, each in their very different manner. For railways remain, as they always were, sturdily national growths, reflecting the character of the individual countries which they did so much to form during the 19th century. From the outset, nations defined themselves by their railways: first whether they had any, then by their relative efficiency. The test did not die with the onset of the motor-car. The post-war Japanese economic miracle was signalled in 1964 with the opening of the New Tokkaido line, with its trains running regularly and safely at over 100 mph.

Even at the height of the delusion that road transport could

"Westward the course of empire takes its way" – how Currier & Ives saw the railroad in North America, 1868.

replace the railways – an aberration which lasted only a generation – many people still believed in them as essential elements in the life of a community. 'Perhaps the trains will disappear from Maine forever', wrote E. B. White, 'I hope it doesn't happen in my lifetime, for I think one well-conducted institution may still regulate a whole country.'

Paul Theroux, a fellow New Englander, provides a clue to the reasoning behind White's lament. Theroux had noticed how trains accurately reflected the culture of a country: 'The seedy, distressed country has seedy, distressed railway trains; the proud, efficient nation is similarly reflected in its rolling stock, as Japan is. There is hope in India because the trains are considered vastly more important than the monkey wagons some Indians drive.'[3] Railway systems represent a country's capacity to organise its transport – and thus, by implication, many less obvious public functions – in a sane and economic manner, keeping a just balance between the interest of the community, the economy, the state, the workers and the customers, be they individual passengers or major industrial concerns. Newspapers, it is said, represent a nation talking to itself. Railways represent a society, a community, in motion; so it is perfectly reasonable to judge its general health by its success or otherwise in organising this, the most public of communal activities, and the priority the society and its elected representatives attach to its railway system.

The balance is a difficult one. If – as in too many countries – the railways are run by the state as a haphazard addition to the welfare state, then the public interest is liable to be forgotten. The interests of employees – or specially-favoured groups of customers – will be given priority over the overall public weal. In the United States by contrast, railways have been condemned as hopelessly outmoded, resulting in another type of imbalance: the ability of private lobbies – motor manufacturers, road hauliers, road builders – to persuade a gullible public that the immense sums they receive in government assistance are somehow morally and economically superior to the minuscule amount of aid required to keep even a skeleton passenger rail service in operation. Considerations of pollution, safety, land use, even the establishment of a basic economic equation between rival forms of transport, were swept aside.

But the United States is now showing signs of catching up, for everywhere we are witnessing the birth of a new railway age as the limitations and inconveniences of the motor car have become increasingly apparent. Railways are again being treated as they were at the time of their first impact, as essential elements in a truly civilised life.

Railway or Railroad?

Originally the two terms were used indistinguishably. The first edition of the Oxford English Dictionary – compiled towards the end of the 19th century – noted that railroad was 'at one time equally (or more) common in Great Britain and still usual in America.'

The first generation of British rail users mostly called them railroads and, in the way that people retain the usages of their youth, continued to use the term throughout their lives – as John Ruskin did into the 1870s. But the two countries had grown apart long before that date. In 1838 a British periodical noted that 'railway seems now we think the more usual term'.[4] And in an unpublished article on 'American and British Railway English' Kurt Moller traces the distinction back to 'the publicity given to the very first railways, the Stockton & Darlington railway in Britain and the South Carolina railroad in the US ... by 1850 'railway' had disappeared almost completely from American English, with two exceptions: printed matter of the more formal kind, and street railways – and even these soon became "streetcars".'

To my mind the British publicity was reinforced by the needs – conscious or sub-conscious – of railway promoters to emphasise that theirs were not public roads but private ways. In this book I follow what I believe is a sensible way (or road) and use 'railroad' only when referring to North America.

I

THE FIRST IMPACT

I will do something in coming time which will astonish all England. – George Stephenson

Stockton to Darlington 1825:

Stephenson on the sparkling iron road –
Chimney-hatted and frock-coated – drives
His locomotive while the Lydian mode
of Opus 132 may actually be
In the course of making. At twelve miles an hour
The century rushes to futurity,
Whose art will be mankind-destroying power.

— Roy Fuller

In the third and fourth decades of the nineteenth century British engineers triumphantly demonstrated that steam locomotives provided adequate power to propel economic loads of passengers or freight along a railway; that such railways could be built over or through the most rugged terrain; and that the resulting lines could be highly profitable for the promoters and benefit the towns and landowners along their route. By 1840, railways had become the most important symbol of industrial, economic and financial power, the most characteristic vehicle for men's dreams of power, wealth and glory. It was soon equally clear that they would also bear an inescapable load of financial malversation.

The idea of a 'rail-way' was not new. For hundreds of years horse-drawn carts had run on tracked ways to carry coal from the face to the pithead and then to the nearest navigable waters.

George Stephenson.

George Stephenson, not a great engineer, but a great visionary.

In 1803, in the face of fierce hostility from the manufacturers of low-pressure steam engines, a high-pressure steam locomotive designed by Richard Trevithick had hauled a ten-ton load along a 'rail-way' near a Cornish tin-mine.

Yet the idea of steam locomotion is indissolubly associated with the name of George Stephenson. His triumph, like that of Winston Churchill over a century later, was based on his character, on an obstinate determination, on fixity of purpose, combined with the luck of being the right man in the right place at the right time. Like Churchill, Stephenson is honoured more in retrospect than during a long career largely spent battling the established order. 'Almost to a man', wrote his biographer L. T. C. Rolt, 'his fellow-engineers dismissed him as an unprincipled and incompetent schemer, but all their shafts broke against the armour of that stubborn determination to succeed which was to triumph over every obstacle, including his own weaknesses.'[1] These included an almost pathological jealousy of other engineers, total autocracy, and a profound managerial incompetence.

The applause is not undeserved. In John Rowland's words,[2] he 'did not originate the steam locomotive, he did not invent a new type of machine; but he used other people's inventions and improved them so completely as to make them peculiarly his own'. Stephenson was lucky: during the first quarter of the nineteenth century the North-East of England, where he first found fame as the leading expert on mining engines, contained a concentration of mines, of rail-ways – and thus of capital – denied to Trevithick in distant Cornwall. Stephenson had lived almost all his life on a 'tramway line' from a mine to navigable water, so he could also draw on the experience of dozens of colleagues, all accustomed to the manufacture and maintenance of steam-engines reliable enough for men's lives to depend on the pumps they powered. So he was backed by both the money and skills required to assemble the package – engine, wheels, track – required to make steam locomotion an economic proposition.

His experiments covered the ten years after the Battle of Waterloo, a period when the price of fodder – and thus of horse-power – was rising rapidly. The resulting replacement of natural fodder with industrial coal was a major step in freeing mankind from dependence on nature. But the railway also improved the very nature of movement. In his *Observations on a General Iron Rail-Way*, Thomas Gray emphasised how 'no animal strength will be able to give that uniform and regular acceleration to our commercial intercourse which may be accomplished by railway'. Without the efforts of Gray and other propagandists the railway promoters could never have mobilised the capital and labour required, and the public would never have accepted the massive upheavals involved in building railways on a large scale.

The first crucial sign that the steam locomotive running on an iron way was the transport medium of the future came in 1818, when Thomas Telford, greatest of canal engineers, pronounced himself in favour of an iron way rather than a canal for a new route between a mine and a river. That same year George Overton, builder of the tramways used by Trevithick, wrote that: 'Railways are now generally adopted and the cutting of canals nearly discontinued.'

Overton's report, and Stephenson's insistence on steam traction, led to the construction of the Stockton & Darlington Railway, financed by local Quaker capital, the first railway line designed from the outset to employ steam locomotives as well as the horses used exclusively on earlier railways. The S & D – 'the Quakers' Line' – opened in 1825 – the same year that Beethoven was writing his last quartets. It used the 15-ft long, malleable iron rails invented by a local engineer the previous year which immediately replaced the existing and inadequate wrought-iron

The very first railway linking Darlington with the nearest waterway at Stockton, 1825.

rails. Stephenson had already proved that locomotives with flanged wheels could run on edged rails, a great improvement in efficiency. By that time it was understood, as a French author put it in 1821, that: 'The railroad and its carriages [should] be considered as one machine.'

The Stockton & Darlington, the world's first public railway, did not involve much technical innovation. Appropriately it was the sun which provided the fire for the first run of 'Locomotion', the Stockton & Darlington's first locomotive. In the words of an old labourer, that day: 'Lantern and candle was to no use so No 1 fire was put to her on line by the pour of the sun.' Thus, accidentally, through impatience rather than design, a direct link was established between the fire in heaven and a man-made flame which was to travel round the globe.

From its opening in 1825 the Stockton & Darlington was a triumphant success. Unexpectedly, it carried not only passengers by their thousands, but also coal by the hundreds of thousands of tons. A local grandee, Mr Lambton, had tried to sabotage the prospects of the line as a freight railway by ensuring that coal destined to be sent onwards by sea would pay only the apparently ruinously low railway freight rate of one shilling and twopence per ton per mile, an eighth of the rate to be charged if the coal were to be used locally. Yet, far from ruining the S & D, the low rate enabled the new means of transport to show its economic potential. It was soon carrying half a million tons of coal annually, fifty times the anticipated figure.

The S & D also gave birth to Middlesbrough, the first town which owed its very existence to the railway. Like so many of its future brethren it grew up where a busy railway line reached navigable water. According to Samuel Smiles:[3] 'When the railway was opened in 1825 the site of the future metropolis of Cleveland was occupied by one solitary farmhouse and its outbuildings. All round was pasture-land or mud-banks; scarcely another house was within sight.' The local municipality wouldn't help, so four years after the S & D was opened 'Mr Edward Pease . . . joined by a few of his Quaker friends, bought about 500 or 600 acres of land, five miles lower down the river

– the site of the modern Middles-brough – for the purpose of there forming a new seaport for the shipment of coals brought to the Tees by the railway. The line was accordingly extended thither; docks were excavated; a town sprang up; churches, chapels and schools were built, with a custom-house, mechanics' institute, banks, shipbuilding yards, and iron-factories. By Smiles's time, a couple of decades later, the port of Middles-brough had a population of 20,000, and was one of the busiest ports in the North East of England.'[4]

While the Stockton & Darlington was being built William James, the true 'Father of the Railways'*, had surveyed an ambitious national rail network to be worked by steam engines. In doing so he freed railways from their previous automatic connection with mining. James was almost a second father to young Robert Stephenson, who clearly found his real father, George, such an unbearable autocrat that he spent some years seeking his fortune in the mines of Latin America.

James's dreams had one major practical result: they awoke the merchants of Liverpool and Manchester to the potential the railway offered to break the monopoly of transport between the two towns held for fifty years by the Bridgewater Canal Company. As recounted in the note about him at the end of this chapter James got into financial difficulties and the scheme was transformed into a practical project by a local man, Joseph Saunders, who called in George Stephenson. In the absence abroad of his son, the father made virtually no progress in improving his locomotives. His limitations were further exposed during Parliamentary hearings over the vague and unsatisfactory survey he had conducted for the projected line.

However, after the early setbacks he demonstrated the confidence and the innovatory common-sense required of all railway and locomotive builders, when he showed how to tackle Chat Moss, the much-dreaded marsh between the two cities. Ortho-dox drainage ditches simply filled with water, but George Ste-phenson triumphantly showed that railways would be able to overcome natural obstacles previously considered to be impass-

* See page 32.

Robert Stevenson. A greater engineer than his father.

able. In L. T. C. Rolt's words: 'Stephenson's plan of floating his railway embankment across the Moss on a raft of brushwood and heather was put into operation. A vast tonnage of spoil was tipped only to be swallowed up, but Stephenson never lost heart and gradually a firm causeway began to stretch out into the Moss to confound the sceptics.'

It was Robert Stephenson who finally ensured that the mobile steam engine would triumph over its stationary equivalent, which, it was generally assumed at the time, would be required if any

14

substantial load were to be hauled up any kind of gradient. Trevithick had already shown that the power of a locomotive could be greatly increased by diverting the exhaust steam into a specially narrowed chimney. In the late 1820s both Henry Booth, the treasurer of the Liverpool & Manchester, and the French engineer Marc Séguin, suggested that the two tubes in the boiler be replaced with a host of smaller ones, thus 'drawing hot gases from a separate fire box and so greatly increasing the heating surface . . . at last they had solved the steam-raising problem and ensured that the locomotive would be capable of a sustained power output over long distances.' But it was Robert who put these ideas into practice with a quick succession of improved engines.

As a result of the partnership between father and son the modern world was conceived on 8th October, 1829, during the trials held at Rainhill to decide how the trains on the Liverpool & Manchester would be powered. Robert Stephenson's *Rocket* attained a steady 29 mph on his later runs, proving that his design was far more reliable than the competing locomotives.

These came from two sources: other engines from Northumbria and, also, and more fundamentally, entries from London. In the capital a whole group of manufacturers had developed steam-powered locomotives designed to haul economic loads on ordinary roads, and these were the clear favourites before the Rainhill trials. The Stephensons' triumph at Rainhill, therefore, was not only personal: it also deprived roads of their hopes of carrying mechanically-propelled vehicles for three quarters of a century.

In the year between the trials and the opening of the railway itself Stephenson garnered a great deal of mostly favourable publicity by driving specially-favoured visitors along the completed sections of the line. The ecstatic reactions of the actress Fanny Kemble quoted below* were not necessarily typical. The gossip and man-about-town, Thomas Creevey, was scared stiff. At twenty miles an hour, 'the quickest motion is to me frightful; it is really flying and it is impossible to divest yourself of the notion of instant death to all upon the least accident

* See page 37.

happening. It gave me a headache which has not left me yet.' But even he had to admit that at 23 mph they were travelling 'with the same ease as to motion or absence of friction as the other reduced pace' – the passengers were comparing travel in the four-wheeled unsprung carts used as railway carriages with even rattlier horse-drawn coaches. Moreover he – and the equally frightened Lord Sefton – were in the minority. 'He and I seem more struck with apprehension than the others.'

On 15th September, 1830, the Liverpool & Manchester Railway was officially opened. After what today would be termed amazing media hype, and amid scenes which combined tragedy and farce in equal proportions, eight special trains carried six hundred important guests between the two cities. These included the Tory Prime Minister, the much-hated Duke of Wellington, and the most out-spoken Tory reformer, William Huskisson, MP for Liverpool and friend of the city's merchants, victim that day of the world's first and most-publicised railway accident, which also nearly cost the life of the Austrian ambassador, Prince Esterhazy.

(The Duke had to be protected from the mobs which swarmed all over the tracks. Uncharacteristically this war hero was so scared that it took considerable persuasion to get him to complete the journey to Manchester. The whole episode, including Huskisson's death, was so traumatic that he could not be tempted onto another train for thirteen years.)

Less publicly, Rainhill had also introduced the idea of technological obsolescence. The railways replaced canals built in the previous half-century, and the post-coaches running over macadamised road surfaces introduced in the previous two decades. Yet these had represented the biggest advance in road transport since the Romans left Britain fourteen centuries earlier. Travelling time between major British cities had halved between 1770 and 1830.

But the locomotives themselves became obsolescent in a matter of months, not decades. By the end of 1830 *Rocket* had been replaced by *Northumbrian*, another of Robert Stephenson's designs. 'In all essential particulars,' in L. T. C. Rolt's words, 'the

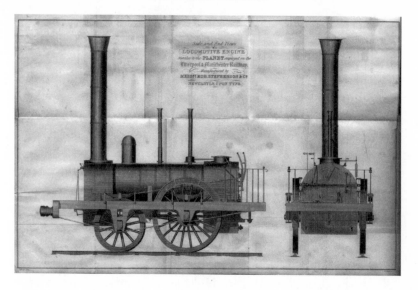

Side and end views of a locomotive engine similar to the Planet, one of the Stephensons' triumphant designs.

boiler of the *Northumbrian* was the same as that fitted to every orthodox locomotive from that day to this.' Within a few years the immortal *Rocket* had been relegated to the sidings. But it had served its purpose. It had seen off the opposition and proved that a mobile steam locomotive could replace horses, fixed engines and steam-powered road carriages.

The immediate success of the Liverpool & Manchester sent shock waves, first throughout Britain, and then, with some delay, round the world. By 1833 a *Railway Companion* describing an excursion along the line could claim that 'already locomotive power is rapidly superseding every other species of conveyance throughout the civilised world.'

Within fifteen years lines had been built between London and most of Britain's major cities, although London's first line (and the first urban railway in the world) from London Bridge to Greenwich, was completed only in 1838, its arches soaring high over the slums and market gardens along the way. Robert Stephenson's line between London and Birmingham was even more significant, and its parliamentary passage a crucial battle between the railway and the canal interests. It was not only the first link between the capital and a major provincial city (and thus, albeit indirectly, between the capital, Liverpool and Manchester), but it also ran parallel – and often very close to – the country's foremost man-made waterway, the Grand Junction Canal, with its twenty-six speedy daily flyboats for urgent goods, and Watling Street, with its sixteen coaches daily between the two towns. With the London & Birmingham the newly almighty – private – railway interest had dealt a deadly blow to the public, communal thoroughfares, canal and road, where the small man could compete on equal terms with major carriers.

However, no-one yet believed that canals had had their day; indeed more miles of canals than railways were built between 1830 and 1840. John Francis[5] quoted one wiseacre that, 'long before the London & Birmingham is ready, such are the improvements now making in canals, that not only may the charge be expected to be many times less than the railway, but the time will be considerably saved.'

By contrast post-coaches, and turnpike traffic in general, were seen as obviously doomed. The Greenwich line, a mere four miles long, saved fifty minutes over the turnpike and showed how even a short line could prosper. The London to Brighton line, opened in 1841, proved that the railway could supersede even the most efficient stage coach service. The coaches to Brighton ran every hour, covering the 90 km to London in under five hours, yet within a couple of years they were mere relics of a bygone age.

With the post-coaches went the coaching inns, the ostlers, and the carters, some of them substantial businesses. Only a few coaching entrepreneurs managed to switch businesses, most famously William James Chaplin, who sold his firm, and invested the proceeds in the London & Southampton railway, of which he became chairman.

By the time the London & Birmingham opened in 1839 the public was so used to railways that there were great complaints when passengers were ferried by coach at the previously respectable speed of eleven miles an hour over a stretch of line which could not be completed for several months because of the difficulty in building the Kilsby tunnel. The public's astonishingly speedy acceptance of this fearsome new form of transport was largely due to its excellent safety record. Only two of the five million or so passengers carried by the Liverpool & Manchester in its first decade of operation lost their lives. 'During the same period,' noted Samuel Smiles, 'the loss of life by the upsetting of stage-coaches had been immensely greater in proportion.'

Many less exalted passengers obviously shared the feelings of Charles Greville, the Clerk to the Privy Council. In 1837 he decided, on an impulse, to 'run down' to see the Earl of Derby by train. He was delighted. 'The first sensation,' he wrote, 'is a slight degree of nervousness and a feeling of being run away with, but a sense of security soon supervenes . . . it entirely renders all other travelling irksome and tedious by comparison.' The next year he records how, as a matter of course, he took the train to Slough and then walked to Windsor Castle when he was summoned there by Queen Victoria.

The Liverpool & Manchester immediately bred a new world of hustling at a previously unimaginable pace. According to Francis, 'Men talk of "getting up the steam", of "railway speed" and reckon distances by hours and minutes. The press never got tired of one particular story, of a gentleman who left Manchester in the morning, went thence to Liverpool, purchased and took back with him one hundred and fifty tons of cotton, and having sold it, returned to Liverpool on a similar errand with similar success.'

At a more humble level Manchester weavers found they could use the railway to reduce the time they spent carrying their loads to their customers. Three of them would give their packages to one of their number. But, in Francis's words, 'railway managers are political economists', and for a time they allowed each passenger to carry only a single pack. The weavers retorted by boycotting the line, and won their point – the first recorded instance of a populist revolt against excessive charges or unreasonable regulations imposed by the almighty, monopolistic, railway.

Traditional railway histories have made much of the opposition to railways mounted by the landowning aristocracy.

Its members undeniably made life a misery for the promoters, especially when House of Lords committees' examined railway bills. A few objected on principle, but most were practical men. They did not want their hunting and shooting interfered with or their views spoiled; they were appalled at the behaviour of the promoters and their surveyors. (The most often-quoted, the Lincolnshire MP Colonel Sibthorp, was clearly regarded as something of an eccentric even at the time.)

The need to avoid the coverts where foxes lurked and game bred led to a number of diversions. However, the railway people added to their own problems by trampling over territory sacred to squire and parson since time immemorial. In an anonymous volume of 'Railroad Eclogues' published in 1846 the Squire moans about:

> These railway bores, who, papers in each hand,
> Request permission to cut up our land –
> Request permission! I should rather say
> Who, leave unasked, invade our lands, survey
> temples and trespass . . .
> . . . No dies non, no Sabbath to projectors.
> 'Sir we're the crooked-railroad deputation,
> And merely want your greenhouse for a station.'

At which point the parson chimes in with his complaint:

> A grand connecting line will tunnel under
> My rectory, and cut my glebe asunder.
> The church they don't intend to touch at present.

But the landowners were greedy, and soon found that opposition could be astonishingly profitable. Cash, and lots of it, soon placated them. 'By paying out £750,000 for land originally valued at £250,000', wrote L. T. C. Rolt, 'the most strenuous objectors were silenced.'

In his splendid novel *Mr Facey Romford's Hounds*, R. S. Surtees recounts how a certain Mr Mellowfield 'who had retired from the troubles of fish-curing to enjoy his filberts and his madeira in the evening of life was so shocked at the invasion of his privacy by the arrival of a railway that "nothing but a strong application of golden ointment could have got over the difficulty. Ten thousand pounds for two thousand pounds" of property mollified him.'

The landowners' profits continued after they had held the promoters up to ransom. Francis noted that 'Some agriculturalists, who had vehemently declared it would ruin their property, discovered that property was increased in value and withdrew from the contest; and some landowners, who had combatted it because it was to ruin the country, found that houses grew in the place of corn, and that ground rents more than compensated for grain.'

At first, the upper classes kept their distance by travelling in their own carriages. 'To enable private carriages to travel along the railway,' wrote A Tourist,* flat forms are provided, upon which the carriage is raised and its wheels firmly secured upon the platforms by moveable grooves.' But these were uncomfortable and inconvenient and by the end of the decade most of their owners travelled like everyone else. By 1840 the first special royal coach had been built for the Dowager Queen Adelaide. Prince Albert, apostle of modernity, was naturally an early enthusiast, and soon converted his wife. By 1842 Queen Victoria noted how she had come to London 'by the railroad from Windsor, in half an hour, free from the dust and crowd and heat, and I am quite charmed with it'.

In the 1830s two great engineers improved on the Stephensons' ideas. George's former pupil, Joseph Locke, refused to accept that lines had to be relatively level because of the low power of existing engines, arguing that locomotive power would increase sufficiently for gradients to be relatively steep. As a result Locke surveyed and built a much shorter though steeper alternative to the lengthy coastal route proposed by the Stephensons for the West Coast route to Scotland.

The second challenge was mounted by the greatest of all Victorian engineers, Isambard Kingdom Brunel, with his 7-foot

---

* Quoted by Francis, op. cit.

Isambard Kingdom Brunel: greatest genius of rail's early years

gauge line[*] to Bristol and the west. Thanks to the superb, level track he laid down, his broad-gauge system set incredible standards of speed. By the mid-1840s his trains were averaging over forty miles an hour to Bristol (a speed which only doubled in the subsequent century), averaging over fifty mph from Bristol to Taunton on their way to Exeter. By the mid-1840s Brunel's trains were reaching this town, over two hundred miles from London, in a mere five hours. Almost incidentally, Brunel established the first town specifically developed to cater for

[*] For a full discussion of gauges see 'The Battle of the Gauges', p. 34.

railways at Swindon, then merely a little village at the pointwhere engines were changed.

Brunel's swaggering success put the proponents of the normal 'narrow-gauge' on their mettle. The competition between the two gauges ensured that by the end of the 1840s most of the major towns in the country were linked by trains averaging over thirty miles an hour, for the potential of the steam locomotive was exploited more quickly and more effectively than that of the internal combustion engine was to be seventy-five years later.

The pressures of the 1830s dealt a final blow to the idea of the 'Renaissance engineer', able to design an engine or a railway line at will. Although Robert Stephenson's original contribution had been as a mechanical engineer, in the 1830s and 1840s he was forced to concentrate on his work as a civil engineer, while Brunel's interference in the design of the locomotives he required was often rather unhappy. Their successors rarely combined civil and mechanical engineering work.

Brunel was also the first of the many visionaries who perceived a railway line as merely one link in an intercontinental transport chain (see Chapter VI). To him the railway to Bristol was merely one step on the route across the Atlantic, and his magnificent steamship, the *Great Western*, forced Edward Cunard and the 'Liverpool Interest' to develop steamships which revolutionised travel on the North Atlantic within a few years.

The level track demanded by Robert Stephenson for the London to Birmingham line, and the broad swathe cut through the countryside by the Great Western, involved earthworks of a size not required even by the most ambitious canals. Stephenson demanded cuttings of previously unimaginable length and depth, and both he and Brunel required longer tunnels than had ever been dug before, ideas which naturally produced the usual buzz of scepticism. They were more expensive and more difficult to dig than anticipated, but proved practicable and profitable. The engineers, however, soon found that it was useless to rely on a horde of small sub-contractors for such vast projects. They gave contracts to single men, like Thomas Brassey and Samuel Morton Peto, the models for the contractors who erupted over the face of the globe in the succeeding decades.

The spread of the railways forced towns to take attitudes towards the intruder. Liverpool was positive, and Liverpool Council was prepared to invest in the tunnel costing well over £100,000 from Edgehill to Lime Street in the centre of the city. As a result Liverpool became by far the biggest English city with a single central station. By contrast Manchester had three disconnected termini. So, originally, did Birmingham, where the first terminus of the first major line linking a capital with a major provincial city was on the edge of the urban area. The burghers of another historic city, York, were so keen that, in Gordon Biddle's words, they 'positively welcomed one inside the medieval walls that required an arch cutting through the fabric . . . the station covered the known sites of three Roman baths'.[6]

The stations themselves quickly assumed their permanent character, as can be seen from Crown Street, Liverpool, the first purpose-built passenger station in the world. Its architect remains unknown, though he was certainly greatly influenced by George Stephenson. It was astonishingly modern. In Carroll Meeks' words[7] it:

> embodied the basic features of the modern station in embryo. The passenger preparing to depart from Liverpool arrived by carriage or omnibus at a vehicle court – foreshadowing the covered driveways of later stations – which was separated from the street traffic by a wall. On entering the building he found himself in a room which combined the function of ticket selling and waiting, as in the great concourse of today's terminals. From the waiting-room he passed onto the platform and into his carriage under the cover of a train-shed, the degree of protection was greater than it is in many recent stations.

During the 1830s architects used a variety of styles to glorify the new form of transport. The most astonishing was at Euston, where in the mid-1840s Philip Hardwicke built a magnificent, classical Great Hall. A grand staircase led to the equally grand offices for the Directors of the London & North Western Railway, the largest railway company – and thus the biggest enterprise – in the land, and the prototype of the arrogant, self-sufficient, lordly railway company.

The magnificence of Euston was echoed at the other end of the line, where Birmingham's first station boasted an Ionic portico, the Midlands' equivalent of the triumphal arch at Euston. And both Euston and Birmingham boasted another convenience, a station hotel. On the 18th September 1838 *The Times* reported that 'part of the magnificent Station house in Birmingham has recently been licensed as an hotel . . . so that passengers, if they think proper, may be accommodated with every good thing without leaving the company's premises'.

These schemes required more capital more quickly than any previous form of capital investment. Fortunately for the promoters, no-one really believed that a railway could be unprofitable. In the dry words of a modern economic historian,[8] 'Private capital was forthcoming for railway investment in the later 1830s and early 1840s only because the eventual lowness of the private rate of return on some projects was not anticipated.'

Francis, looking back fifteen years later, saw the 1830s as a period of relative innocence. 'The established lines were conducted by men who could not have done a mean action had they tried, and would not have done if they could. The monied public felt this, and purchased freely where they trusted fully.' Nevertheless even this Golden Age of Innocence was full of dubious schemes, each promoted in a separate Parliamentary Bill which provided opportunities for much debate and more bribery.

The sums involved were gigantic: Thomas Brassey built sixty miles of difficult line in Northern Italy for the same sum – £430,000 – as it cost to put through the Bill for a single English railway, the Lancs & Yorks. Even worse, in John Francis's words, 'scarcely was it recognised as an object of legitimate investment than it became a subject of illegitimate speculation.'

The success of the 'railway interest' provoked the complaint that 'in our country, alone, has the right of possession in perpetuity been granted by the government'.[9] From the beginning their profits attracted envy, naturally expressed in demands for government control. This was somewhat unfair. As John Francis put it, 'It was said, and with much justice, that railways were as beneficial as canals, but that, though the latter averaged 33 per cent, there had been no restriction on their dividends, no claim on their profits.'

By the early 1840s politicians were already heavily involved. Lord Dalhousie, who carried his enthusiasm for railways – and for government control over them – to India when he became Governor-General, went so far as to suggest that the government should be given the power to nationalise the railways if their profits had been found excessive over a ten-year period. Before a railway could be built a board should examine the promoters' capacities and their forecasts of costs, revenue and profits. In the event these ideas were swept away. A York-born promoter, George Hudson, did a private deal with William Gladstone to water down the original, more restrictive, proposals for controlling the railways.

Francis recognised that 'The spirit of unreasoning optimism was in the air; the possibilities and advantages which the country was to attain with liberal railway communication were deemed to be boundless.' The railway spirit was epitomised by Hudson, the very archetype of the vulgar, swaggering adventurer bred world-wide by the railways. In the words of his biographer[10] 'his energies flowed into four distinct channels: first, railway, dock and other industrial enterprises; secondly, banking and finance; thirdly, the acquisition and management of landed property; lastly, politics local and national' – he naturally represented his native York in Parliament. But, inevitably in a railway-mad age, railways came first.

At the height of his powers he controlled 'a vast network of enterprises such as no one man before his time had dared to try and combine'. To the majority who fawned on him 'he was as a mountebank upon a platform at a fair – one who could draw money from their pockets by tricks which kept them perpetually gaping'. He had the nerve and the bulldozing drive to push through the bills, the amalgamations, required. His basic aim, as he told a House of Commons committee in 1844, was a controlled monopoly through a mixture of amalgamations, leases and purchases. To achieve his aim he perfected most of the fraudulent devices employed by his successors the world over. He manipulated the stocks of the many companies in which he was interested; sold land from his own estate to his own railways; bought rails and other equipment cheap and sold it dear to his railways, and withheld the money he owed to landowners and contractors.

Yet, at the height of his fame, he was, almost literally, worshipped; his grand mansion in Kensington was besieged by the great and good, his every move an object of wonder. In such an atmosphere it was not surprising that earlier 'canal manias' were soon eclipsed by the railway boom which erupted in 1845. The press whipped up the excitement, and the hype was often memorable. The line from London to Exeter was proposed partly because 'it was nearly the road adopted by the Romans'. Were not 'railways the emblems of internal confidence and prosperity . . . the great levellers, bringing the producer and consumer into immediate contact . . . by railways the whole country may be, and will be, under the blessing of divine providence, cultivated as a garden.'[11]

In 1845 Parliament passed 225 Railway Bills, with a further 270 in the following session, providing for 4,540 miles of track, costing nearly £100 million. Members were not exactly impartial. In 1845, a total of 157 had their names on the registers of new railway companies – one company boasted of being able to command a hundred votes in the House of Commons alone. Titled personages were naturally much sought after by promoters; one man was a director in twenty-three railway companies, a second in twenty-two.

The mania was universal. In a Yorkshire vicarage Emily and Anne Brontë ignored the warning of their sister Charlotte and invested their meagre savings in the Yorkshire & Midland railway. In London, 'Men were pointed out in the streets who had made their tens of thousands. [Sober citizens] saw the whole world railway mad . . . they entered the whorlpool and were carried away by the vortex . . . their infant daughters were large subscribers; their youthful sons were down for thousands. Like drunken men they lost their caution and gave their signatures for everything that was offered.'[12] Even Charles Greville dabbled, although he had been warned by the Governor of the Bank of England who 'never remembered in all his experience anything like the present speculation . . . and that there could not fail to be a fearful reaction.'

Inevitably the pot boiled over; but while the crash of 1847 inflicted severe losses on thousands of investors and permanently cooled the ardour of the British investing classes towards their native railway system, it did not inflict anything like the damage caused by bigger Victorian crashes. Although at the time the panic was, naturally, blamed on the railway promoters, Lewin sensibly blames the general economic situation: the failure of the Irish potato crop and the famine which followed; the repeal of the Corn Laws and the subsequent sharp reduction in the price of grain; and a consequent severe shortage of spare capital for investment.

The greatest of all promoters survived the mania. Hudson's downfall came two years after the general crash, sparked off by a crisis in the affairs of the Eastern Counties railway. The chairman of the investigating committee was a Quaker, which added moral and linguistic force to his questions – 'Didst thou, after the accountant had made up the yearly accounts, alter any of the figures? . . . wilt thou give the committee an answer, yea or nay?'. Hudson fell because, although he controlled 1,450 out of the 5,000 miles of railway in Britain, they never formed a natural system, and his doom was inevitable once his enemies had managed to promote a direct line from London to York, thus greatly reducing the value of the roundabout routes he controlled between the two cities.

Not even the crash and Hudson's fall deterred the promoters for long, however, and by the end of the century Britain was saddled with an unnecessarily complex, over-competitive railway system with innumerable, inevitably uncommercial branch lines. Every major system strove to squeeze every possible drop of traffic from its hinterland. The sequence of events left the British public ambivalent: pride in the world's first railway system combined with a sceptical, if not downright hostile attitude

28

The Stourbridge Lion, the first imported locomotive on American soil, 1829

towards railway promoters and railway directors. But by that time they had infected the rest of the world. Thomas Gray's 'Observations on a General Iron Way', translated into French and German, had spread the railway gospel, notably into Germany and Belgium, where George Stephenson was treated as a heroic figure. But then he had always been confident that, as he told a devout Methodist friend 'I will send the locomotive as the great missionary over the world'.

*

The Americans had started early. In 1827 a few farsighted citizens of Baltimore visited Britain and on their return promoted the grandiosely-named Baltimore & Ohio Railroad, the city's attempt to counter the dominance of New York – a dominance reinforced by the triumphal opening two years earlier of the Erie Canal to the Great Lakes. The Baltimoreans went about their work in style.

'Best Friend'. The first all-American locomotive, built in 1831.

In 1827 the first spadeful of earth was dug (naturally on 4th July) by Charles Carroll, the last surviving signatory of the Declaration of Independence, while the incumbent President, John Quincy Adams, was inaugurating work on a nearby canal.

The same impetus – the desire by a seaport to capture the trade of a hinterland at a convenient point on a river – was behind America's second real railroad, between Charleston and Hamburg on the Savannah River. Throughout the 1830s numerous lines in Pennsylvania repeated the pattern set by the Stockton & Darlington, joining coal fields and navigable waters. But 'even these earliest railroads were new and largely independent agents of transportation, sturdy rivals of the older canals', noted George Rogers Taylor.[13] Over 3,300 miles of railways were built during the decade (in which 2,000 miles of canals were constructed) so that by 1840 the Americans had built over half the railways in the world. But in so enormous a country even the rapidly-growing web of rails in New York and New England made far less of an impact than a comparable mileage in Britain.

Moreover, the Americans gained their independence from British engineering influence only slowly. A dozen American engineers visited Britain between 1825 and 1840. The resulting influence (particularly of the solid construction on the Liverpool & Manchester) was felt on the whole 'technological package', including the rails and the locomotives, especially in the south and in New England.

The story in Continental Europe was rather different, if only because no other country was as industrially well-equipped as Britain to grasp the railways' potential. The French, typically, started by theorising.* Most of their early railways were designed to be used by horses, or stationary engines, and during the 1830s the French devoted more of their energies to discussing the long-term results of railways than to planning, let alone building them.

Frederic Barthlony, chairman of the Orleans company, hailed railways as comparable in importance to printing and the discovery of America, a herald of an age of universal peace. An anonymous deputy greeted them as a means of binding together the peoples of France even more tightly, though Proudhon the Socialist sourly proposed that the French improve the lot of their own people before embarking on the construction of railways. Railways were also denounced as an example of the irrational times. Nevertheless some lines were built, notably from Paris to Saint Germain and Versailles, both under the aegis of the Pereire brothers, Saint-Simonians,† for whom railways were, in a sense, the crucial instrument of their creed.

During the 1830s and 1840s lines, generally short and unconnected, were built in most European countries, in Prussia, in other German states, in Russia, Holland, Denmark and Austria. Outside Europe a short line was opened in Cuba, then a Spanish colony, to transport sugar, before there were any lines in the mother country. But only the Belgians seized on the new form of transport to bind a country together in a systematic fashion, a lead which resulted in the first international railway, from Cologne through Brussels to Antwerp, which opened in 1843.

Globally, the railways' age of glory started in 1840, when there were a mere 5,500 miles in operation. By 1880 there were over 220,000 throughout the world. The Europeans, in particular, had overtaken the British in mileage, and, often, in techniques as

---

* In the words of Baron de Jouvenel: '*Le génie de notre nation a cela de particulier qu'il faut toujours un mouvement intellectuel pour préparer une réforme, même de l'ordre industriel et commercial.*' ('The genius of our people has the special characteristic that it requires an intellectual movement to prepare a reform, even in the commercial or industrial sphere'.) Quoted by H. Peyret, *Les Chemins de fer en France et dans le monde.*

† Followers of Claude Henri de Saint-Simon, whose creed was the paramountcy of useful, productive labour, of which railways were the supreme servant. See section on the Pereires on page 96.

well. By 1880 not only Jules Verne's fictional hero, Phileas Fogg, but also a real-life journalist, Nelly Bly, could use the world's vastly expanded railway network to go round the world in less than three months. As Eric Hobsbawm points out,[14], without railways the journey would have taken Phileas Fogg or Nelly Bly nearly four times eighty days.

The world's rail mileage doubled again in the last two decades of the century, partly because of explosive growth in Russia, Latin America, Africa and Australia, which had had a mere 2,500 miles of line between them, less than a twentieth of the world total, as late as 1860. But even in Europe as many miles were built between 1880 and 1913 as in the preceding thirty years. France, Germany, Sweden Switzerland and the Netherlands all more or less doubled their networks in the thirty years before World War I – although these were mainly branch and feeder lines, which proved uneconomic with the arrival of the internal combustion engine.

By the 1880s the railway was no longer the wonder of the age. Electric power – in the form of motors, telephones, lighting – was replacing steam as the miracle worker. It is not surprising, therefore, that most of the examples in this book inevitably come from the period between 1840 and 1890 when the railways ruled unchallenged as the great, general, exemplar of progress.

William James – the Forgotten Pioneer

It was William James[15] not George Stephenson, who first projected the idea of a national network of railways to replace the canals, and he was well placed to carry his ideas through to reality. Indeed, it was only a financial crisis in the early 1820s, which ruined him, that prevented him reaping the reward of his efforts.

He was a distinguished land agent with so lucrative a business that he was a multi-millionaire by today's standards by the middle of the second decade of the century. He devised improved means of transport for the coal produced under his employers' lands, projecting new turnpike roads and new canals to carry coals from Staffordshire to Birmingham. These plans came to naught, so he spent the early 1820s planning a railway system, centred on Birmingham, running from Wolverhampton to London via Oxford (avoiding the expensive tunnels, cuttings and embankments required by the alternative route eventually followed) and to Liverpool (the future Grand Junction railway). He also sketched a dozen other lines, notably from London to Brighton, Portsmouth and Chatham, all realised in the 1830s and 1840s.

More immediately he grasped the need for a railway connecting Liverpool with Manchester and other cotton towns to compete with the inordinately expensive Bridgewater Canal. In 1821 he formed a company to build the line, intended from the beginning to be powered by steam locomotives. 'He did not discover the locomotive,' as Samuel Smiles put it, 'he did what was next best to it, he discovered George Stephenson.' At the time it was James, rather than the Quakers promoting the Stockton & Darlington, who appeared best-placed to exploit the locomotives Stephenson was producing.

James carried out a thorough survey of the line, but was caught short of cash in the financial crisis of the early 1820s and crashed – he was so important a figure that his case occupied the Bankruptcy Commissioners for twenty years and the lawyers' fees amounted to hundreds of thousands of pounds in modern money. The first vulture to profit from his misfortunes was Joseph Saunders, a local man to whom James had brought his ideas, who underwrote the survey of the line and subsequently became its managing director. He forced James to hand over control, assuring him that 'your name shall be prominent in the proceedings . . . you may rely on my zeal for you in every point connected with your reputation . . . the appointment of George Stephenson will, under the circumstances, be agreeable to you.'

James had to agree. He was pushed aside and died, a broken man, in 1837. But he was not forgotten. Maunder's *Biographical Treasury* noted that James: 'may be in truth regarded as the father of the railway system', and nine years after his death all the country's leading engineers, with the single exception of

George Stephenson, formed a committee to compensate James's children for the fact that their father's 'successful exertions and great pecuniary sacrifices' had deprived his family of all patrimony. The letter spelt out the 'acknowledged fact that, to their father's labours, the public are indebted for the establishment of the present railroad system'.

George Stephenson could not bear the implication that he was not the sole creator of the railway – especially as he was in the best position to know the truth. He was furious, and forced his son to withdraw his signature from the letter.

The Battle of the Gauges

For centuries, some say since the Romans, mining engineers had been accustomed to rail-ways laid to a gauge of about 4' 8½" – 1,435 mm. George Stephenson followed the tradition – using a 4' 8" gauge for the Stockton & Darlington and, for some unknown reason, added an extra half-inch when he came to construct the Liverpool to Manchester. The Stephensons, partly accidentally, institutionalised the gauge, because the locomotives built in their Newcastle factory – the first to be used in a dozen countries – were built to that gauge.

George Stephenson later claimed that he had originally preferred a 5' 2" gauge, but had reverted to the earlier measure after discussing the matter with his son. Most of the other major engineers at the time preferred a slightly broader gauge of between 5 ft and 5' 6". They needed room for the biggest possible boilers and were looking for the lowest possible centre of gravity, both aims helped by a broader gauge.

Only one man in Britain, Isambard Kingdom Brunel, dared challenge the Stephensons. 'Looking at the speeds which I contemplated would be adopted on railways and the masses to be moved,' he later told a government committee, 'it seemed to me that the whole machine was too small for the work to be done, and that it required that the parts should be on a scale more commensurate with the mass and the velocity to be attained.' But by 1835 when he proposed his alternative – and technically superior – 7-ft gauge, it was already too late: too many railway lines had already been built, or planned, at the narrower gauge. Although broad-gauge trains ran on Brunel's Great Western until 1892 the doom of the 7-ft gauge had been sealed half a century earlier.

The Gauge Act, passed in 1844, effectively confined the broad-gauge system to its existing territory, but allowed the two to co-exist. At that point Joseph Locke, one of Britain's leading engineers, and normally an equable man, exploded with rage. England, mother of railways, would see uniformity everywhere else, but 'would stand alone in the anomalous position of having (because one man of great genius disdained to pursue the path pursued by others, and because Parliament, being careless and indifferent to the subject, allowed one company to deviate from the general plan) engraved on her railway a duplication, a complexity and a ruinous expense, of which I am satisfied it would be said that could they have been foreseen they would never have been tolerated.'

Once the continental pioneers, the Belgians, had adopted 4' 8½", their western European neighbours were, eventually, bound to follow suit, as the Dutch found to their cost. Against the advice of their British contractors and engineers they used a gauge of 6' 6" for their first railways, but these proved unprofitable. Nevertheless the infrastructure of tunnels, viaducts and bridges in Continental Europe allowed broader, taller trains, wagons and coaches than most British lines – a discrepancy in 'loading gauges' which is hampering development today of the truly European railway system which will radiate from the Channel Tunnel.

To remain different, you had to be isolated. Irish rails were 5' 3" apart, the Russians and the Spanish, on the edges of the continent, 5' 6" – though the Spanish are now having to convert to the standard 4' 8½" gauge to enable the ultra-fast lines they are building to be used by international expresses.

The British, by choosing 5' 6" for main lines in India, also, accidentally, imposed the same gauge on the budding Argentine network. The first locomotives bought by the Argentine Western

Railway had been destined for India, had been sent to Sebastopol to haul troops and equipment during the Crimean war, had returned to England, been rejected as unserviceable, and were snapped up by the Argentines at a bargain price. Later lines had to follow suit.

In the United States individual railroads often chose non-standard gauges as a gesture of independence, an affirmation of their territorial imperatives. Even though the powerful 'Commonwealth' of Pennsylvania stipulated the use of the 4' 8½" gauge as from 1852, there were at least eleven different gauges in the North, including the 6-ft gauge adopted by the mighty and mightily contrary Erie railroad. In the Southern states many, though not all, the major lines were of 5-ft gauge. As a result there were at least eight changes in track width between Philadelphia and Charleston. Territorial imperatives were not confined to the railways. The town of Portland in Maine imposed a gauge of 5' 6" on the Grand Trunk railroad to exclude its better-established rivals like Boston and New York from the traffic it hoped to attract from Canada.

During the Civil War the need for through traffic overrode narrow corporate considerations and some mileage was standardised, at least in the North, though even after the war the mileage of 5 ft gauge line in the former Confederate states nearly doubled. During the 1880s however all the major lines, North and South, shifted to 4' 8½" as the requirements of an increasingly-integrated national market demanded through transport.

The individualistic Australian colonies added a political dimension to deliberate bloody-mindedness and built their lines with gauges ranging from 2' 6" to 5' 3". What Mark Twain described as 'the jealousy between the colonies' ensured that through trains could not run between the country's two biggest cities, Sydney and Melbourne, for half a century.

Even Brunel recognised that mountainous railways demanded narrower gauges to enable curves to be tighter (although the 'narrow' gauge he recommended for the Taff Vale railway was 4' 8½". But he would not have approved of the other reason – simple economy of construction – for the plethora of truly narrow-gauge railways, often of a metre or less, built, especially in the developing world. These greatly hampered and still hamper integration. It has proved too costly and inconvenient to convert most of the world's narrow-gauge railways to 4' 8½" or even to match the width of their neighbour's lines.

Actress and worshipper of George Stephenson, Fanny Kemble.

Fanny Kemble in Love

Fanny Kemble was not what was usually meant by an 'actress' in the early 19th century – part music-hall artist, part courtesan. The Kembles were the most distinguished theatrical family in London and she herself was received, in the contemporary phrase, in the highest society. She was pretty, witty and delightful, so naturally Stephenson was at his most charming when she climbed aboard the *Northumbrian* on the newly-built Liverpool & Manchester railway. The conquest was mutual.

> We were introduced to the little engine which was to drag us along the rails. She (for they make these curious little firehorses all mares) consisted of a boiler, a stove, a small platform, a bench, and behind the bench a barrel containing enough water to prevent her being thirsty for fifteen miles – the whole machine not bigger than a common fire-engine.
>
> ... This snorting little animal, which I felt rather inclined to pat, was then harnessed to our carriage, and, Mr Stephenson having taken me on the bench of the engine with him, we started at about ten miles an hour. The steam-horse being ill-adapted for going up and down hill, the road was kept at a certain level, and appeared, sometimes to sink below the surface of the earth and sometimes to rise above it. Almost at starting it was cut through the solid rock, which formed a wall on either side of it, about sixty feet high. You can't imagine how strange it seemed to be journeying on thus, without any visible cause of progress other than the magical machine, with its flying white breath and rhythmical, unvarying pace, between these rocky walls, which are already clothed with moss and ferns and grasses; and when I reflected that these great masses of stone had been cut asunder to allow our passage thus far below the surface of the earth, I felt as if no fairy tale was ever half so wonderful as what I saw. Bridges were thrown from side to side across the top of these cliffs, and the people looking down upon us from them seemed like pygmies standing in the sky . . . After proceeding through this rocky defile, we presently found ourselves raised upon embankments ten or twelve feet high; we then came to a moss, or swamp, of considerable extent, on which no human foot could tread without sinking, and yet it bore the rod which bore us.
>
> . . . the engine having received its supply of water, the carriage was placed behind it, for it cannot turn, and was set

off at its utmost speed, thirty-five miles an hour, swifter than a bird flies (for they tried the experiment with a snipe). You cannot conceive what the sensation of cutting the air was; the motion is as smooth as possible, too. I could either have read or written; and as it was, I stood up and with my bonnet off 'drank the air before me'. The wind, which was strong, or perhaps the force of our own thrusting against it, absolutely weighed my eyelids down . . . when I closed my eyes this sensation of flying was quite delightful and strange beyond description; yet strange as it was, I had a perfect sense of security, and not the slightest fear.

Part of the security clearly came from 'the master of all these marvels' George Stephenson with whom she claimed to being 'most horribly in love'.

. . . A common sheet of paper is enough for love, but a foolscap can alone contain a railroad and my ecstasies. There was once a man, who was born at Newcastle-upon-Tyne, who was a common coal-digger; this man had an immense constructiveness, which displayed itself in pulling his watch to pieces and putting it together again; in making a pair of shoes when he happened to be some days without occupation . . . he is a man of from fifty to fifty-five years of age; his face is fine, though careworn, and bears an expression of deep thoughtfulness; his mode of explaining his ideas is peculiar and very original, striking and forcible; and although his accent indicates strongly his north-country birth, his language has not the slightest touch of vulgarity or coarseness. He has certainly turned my head.

In the event the enchanting Fanny married a rich American slave-owner and disappeared from the British social scene. Her deservedly famous account is contained in a letter published in her *Record of a Girlhood*.

II

THE HOPES AND FEARS OF ALL
THE YEARS

Railways proved able to absorb and reflect the theories and fantasies of generations of writers. Novelists, poets, men of letters, recognised the incomparable opportunity they offered. As Robert Louis Stevenson rattled across the United States he noted that railways 'brought together into one plot all the ends of the world and all the degrees of social ranks'. They 'offered to some great writer the busiest, the most extended, and the most varied subject for an enduring literary work. If it be romance, if it be contrast, if it be heroism that we require, what was Troy town to this? (*The Amateur Emigrant*).

Writers naturally exploited railways for their own purposes, as backdrops, as symbols, as points of departure for their imaginings, revealing their own deeper selves in their attitudes. In later years Rupert Brooke was racialist, Frances Cornford superior (and was duly slapped down by G. K. Chesterton),[*] Hardy was melancholy, contemplative[†], Jack Kerouac naturally focused on the railway bums. From the very beginning the balladeers seized on the numerous tales of heroism, romance and accident involved. Railways – and more especially stations – were the ideal setting for farewells and greetings, redolent of first ventures into new worlds, memorable punctuation marks in people's lives.

[*] See pages 60–61.

[†] 'In the 3rd class seat sat the journeying boy,
And the roof lamp's oily flame
played down on his listless form and face,
Bewrapt past knowing to what he was going
or whence he came'

The railways exploded on the scene at a time when spoken and written English were both incomparably vivid, without any of the pomposities of the eighteenth or later nineteenth centuries. So any quotation, from a politician, a man about town or – as is shown by Fanny Kemble's reaction – by a young actress, was expressed in irresistibly quotable language. Professional writers and lay observers alike illuminated many a railway scene, and contemporary accounts remain invaluable and colourful witnesses to the themes explored in this book, though some of the hopes and fears the railways evoked related specifically to the writer's internal experiences, his psyche as much as his travels.

The amateurs who transmuted their often extraordinary experiences into such memorable prose presented a considerable challenge to professional writers, even though the latter could interiorise the railway, exploit its symbolic or allegorical importance. Nevertheless, some writers, most obviously Rudyard Kipling, had the confidence to meet the 'descriptive' challenge from the amateurs head-on. Not for nothing had his earliest work appeared in a series designed to while away the hours spent on travelling on Indian railways.

Rail travel itself was an unprecedented experience. It evoked the enchanting temptations offered by a new world, their trains' destination. In Edna St Vincent Millay's words:

My heart is warm with the friends I make,
And better friends I'll not be knowing,
Yet there isn't a train I wouldn't take
No matter where it's going.

Her yearnings were echoed a century later by Paul Theroux: 'Ever since childhood when I lived within earshot of the Boston & Maine, I have seldom heard a train go by and not wished I was on it.'[1]

Sometimes the dream was more narrowly targeted. To the provincial they symbolised the metropolis at the other end of the line. Even in the 1950s William Whyte, a trainee cosmetic salesman stranded in the hills of Eastern Kentucky, could write

how 'often in the evening I would somehow find myself by the C
& O tracks when the *George Washington* swept by, its steamy
windows a reminder of civilisation left behind.'[2]

The first generation of railway travellers all felt what Humphrey
House calls 'an early astonishment which we can never recapture'.[3]
The philosopher-naturalist Henry David Thoreau, while aghast at
the effects on the nature he loved, was in awe of the challenge it
presented to mere mortals. 'When I hear the Iron Horse make the
hills echo with his snort like thunder, shaking the earth with his
feet, and breathing fire and smoke from his nostrils (what kind of
winged horse or fiery dragon they will put into the new mythology
I don't know) it seems as if the earth had sent a race now worthy
to inhabit it.' More simply, frightened negroes in the Southern
states called trains 'Hell in harness'.

Once aboard the train, travellers found, often to their
astonishment, that rail travel was much smoother than any
means of transport involving a horse-drawn vehicle. 'The animal
advances not with a continued progressive motion, but with a
sort of irregular hobbling, which raises and sinks its body at
every alternate motion of the limbs,' wrote one early observer.[4]
'With machinery this inconvenience is not felt; the locomotive
engine rolls regularly and progressively along the smooth tracks
of the way.' 'Mechanic power is uniform and regular,' emphasised
Thomas Gray, 'whilst horse-power, as we all very well know, is
quite the reverse.' 'People talk of the dangers of railways,' wrote
R. S. Surtees, 'but all horse owners know that there was no little
danger attendant on the coaches. If a man had a vicious animal
he always sold it to a coach proprietor.'[5]

Comfort was a relative term. Early trains were not only
bumpy, noisy and uncomfortable, they also smelt strongly, not
only from their human cargo but also because vegetable oil or
animal fat was used as lubricating fluid until mineral oil was
introduced in the third quarter of the century. Nevertheless
coaching had been worse at least for those without romantic
preconceptions. Samuel Smiles recalled how 'to be perched for
twenty hours, exposed to all weathers, on the outside of a coach,
trying in vain to find a soft seat . . . was a miserable undertaking . . .

Nor were the inside passengers more agreeably accommodated. To be closely packed up in a little, inconvenient straight-backed vehicle, where the cramped limbs could not be in the least extended, nor the wearied frame indulge in any change of posture, was felt by many to be a terrible thing.'[6]

But, quite naturally, it was the speed which most immediately impressed the average observer. Charles Greville found 'the velocity' of rail travel delightful 'and the continual bustle and animation of the changes and stoppages make the journey very entertaining ... it certainly renders all other travelling irksome and tedious by comparison.' The Reverend Sydney Smith waxed lyrical: 'Before this invention man, richly endowed with many gifts of mind and body, was deficient in locomotive powers; he could walk four miles an hour while a wild Goose could fly eighty in the same time; I can run now much faster than a fox or an Hare and beat a Carrier pigeon or an eagle for a hundred miles.'[7]

Smith and Surtees were both realists, men of the world, and therefore natural supporters of the railways. So was Balzac. Loving risk, he invested his own and his mistress's money in the shares of the Compagnie du Nord; loving modernity, he berated the French for their tardiness in building railways; an impatient traveller, he bemoaned the problems created by the lack of connections when he travelled on the railways in Russia, and looked forward to the day when Europe would be covered with an iron web.

Nevertheless for many British writers of the same generation travel by train provoked a sense of loss, primarily because it removed the excitements, the petty dramas, associated with horse-drawn travel. The stage coach represented the glamour of travel as perceived by their childish selves. The stage coach had been a short-lived phenomenon, coming into its full glory only in the 1820s and 1830s. In *The Dickens World* Humphrey House noted that:

The boys of Dickens's generation were coach-conscious as their predecessors had never been. Power over speed and efficiency of movement was then first becoming a focus of

43

childish admiration: boys were ambitious to be coachmen, as later to be engine-drivers ... A young man of 1836, whose earlier ambition had focused on the box seat of the Birmingham Mail, found it very difficult to transfer the thrill and glamour to the footplate of an engine on the London and Birmingham Railway ... a whole generation, in which were many writers, caught by admiration of the coaches in their short-lived pride, was unable to work off in the boredom of adult experience the glamorous ambitions of boyhood ... It is often said that Dickens never grew up: in this respect the course of history made it hard for him to do so.

Dickens was not alone. In his autobiography, Anthony Trollope recalled that 'A journey on the box of the mail was a great delight to me in those days – days somewhere in the third decade of the century; and faith! I believe would be still, if there were any mails available for the purpose.' 'We who have lived before railways were made,' wrote Thackeray, 'belong to another world'; while in France Alfred de Vigny and Théophile Gautier, of the same generation, experienced the same gut reactions – although Vigny did allow for the railways' practical advantages.

Their childhood love was inevitably veiled in a nostalgic mist, to the detriment of the railways' reputation. The recorders remember the stagecoach as part of the excitement of youth, not as an inconvenient and relatively slow means of transport. Similarly, for my own generation the dirt and inconvenience of steam travel is veiled with a romantic patina.

Because, as we see in Chapter III, railways were associated with democracy they naturally induced a new type of snobbery, one which was to be repeated in turn with every new form of transport. Each novelty has produced its own automatic glorification of an automatically romanticised past.* William T. Brigham, an early American traveller in Central America, showed all the symptoms. 'When the northern railroad extends through Guatemala,' he wrote, 'and the Nicaraguan canal unites the

---

* The snobbery extends to any democratising invention – remember all the 'intellectual' sneers which accompanied the spread of television in Britain.

Atlantic and the Pacific, the charm will be broken, the mulepath and the *mozo de cargo* [carrier of bundles] will be supplanted, and a journey across Central America become almost as dull as a journey from Chicago to Cheyenne.'*

Previous travel methods had been organic, inextricably linked with nature, with the horses, with the country, with the coachmen. It was production on a small scale, 'artisanal' as the French would say. Rail travel was impersonal, its scale inevitably industrial, its instruments made of hard, unyielding iron, not sympathetic wood and leather. 'Seated in the old mail-coach we needed no evidence out of ourselves to indicate the velocity' wrote Thomas de Quincey, 'we heard our speed, we saw it, we felt it as a thrilling; and this speed was not the product of blind insensate agencies, that had no sympathy to give, but was incarnated in the fiery eye-balls of the noblest among brutes, in his dilated nostril, spasmodic muscles, and thunder-beating hoofs.'[8]

Rail travel, unlike any previous form of transport, but like all its successors, was mechanical, speedy, inhuman, alienating. You were distanced from reality, cut off as never before from the natural world. 'The echoes in this place are very distinct,' wrote one early traveller, 'and whilst traversing its extent you seem shut out from all communication with the world.' The traveller perceived the landscape through a filter provided by the machinery of the train itself as well as its rhythmic progress. 'Looking out a train window in Asia', wrote Paul Theroux, 'is like watching an unedited travelogue without the obnoxious soundtrack.' And yet, this apparently 'inhuman' method of transportation now appears human compared with travel by air.

With alienation came dehumanisation. In the words of a recent observer:[9]

Just as the path of travel was transformed from the road that fits itself to the contours of land to a railroad that flattens and

* Quoted by Paul Theroux in *The Patagonian Express*. 'How wrong he was,' writes Theroux. But he proved susceptible to the same urge. In Lhasa he understood that 'The Kun Lun range is a guarantee that the railway will never get to Lhasa. That is probably a good thing. I thought I liked railways until I saw Tibet, and then realised that I liked wilderness much more.'

subdues land to fit its own needs for regularity, the traveller is made over into a bulk of weight, a 'parcel' as many travellers confessed themselves to feel ... mechanized by seating arrangements, and by new perceptual coercions (including new kinds of shock), routinized by schedules, by undeviating pathways, the railroad traveller underwent experiences analagous to military regimentation – not to say 'nature' transformed into 'commodity'. He was converted from a private individual into one of a mass public – a mere consumer.

Contemporaries knew perfectly well what was happening to them. John Ruskin combined the ideas of speed and dehumanisation. 'All travelling becomes dull in exact proportion to its rapidity. Going by railroad I do not consider as travelling at all; it is merely "being sent" to a place, and very little different from being a parcel.' Two German authors[10] found that man 'demotes himself to a parcel of goods and relinquishes his senses, his independence ... one ceases to be a person and becomes an object, a piece of freight'.

Even the noblest traveller lost control of his environment to the employees of the railway company, an unnerving experience. As early as 1838 an anonymous witness complained that 'a railway conveyance is a locomotive prison. At a certain period you are compelled to place your person and property in the custody of a set of men exceedingly independent and who have little regard for your accommodation. Till your journey is accomplished, you are completely subservient to their demands.' Marching to someone else's drum naturally agitated such querulous travellers as Thomas Carlyle. He reached Liverpool 'after a flight (for it can be called nothing else) of thirty-four miles within an hour and a quarter. I was dreadfully frightened before the train started; in the nervous state I was in, it seemed to me certain that I should faint, from the impossibility of getting the horrid thing stopt.'

However, the railways' biggest disturbance to the nervous system was not in the loss of independence, or the physical shocks it involved, the hurtling, the change in the perception of place, but in the way they telescoped distance and time. Henry Booth, treasurer of the Liverpool & Manchester perceived how the railway had effected a 'sudden and marvellous change . . . in our ideas of time and space. Notions which we have received from our ancestors, and verified by our own experience, are overthrown in a day and a new standard erected, by which to form our own ideas for the future. Speed – despatch – distance – are still relative terms, but their meaning has been totally changed within a few months.'[11] When Dickens travelled from London to Paris he called the report *A Flight*. (Via Folkestone it took only eleven hours as early as 1851.) 'Enchanted' by the magical experience, he blessed the South-Eastern Railway Company 'for realising the Arabian Nights in these prose days'.

The journey could be an end in itself. In *Gryll Grange* Thomas Love Peacock claims that:

'Men are become as birds and skim like swallows the surface of the world.'
'To what good purpose?'
'The end is in itself – the end of skimming the surface of the world.'

In the words of the modern English writer Michael Frayn 'The Journey is the Goal'.

The shrinking of space, the upsetting of all previous notions of the relationship between time and distance, inevitably excited fears that, as the *Quarterly Review* remarked, 'the metropolis would engulf the whole country', while the French naturally envisaged their whole country fitting into Paris and its immediate vicinity. 'Even the elementary concepts of time and space have begun to oscillate,' wrote Heine in *Lutetzia*. 'Space is killed by the railways and we are left with time alone . . . I feel as if the mountains and forests of all the countries were advancing on Paris. Even now, I can smell the German linden trees; the North Sea's breakers are rolling against my door.'

For nearly a century after the 1830s any journey of more than a few miles through a civilised country was by rail, and it still remains the best, most intimate way to see a country, its internal essences as well as its outward physical appearance. 'A train isn't a vehicle. A train is part of a country. It's a place,' wrote Paul Theroux as he travelled round China.[12] 'It allowed one to make visual connections in a place that was otherwise full of bafflements. Every other mode of travel made the country seem incomprehensible.'

Yet it could be presented entirely otherwise, as a deliberate blank in people's lives. To Mallarmé,[13] the Parisians who flocked south in the winter were 'calm, self-absorbed people, paying no attention to the invisible landscapes of the journey. To leave Paris and to get to where the sky is clear, that is their desire.'

In reality these apparently 'self-absorbed' people were probably simply terrified, blotting out their fears through a feigned indifference to the landscape hurtling past. If so, they were in distinguished company. Gustave Flaubert used to stay up all night before a journey in order to sleep through it and obliterate the whole experience from his consciousness. Like many air travellers today he covered real terror with an unconvincing veil of indifference. In 1864 he claimed that he got 'so bored on the train that I am about to howl with tedium after five minutes of it. One might think that it's a dog someone has forgotten in the compartment; not at all, it is M. Flaubert groaning.'

Freud was more honest. 'At the age of three,' he once admitted, 'I passed through the station when we moved from Freiburg to Leipzig, and the gas jets, which were the first I had seen, reminded me of souls burning in hell. I know something of the context here, the anxiety about travel which I have had to overcome is also bound up with it.'

In physical terms railways were the first industrial intrusion on most of the world's landscape. In Britain the landscape had been changing since the middle of the 18th century – the fields had been enclosed and enlarged, the landscape pierced by canals and turnpikes – yet these were relatively gentle interruptions compared with the territorial imperatives asserted by the railway. Previously the Industrial Revolution had been confined to a handful of towns and cities. Railways were inescapable, omnipresent evidence of a new, brutally mechanical world. In 1844 an anonymous author lamented how 'in travelling on most of the railways the face of nature, the beautiful prospects of hill and dale, the healthful breeze, and all those exhilarating associations connected with "the Road", are lost or changed to doleful cuttings, dismal tunnels, and the obnoxious effluvia of the screaming engine.'

Not surprisingly John Ruskin went the furthest in associating what he called an 'infernal means of mischievous locomotion' with the horrors of the industrial revolution: 'when the iron roads are tearing up the surface of Europe, as grapeshot do the sea, when their great net is . . . contracting all its various life, its rocky arms and rural heart, into a narrow, finite, calculating metropolis of manufactures'. A famous passage in *Praeterita* denounces a railroad enterprise. 'You enterprised a railway through the valley,' he thundered, 'you blasted its rocks away, heaped thousands of tons of shale into its lovely stream. The valley is gone, and the Gods with it; and now, every fool in Buxton can be in Bakewell in half an hour, and every fool in Bakewell in Buxton; which you think a lucrative process of exchange, you Fools everywhere.'

For later generations, when no one remembered the shape of the landscape before the railways were embedded in them, they became a deeply cherished part of the national heritage, and roads took their place as the despoilers of the landscape. But at the time intellectuals outside Britain echoed Ruskin's attitude. Nathaniel Hawthorne emphasised that 'the locomotive brings the noisy world into the midst of . . . slumbrous peace.' 'People of today sacrifice, if they must, all their own particular literature and culture in favour of "night through-trains" ' wrote the Swiss historian Jacob Burckhardt in disgust, while France spawned a whole school of romantic anti-railwayites. Alfred de Musset, among many others, took the railway as the preeminent symbol of a modern barbarism which had swept away all the beauties of the world.

In France the battle was more formal than in Britain. The modernising Saint-Simonians were as ideologically motivated as their romantic opponents, the Parnassiens, who rallied most of the country's major literary figures in rejecting modern life as exemplified by the railways. In the words of Marc Baroli 'literary history offers few examples of failures more complete than that of Maxime du Camp's Chants Modernes', which hymned their delights.[14]

The damage the railways caused was obvious even to those perpetrating them. Railways were 'unholy devastators of the soil'

Not everybody welcomed the railways.

in the words of the great engineer Joseph Locke ('Shareholders do not want works of art,' added his biographer, J. Devey, 'they want half-yearly dividends'). As always the greatest engineers – like Locke – managed to combine the functional and the beautiful. Nevertheless the sheer scale and insensitivity of the intrusion inevitably bred the Nimby*, most illustriously William Wordsworth.

Wordsworth was not alone. The garden of the country retreat owned by Dr Flaubert, Gustave's father, was bisected by the railway line from Paris to Le Havre, while the Goncourt brothers' notorious insomnia was exacerbated by the trains which thundered past their house at Auteuil. Later, poachers turned gamekeepers. The railway from Leatherhead to Dorking was opposed by Thomas Grissell, a celebrated contractor retired to enjoy some country peace nearby.

Nevertheless the ever-changing vista offered by the sheer speed of the train enchanted and finally converted even the most sensitive travellers. In the process they were succumbing to the lure of the travel 'product' they were 'consuming.'† Late in life, looking out from a carriage on the line from Amiens to Beauvais, Ruskin obviously did not see the intrusions caused by the railway on which he was travelling but 'every instant a nearly divine landscape of wood, harvest-field and *côteau*' and at Aix recounted that 'yesterday an entirely divine railway coupé drive from Aix by the river gorges – one enchantment of golden trees and ruby hills.'

Victor Hugo, no railway lover, perceived that 'The flowers by the side of the road are no longer flowers but flecks, or rather streaks, of red or white; there are no longer any points, everything becomes a streak; the grainfields are great shocks of yellow hair; fields of alfalfa, long green tresses; the towns, the steeples and the trees perform a crazy mingling dance on the horizon.'

By the time of Hugo's conversion to their virtues, railways had entered the very fabric of the language. The Americans had

* Short for Not In My Back Yard.

† In Schievelbusch's words, the traveller 'is experiencing industrial production, although from the consumer's standpoint. The railway's industrial product is transportation, change of locality. What makes this production fundamentally different from all other industrial production is exactly the simultaneity of production and consumption'.

hoped to domesticate this strange new fire-eating beast through using horsey words. The locomotive was named the 'iron horse'. When an engine ran away: 'so much for leaving a horse in the street without being made fast'. As for the railway lines, why, they were like trees, there were trunk routes, branch lines, feeders 'like tributaries feeding rivers'. The escape route for runaway slaves was known as the 'underground railroad' because it was so reliable. In *Moby Dick*, Melville elevates the comparisons to poetry when Ahab ruminates 'swerve me? The path to my fixed purpose is laid with iron rails, whereon my soul is grooved to run ... through the rifled hearts of mountains, under torrents' beds, unerringly I rush! Naught's an obstacle, naught's an angle to the iron way.'

Every novelist of the first generation absorbed the railway into his skin, and thence into his writings. But for Dickens, the railway had a universal significance. It destroyed towns and created new ones, it was life, it was death. It was the supreme sign of Dickens's awareness of living in a world of change, symbolised above all by the ubiquitous railway lines.

Railways play a particularly significant role in *Dombey and Son*, written at the height of the railway mania of the mid-1840s. Although they are mentioned in only a dozen of its near nine hundred pages, every word of each passage provides a clue to the inner meaning of the work as a whole. Railways are 'the power that forced itself upon its iron way – its own – defiant of all paths and roads, piercing through the heart of every obstacle, and dragging living creatures of all classes, ages and degrees behind it.'

The book's most dramatic moment occurs when a train runs over the evil Mr Carker at the moment he felt that 'Death was on him'. Of course Dickens was not alone in finding railways a convenient, and conveniently dramatic, means of disposing of unwanted characters. But comparing Mr Carker's death with, say, that of Anna Karenina or the adventurer Ferdinand Lopez in Trollope's *The Prime Minister* is a matter for students of the novelists concerned.[15] The deaths are not comparable, only the means are the same (although both Carker and Lopez plucked up courage to throw themselves under trains only when they realised they were being pursued).

But no novelist could ever have conjured up the 'Death Road' described to Paul Theroux during his travels in China.[16] 'During the Cultural Revolution people used to kill themselves on this section of track. One person a day, and sometimes more, jumped in front of the train. In those days the buildings in Pekin weren't very tall – you couldn't kill yourself by jumping out of the window of a bungalow. So they chose the train, because they were too poor to buy poison. Also if you were killed by a train China Railways was obliged to bury you free of charge.'

For Dickens in *Dombey and Son* the railway embraces both life and death. This universality is most obvious in the famous account of Mr Dombey's journey to Leamington. 'It has generally been interpreted either as Dickens's great paean to the advent of a revolutionary new transport system, or as an expression of doubt as to its benefits,' wrote Andrew Sanders.[17] Although the journey, dominated by memories of the recent death of Mr Dombey's son, Paul, may strike readers as the 'Victorian equivalent of the chariot of Death in some medieval pageant . . . only to the particular traveller Dickens is describing, one who carries the blight of death with him like a carrier of an infection.' To present the journey Dickens used a sort of prosodic doggerel, the clackety-clackety rhythm associated with railway travel until the coming of longer welded rails in recent years:

Away, with a shriek, and a roar, and a rattle . . . Through the hollow, on the height, by the heath, by the orchard, by the park, by the garden, over the canal, across the river, where the sheep are feeding, where the mill is going, where the barge is floating, where the dead are lying, where the factory is smoking, where the stream is running, where the village clusters, where the great cathedral rises, where the bleak moor lies, and the wild breeze smooths or ruffles it at its inconstant will; away with a shriek and a roar and a rattle, and no trace to leave behind but dust and vapour: like as in the track of the remorseless monster, Death!

Robert Louis Stevenson tamed the same rhythm, transformed it in an innocent nursery rhyme, 'From a Railway Carriage':

Faster than fairies, faster than witches,
Bridges and houses, hedges and ditches;
And charging along like troops in a battle,
All through the meadows the horses and cattle;
All of the sights of the hill and the plain
Fly as thick as driving rain;
And ever again, in the wink of an eye,
Painted stations whistle by.

The rhythm proved durable. In the late 1930s W. H. Auden used it for the film *Night Mail*:

This is the Night Mail crossing the border,
Bringing the cheque and the postal order . . .

But behind the apparent innocence of the rhythm Peter Gay insists that 'the erotic desires and fears stimulated by the rhythmic experience of the train ride were never far beneath the surface'. Freud attributed boys' desire to be an engine driver (or a coachman for that matter) to the fascination provided when the body (and the libido) were thoroughly shaken by travel by coach or train. He went on to insist on the 'exquisite sexual symbolism' in railway travel and a 'compulsive link' between the two, springing clearly 'from the pleasurable character of the sensations of movement'.

It was two lady poets who best seized the erotic nature of train travel. In her poem 'To the Railway', written in 1844, the German Luise von Plonnies tells of her experiences:[*]

Fast flash which carries me
As fast as an arrow powered by fire
Rushing through the glory of the day,

* I have to thank Rupert Wickham for the translation.

Roaring through the darkling night,
Thundering over the foam of the current,
Going like lightning around the edge of the abyss

(Rascher Blitz, der hin mich tragt,
Pfeilschnell von der Gluth bewegt,
Sausend durch des Tages Pracht,
Brausend durch die dunkle Nacht,
Donnernd uber Stromesschaumen,
Blitzend an de Abgrunds Saumen)

Elizabeth Barrett Browning's imagery was even more blatantly sexual in her poem 'Through the Tunnels' from *Aurora Leigh*:[18]

So we passed
The liberal open country and the close,
And shot through tunnels, like a lightning-wedge
By great Thor-hammers driven through the rock,
Which, quivering through the intestine blackness, splits
And lets it in at once: the train swept in
Athrob with effort, trembling with resolve
The fierce denouncing whistle wailing on
And dying oft-smothered in the shuddering dark
While we, self-awed, drew troubled breath, oppressed
As other Titans underneath the pile
And nightmare of the mountains, out, at last,
To catch the dawn afloat upon the land.

The sexual side of rail travel was not always mere fantasy. Love overcame Gustave Flaubert's fears of rail travel. He regularly used the line from Rouen to meet his mistress, Louise Colet, half way between his home and hers. Other French novelists seized on railways as a natural locale for sexual encounters.[19] But it was a writer of a much later generation, Emile Zola, who managed to combine all his obsessions, with sex, crime and the railways, in his famous novel *La Bête Humaine*. The railway landscape provided a suspense-saturated atmosphere for the

novel's melodramatic plot: the trains and locomotives are important characters in it.*

For painters, as for writers, railways proved a universal
inspiration. In the words of Louis Armand, 'The Impressionists
fixed on forms moving through the countryside and on the
wisps of steam which provide movement in even the most
tranquil sky. The Fauves discovered an imposing force in the
railways which provided the effect of weightiness they were
looking for. More modern artists have perceived in the railways
an ensemble of lines and curves which responded to the new
rules of painting. All of them have found something to take
because the train, the station, the tracks themselves are all part
of living reality.'[20]

In the first days of railways a number of sometimes
distinguished artists were employed by British railway promoters
to provide an unfairly picturesque image of their activities. In
Gareth Rees's words, the railway prints:

> stressed the grace and order of the railway in the landscape . . .
> Bury's prints, for example, always depict well-to-do people
> associating with trains in bright sunlight in excessively tidy
> stations. Animals near or on trains seem unfrightened by the
> experience. Cuttings and embankments are grassed over and
> station crowds well disciplined. Although the actual
> appearance of the railway in its first few years must have
> been as raw as a new motorway it never appears so . . .
> railway prints helped to subdue the alarms felt by ordinary
> people at the noise, smoke, danger to life, and the very sight
> of something that apparently moved without natural cause.[21]

Richard Bourne produced the finest views of them all in his
majestic series depicting the London to Birmingham Railway. In
them he minimises the railway's impact by presenting it from a
distance, reducing its obtrusive nature, integrating it with the

---

* In *L'Eve Future* by Villiers de l'Isle Adam a certain Lord Ewald picks up a
young innocent unable to find a seat in a crowded train by offering her a place
in his reserved compartment.

landscape. But the vision soon faded. A few years later, when Bourne came to celebrate the opening of the Great Western Railway, the prints were less dramatic and the volume sold less well. The line was less spectacular, and railways were no longer the exciting novelty they had been a few years earlier.

After the financial crash of 1846 the companies no longer had time for such fripperies and the artists scattered. Bourne went off to Russia while Richard Tait produced equally romantic visions for Currier & Ives in the United States, where the railroads still had the funds to commission suitably idealised publicity material. One typical product, *The Lackawanna Valley*, by George Innes, was commissioned by the railroad to demonstrate its integration with the landscape. By then the relatively impersonal, 'industrial' art of the photograph was beginning to replace the individual, personally involved eye of the landscape artist.

Luckily for lovers of railway art, in 1866 a group of Impressionists started to meet regularly at the Café Guerbois in

The Lackawanna Valley, by George Innes, an idealised vision of the railroad.

One of Monet's impressions of the Gare St Lazare.

the Grande Rue des Batignolles, on the approaches to the new Gare St Lazare. Other Impressionists soon followed, indeed became known as 'La Groupe des Batignolles'. They became fascinated by everything about trains: their air of imprecision, the transitory nature of the train passing by, the steam – indeed the sheer power – of the locomotive, the bustle of the station, the train in the landscape on their favourite line from St Lazare to Rouen and the coast of Normandy.

In 1876–77 Monet spent a year painting the station, a perfect subject. As John Rewald put it,

Monet felt attracted by the huge enclosure, with its glass roof against which the heavy locomotives threw their opaque vapour, the incoming trains, the crowds, the contrast between the limpid sky in the background and the steaming engines – all this offered unusual and exciting subjects, and Monet intriguingly put up his easel in different corners of the station. As Degas liked to do, he explored the same motif from a variety of angles, proceeding with both vigor and subtlety to seize the specific character of the place and its atmosphere.[22]

But as Rewald goes on to say, Monet was no Ruskin; neither he nor the other Impressionists associated the station with its industrial purpose. Monet found it 'a pretext rather than an end in itself; he discovered and probed the pictorial aspects of machinery but did not comment on its ugliness or usefulness or beauty, nor upon its relationship to man.' Neither, of course, did J. M. W. Turner in his famous painting, *Rain, Steam and Speed*, which predated – and outdid – the Impressionists. Like their paintings, Turner's was taken from real life. And, as Hamilton Ellis records in *Railway Art*, there was a witness, one Lady Simon, who happened to be travelling from Exeter to London in the same compartment as:

> an elderly gentleman, short and stout, with a red face, and a curious prominent nose. The weather was very wild, and by-and-by a violent storm swept over the country, blotting out the sunshine and the blue sky and hanging like a pall over the landscape. The old gentleman seemed strangely excited at this, jumping up to open the window, craning his head out, and finally calling to her to come and observe a curious effect of light. A train was coming in their direction, through the blackness, over one of Brunel's bridges, and the effect of the locomotive, lit by the crimson flame and seen through driving rain and whirling tempest, gave a peculiar impression of power, speed and stress.[23]

Lady Simon thought no more of the incident until she recognised the scene when she saw Turner – and the painting – at a private viewing at the Royal Academy. 'Overhearing a critical bystander say, "Just like Turner, ain't it? Whoever saw such a ridiculous conglomeration?", she is reported to have contemplated the Philistine with an icy disdain, and to have replied, "I did." '

Turner's incomparable vision of crossing Maidenhead bridge in a rainstorm.

Poets often tell more about themselves than about the subject when they use railways as a peg.

DAWN
by Rupert Brooke

Opposite me two Germans snore and sweat.
Through sullen swirling gloom we jolt and roar.
We have been here for ever: even yet
A dim watch tells two hours, two aeons, more
The windows are tight shut and slimy-wet
With a night's foetor. There are two hours more;
Two hours to dawn and Milan; two hours yet.
Opposite me two Germans sweat and snore . . .

One of them wakes, and spits, and sleeps again.
The darkness shivers. A wan light through the rain
Strikes on our faces, drawn and white. Somewhere
A new day sprawls; and, inside, the foul air
Is chill, and damp, and fouler than before . . .
Opposite me two Germans sweat and snore.

A FAT LADY AS SEEN FROM THE TRAIN
A triolet by Frances Cornford

O why do you walk through the fields in gloves,
Missing so much and so much?
O fat white woman whom nobody loves,
Why do you walk through the fields in gloves,
When the grass is soft as the breast of doves
And shivering-sweet to the touch?
O why do you walk through the fields in gloves,
Missing so much and so much?

THE FAT WHITE WOMAN SPEAKS
by G. K. Chesterton

Why do you rush through the field in trains,
Guessing so much and so much.
Why do you flash through the flowery meads,
Fat-head poet that nobody reads;
And why do you know such a frightful lot
About people in gloves as such?

And how the devil can you be sure,
Guessing so much and so much,
How do you know but what someone who loves
Always to see me in nice white gloves
At the end of the field you are rushing by,
Is waiting for his Old Dutch?

The First Nimby

William Wordsworth had given railways a somewhat ambiguous welcome in his sonnet 'Steamboats, Viaducts and Railways', written in 1833.

> 'In spite of all that beauty may disown
> In your harsh features, Nature doth embrace
> Her lawful offspring in Man's art.'

Eleven years later he was up in arms, a vigorous seventy-five-year-old aghast at the idea of a railway penetrating as far as the shore of Lake Windermere. In October he dashed off a famous sonnet, which has since become the national anthem of Nimbies the world over:

> Is there no nook of English ground secure
> From rash assault? Schemes of retirement sown
> In youth, and 'mid the busy world kept pure
> As when their earliest flowers of hope were blown
> Must perish; – how can they this blight endure?
> And must he too the ruthless change bemoan
> Who scorns a false utilitarian lure
> 'Mid his paternal fields at random thrown?
> Baffle the threat, bright Scene, from Orrest-head
> Given to the pausing traveller's rapturous glance:
> Plead for thy peace, thou beautiful romance
> Of nature; and, if human hearts be dead,
> Speak, passing winds; ye torrents, with your strong
> And constant voice, protest against the wrong.

He broadened his attack in a number of letters to the *Morning Post*, emphasising that love of the Natural and Picturesque was a relative novelty. It was 'so far from being intuitive, that it can be produced only by a slow and gradual process of culture . . .' Better to leave it to 'those who have been in the habit of observing and studying the peculiar character of such scenes'. Instead of invading the Lake District 'artisans and labourers, and the humbler classes of shopkeepers' should be content with 'little excursions . . . after having attended divine worship'.[24]

The condescending tone of his attack made him wildly unpopular. The official report recommending the railway's construction noted only one objection 'which has been strongly urged' that the comfort and privacy of existing inhabitants would be affected. To which the report gave the magnificently democratic response that:

> to deprive the artisan of the offered means of occasionally changing his narrow abode, his crowded streets, his wearisome task and his ungrateful toil, for the fresh air, and the healthful holiday which send him back to his work refreshed and invigorated – simply that individuals who object on the grounds above stated may retain to themselves the exclusive enjoyment of scenes which should be open alike to all . . . appears to us an argument wholly untenable.

Even after the scheme had gone through Parliament Wordsworth addressed a protest meeting attended also by the young Matthew Arnold, whose father, Dr Arnold, had rapturously welcomed the railway when it passed by Rugby School, but who reacted very differently when his family house, Fox How, was threatened by the projected line. In the event more mundane considerations prevented the railway reaching the lake itself. The line ended, then as now, a mile away simply because of engineering difficulties and 'a great deal of opposition from landowners such as the Earl of Bradford'. Nevertheless, as Wordsworth had feared, the hordes from Lancashire did descend on Windermere, and its peace was spoilt.[25]

Thirty years later, following a new railway scare, John Ruskin immediately took up his pen, claiming that the scenery made accessible by the new railway would no longer be the same as before. While claiming that his interest was unselfish (by implication, unlike Wordsworth's forty years earlier) he echoed his predecessor in recommending that the populace content themselves with paying for a chaise and pony and picnicking 'on a mossy bank' nearer home. He added that it was 'precisely because I passionately wish to improve the minds of the populace, and because I am spending my own mind, strength and fortune, wholly on that object, that I don't want to let them see Helvellyn while they are drunk.'[26]

The episode led to the formation of the first-ever conservation society, the Lake District Defence Association. Inspired by its success – and a suggestion of Ruskin's – its founders, including a local cleric, Canon Rawnsley, went on to help found the National Trust, oldest and most effective of the institutions designed to save Britain's heritage.

Thomas Hardy and the Gravediggers

Building a railway through old St Pancras churchyard created a scandal when the contractor, the redoubtable Joseph Firbank, (see page 93) was asked to look for the bones of a French bishop, buried there as a refugee from the revolution. Firbank simply set aside the darkest set of bones he could find, reasoning that all foreigners, whatever their nationality, were dark.[27]

Enter Thomas Hardy, apprentice architect. His master, Arthur Blomfield, son of the late Bishop of London, was considered the most suitable man to prevent any repetition of so unseemly an episode, and so the young Hardy was despatched every evening to supervise the removal of the bodies. According to his widow, 'there after nightfall, within a high hoarding that could not be overlooked, and by the light of flare-lamps, the exhumation went on continuously of the coffins that had been uncovered during the day, new coffins being provided for those that came apart in lifting, and for loose skeletons.'[28]

The episode obviously made a vivid impression on Hardy, as witness his evocative poem 'The Levelled Churchyard':

O passenger, pray list and catch
Our sighs and piteous groans,

Half stifled in this humbled patch
Of wrenched memorial stones!
We late-lamented resting here,
Are mixed to human jam,
And each to each exclaims in fear,
'I know not which I am.'

Having got that off his chest, Hardy could afford to be jocular about the whole episode. As his widow recounts, 'In one coffin that fell apart was a skeleton and two skulls. He used to tell that when, after some fifteen years of separation, he met Arthur Blomfield again and their friendship was fully renewed, among the latter's first words were "Do you remember how we found the man with two heads at St Pancras?" '

III

RAILPOLITIK

1

Progressive, Modern, Democratic and above all National

In early September, 1850, the great French historian Jules Michelet took his wife to Fontainebleau to recuperate from the death of their six-week-old son a few days earlier. He was naturally deeply troubled on his wife's account, anguished that his attempts at sympathy were inarticulate, badly expressed.

He took refuge in contemplating the grandeurs of the ancient site. In his strolls round the ramparts he reflected on the enormous contrast between

> old Fontainebleau, now simply a museum, a royal residence denuded of royalty, on the other side the railway line, inaugurated but yesterday, marked by the grandeur of its elegant and powerful curves, seated on arches a hundred metres high. The whole is connected by a lovely hyphen, the canal and its deep and lengthy shadows, cold and majestic, which link man's two worlds, the ancient and the modern, with nature's fine impartiality. Unlike nature, I am not impartial: the chateau represents pleasure, the caprice of one man; the railway is for everyone's use, bringing France together, bringing Lyons and Paris into communion with one another.[1]

*

He was not alone in associating railways with progress, modernity, a brighter future, liberation from ancient autocracies. As Dr Arnold watched a train thunder past Rugby School on its way from Birmingham to London he rejoiced 'to see it and think that feudality has gone for ever. It is so great a blessing to think that any one evil is really extinct.' John Stuart Mill wrote how 'the more visible fruits of scientific progress ... the mechanical improvements, the steam engines, the railroads, carry the feeling of admiration for modern, and disrespect for ancient times, down even to the most uneducated classes.'

In Uruguay a progressive political journal, which had nothing specifically to do with railways was named *Ferrocaril* [railways]. When British engineers were completing the first railway bridge over the River Tiber, Pope Pius IX came down to look. When the chief engineer was presented to him as the 'British Minister of Public Works' the Pontiff told him, 'now you can say that the Roman Pontiff is not always at prayer surrounded by incense, monks and priests. Tell the Queen that Her Majesty's Minister of Public Works found the old Pope surrounded by his engineers while helping to finish a new bridge over the Tiber.'

Railways, it was supposed, would be a means of uniting the nations, of spreading a progressive gospel of democracy and modernisation the world over. The supposition was only partly correct. They did indeed unite the inhabitants of individual countries, but they were of no help in the quest for international peace; and they proved quite as suitable for authoritarian as for democratic societies.

The more backward the country, the more urgent its need – psychological as much as economic – to modernise, the more eagerly it seized on the railway as the key to progress. A model railway was one of the gifts Commodore Perry presented to the Japanese to demonstrate the power of the West. The Japanese had already grasped the railways' significance. In 1855, before Perry's arrival, they built a crude model of a Russian train. Another, running on a circular track, features in a book on Western civilisation published in Japan in 1867.

To the Japanese, the locomotive was a crucial symbol of foreign, modern technology.

In one important sense the railways were undeniably democratic. For the first time in history the poor could travel in the same conveyance, at the same speed as the rich – though, as we shall see, railway companies soon found a way of ensuring that the rich could travel faster, as well as more comfortably than the poor. The railways' fundamentally democratic nature was welcomed by progressives the world over. In France Walter Pecqueur, a leading Saint-Simonian, waxed suitably eloquent:

by causing all classes of society to travel together and thus juxtaposing them into a kind of mosaic of all the fortunes, positions, characters, manners, customs and modes of dress that each and every nation has to offer, the railways quite prodigiously advance the reign of truly fraternal social relations and do more for the sentiments of equality than the most exalted sermons of the tribunes of democracy ... It is the same convoy, the same power that carries the great and the small, the rich and the poor; thus the railways most generally provide a continuous lesson in equality and fraternity.

Conversely the railways were hated by elitists like Thomas Carlyle and, more importantly, by reactionary autocrats – the Emperor Francis II of Austria opposed railways which he assumed would bring 'rebellion' in the shape of democratic ideas into his empire.

With progress and democracy went the association of railways with the specific identity, the unity, the national aspirations of countries old and new. This association was not confined to politicians and philosophers. Robert Stephenson was moved to describe the opening of the Royal Border bridge at Berwick-on-Tweed as 'the last act of Union' between England and Scotland. A twentieth-century Governor of Kenya was typical in asserting that 'the railway is the beginning of all history in Kenya. Without it there would be no history of Kenya.'

The precedent was set by the Belgians. In 1830 they had successfully revolted against their former Dutch masters. For the new country, building a rail network was conclusive proof of their country's existence, that it could survive without Dutch supervision or Dutch finance. As one Belgian put it,[2] 'Without the revolution the railway could never have existed, without the railway the revolution would have been compromised.' In 1834 they defined their country by establishing a state-owned railway network. Not only would it tie the country together, it would also be international, with links extending to the country's frontiers, anticipating that the French and the states of the Rhineland would build railways to their own side of the frontier.

The railways were also designed for strategic purposes, to act as an alternative transport network in case the Dutch tried to block Antwerp's access to the sea.* This necessity had been foreseen as early as October 1830, when the Liègeois asked the provisional government to find ways of using railways to replace the Dutch waterways between the Rhine and the Escaut which provided access to Antwerp, Belgium's principal port. Naturally the network was to be nationally-controlled – any private railways were granted only twenty-year licences before they reverted to state control.

The Germans followed the Belgian example. In the 1830s the then-independent state of Baden was shocked into action when the French started building lines in Lorraine the other side of the Rhine, but Baden went it alone, proudly refusing to adopt the common English gauge used by every other German state. Baden and its neighbour, Hesse, genuinely wished to construct a railway linking them, yet 'six valuable years were spent merely coming to a political agreement on a railroad project vital to the development of both states immediately involved'.[3]

Most of Germany's dozens of states ignored the success (and profitability) of the economic activity generated by railways in other countries, basing their calculations on the share of existing traffic the trains could hope to attract. Their motives changed when railways became a symbol of national unity, of economic progress, of military preparedness. The creation of a united railway network was a demonstration of German capacity to join in a common aim. By 1846, only eleven years after the opening of Germany's first railway, the German states had formed a Union of German Railway Administrations, ensuring a uniform tariff throughout the country. 'The frontiers of the races and the states', wrote the philosopher William Treitschke, 'lost their disruptive power, rivalries were forgotten and the Germans discovered the pleasure of getting to know each other.'

Prussian generals, notably von Moltke, have often been credited with determining the shape of Germany's rail system. In fact the network was developed earlier for strict economic

---

* Previously the same role had been played by plans for canals designed to link Belgium and Germany. By 1833 railways already offered better value.

considerations, combined with a spirit of emulation among the German states and a desire for national unity. When Germany was first united in 1871 the railways had remained under the control of individual states, but for Bismarck, architect of the country's unity, 'railways were too serious a matter to be left to the market or to the particularist forces within the Reich'. He fought long and hard 'to have the Reich acquire the country's railways and organise them into an efficient national system – as a functional and symbolic demonstration of the newly-found national unity.'[4]

For the Italians, another people searching for national unity during the first railway generation, both the idea and the reality of railways was supremely important. Count Camillo di Cavour, the Piedmontese founder of the modern Italian state, was obsessed by them – he even planned and supervised his country's timetables. They were proof that Italians could govern themselves without the tutelage of their former Austrian masters. As early as 1857, when Piedmont was still a small, isolated kingdom, he persuaded its parliament to pledge the country's credit for ludicrously large sums to enable work to start on a tunnel under the Mont Cenis pass, the vital route to France, the first of many prodigious achievements of Italian engineers. (Described in Chapter VII)

Although the first railway in Italy had been in the Kingdom of the reactionary Bourbon King of Naples by 1860 Piedmont, the country's most advanced and industrialised state, naturally accounted for half the miles of track in the whole peninsula. Following the Belgian example the network extended to the kingdom's frontiers. After the creation of a united Italy in 1861 Cavour envisaged railways as the crucial force for Italian unity, and in the state's early years investment in railways accounted for a full fifth of the national budget.

There were a few exceptions to the rule that national pride automatically led to the promotion of a rail network as an instrument of national development. For a variety of reasons, economic, cultural, social, political, Spain, already a united country before the railway age, signally failed to take the

How Swiss railway builders conquered the Alps.

opportunities for increased political cohesion and economic development they offered. Initially the Swiss deliberately refused to use their burgeoning railway system to unite a country which had been the loosest of confederations for over five centuries until 1848. The Swiss remained parochial, far more attached to their cantons and to their own narrow financial interests than to the Confederation. Hence, in the words of an official report, '*a priori* the Swiss will find it difficult to accept a rail network providing uniform services to different regions and different inhabitants, crowded industrial cities and other major traffic centres, following the example of Belgium which is presented to us as a model.'[5]

The decision did not reflect national indifference. While the majority of economic arguments did not interest the average Swiss, 'the railway question actively interested the common people'.[6] They were faced with a choice between railways financed by private capital, much of it from abroad, and a 'link between all states and cities [which] should be the monument of living democracy'. At the outset they chose the private path – though many of them lived to regret it.

They were galvanised into action only in 1867, when two trans-Alpine rail routes were opened – in the west through the Mont Cenis tunnel and in the east by way of the Brenner Pass – neither of which passed through their country. As a result the Swiss lost much of their precious transit traffic. They were so heavily involved in international overland transport through their control of key Alpine passes that existing vested interests, carriers, innkeepers and the like, their power reinforced by the country's deeply decentralised political structure, had been able to block progress on trans-Alpine rail links through Switzerland.

Only when faced by competition did they take seriously the idea of building a tunnel under the St Gotthard pass to Italy, the historic route over the Alps which had been the key to Swiss prosperity down the centuries. To be fair to the Swiss, concerted action over such a route was possible only when all the countries involved – Germany and Italy as well as Switzerland – had cohesive national governments of their own. Even in the late 1860s Germany was still a loose confederation while Italy was only a few years old.

In 1883, when the concessions came up for renewal, re-purchase by the state was rejected by only a small majority. Eight years later nationalisation had become the subject of probably the single most passionate political debate in which the Swiss have ever engaged. The agreed purchase of the Central, the biggest of the railways, was overturned in a referendum but,

Across the desert from Cairo to Alexandria

nothing daunted, the nationalisers rallied their countrymen under the slogan, 'The Swiss railways for the Swiss people', playing heavily on the fact that the railways were controlled by foreign capitalists, many of them Jewish. Their private-enterprise opponents, uniting under the equally apposite banner 'The Swiss debt for the Swiss people', and thus emphasising the cost of the purchase, were swamped in a vote which surprised everyone, for it marked a considerable advance in federal involvement in national affairs. If the Swiss, staunchest of free-marketeers, could be persuaded that government control of railways was a national necessity, then protagonists of private railways elsewhere in Continental Europe were clearly doomed.

Throughout the world a national railway system was as much a proof of national identity as an airline is today. Then as now the smaller and poorer the country the more insistent the pressure. In Central America the Costa Ricans, seeing that the Hondurans were building a railway from sea to sea with money

borrowed in London, resolved not to be outdone by their poorer neighbours.

Throughout the less-developed world, any megalomaniac ruler naturally dreamed of railways. Ismail Pasha of Egypt was a perfect case.[7] He planned a railway a thousand kilometres long linking Cairo with Khartoum to help develop what he believed were the fabled agricultural riches of the Sudan – rejecting a cheaper route using the Red Sea for part of the journey on the specious grounds that it would expose traffic to possible naval action.

Railways as a symbol of nationalist autocratic megalomania lasted until well into the twentieth century. When the former corporal Reza seized the Persian throne in 1922 one of his first acts was to order the construction of a railway across his country from the Caspian Sea to the Persian Gulf. Even though the Government of India offered to help, the Shah 'was not disposed to adopt such half measures'. The line of his dream was to be purely Persian, 'its ownership, management and maintenance Persian, its finances untainted by foreign loans. We may doubt the wisdom of his policy: but we cannot withhold our admiration from the originator of the grandiose scheme.'[8] The line, built by forty thousand workers under an international consortium, overcame appalling obstacles and provided a vital route for supplies to Russia between 1941 and 1945.

In the New World railways found their greatest scope for creating nations, if only by connecting previously isolated settlements. In Argentina Juan Batista Alberdi, a 'liberal' (i.e. capitalist) statesman could enthuse that the railway 'will unify the Argentine republic better than any congress. A congress can declare a country one and indivisible; but without the iron road, which draws together a nation's far-flung extremes, the country will for ever remain divisible and divided in spite of all legislative mandates. Thus political unity must begin with territorial unity, and only the railroad can make a single area out of two places separated by 500 leagues.'[9]

But an undeveloped country needed a strong sense of national identity to use foreign capital without lasting damage. Not surprisingly, the masters at this difficult task were the Japanese, who first showed their uncanny capacity to absorb foreign technology and improve on it when building up their rail network in the last quarter of the century. In the New World only two countries, Canada and the United States, were strong enough to use foreign capital as an instrument of their own national creation.

Every single step in the creation of a united Canada seemingly demanded a major railway. One of the first, the Intercolonial across the Maritime Provinces, was an explicit part of their willingness to join the fledgling country. 'No railway, no Federation,' was in effect the attitude of their delegates; an attitude which was clearly appreciated by the Canadians. The Intercolonial had to be promised and promised definitely.[10]

Two more provinces demanded a railway link in return for adherence to the Canadian Federation. One case was fundamental to Canadian history: in 1872 the veteran politician Alfred Waddington insisted that the federal government promise to build a transcontinental railway within a decade as a condition of bringing British Columbia into the federation. The other instance was pure farce: the inhabitants of Prince Edward island in the Gulf of the St Lawrence forced the federal government to assume the debts of its railway system (120 miles, costing $12,000 annually in interest payments) as part of its price of entry.

The Intercolonial, wrote a contemporary historian, 'was one of those great projects essential to an independent Canadian nationality which have been forced on this country by the proximity of the United States'[11] – a proximity which dominated Canadian thinking about railways, as about every other aspect of economic and political life. The Canadians used railways not only to define their national boundaries, but also to repel the opportunities they offered the Americans to integrate the two countries' economies and thus, in Canadian eyes, subjugate them to the American yoke, using them quite consciously to rebuff repeated American attempts at colonisation through railways.

This theme recurred throughout the first fifty years of Canadian railway development. In the 1840s one new line was designed to pass to the (Canadian) north of Lake Erie to link two American cities, Buffalo and Detroit. The Grand Trunk, Canada's first ambitious railway venture, at the time the biggest in the world, nine hundred miles of track, using English finance and engineering know-how, was designed to drain Canadian traffic south to Portland in Maine. The idea was actively supported by the inhabitants of the lowlands round the St Lawrence who wanted an outlet to improve their ties with Great Britain. For over half a century, until it was nationalised just after World War I, the Grand Trunk was considered an intruder, its London-based board assumed to be unsympathetic to Canadian interests. Nevertheless it was, essentially, the product of a Canadian dream. 'Canadians saw that Britain and the United States were thriving. They knew that both these countries had many miles of rail and, so they said, if Canada had railways, she would be united and prosperous too.'[12]

Inevitably the theme of national unity was prominent during the long, tangled, story of the Canadian Pacific, the country's first transcontinental railroad. A Canadian–American project in the early 1870s was defeated after one of the most bitter political battles the new country had ever seen. But the dream remained. 'Until this great work is completed,' said the Prime Minister, Sir John Macdonald, 'our Dominion is little more than a geographical expression.'

A few years later these feelings defeated the great American railroad-builder, Jim Hill, when he proposed an economically-sensible transcontinental southern route through Minneapolis and Chicago, thus depriving Canada of a purely national route to the Pacific. Defeated, he withdrew and constructed the Great Northern, his own, purely American, route to the Pacific just south of the Canadian border. Despite continuing American sniping and a financial situation of continuing precariousness the Canadians showed the world that they could build a trans-continental railway honestly and quickly.

They were lucky: the builders were led by George Stephen, called 'the greatest genius in the whole history of Canadian finance', his cousin, another Scot, Donald Smith, later Lord Strathcona, a brilliant businessman, and William van Horne, one of the ablest of all railway generals. All were honest; all prepared to commit their last pennies, their whole personal credit, to the completion of the CPR.

The automatic association of railroads, especially those across the continent, with Canadian national pride continued even after the triumphant completion of the Canadian Pacific. The CPR had been the dream of Sir John Macdonald. His disciple and successor, Sir Wilfred Laurier, echoed his master's vision with the idea of building the more northerly railroad, parallel to the CPR, a plan which emerged as the ill-fated Canadian National. In the words of an English writer, 'The illusions of grandeur which made the Dominion, with a population of only ten million, build railways sufficient for fifty million people, seemed to have become an integral part of the Canadian soul, destined to outlive the generation that was their birth.'[13]

In the United States the association of railroads with the country was even more obvious if only because they were basic to the country's very existence. 'In America a railway is like a river', wrote Sir Arthur Helps in his life of the great contractor Thomas Brassey, 'and is regarded as a natural channel of civilisation; it precedes population; and is laid down even before common roads are thought of.' Moreover it was a universal, democratic blessing. 'The railway is the poor man's road,' said a speaker at the Internal Improvements convention held in New York in 1836. 'It is the rich man's money expended for the benefit of himself and the poor man.' 'Early railroad enthusiasts always strove to promote their prejudices as national in character and destined to improve the common weal,' wrote James A. Ward.[14] 'The new form of transport could unite discordant existing images; railways could at the same time serve individual betterment and the public good.'

They quickly became a symbol of all the qualities on which the Americans prided themselves, their vigour, their optimism, their unconquerable pioneering spirit. As early as 1832 Charles Caldwell was confident that the 'vastness and magnificence' of 'our system of railroads ... will prove communicable, and add to the standing of the intellect of our country'. Not surprisingly the Americans were soon proud to be thought of as 'a locomotive people'. 'I really think there must be some affinity between Yankee "keep-moving" nature and a locomotive engine,' wrote an English tourist in the 1850s, 'whatever the cause, it is certain that the "humans" treat the "ingine" as they call it, more like a familiar friend than as the dangerous and desperate thing it really is.'

Not surprisingly the Americans tended to forget whose idea railroads were in the first place. 'There is one agent which we can call peculiarly our own and in the application of which the nation is destined to excel,' said one orator.[15] 'What is more,' he added, 'the agent has appeared at a providential moment, just when our Manifest Destiny requires it.' He was right: the railroad symbolised and inaugurated the whole dangerous concept.

The symbol endured. As late as the mid-1960s, when American railroads were in near-terminal decline, they were perceived as still synonymous with the country's national identity. 'All social inventions take place in terms of a national "style", which strongly affects both their emergence and their impact,' wrote

Bruce Mazlish in *The Railroad and the Space Program*. This study was commissioned by NASA to try and persuade the American public that the space programme was as crucial to the American sense of their national identity as the railroad had been a century earlier. 'By accentuating existing cultural differentials, the railroad presumably made Americans more "American" ', wrote Thomas C. Cochran in the same volume; adding hopefully that 'it seems quite possible that space travel may have similar reinforcing effects.'

Even sophisticated foreign observers were persuaded that before the coming of the railways the United States was a mere wilderness. Max Maria von Weber* asserted that 'with the construction of railroads American culture *began* what European culture completed with them . . . *before* the humble footpath, before the cattle road, the railroad stretched itself through the wild savannah and primeval forest. In *Europe* the railroad system *facilitates* traffic: in America it creates it' – a vision true in the West, but certainly not along the Mississippi and the many natural and man-made waterways between the river and the Atlantic.

Above all the railroad symbolised the unity of a nation uncomfortably aware, even before the Civil War, of its deep cultural divisions. Emerson told his audiences that railroads, 'like enormous shuttles, shoot every day across the thousand various threads of national descent and employment and bind them fast in one web'. 'Many of the metaphorical expressions display a nervous edge,' noted Ward, 'they reveal a deep fear that the nation will not endure, much less prevail.'

Not surprisingly Lincoln equated the idea of a transcontinental railroad with the unity of the continent under one flag. He ensured that the Pacific Railroad Act† was passed in 1862, at a dark time for the Unionist cause. Four years after his death the 'Golden Spike' finally united a country whose diversity was kept in check

---

* Quoted by Wolfgang Schievelbusch, op. cit., who describes him as 'a philosophically-minded railroad expert and son of the well-known composer'.

† The absence of Southern members of Congress during the war helped. Before the war they had tried to ensure that any transcontinental railroad would take a, necessarily longer, route through the South.

Driving the last spike on the Candian Pacific Railway: all Canada is now connected.

largely by an iron grid of railroad lines. The very idea of the Union Station, a feature of almost every major American city in the decades after 1865, symbolised a nation finally united after the agonies of the Civil War. The idea reaches its most magnificent and symbolically appropriate form in Union Station in Washington, at one corner of the magnificent site above the city which houses so many of the symbols of American unity, the Supreme Court, the Library of Congress as well as the Congress itself.

But once the continent had been united, the railroad dream turned abruptly into a nightmare for the railroad interest. Within a couple of years the names of the transcontinental's promoters had become synonymous with greed and crookery. The dream had become reality, and once the reality was examined at all closely it turned, not into ashes, but into a mass of human frailties. And inevitably, because the hopes had been so unrealistic, and expressed in such elevated language, the subsequent let-down was the more extreme, the anti-railroad bias more deeply entrenched.

2

Politics and Politicians

As the Americans had discovered, the railways' sheer size and scope ensured that they were the first industry whose very existence was inevitably bound up with politics, politicians, governments, legislatures. Because of their size – and the absence of effective competition from other means of transport – the public interest, itself largely defined by their impact, demanded that politicians provide protection against the over-mighty railway companies.

In one of the most significant demonstrations that technical changes do not, in themselves, obliterate the differences between national cultures, but merely heighten them, the response, the patterns of investment, of construction and control varied from country to country. Every government faced similar problems in controlling these enormous, octopoidal intruders, and every government reacted differently. The railways' existence did not impose any uniform international pattern, did not lead to any convergence of national habits.

There was, however, one fundamental divergence, between Anglo-Saxons and the 'rest'. Almost instinctively, Britons and Americans left the shape of their railwork to market forces, to individual promoters. In Britain this relatively unregulated competition led merely to the duplication of a few lines. In the United States duplication ran riot. Even after the rationalisation of the 1890s there were twenty-one different routes between New York and Chicago, varying in length between 912 and 1376 miles, and no fewer than ninety 'all-rail' routes between New York and New Orleans.

By contrast the Continental Europeans adopted the orderly 'Belgian' pattern, by which railways were planned and regimented, because they were deemed to be of crucial national interest. The government would ensure that the promoters received a 'normal' rate of return during construction. In return, the state ensured that the railways' assets would revert to public ownership at the end of a specific period.

The French went the furthest. They had planned a coherent rail system before a single mile of main-line track had been laid. As a result there is only one line between any two major towns: but because the network radiates from Paris connections between some major provincial centres – most obviously Lyons and Bordeaux – have ranged from the poor to the disgraceful.

Planning did not preclude political conflict even before any main lines had been built. By 1848 the railways represented symbols of bourgeois capitalism powerful enough for the French revolutionaries of that year to call for their nationalisation. In the event their relationship to the state was worked out only during the reign of the Emperor Napoleon III, most notably by those dedicated Saint-Simonians the Pereire brothers, whose career is covered in a note on page 85.

Following the Crimean War, Haussmann's enormously expensive reconstruction of Paris and a financial crisis in 1857, the French railway companies were forced to ask for financial help. The next year the system was divided into two, the 7,774 kilometres already built and the 8,578 kilometres of lines being promoted at the time. In a typically French carve-up the network was divided between six great companies. The state guaranteed the interest due on loans required to build the new network, receiving a small percentage on the revenues of the railway companies, which, effectively, became the state's partners. As usual the capital required was underestimated and the agreement had to be revised, but it provided France with a coherent network and allowed the state to intervene if it thought rates were too high.

However, the politicians would not let well alone. By the mid-1860s the opposition was demanding the construction of socially useful but economically marginal local lines, and the railway companies, with their close links to the Emperor, became symbols of his over-centralised regime and its grasping supporters. After the 1870 war the opposition's views prevailed and an elaborate network of smaller, local lines was built, largely for electoral reasons. This 'Freycinet network' was much abused at the time, although it made an enormous contribution to the unity of rural France.[16] But the unfortunate Chemins de Fer de l'Ouest, which included a high proportion of branch lines running through thinly-populated rural areas, got into terrible financial trouble and had to be nationalised. The first lines to be taken over were in a poor financial and operational condition, so their nationalisation inevitably led to perfectly justified accusations of incompetence and over-manning. Nevertheless the French state gradually increased its influence until a unified network was formed under national control just before World War II.*

In Germany the individual states had originally perceived the railways as a further opportunity to assert their identity. In most cases, even when private money was involved, there seems to have been a tacit understanding that eventually the state would take over. To build the line between Cologne and Minden the government provided a guarantee that the bonds would pay 3½ per cent interest. The state would also buy a seventh of the original share capital, which was arranged so that eventually the government would own the whole lot.†

But arrangements varied. Baden modelled its system on that of Belgium. In the neighbouring state of the Pfalz, private enterprise held sway. One bemused observer[17] points out that 'both of these systems involved serious time losses and periods of indecision at the start and both slowly created a viable and profitable railroad system in the end.' What mattered more than the system was 'the basic determination to decisively and energetically develop the railroad through one system or another.'

To Bismarck it was essential that the railways, the most potent symbol of German unity, should be in public hands. In 1873 he insisted on the creation of a new Imperial railway agency for the newly-united German Empire, ostensibly to work towards greater uniformity in rates, in fact to promote eventual nationalisation of the few lines in Prussia not already in the state's hands.

It took even the supposedly all-powerful Bismarck several years to create a Ministry of Public Works designed to take

* The Société Nationale des Chemins de Fer was formed as a private company, albeit one in which the state retained the majority of the shares.

† The railway was so valuable that its gradual sale enabled Bismarck to finance the Prussian war against Austria in 1866.

charge of the nationalisation process. Meanwhile his friend and banker, Gerson Bleichroder, was busy buying shares in lines he expected to be nationalised. In 1863 Bleichroder had enabled Bismarck to acquire cheap options on shares in a couple of railways, but his later investments were on a much larger scale. Fritz Stern, in *Gold and Iron* reckons that 'at some points, roughly half of his liquid capital was invested in these shares.' For Stern the investment represented 'the clearest commitment to his own policy of nationalization, because failure or even undue delay in nationalizing could have cost him money.' The commitment 'sustained his intense interest in the nationalization of railroads.' Less sympathetic commentators would simply have labelled Bismarck an 'insider trader'.

The truly enthusiastic railway politician, like Cavour, was less interested in the relationship between them and the state than simply in getting them built. 'His methods were eclectic,' wrote P.M. Kalla-Bishop in *Italian Railways* 'there was a state plan and a state railway system, yes; but should a private company wish to build a railway it was encouraged, and, as well, there were railways jointly owned by a company and the state. The object was to get railways built by any means.'

Even the knowledgeable Cavour assumed that politically-motivated lines – in his case those running down the Italian peninsula, specifically designed to encourage national unity – would also prove economically viable. They didn't. Similar mistakes were made in Spain and Austria-Hungary, which both 'constructed "star" systems, centring inappropriately upon their capital cities'.[18] In Austria-Hungary like Italy, a state with more ambitions than capital, government policy was often dictated by the financial needs of the Emperor. As a result the railways changed from private ownership with state guarantees, into state ownership; then, in 1885, the state lines were leased to private companies in three networks, the Mediterranean, the Adriatic, and the Sicilian. Although these corresponded to France's six great companies, they were far less economically successful, and nationalisation was required a mere twenty years later.

The smaller, and generally even poorer, European countries

often suffered from the depredations of British promoters. Portugal had some especially unhappy experiences, while the Swedes, after experiencing the misdeeds of the unscrupulous John Sadleir,* reverted to an earlier pattern by which the Gota canal had been built as a private monopoly under strict state supervision, using government-guaranteed funds.

The pendulum swung the same way outside Europe. In Japan the Meiji Emperor was so anxious to encourage railway construction that the government's own Railway Bureau actually surveyed and built the first lines, while the company received a guaranteed eight per cent yield on its capital. In India the first railways were built under a system which combined profit-sharing and a generous state guarantee. In 1869 an increasingly self-confident Imperial administration decided to take over the task of construction itself. The task proved too burdensome so private enterprise was allowed to enjoy the rewards from profitable lines, albeit with a smaller guarantee, while the state took on the burden of unprofitable routes. The government investment proved immensely worthwhile: by 1914 the government-owned railways were providing a fifth of India's total government revenue, more than customs and excise combined.

In the absence of such a firm imperial hand the whole messy process of construction, operation and attempted regulation of such natural monopolies provided innumerable opportunities for politicians to sell the valuable gifts they had in their power: construction rights, permission for compulsory land purchase, government backing for their loans, preventing competition once the lines were built. Individual politicians, or fleeting pro-railway majorities in Parliament or Congress, are sometimes denounced as corrupt, but, somewhat unfairly, the railway promoters have borne most of the blame. But the moralising was, and is, largely confined to Britain, Canada and the United States. In non-Anglo-Saxon countries people have lower expectations of honesty from their politicians.

Time and again politicians everywhere proved themselves eager to be corrupted. Their underlying corruption is probably

* The model for Merdle in Dickens's *Little Dorrit*.

best seen during the construction of the first American transcontinental railroad. The correspondence of Collis Huntingdon, the Washington representative of the Central Pacific, which was building the Western half of the railroad, is filled with the grasping demands of politicians whom he was

"The Railroad States of America": how the railways bought the US Senate.

exceedingly anxious not to have to pay, if only because his railroad was, effectively, bankrupt at the time.

As we saw with Bismarck, contemporary attitudes were very different from those imposed by later historians. William Cobden, the apostle of Free Trade in Britain, speculated up to his neck in the shares of the Illinois Central.[19] He had received the equivalent of $400,000 from grateful British manufacturers after the repeal of the Corn Laws and put most of it into the railway's stock, then a pure speculation. When he was unable to meet calls for further capital, his friends had to rally round. In 1859 he paid a quick visit to the railway and wrote some enthusiastic letters which were widely publicised by a grateful chairman, but at the time no-one seems to have worried about this attempt by a man regarded as more of a prophet than a mere politician to salvage his personal fortune in this way.

The two protagonists in the great debates which dominated the American presidential election a year later had both speculated in the increased land values which accompanied even the rumour of a new railway. Stephen Douglas had enhanced the value of his real estate holdings in Chicago by securing a federal land grant for a railroad from that city to Mobile. His opponent, Abraham Lincoln, made a more modest return on his investment in land in Omaha, presumed to be the terminus for a projected railway west to the Pacific. By today's standards, of course, Lincoln would have been perceived as a mere tool of the railroad lobby, for his fame as a formidable national figure sprang not from his few short years in Congress but as advocate for the Illinois Central. His biggest coup had been in showing how the destruction of his clients' bridge across the Mississippi was due to deliberate action by ferrymen afraid of railroad competition and was not, as they had claimed, a mere accident.

Canada and the United States both felt that their very existence as coherent countries depended on the construction of transcontinental railroads, but they followed dramatically different paths. The Canadians started with a major political scandal, and triumphantly produced a splendidly honest railroad. The Americans started with high hopes and ended, a mere seven years after the passage of the act authorising the building of the railroad, with a traumatic scandal following the discovery that a construction company, the Credit Mobilier, controlled by the railroad's promoters, was siphoning off most of the considerable profits available from building the railroad. The original Credit Mobilier was a French bank, promoted by the Pereires, designed to widen the investment possibilities open to the petit bourgeoisie. It often invested in railways, but did not otherwise resemble its American namesake, which was a conspiracy of insiders, the opposite of the French original.

At the time the 'Big Four'* who had pledged their credit to achieve the Western section of the railroad, were more successful in escaping public odium than their Eastern counterparts. But their exploitation of the Central Pacific's monopoly position created a radical strain in Californian politics which lasted for several generations.

Canadian politicians were as bad as their American equivalents. In the late 1840s a British businessman, Sir Edmund Hornby, crossed the Atlantic to lobby for the Grand Trunk railway and found that 'some twenty-five members, contractors, etc were simply waiting to be squared either by promises of contracts or money, and as I had no authority to bribe they simply abstained from voting and the Bill was thrown out. Twenty-five thousand pounds would have bought the lot, but I would rather someone else had the job than myself . . . As usual it was a psalm-singing Protestant Dissenter who, holding seven or eight votes in the palm of his hand, volunteered to do the greasing job for a consideration.' (*Autobiography*)

The inter-provincial balancing act, complete with politically-inspired payments and subsidies, continued in full flood even after the provinces had received their railroad mileage in return for adherence to the Federation. The same atmosphere hung over the first attempt at a Canadian transcontinental railroad. This ended in the disgrace of the Prime Minister, Sir John Macdonald,

* Mark Hopkins, Leland Stanford, Collis Huntingdon and Charles Crocker, names attached to most of California's most venerable and reputable institutions, from banks and hotels to universities and museums.

after smashing attacks on him for being in the hands (and the pay) of Sir Hugh Allan, the financier behind the scheme.

In the United States, General Grant was re-elected President even after the Credit Mobilier scandal, but the Canadians took their principles seriously enough to get rid of the politicians they believed to be guilty. In fact, Macdonald and his colleagues had merely been indiscreet, but a verdict of not proven did not satisfy the electorate at the time. The government's own attempts to survey the route were no more successful. In 1880 a Royal Commission found that the work 'was carried on as a Public Work at a sacrifice of money, time and efficiency', largely because everyone involved had been selected because of their political allegiances, not their qualifications for the job.

Even when the Canadians found themselves with an honestly-built transcontinental railroad, the politicians would not let well alone. The CPR's monopoly provided a splendid excuse for Sir Wilfred Laurier to promote his idea of a rival road, a dream naturally exploited by two ambitious financiers, Mackenzie and Mann.

The eventual result, the Canadian National, involved decades of political shenanigans. When Mackenzie and Mann asked for federal guarantees to build the line between Saskatoon and Calgary, the Canadian Conservative politicians 'failed to oppose the scheme in Parliament, probably because Tory insiders were shown the route of the proposed line, a piece of information that allowed a favoured few to buy up land close to the right of way.'[20] Almost inevitably the CNR was always struggling and was duly nationalised just after World War I.

Even privately-owned railways were subject to government supervision. In Britain the railways division of the British Board of Trade dates back to 1841. However it was subject not only to politicians' whims but also to the prevailing mood of the day, and thus swung between allowing the railways to regulate their own affairs and – a mood particularly prevalent after a major crash – a determination to assert the primacy of the public interest.

The companies became adept at delaying or evading regulations. For instance the 1844 Regulating Act provided that every company had to run at least one train every day to serve all the inhabitants along its route. The train had to stop at every station, cheap fares would be available, and the train had to average at least 12 mph. These 'Parliamentary trains' became a long-standing joke, famous for their inconvenience, discomfort and snail-like pace.

The companies' long-term rear-guard action against regulation was helped by the 'railway interest', the first major, organised, feared – and overrated – industrial lobby. Opponents alleged that the legislature was dominated by members dedicated more to the railways than to the common good.

On the face of it the critics seemed to have a case. For a generation after the great influx resulting from the railway boom of the 1840s there were never fewer than a hundred Members of Parliament with some railway connections. Nevertheless, as Geoffrey Alderman has shown,[21] there was a gulf between appearance and reality. Most of the members of the 'interest' were directors of local railways; they were not tied to the major companies most likely to come into conflict with government. However, they were powerful enough to block much legislation for the twenty years after 1846, a period when Parliament was dominated by interest groups rather than parties. In this atmosphere political pressure for effective control or eventual nationalisation naturally evaporated. It was only after the Reform Bill of 1867, and the resulting reinforcement of party discipline, that Parliament started to act, albeit mainly on settlements of railway disputes. Earlier regulations had assumed that the railways would play fair, would reduce their charges in return for protection from competition. Of course they didn't.

Yet even after a series of crashes in the early 1870s, even after the companies had refused to accept government-imposed brakes (partly because they could not agree on the type they would fit) the Board of Trade's inspectors were still divided as to whether legislation was needed or whether they could rely on 'the persuasive power of public opinion as a means of securing the adoption of safety devices'. Not surprisingly by 1884 even The Times was calling for government regulation of railways on behalf of the public.

The laissez-faire attitude was still far more powerful than it was in Continental Europe. The British companies, for instance, waged a long campaign to avoid granting automatic protection to workmen injured at work, whereas in France railway companies were bound to provide compensation even if they were in no way to blame.

Even in Britain, however, nationalisation had had its advocates from the very beginning. John Ruskin, for one, had always believed that 'all means of public transport should be provided at public expense, by public determination where such means are needed, and the public should be its own "shareholder".' During the debates of the early 1840s many pioneers, including the great contractor Thomas Brassey and, more surprisingly, George Hudson, the Railway King, testified that a controlled monopoly was the best form of railway management. Competition, Hudson pointed out – and later experience in the United States proved his point – led to ruinous undercutting of rates, inevitably succeeded by agreements not to compete, what the Americans called 'pools'. In the United States, freight railroads are still privately owned and in Britain it took until 1923 to group the companies into four giant concerns, and a further quarter of a century before Britain followed the rest of Europe and nationalised its lines.

Government ownership provided ample opportunity for direct electoral profit. The Canadians soon saw the possibilities. In the Maritime Provinces, particularly, 'railway employees were not allowed to vote as they pleased but "were driven to the polls like sheep".'[22] Such behaviour naturally provided considerable opportunities for the opposition. 'Government management of the Inter-colonial is monstrous. The next thing that Ottawa will try to manage will be the weather.'

Australia probably had the greediest politicians in the English-speaking world. As The Times reported in May, 1913: 'not only were railways constructed so as to maintain a Ministry's majority in Parliament, but ministerialists obtained contracts for supplies, and even jobbed their constituents into places and procured the adoption of their own inferior inventions on the lines.'

Not unexpectedly the battle between the companies and the 'public interest' was waged most fiercely in the United States, where public support had never implied public ownership but, equally, private ownership did not imply public approval. Popular opinion was first mobilised by two scandals which erupted almost as soon as the Transcontinental railroad had been completed: the Credit Mobilier and the uproar on Wall Street known as the Erie Scandal.* To the average American it seemed that railway construction was inevitably crooked, a corruption matched only by that of politicians benefiting from dealing in the stocks of railroad companies.

The railroads represented a frightening new phenomenon, an industrial monster which dictated its terms to politicians, farmers, businessmen, as well as its employees. By their arrogance, their greed, they had alienated almost everyone not directly in their pay. During the 1870s the only power strong enough to face them was John D. Rockefeller's Standard Oil, a trust more unified, more sophisticated, and thus more powerful than any combination of railroads. Popular opposition was only patchily effective until it was reinforced by the commercial interest, the manufacturers and merchants who also suffered from railway power.

The first effective opposition movement brought mid-Western farmers together in the famous 'Grange movement'. Their official name was the Patrons of Husbandry, their leader, Oliver Hudson Kelley, a clerk in the Agricultural Bureau in Washington. Their organisation echoed that of the Masons, but was open to both sexes. Women were Gleaners and Shepherdesses, their menfolk Harvesters and Husbandmen. Their objective was simple, 'protection from the intolerable wrongs now inflicted on us by the railroads'.

Their strength grew after 1873 as the effects of a major financial crisis spread to the western plains. By early 1875 the Grange's 21,000 branches had 700,000 members concentrated in the Mid-West. They were not political activists but a single-issue pressure group, forcing politicians to pledge their opposition to the railroads, above all the crippling freight rates they charged

* See page 109–10.

93

small farmers. Within a few years several states had passed 'Granger Laws' prohibiting free passes, establishing state railroad commissions, ensuring that railroads did not discriminate against short-haul traffic and even laying down detailed freight rates aimed at the infamous 'pools' by which major companies removed any competition.

The Grangers were joined by manufacturers in the Eastern states, mostly too small to benefit from the rebates granted to the likes of Standard Oil. Indeed it was one Mr Sterne, a member of the ultra-respectable New York Board of Trade and Transportation, who complained that[23] 'railroading can never be considered a private business'. Not only did 'the roads exercise the right of eminent domain'. More importantly 'they had abandoned even the pretence of competition between themselves, and have cast aside the whole basis of American legislation which proceeded on the principle of competition'. The railroads had 'outgrown all state limits'. They were licensed bandits, comparable to the 'fermiers généraux' of 18th-century France, able to tax the people at will. Only federal legislation would suffice to control them.* In Britain the same type of opposition from businessmen confronted by the railways' power meant that in the last two decades of the century the normally conservative Chambers of Commerce anticipated later Socialist demands for railway nationalisation.

The sea change in attitudes was summed up by the history of the free passes granted by railways to anyone of influence. In Britain they were largely tokens of the passenger's importance. In later life George Stephenson took a childish pleasure in flourishing his free pass and being led deferentially to a first-class compartment. The last politician to possess one was also British, the late Earl of Stockton, better known as Harold Macmillan. But this was the result, not of his political activities, but of his directorship of the Great Western Railway before World War II. In the United States they became a sort of currency, which soon

---

* For a striking instance when a railroad allegedly took extreme measures against a determined opponent, see the note at the end of this chapter, 'Was the Curmudgeon also a Murderer?'

became a substantial burden on the railways, who were forced to buy goodwill from all sides of every legislative body with which they came into contact. Politicians came to assume that the pass was theirs as of right, not because the railroads expected their services in return. Ignatius Donnelly, a future populist leader, actually wrote to a railroad president asking for a pass. A few years later he declared passes an abomination.

By the end of the 1870s the American railroads felt beleaguered. With astonishing confidence and political sophistication they turned to the government for protection against their own customers, becoming the leading advocates of federal regulation. In Gabriel Kolko's words 'the ogre of government intervention could not have appeared too formidable to men with important political connections' (*Railroads and Regulation*).

The result was the Interstate Commerce Commission, the first of many regulatory agencies. Like many of its successors it became a 'captive' of the industry it was supposed to regulate within a few years of its establishment in 1887. 'Well before the end of the century the ICC had reached the stage, described in the writings of political scientists dealing with regulatory commissions in later periods, in which its primary function was to minister to the needs of the industry which it was ostensibly to regulate on behalf of an amorphous, implicitly classless public interest.'[24] Even when the ICC took the carriers to court, the railroads' lawyers ensured that the cases were long-drawn-out (averaging four years) and the judges were generally unfriendly to the regulators. (The Commission won only one of the sixteen cases which reached the Supreme Court between 1887 and 1913.)

But succeeding generations of railwaymen reaped a bitter harvest. A revolt against the cosiness of the early ICC was to lead to sixty years of over-regulation which prevented the railroads from competing effectively with the internal combustion engine.

The Pereires: The Pure Believers

Only in France did – only in France could – railways become a doctrine. Yet they were the rallying cry of a small but dedicated group, called the Saint-Simonians after their founder, Claude Henri de Saint-Simon. They were firm believers in a creed which placed useful, productive labour above all else, and proposed to organise the political process to reflect economic realities as they saw them. To the Saint-Simonians railways were the supreme example of public industrial utility and they worshipped them accordingly.

The Saint-Simonians believed in a corporate state in which everyone's interests would be represented for them. So they replaced ordinary democracy with an ideal parliament with three chambers: *d'invention* for artists, *examen*, effectively the legislature, and *execution*, corresponding to the executive branch of government. Their high-minded, albeit patronising and autocratic, political ideals were translated into practice during the 1850s and 1860s, during the reign of the Emperor Napoleon III, who found their undoubted capacities enormously useful.

The Saint-Simonian creed struck a particular chord amongst France's increasingly important technocrats, the naturally autocratic, invariably intelligent, hard-working, logical and supremely well-educated graduates of France's already-powerful Grandes Ecoles, most notably the Polytechnique. Believers included Paulin Talabot, the brilliant engineer responsible for the line from Paris to Marseilles, the influential Michel Chevalier and that visionary diplomat, Ferdinand de Lesseps, creator of the Suez Canal.

But even in this distinguished group the Pereires stood out.[25] The brothers Emile and Isaac came from a distinguished Jewish family long-established in France – their grandfather was the first doctor to teach the deaf and make a proper study of their problems. As early as 1832 Isaac propounded the theory, which soon became part of the group's core beliefs, that railways were more than a mere means of transport, that they were instruments of civilisation itself. France, he continued, was an isthmus providing the shortest route by land between two great seas. So routes between the North Sea and the channel to the Mediterranean, from say, Le Havre to Marseilles (naturally via Paris) should take precedence over alien routes (Hamburg to Trieste for example).

For the Saint-Simonians, indeed for all the apostles of centrally-directed progress in France, railways quickly became the outstanding symbol of modernity, of scientific progress, all directed by a small group of high-minded, almost Platonic guardians.

Inevitably their high-mindedness brought them into conflict with almost everyone. The Parisians revolted, successfully, when they planned a station, albeit quite a modest, Italianate affair, on the Place de la Madeleine in the heart of their city. And in their subsequent schemes they came up against the great James Rothschild, at first their ally (for some time Emile even had an office in the Rothschild bank), and then their enemy. For him the profit to be made from railways – or any other venture for that matter – was an end in itself. For the Pereires the railways, not just in France, but all over Europe, in Italy and Austria–Hungary in particular, were a crucial element in their vision of the triumph of the good and the efficient.

The Saint-Simonians' influence and ideas were not confined to railways. The Pereires' biggest innovation, indeed, was the Credit Mobilier, the first attempt in France to tap the savings of the mass of the population for productive purposes – like railways.

In the end the brothers overstretched themselves, and it was the canny, practical James Rothschild who in a sense 'won'; though the Pereires came through their financial embarrassments with their fortune merely dented and their ideals barely scratched at all. And why not? It is largely to the Saint-Simonians that France owes its magnificent railway system.

Was the Curmudgeon also a Murderer?

American railroads were accused of many crimes, but none has entered more vividly into local folklore than the murder of William Goebel, the 'dark, taciturn figure . . . considered by some to be the most controversial figure in modern Kentucky

Kentucky's martyr to the power of the railroad.

history'. To this day it is difficult to find anyone in Kentucky who does not believe that William Smith was responsible for his death.

Smith, president of the Louisville & Nashville Railroad from 1884 to 1921 was a 'curmudgeon for all seasons' in the words of Maury Klein.[26] He was gruff, sardonic, a brilliant railroad

98

manager, but also 'a symbol of rugged individualism' in an increasingly corporate era.

He was a man of vision, playing a crucial role in developing Birmingham, Alabama as a major steel centre. Not surprisingly he hated government regulation, which he viewed as a mere preliminary towards public ownership. His hatred focused on the progressive forces which flourished in the depression which hit Kentucky hard in the 1890s. The anti-railroad agitation resulted in a stringent regulatory bill, known as the McChord Bill, which the Republican governor duly vetoed on behalf of the L & N.

In the gubernatorial election of 1898 Goebel led the progressive forces. The L & N naturally fought hard to deny him the Democratic nomination, but succeeded only in splitting the party. In the subsequent election the Republican William S. Taylor gained a narrow victory. The Democrat-controlled legislature immediately cried foul, the L & N carried car-loads of rugged mountaineers 'equipped with rifles, pistols and an ample supply of corn liquor' into Frankfurt, the state capital, to support Goebel.

The inevitable explosion came when Goebel was shot, removed to a hotel, where he was sworn in as governor, and, three days later, died from his wounds. His lieutenant-governor was immediately sworn in as his successor. Eventually the Democrats gained the day and the McChord Bill was passed. Although three men, including the Republican Secretary of State, were tried and convicted of Goebel's murder, no one knows who fired the fatal shot, or whether Smith ordered it.

Whistle Stops and Other Political Tours

Politicians found railways convenient from the very outset. In the early 1830s the record for the journey from Manchester to Liverpool was held by an election special which hurled voters between the two cities in a single hour, at a time when the journey normally took two and a half hours.

Naturally politicians employed railways as a means of getting their messages through to more, and more scattered, audiences than ever before. In the United States the idea became a symbol of the whole democratic process, the mobile equivalent of the 'town meeting' which had been at the very base of American democracy in New England. But inevitably the politicians going on what became known as 'whistle-stop tours' (stopping at even the most insignificant stops) were the outsiders. Until well into the twentieth century, incumbent presidents seeking re-election did not deign to tour the country.

The precedent was set by Lincoln's successor, Andrew Johnson, with what became known as a 'Swing Around the Circle of the Union', a tour which took in all the major cities of the North between Washington, New York, Detroit and Chicago in an attempt to preach his gospel of reconciliation after the Civil War. Johnson was heckled by increasingly well-organised crowds of Radicals and his ideas were doomed to failure. Nevertheless the journey set a fashion for those bold enough to take their cause to the country by train which was to last for eighty years.

One of the most famous 'outsiders' to specialise in such tours was the silver-tongued William Jennings Bryan, an orator so in love with the sound of his own voice that his special train was always late. According to James Marshall,[27] the trainmaster 'conceived the idea of getting the candidate onto the back platform and letting him talk from there. Then at starting time, Mr Lake [the trainmaster] simply high-balled the engineer and they pulled out, Mr Bryan still talking to the receding crowd . . . sometimes he was talking when they pulled into the next town'.

President Truman's 'give 'em hell' campaign in the 1948 presidential election was the last burst of populism organised round the country's railroad system. Since then presidential hopefuls have often posed on the cabooses of trains – as late as 1988 the Reverend Jesse Jackson was photographed on one in the course of the New Hampshire primary – but these have been token appearances, attempts to associate the candidate with the earlier populism of the whistle stop. Yet the symbolism remained

Abe Lincoln's funeral train, one of several used to carry Lincoln's body from Washington, D.C., to Springfield, Ill.

powerful even though the private jet had become the effective campaign vehicle.

Trains retained one power: to arouse emotions at the demise of well-loved statesmen. In 1865 the crowds had gathered in their hundreds of thousands to watch President Lincoln's body being transported from Washington to his final resting-place, Springfield, Illinois. A hundred years later crowds just as large, just as affected, swarmed by the tracks to mourn the passage of the funeral train carrying Robert Kennedy's body. As Theodore White put it[28] 'one finally understood aboard the train the purpose of an Irish wake: to make a man come alive again in the affection and memory of his friends.'

IV

CAPITALISM, CAPITALISTS –
AND CONTRACTORS

Railways were by far the biggest projects undertaken since the time of the Romans. Before the railways, the world's financial markets were, at best, primitive affairs, incapable of providing the unprecedented amount of capital railways absorbed, while only a handful of European countries and American states, had raised capital outside their own country. But the railways did more than create markets: miraculously they conjured up whole new breeds of men. The promoters and financiers found the money: the contractors, particularly the English pioneers, worked marvels in actually building the lines.

Much of the process is described in later chapters: the creation of the international markets as part of my discussions of Imperialism, direct and indirect, and of the armies the contractors commanded. But the railways also spawned a new, and deeply involved, breed of capitalist. Robert Louis Stevenson in *The Amateur Emigrant* was typical in associating them with the cartoon figures of frock-coated, pot-bellied financiers. 'When I go on to remember that all this epical turmoil [the first American transcontinental railroad] was conducted by gentlemen in frockcoats, and with a view to nothing more extraordinary than a fortune and a subsequent visit to Paris, it seems to me, I own, as if this railway were the one typical achievement of the age in which we live.'

For half a century railway securities dominated the world's stock markets. In London they were far and away the biggest gambling counters until they were replaced by 'Kaffirs' after the discovery of gold in South Africa in the 1880s. In New York they were the very stuff of Wall Street's most inglorious era, while even in Germany, where the whole process was relatively sedate, three quarters of the capital invested in Prussian joint-stock companies in the twenty years after 1850 went to railway companies.

Railway securities also established the relationships between markets, corporate owners, and their shareholders, who, then as now, didn't get much of a look-in. In Britain the financial goings-on induced a certain amount of popular concern – in the painful aftermath of the 1845–46 railway mania *Punch*, then a radical journal, even suggested that railway directors be tied to their company's locomotives. The hostility did not die out with the mania. Ten years later a disgusted radical calling himself 'a Lancashire victim' published 'a satire', entitled 'The Railway Meeting – dedicated to the pillaged shareholders of Great Britain'.

At a more philosophical level Herbert Spencer pointed out that while the constitution of the railway companies, like that of the country itself, was democratic, the directors (like Members of Parliament), 'by no means regarded themselves as servants of the shareholders; directors rebel against dictation by them.'[1]

He even perceived how a group of not necessarily dishonest men can, as a board of directors, behave dishonestly. The 'corporate conscience is ever inferior to the individual conscience – that a body of men will commit as a joint act, that which every individual of them would shrink from did he feel individually responsible ... most of these great delinquencies are wrought out, not by the extreme dishonesty of any one man or group of men, but by the combined self-interest of many men and groups of men, whose minor delinquencies are cumulative.'

The directors were often not major shareholders, their involvement was often indirect: as landowners or manufacturers they were more interested in the building of a new branch line than in the company's profits. 'The indirect profits accruing from the prosecution of one of these new undertakings, may more than counter-balance the direct loss upon their railway investments.' So they would not worry too much at those classic malpractices, the dividends not backed by profits, the capital artificially increased to build smaller and smaller, decreasingly-economic, branch lines.

In Britain popular interest was initially concentrated not on the deeds and misdeeds of railway directors but of that peculiarly British breed, the railway contractors. The first generation, at least, were not mere builders. They were part shyster, part entrepreneur, part financier, part civil engineer, wholly typical of an age which bred chancers of all descriptions. On a much larger scale they followed the pattern set by the nabobs of the late 18th century, their fortunes made in India, who 'increased the price of everything, from fresh eggs to rotten boroughs'. They were not the last of their sort. The contractors were succeeded by the 'hard-faced men who had done well out of the war', who had made their fortunes by supplying Britain's armies between 1914 and 1918.

Like the nabobs and the 'hard-faced men', they were, by definition, a transitory phenomenon, a group which took advantage of an unrepeatable opportunity to exploit their peculiar talents. After all their work could only be done once. Moreover their businesses were purely personal. None of them built up a continuing business, not even the greatest of them all, Thomas Brassey, who at times was undertaking a dozen contracts in as many countries. It was left to later entrepreneurs – contractors – who may, like John Mowlem, have started as sub-contractors on railway lines, to found long-lasting industrial dynasties.

The contractors' defenders naturally take Brassey as their archetype. Even in his lifetime he acquired an extraordinary aura thanks to his total honesty, his unflappability and his extraordinary organising capacity, which included the crucial ability to choose reliable subordinates. During the Austro-Prussian war in 1866 one of his agents charged through the battle-lines in an old engine carrying enough money to pay the workers, an incident which earned Brassey a medal from an astounded Austrian Emperor. But Brassey stuck too closely to his work to be typical of the breed. Many of the contractors – most obviously Sir Samuel Morton Peto – had a far more general influence on British public life.

The contractors, again like the nabobs and the 'hard-faced men', enjoyed large-scale, suddenly-earned, greatly-resented wealth. In the words of Sir Edward Watkin, one of the greatest of late-Victorian railway magnates, 'At the opera, if we look at the lady occupants of the best boxes, who are glittering with the best diamonds, and ask who they are, we are told that they are the wife and daughters of Clodd the great railway contractor.' Clodd and his like were reviled, worshipped, sneered at for their pretentions, then gradually absorbed, their expensively-educated offspring merging imperceptibly into the British upper classes. Thomas Brassey's son was typical in turning to good works and thus acquiring a peerage.

Even the earthiest of them all, Joseph Firbank, produced a son who showed every sign of respectability. 'Old Joseph,' wrote R. S. Joby, in *The Railway Builders* 'was a genius at building railways, had a calculating mind that needed no elaborate machinery to check the results, and worked hard and long all his life, devoting more time to public service in his later years. The other side was an intolerance towards leisure, foreigners and paper deals . . . one story is that he even refused a contract in the Isle of Wight because that was abroad.' The son was more broad-minded and was prepared to quote for a railway in the Isle of Wight – though he then became an MP and retired to a life of idle luxury.

It was not only the sons who entered Parliament, but some of the first generation as well. They were greeted with something less than enthusiasm, because most of them – Peto was an exception – clearly regarded their seats as simply a rung in the social ladder and an opportunity to promote their business interests. In the disgusted words of the *Morning Post* in 1865:

A large number of those who seek admission to Parliament now are contractors, speculators, men who take a wonderful interest in the promotion of joint stock companies, in fact what are called businessmen, and who are as indifferent to the fact of political parties as they are ignorant of the distinctions which characterise them. These individuals simply require, for their own special purposes, to have seats in Parliament and are perfectly ready to give any pledges to those who will send them there.[2]

Once the major British lines had been completed, a mere twenty-five years after the opening of the Liverpool & Manchester Railway, the contractors either had to go abroad or conjure up new lines within Britain, the usually unnecessary and uneconomic 'contractors' lines. 'They are as insatiate as millionaires in general,' wrote Herbert Spencer,[3] 'and so long as they continue in business at all, are, in some sort, force0 to provide new undertakings to keep their plant employed . . . lines are fostered into being, which it is known from the beginning will not pay.'

Ambitious local grandees could easily be seduced by a big name – the projectors of a small railway near Bristol demanded a contractor 'of the class of Peto, Brassey and Betts' (Peto's partner). The promoters would then 'make an agreement with a wealthy contractor to construct the line, taking in part payment a portion of the shares, amounting to, perhaps, a third of the whole, and to charge for his work according to a schedule of prices to be thereafter settled between himself and the engineer' – a guarantee of profit, for the contractor would take care to choose an amenable engineer.

Contractors' lines soon, and rightly, got a bad name and the whole breed was finally destroyed by the Overend Gurney crash of 1866. The disaster resulted from the enormous appetite of the whole railway financing machine. The promoters and contractors desperately needed new schemes, but all the most viable had already been constructed. So they were left with a rag-bag of inevitably unsound projects – including contractors' lines, railways in Spain, and the disastrously expensive efforts of the London Chatham & Dover Railway to establish a terminus within the City of London at any cost. In 1864 the contractors began to find it difficult to secure adequate finance. To fill the gap they formed finance companies which borrowed the necessary money. But since these companies' major (or only)

Thomas Brassey, king of contractors.

assets were shares in increasingly unsound new railway companies they were bound to crash. They duly went under, and it was Overend Gurney, the most prominent City house involved in these shenanigans, whose own crash gave its name to the whole disaster. In the ensuing panic Brassey barely survived, Peto was destroyed, and the term 'contractor' took on its modern meaning. They ceased to be self-financing entrepreneurs and became purely the agents of the bankers and promoters backing the railways, rather than principals.

Curiously enough, the only other country which produced 'contractors' similar to the British breed was Russia. There, in the words of J. A. Westwood, in his *History of Russian Railways* there was a whole spectrum of railway kings. There were those 'who had entered the railway field after making their fortunes in other business, men like Bernardaki who became a promoter after making his fortune in the Siberian liquor trade; professional bankers who simply became chairmen of the railways they were financing, and then a new generation which made its fortune solely from railway promotion.'

There was Von Derviz, a schoolmate of Reitern, the Minister of Finance, who had given him concessions to build two major lines from Moscow. After completing a third from Kursk to Kiev, Derviz kept the shares and managed to sell debentures to finance the railway at a difficult time. But he was no villain: he built sturdy and durable lines before he retired to Italy where he built a theatre and hired an opera company to give performances solely for him.

More exotic was Polyakov, a former plasterer and small-time contractor, who, in an anti-Semitic environment, nevertheless flaunted his Jewish origins. He started as sub-contractor, was lucky in attracting Count Tolstoi as his patron, and made a vast fortune from building a number of major lines below the estimated cost.

But Russia was an exception. Outside Anglo-Saxon countries the business of railway construction depended too closely on the government to allow the development of the contracting breed. The French produced their own special type, the engineer-technocrats closely linked with successive governments and their policies, who had an even greater influence on railways in the rest of Europe than their British equivalents. In Germany, although railways were of crucial economic importance, no great political capital was made out of them, they were relatively uncontentious ventures, no permanent fortunes were made, no reputations made or ruined.

*

As we saw in the last chapter, the Canadians followed a path of their own, with the two Scottish cousins, George Stephen and Donald Smith, prepared to pledge all their personal assets to complete the CPR, which they were promoting. 'If we fail,' said

Smith at a crucial moment, 'you and I, Donald, must not be left with a dollar of personal fortune.'

More typical of the classic contracting breed were the pair of adventurers behind Canada's second transcontinental railroad, William Mackenzie and Donald Mann. Nominally Mackenzie was a Tory, Mann a Liberal, but that was merely a ploy to get help from the Canadian government.* In fact they were pure railwaymen – Mackenzie refused to sell out to the much larger, British-controlled Grand Trunk 'because I like building railroads.'[4]

They both started as contractors, first working together on a small branch line for the CPR. Their earlier major opportunity came when the provincial government of Manitoba, worried at the CPR's monopoly, provided guarantees for a line from Duluth to Winnipeg – a railway starting in another country and ending in another province. Exploiting the gullibility and crookedness of Canadian politicians to the full, they managed to buy cheap land and get federal guarantees for a line between Saskatoon and Calgary, eventually transforming the Canadian Northern 'from a series of disconnected and apparently unconnectable projections of steel hanging in suspense' into a proper network, multiplying its length twenty-fold to over 2,640 miles in the first decade of the twentieth century.

In doing so they received nearly $100 million in bond guarantees from the state and federal governments. But official help was never going to suffice. In their first ten years as railway promoters they borrowed $130 million from investors inside and outside Canada. To do so they marketed twenty-nine bond and stock issues, creating some sort of record for variety and ingenuity with their 'Mortgage Bonds, Gold Mortgage Bonds, Land Grant Bonds, Income Bonds, Prior Lien Bonds, Sinking Fund Gold Bonds, Consolidated Debenture Bonds, Mortgage Debenture Stock and Perpetual Debenture Stock.'[5] It was not only the pure financiers who needed imagination to get their schemes off the ground.

* Their religious beliefs were more profound. When Mackenzie died Mann urged the whole country to pray for him.

In Canada Mackenzie and Mann had been tolerated as useful rogues: in Britain the contractors, after some delay, had been accepted into polite society; in France railway builders were almost heroic figures. Only in the United States did a tradition develop in which the whole class of capitalists associated with the financing and construction of the railroads were automatically assumed to be villains.

Their successors, the magnates who ran the railroads, were an equally tempting target, arrogantly aware of the power they enjoyed. To Lord Bryce, the British Ambassador, they were 'amongst the greatest men, perhaps I may say the greatest men in America . . . they have power, more power – that is more opportunity for making their will prevail – than perhaps anyone in political life, except the President and the Speaker, who after all hold theirs only for four years and two years, while the railroad monarch may keep his for life.'

In reality, and with good reason, they did not feel as secure as Bryce makes them out to be. They clearly felt a compulsive need to assert their power, above all the 'territorial imperatives' of their railroads, providing an early example of that automatic, reflex aggressiveness which became the hallmark of the American brand of capitalism. The southern railroads, noted Maury Klein,[6] continued to expand 'because railroad managers perceived it as a necessity for survival . . . without it the railroad would die of atrophy.' James A. Ward[7] quotes J. Edgar Thomson of the mighty Pennsylvania Railroad, most secure of all, telling anyone who would listen that 'we cannot stand still, for that means slipping back; we must constantly go forward'. Ward goes on to point to the military language habitually employed by Thomson and his rivals – although the battles between these giants, while they seemed bloody at the time, were relatively artificial eighteenth-century affairs which usually ended in a diplomatic gavotte and a cosy carve-up of the eternal enemy, the customers.

Thomson and his successors were not, however, in the front rank. This role was reserved for their predecessors, the first railway tycoons, assaulted by radicals known generically as 'muckrakers', writing a generation or more after the evil deeds they described, the Credit Mobilier affair and the Erie scandal, as well as the abuses which led to the success of the Grangers. While the tycoons were attacked in their lifetime, they were at least judged by contemporary standards. The muckrakers imposed later, stricter standards on their victims.

Fictional accounts like those in *The Octopus* about the grip of the 'Big Four' on California were matched by the whoopings of the exposers. In 1910 Gustavus Myers devoted two of the three volumes of *The History of the Great American Fortunes*, to the 'railroad fortunes.' In these he included those of Morgan and Vanderbilt, whose money came from a number of sources. But the railroad element was perceived, and not only by Myers, as being dominant. He did not spare his victims. 'Through all of these weary pages' he wrote, 'have we searched afar with infinitesimal scrutiny for a fortune acquired by honest means. Nor have the methods been measured by the test of a code of advanced ethics, but solely by the laws as they stood in the respective times' – a rather disingenuous disclaimer.

In the hungry 1930s, when capitalists of any description were fair game, Matthew Josephson naturally found a receptive audience for his enormously influential *The Robber Barons*, in which he quotes freely from 'the historian Myers'. By then the words 'railroad fortunes' had become synonymous with all that was evil in American capitalism.

Myers, Josephson, and their colleagues were unable to explain how the men they portray as criminals left the country the legacy of a railway system which stood it in good stead for a hundred years. They cannot even point to any major mistakes in the routing of the major lines – they can only harp on a single deviation, insisted on by that undoubted rogue, Dr Durant, which led the Union Pacific a dozen or so miles astray in a line which ran for over a thousand miles. Unfortunately 'the devil has the best tunes'; they often wrote well, they were impelled by a genuine moral fervour, and their pen-portraits remain unforgettable even if cold reason says that they were invariably exaggerated and usually distorted.

The muckrakers' victims deserve to be judged according to

Daniel Drew, one of the most notorious speculators.

their contemporaries' lights (this was not necessarily flattering). Nor were they a single group. There were the men who financed the original major lines, the organisers (who came a generation later) and the pure speculators. The latter, who manipulated railroad stocks because they were the biggest game in town, were no better and no worse than their modern equivalents, the Boeskys, the Milkens and their like, except – a crucial distinction – that they were operating at a time when ethical standards were far laxer than those prevailing, at least in theory, on Wall Street today. The best comparison, perhaps, is with another country which combined enormous economic growth with dubious political-financial ethics – post-war Japan. The sheer size of the financiers' operations, like the result of the Cosmos–Recruit affair in Japan,* led to a transformation in public perceptions, and thus in the behaviour of financiers – and the politicians they helped financially.

The speculators most closely associated with the Erie and the other scandals were a lot more fun than their grey, hard-working modern equivalents. There was Daniel Drew who, allegedly invented the practice of watering stock.† But the king of speculators was Jim Fisk. Even Josephson had a soft spot for his:

> verve, his ready jests, his strings of charity – like a Robin Hood – he diverted attention from his monumental unscrupulousness . . . Fisk rejoiced, wrangled and drank while engaged with unequalled zest in the multitudinous details of his office. At the railroad headquarters of Taylor's Castle he installed his buxom mistress, Josie Mansfield, whose dazzling white skin, whose thick black hair and gray eyes enthralled him so long and fatally, for whom he had forsaken his lawful spouse, and upon whom he lavished vast sums of money in his mad infatuation.

Fisk redeemed himself in many people's eyes (including those of the New Yorkers, always ready to applaud a gaudy show, whatever the morals of the impresario) when he was shot by a 'jealous swain' of the lovely Josie.

The costs of railroad construction, in the United States as every-where else in the world, were systematically underestimated – even if the true, usually frighteningly large, figures, had been

---

* In which the company chairman systematically financed numerous important politicians and their staffs to obtain political favours.

† As a drover, he gave salt to his cattle as he led them across the Alleghenies: as a result they drank too much water, swelled in weight and thus in value. Soon the term came to be used when paper stocks were multiplied to the detriment of the original owners.

HELEN JOSEPHINE MANSFIELD.

The pin-up of the Railway Kings.

grasped by the builders, which wasn't usually the case, they would have scared off potential investors. So even the real visionaries could never be entirely honest. Moreover the builders of the original network included a fair selection of straightforward swindlers, like G. C. Chapman. When he had completed the Kansas Midland he 'cashed in his bonds, left many material bills unpaid and lit out for Ohio. Here he built a line from Chilicothe to Columbus and cleaned up again. Last heard he was living high in Venice, Italy.'[8]

But the best sample can be gained from the building of the three great transcontinental railroads. The first was divided into two sections. The Union Pacific had a chequered history with a fair amount of financial trickery, including the Credit Mobilier

114

affair; but the western half, the Central Pacific, was honestly built. The Big Four, like their equivalents on the CPR, were visionaries who pledged their last penny to build the line at a time when no one else in California would support their apparently hopeless venture. Unfortunately their success left them with the feeling afterwards that their courage entitled them to act as dictators of the state.

The Northern Pacific was a classic example of initial underfunding and the tricks required to combat the problems it created, while the Great Northern, last and in theory least economic of the three, was a triumphant success thanks to a railroad genius, Jim Hill, whom even Josephson called 'sounder' and 'more efficient' than the usual run of villains – though he uses quotation marks to indicate how grudging was his approval. Josephson had to admit that Hill 'became something of an engineer . . . an undoubtedly able administrator, augmented by shrewd buying and selling and ruthless "hiring and firing", brought fundamental economies year after year, and cleared the way for tremendous expansion.'

How the cartoonists saw the great Erie scandal.

Within a generation after they were built most of the railways needed a fair amount of reconstruction. To the muckrakers this was proof that the original builders were crooked. In fact the economics of railway construction in virgin territory everywhere demanded quick and thus shoddy work, whether the line was being constructed by American speculators or the Tsar of All the Russias. Even William Van Home of the CPR felt it was vital to 'get a workable line going which would stand up for six years, make it pay and then begin improving it'. An American financier promoting a railway in Mexico put it more cynically. 'No railroad,' he said, 'has ever been placed on a paying basis until it has been through a receivership.'

To rebuild and reorganise a railroad (let alone combine two or more) demanded the flair of the financier and the organising ability of a Jim Hill. The great E. H. Harriman was generally recognised to have both qualities, to the great benefit of the Union Pacific and his other systems: even Josephson admitted that 'thanks to his great mental agility he did learn much about managing railroad systems'.

Much more controversial is the role played by Jay Gould, the most-hated, most misunderstood figure of all. To Myers he 'became invested with a sinister distinction as the most cold-blooded corruptionist, spoliator and financial pirate of his time, and so thoroughly did he earn his reputation that to the end of his days it confronted him at every step, and survived to become the standing reproach and terror of his descendants. For nearly half a century the very name of Jay Gould was a persisting jeer and byword, an object of popular contumely and hatred, the signification of every foul and base crime by which greed triumphs.'

The truth was more complicated and more interesting. Gould – a sick man for the whole thirty years he was involved in the railroad business – was an intellectual. In the words of Maury Klein, 'there was something of the mathematician in all Gould did, something of the theorist striving to impose his models on a stubborn reality.' He was also breathtakingly ambitious, dreaming of his own transcontinental railroad. He actually loved railroads. When asked by reporters why he had recaptured the

116

Jay Gould, the most unfairly maligned railroad tycoon.

Union Pacific he replied simply: 'There is nothing strange or mysterious about it. I knew it intimately when it was a child and I have merely returned to my first love.' Gould did a great deal towards rebuilding the Union Pacific's tracks and business, attracting traffic from coal and sulphur mines, and encouraging the stockmen on whom the UP depended for much of its income.

His reputation suffered because he was indifferent to his public reputation. As the *Atlanta Constitution* put it: 'The trouble with Mr Gould was that he did not make arrangements with the newspapers to herald his deeds of benevolence, and the result was that no-one outside of his small circle of intimates and familiars knew the extent of them.' He was a man of 'domestic inclinations . . . they are not calculated to make me particularly popular in Wall Street, and I cannot help that.'

JAY GOULD'S PRIVATE BOWLING ALLEY.

Jay Gould bowls Wall Street over.

Gould suffered for his indifference. Klein points to 'the extraordinary extent to which the Gould of legend was a creation of the press . . . twentieth-century biographers relied heavily on the hack biographies that appeared shortly after Gould's death. Without exception these works were compilations of material lifted, often verbatim, from the newspapers.'

Inevitably Gould was involved up to the hilt in all the dubious financial wheeling and dealing which surrounded railroad stocks. But to gauge his real stature you have only to compare him with the gang of well-placed, highly-respected financiers who raped the Penn Central of its assets at the end of the 1960s, leaving the railroad itself crippled. They were pure speculators, whereas Gould left the railroads he ran in better shape than he found them.

His vision made him bolder than his contemporaries. In Klein's words, when Gould took over the Missouri Pacific he assumed 'that profits could be had by developing untapped territory where competition was minimal, and that Saint Louis could be developed into a transportation entrepot rivalling Chicago' – even though the Missouri Pacific was not a major trunk line, and it was assumed that one was needed as the centre of any system. But the best witness to Gould's real stature was General Grenville Dodge, the chief engineer to the Union Pacific. Gould, he said, would 'stand in history as having risked and planted his millions in developing a new country while others merely risked and planted their millions in a country . . . where there was no risk as to returns.'

The Goulds and the Harrimans were exceptions. 'Reorganisation' in the United States usually meant the final triumph of the bankers, rather than individual railwaymen. During the heroic era the bankers had remained in the background. The first local lines had usually been built with capital provided by locals anxious to boost their towns – and to increase the value of their land holdings along the tracks. But longer lines involved external capital. First raised in regional centres, as the demands grew greater it was provided by a handful of national, indeed international financial markets, notably New York and Boston, able to attract foreign capital and to provide integrated financial services.

At the outbreak of the Civil War capitalism in the United States, apart from railroads, was so small-scale that it did not require the services of pure investment banking houses. But in Vincent Carosso's words in *Investment Banking in America*:

Financing the railroad construction boom of the last two decades of the nineteenth century resulted in the extension and institutionalization of several investment banking practices that previously had been provided informally. The banker's relationship as the financial adviser and fiscal or transfer agent of the railroads he sponsored dated back to the late 1840s and early 1850s; the rise of railroad-banking alliances occurred in the 1860s, if not earlier; and the use of

119

the syndicate to introduce and distribute railroad bonds was introduced in the 1870s.

Bank representation on railroad directorates and finance committees after 1880 was an institutionalization of the close personal ties that commonly had existed between bankers and railroad officials before that date.

A banker's presence on the board of a railroad gave investors a feeling of security, for they could rely on the bankers to move in when things went wrong. When the Santa Fe got into difficulties in 1887, for instance, Kidder Peabody imposed stringent financial disciplines, sharpened accounting systems, and imposed close controls over expenditure and capital investment. The great J. P. Morgan spent fifteen years reorganising unprofitable railroads – although even he could not induce the quarrelling Western railroads to cooperate until they were all nearly (or totally) bankrupted in the panic of 1893.

The solutions the bankers imposed varied in form and effectiveness, but, in Carosso's words, 'in the short term they brought added prestige, influence and alleged huge profits to the investment houses that negotiated them' – a foretaste of the mergers and acquisitions which have made bankers' fortunes in the past twenty years. For by the end of the century American railroads had become just another business, unable to escape the laws which governed less exciting sectors.

Sir Samuel Morton Peto

To contemporaries Sir Samuel Morton Peto was seen as the very archetype of the railway contractor. In John Francis's words, 'to the railway contractor who has arisen with the railway power, this gentleman should be an example and a type. Born of that great middle class to which England owes so much of her grandeur, leaving school at an early age to serve an apprenticeship, it is to his honour that, determined to attain a practical knowledge of the work to which he was devoted, the future legislator

Sir Samuel Morton Peto, the unluckiest of the great contractors.

handled the trowel of the mason, and worked with the chisel of the carpenter, with characteristic energy.'

Peto enjoyed a better start than Francis made out. He was indeed a first-class bricklayer, and did indeed start as an apprentice, but to his uncle, one of the biggest builders in England. In 1831, at the age of twenty-one, he inherited his uncle's business and immediately showed his willingness to tackle the largest projects. In Francis's words, he and his partner Thomas Grissell 'devised Hungerford market and rebuilt the Houses of Parliament; they erected clubs and formed model prisons; contracted for theatres, built castles, and constructed docks of the most perfect character in the kingdom.'

In 1834 he spotted the potential of railways, dissolved his connection with his uncle's building firm and became a railway contractor. As a builder based in the Thames Valley he was ideally placed to find business. From the very beginning his operations were marked with a boldness remarkable even in a confident age. In Francis's words 'he has been first and foremost in singly taking contracts at which companies would once have hesitated; and he has been one of the few who, holding a moral and physical sway over thousands, have not betrayed their trust.'

He refused to increase his profits through the infamous truck system, treated his navvies as human beings, 'supplied them with books, and engaged for them teachers. He formed sick-clubs, introduced benefit societies, and taught them the use of savings banks. He built temporary cottages and let them at a proper price.'

By 1846 Grissell had become nervous of the risks Peto habitually undertook, and dissolved the partnership; so Peto took on Edward Betts, who had married his sister Ann. Grissell's nervousness was understandable. Peto was involved in some seven hundred miles of construction in Britain alone, and, through the Eastern Counties Railway, was involved in large-scale development in East Anglia. As his son recorded, his father was used to crises: 'I have never passed through such a crisis,' he wrote in 1857, 'I have now £200,000 owing to me, and get it I cannot; but I trust my way will be made clear without sacrifice; but it must be some time before the clouds clear away, and it has been anxious work – these things come perfectly unexpectedly, and are not to be guarded against in large affairs.'9

Peto had become a Member of Parliament in 1847. From a Dissenting background, a Baptist after his second marriage, he pushed for the rights of Dissenters, most publicly their right to be buried in Church of England graveyards.

His public fame and his baronetcy both derived from his success in building the railway from Balaclava to the Anglo-French lines above Sebastopol during the Crimean War. He suggested the idea to Lord Palmerston, and carried it through at no profit to himself after the army had made a mess of the line.

He even resigned his seat in Parliament so as not to be accused of taking advantage of his position.

Despite his reputation, the general contemporary bitterness toward the whole contracting breed was reflected in *Dr Thorne*, where the author, Anthony Trollope, paints Peto – in the character of Sir Roger Scatcherd – in scathing terms. Scatcherd

> was whilom a drunken stone-mason in Barchester . . . there had been a time when the government wanted the performance of some extraordinary piece of work, and Sir Roger Scatcherd had been the man to do it. There had been some extremely necessary bit of railway to be made in half the time that such work would properly demand, some speculation to be incurred requiring great means and courage as well, and Roger Scatcherd had been found to be the man for the time. He was then elevated for the moment to the dizzy pinnacle of a newspaper hero . . . He went up one day to court to kiss her Majesty's hand, and came down to his grand new house at Box Hill, Sir Roger Scatcherd Bart.

In the twenty years after he entered Parliament Peto was one of the most prominent figures in public life. He provided the first crucial guarantee which led to the financing of the Great Exhibition and backed Joseph Paxton's revolutionary Crystal Palace. His religious beliefs did not prevent him cutting a dashing figure. His son quoted an old engineer as remembering: 'In those days there still survived the tradition of dandyism among men of distinction . . . I have often thought that the dignified, courtly presence of Mr Peto in those days, enhanced by his exquisitely-frilled shirt, diamond pin, and faultless coat with velvet facing, was a sort of index of the magnificent style and elevation of the whole manner of his firm and of their style – dignified, yet not extravagant.'

Inevitably he expanded his activities abroad. Already in the 1840s he was involved, with Thomas Brassey, in the ill-fated Grand Trunk Railway in Canada and, on his own, in the Great Southern railway from Buenos Aires. In the late 1850s he helped build the first railway in Algeria, observing that 'the country wanted only a good railway system to enable her agricultural resources to be developed'. He made no fewer than fourteen journeys to Paris in connection with the railway and accompanied Napoleon III to the opening in Algiers.

By then he was a major international figure – the King of Denmark travelled from his castle to Copenhagen for the opening of the country's first railway to save Peto's time. He was treated with a similar respect in Portugal, where three barges accompanied him on the first stage of his return from Oporto. But his scruples prevented him getting the contract for the railway up the Douro to the Spanish frontier. As he wrote, 'I find that since I was last here a French party has been intriguing and using money among the employees of the Board of Works.' Peto refused to spend the £5,000 required to buy up the officials.

In 1865 he organised a Transatlantic trip for an influential group to inspect the Atlantic and Great Western. On his return, as well as publishing a book on the resources and prospects of America, he conceived a plan to link the Atlantic and Great Western with the whole of the East and the Mid-West. Peto was thus 'one of the first entrepreneurs to consider the consolidation of a single system reaching from the Mississippi to the Atlantic seaboard that would transcend several state boundaries.'[10]

His downfall came the following year in the Overend Gurney crisis. Instead of demanding cash payment Peto had taken shares in the London Chatham & Dover Railway to enable it to complete its ill-fated extension to Blackfriars. He was caught up in the scandal, and was viciously pursued by the *Daily Telegraph*. Although everyone acknowledged that he was an honest victim of the crash it was a pitiless age. Peto felt obliged to resign his seat in Parliament and sell his new, specially built, town house in Kensington Palace Gardens.

His partner Betts retired to the country, while poor Peto exiled himself to Budapest for three years. He became a consultant, trying, unsuccessfully, to promote railways in Russia as well as Hungary. On his return he tried to launch a small mineral railway in Cornwall, failed, but lingered on, a forgotten figure, dying in obscurity in 1889.

Charles Francis Adams: the Patrician Fights Back

American railroads created their own elites. In doing so they displaced the groups which had run the United States since 1776. The process can be seen at its most vivid in the career of Charles Francis Adams Jnr, grandson and great-grandson of presidents. Adams believed 'that he could make a living by wedding railroads and reform.'[11] As one of the three commissioners in Massachusetts he put into practice his firm belief that railroads could be controlled by voluntary agreements. But this gentlemanly, voluntaristic approach could not cope with the railroad industry – nor the characters of the men who dominated it.

Adams realised this when he served as deputy to Albert Fink of the Louisville & Nashville railroad, who headed a committee which tried to control national freight rates. Competition from new lines undermined the pool, and Adams concluded that Fink was 'fighting the stars in their courses – laboring through organization to defeat in its workings the great law of the survival of the fittest.' This experience converted him to the need for a legal system to control the railroads' activities, a conclusion reached by Congress less than a decade later.

As a railroad manager, president of the troubled Union Pacific, Adams was not a success, for his patrician attitude prevented him appointing or inspiring efficient managers. Apart from his symbolic importance, his lasting fame derives from a single book, *A Chapter of Erie*, his account of the stormiest episode in the history of American railroad finance: the Erie scandal of 1869. Adams, a firm believer in 'the eventual supremacy of an enlightened public opinion', originally wrote the account for the *North American Review* and published an enlarged version as *A Chapter of Erie* later the same year. Adams was a contemporary who thoroughly understood the markets and the mentalities of the operators involved. His indignation at the comprehensive dishonesty of everyone concerned was conveyed in a springy prose which exposes, clearly and completely, an exceedingly murky and tangled story.

Part of its power derived from his closeness to the scene. In his autobiography he wrote, 'I have known, and known tolerably well, a good many "successful" men – "big" financially – men famous during the last half century; and a less interesting crowd I do not care to encounter. Not one that I have ever known would I care to meet again, either in this world or the next; nor is one of them associated in my mind with the idea of humor, thought or refinement. A set of mere money-getters and traders; they were essentially unattractive and uninteresting.'*

His rather unappetising patrician disdain was diluted by his appreciation of the size of the characters involved, and an awareness that he, too, was touched with their sins of greed and opportunism. When Jim Fisk was murdered Adams reflected how 'the damned rascal was a good friend to me but the state's prison has been cheated of an inmate.' And after taking a flyer in the Denver & Rio Grande he wrote that it was 'a pure little gamble by the way, wholly reprehensible, but pleasant – if it wins'. Financially Adams was very shrewd, making several million dollars through systematic property speculation and development in Kansas City.

The Erie was originally founded in 1832 but it took nineteen years and several rescues for it 'to reach Lake Erie from tidewater'. The 'affair' started when 'Commodore' Vanderbilt, already master of the New York Central, tried to buy the Erie and thus 'make himself master in his own right of the great channels of communications which connect the city of New York with the interior of the continent, and to control them as his private property.'

Vanderbilt had already seized control of two of the approach roads, but his 'pitiless energy which has seemed to have in it an element of fate' brought him up against those equally pitiless operators, Messrs Fisk, Gould and Drew. While Vanderbilt was trying to buy control of Erie in the market his opponents were trying to thwart him by the endless creation of new stock and new bonds convertible into stock – a technique perfected by Daniel Drew as treasurer of the Erie.

Inevitably the dispute reached the state courts, with both sides controlling their own judges, who were elected officials.

* This, and the following quotes come from 'A Chapter of Erie'.

Charles Francis Adams, railway boss – and investigative author.

127

Commodore William Henry Vanderbilt as the 'Colossus of Railroads'.

'When the ermine of the judge is flung into the kennel of party politics and becomes a part of the spoils of political victory, when by any chance partisanship, brutality and corruption become the qualities which specially recommend the successful aspirant to judicial honours, then the system described will be found to furnish peculiar facilities for the display of these characteristics.'

Vanderbilt won the first battles in the legal war:

'The Drew party were enjoined in every direction. One magistrate had forbidden them to move, and another magistrate had ordered them not to stand still. If the Erie board held meetings and transacted business, it violated one injunction; if it abstained from doing so, it violated another. By the further conversion of bonds into stock, pains and penalties would be incurred at the hands of Judge Barnard; the refusal to convert would be an act of disobedience to Judge Gilbert.'

To escape from the jurisdiction of the New York courts the directors, 'looking more like a frightened gang of thieves disturbed in the possession of their plunder than like the wealthy representatives of a great corporation', simply took the ferry to New Jersey. But they did not forget their liquid assets. 'One individual bore away with him in a hackney-coach bales containing six million dollars in greenbacks.' From the safety of the Jersey shore they dumped millions of dollars of stock onto the market, so depressing the price that at one point Vanderbilt stood to lose $7 million.

The continuing legal skirmishings were overshadowed by both sides' systematic bribery of the members of the New York state legislature in Albany. This splendid body of rogues promptly appointed a committee of investigation (a sure source of profit for the members). At first Vanderbilt had his own way, but Gould, escaping his not very vigilant bailiff, camped in Albany where 'he assiduously cultivated a thorough understanding between himself and the legislature'. This 'understanding' later appeared as an extraordinary item of $1 million in the railroad's balance sheet.

Within a few weeks Vanderbilt had had enough. 'He could easily buy up the Erie Railway but he could not buy up the printing press' used so liberally to provide his opponents with new shares. He did a deal, leaving Messrs Fisk and Gould in charge of a battered railroad. But the victorious conspirators then over-reached themselves. In conjunction with the Tweed gang, which dominated New York politics, they failed in a spectacular attempt to corner the gold market.

The whole episode confirmed Adams in the pessimism typical of his generation of his family. He feared that a future dictator would combine Vanderbilt's 'Caesarism' and the 'combination of the corporation and the hired proletariat' represented by the Erie-Tweed ring. It was true that 'evils ever work their own cure, but the cure for the evils of Roman civilization was worked out through ten centuries of barbarism.'

But, as so often happens, the tide was turning at the very moment that current trends were being projected into the distant future. Despite Adams's gloom that the affair had not 'led to any persistent effort at reform', the Erie affair – and the almost contemporary Credit Mobilier scandal – did mark the high-water mark of institutionalised corruption. The history of the United States in the next half century was to be dominated by persistent attempts to control the abuses Adams had so vividly exposed. He was less of a failure than he liked to imagine.

V

THE ECONOMY OF RAIL

Economists have always been fascinated by railways, which developed at much the same time as the 'dismal science' itself. Early in their joint lives the theory of imperfect competition was developed from observing the operations of those giant enterprises, the railway companies. But more recently academics have played a more questionable role in trying to understand the railways' economic effects.

Since the 1950s a whole school, the so-called New Economic Historians, have queried the historic assumption that railways were of supreme economic importance, by measuring what they called the 'social savings' attributable to the railways. Using the available statistics (themselves not always complete, let alone reliable), they calculated the actual cost of the services the railways provided in a given year, and the hypothetical cost of the same services using the best transportation methods available if the railways had never been built. The difference between the two costs formed the 'social savings'.

The result of their efforts has been a long and acrimonious series of arguments in the learned journals, which have distracted scholar power from more positive endeavours. To make matters worse, as Professor Douglas North pointed out,[1] by its very nature New Economic History was 'unteachable at undergraduate level because of its failure ... to provide any integrated explanation of man's economic past'.

The debate originated in the United States, in the attempt by R. W. Fogel[2] to quantify the contribution made by the railways to American economic development and in doing so to counter

FRANK LESLIE'S ILLUSTRATED NEWSPAPER. [MAY 29, 1869.

SAN FRANCISCO

NEW YORK

"DOES NOT SUCH A MEETING MAKE AMENDS?"

A cartoon weighs the costs of the Trans-Continental railroad against its future economic benefits.

the previous 'progressive' image of American history, in which each era is portrayed as an advance on its predecessors. More narrowly it was an echo of a general and increasing American disenchantment with the railways, an attempt to minimise their contemporary and historical role.

Not unexpectedly this counter-factual, 'what-if', historical approach has now proved self-defeating. As David Lightner put it:

> to demonstrate that many of the economic changes wrought by the railroad could have been achieved by other means does not alter the fact that railroads did what they did. No historian will ever again say that railroads were indispensable to American economic growth – in that narrow sense the Fogel theory is triumphant – but there is no reason for historians otherwise to alter their customary practice of assigning to the railroad a central role in any narrative account of American economic history.[3]

Moreover 'social saving' provides an inadequate measure of the railways' impact. As Stanley Libergott pointed out, 'a tiny percentage may be economically very significant. If . . . products were carried by magic carpet, at absolutely zero cost, the "social saving" would still compute to less than three per cent of national income. Similarly tiny numbers would describe the "social saving" from the coming of electricity, the automobile, hybrid corn, or anything else.'[4] If, for example, the railways had ceased to carry any fish in 1865 the saving would have been less than 0.1 per cent, yet, as we see later the 'fish traffic' was part of a dietary revolution.

Focusing on 'social saving' overshadowed the railways' indirect benefits. Economic progress, so often linked to railway construction, tended to be a self-justifying proposition of great but totally unquantifiable importance. For the Saint-Simonians in France, for Bismarck in Germany, for Count Witte in Russia, for Sun Yat-Sen in China, railways were a symbol of economic as well as political progress. The Tsar's belief, expressed in his 'railway *ukaz*' of 1857, that 'our fatherland, equipped by nature with abundant gifts, but divided by huge spaces, especially needs suitable communications' did more than spur on the construction of thousands of miles of railways. A mere two years later the Minister of Finance, in urging the creation of a modern banking system, was looking for 'the revival of industrial entrepreneurship . . . and the anticipated construction of railways'.

For their greatest stimulus was not measurable. Repeatedly the railways disproved pessimists' fears the world over. In Eric Hobsbawm's words, 'even in the late 1840s intelligent and informed observers in Germany – on the eve of the industrial explosion in that country – could still assume, as they do today in undeveloped countries, that no conceivable industrialization could provide employment for the vast and growing "surplus population" of the poor'.[5] Quite simply, railways lifted man's economic horizons.

By definition the railway was an instrument of economic development, if only because of the enormous investment and industrial efforts required to build it. Moreover, notably unlike investment in roads, the railways had a continuing economic effect through the organisation required to operate them. The financing and construction of railways – and the equipment they used – formed one such effect: the need to manage such enterprises was another; while the opportunities they provided for new economic activity, both immediately and, rather separately, for generations after they were built, provided yet another stimulus. Many of the effects were unquantifiable. 'It is precisely such effects as spin-offs to the training of labor and management, the diffusion of skills and technology between and within industries, economies of scale and the whole learning process inherent in economic development that cannot be captured within the conceptual folds of social saving.'[6]

Economists divide the effects of technical innovations like railways into what they term 'forward' and 'backward' linkages. Forward linkages measure the gains because the railways were faster, more convenient, cheaper than alternative means of transport. 'Backward linkages' measure the effects of the railways' own demands for such commodities as coal and iron. But even this distinction does not cover all their economic and technical contributions.

Fogel minimised the railways' technological contributions by affirming that their effects were confined to the railways themselves. He was clearly wrong. The techno-economic effects were both wide-ranging and lasted beyond the half-century when they were the technological advance guard. They helped to spur innovations generally associated with the second industrial revolution – harder and more durable steels, the increasing use of electricity, above all for motive power. Throughout the century only the railways' alliance with the telegraph and the steamship provided means of communication adequate for modern methods of production. The telegraph's poles marched alongside railway tracks the world over. The synergy between the two was obvious. The telegraph vastly increased the speed and frequency with which trains could run over a given line. But the railways' needs also spread the telegraph far more quickly and universally than would otherwise have been possible.

Economically the figures for 'social savings' are often too vague to be meaningful – estimates for the railways' contribution

How the railroads got grain to market.

to Mexico's economy vary between 25 and 39 per cent, figures which tell us nothing at all except that they were extremely important. The very existence of the railways had a continuing effect on economic development, yet 'social savings' are measured in a particular year soon after the railways were built and thus do not allow for their longer-term effects. They also ignore the growing importance of the transport sector, which doubled its share of Europe's economic output in the course of the 19th century by encouraging not only new industries, but the new service of mass passenger travel. And the very efficiency of rail transport made its own contribution to economic growth, acting as what the economists call a 'leading sector' in economic development.

For new industries did not spring up ready-made immediately the tracks were laid. Even the most obvious effects were not immediate – it took fifteen years for the Silesians to replace British coal in the hearths of Berlin. Even by the social savers' own measurements the percentages grew. Railways had contributed a mere 4.1 per cent to Britain's economy in 1865: twenty-five years later the figure had risen to 11 per cent. In the United States the figures were 3.7 and 8.9 per cent, and in Belgium 2.5 and 4.5 per cent.*

Many of the consequences were part of more complicated socio-economic events. The great boost to American railroad construction in the late 1840s came from two forces which had nothing to do with that country: the repeal of the British Corn Laws in 1846, which greatly increased demand, combined with the Irish famine of 1846–47. Within two decades the Mid-West had become the breadbasket of the world. Its only competitor was Russia, which constructed a vast network of railways in the major grain-growing regions between 1860 and 1875.

But the Russian agricultural boom could be attributed to a totally separate factor – in this case the abolition of serfdom, beginning in 1858, which brought millions of former serfs into the money economy for the first time. By the end of the 1860s capitalism had penetrated the countryside through 6,500 rural fairs which ensured an effective exchange between agricultural and industrial products, both of which relied on the railways: as a result the value of agricultural production rose from 360 to 460 million roubles between 1860 and 1863.

In Russia, as elsewhere, unprecedentedly large concerns were indeed required to build and operate railways, but they provided as much, if not more, help to smaller entrepreneurs. The increasing ability to turn their produce into cash reduced the villagers' dependence on the classic rural plague, the village usurer.

In place of the great Moscow or Kolomna merchant, the Nizhny Novgorod miller, the Moscow flax or hemp-factory owner, the large export wholesaler, and the old 'flour dealers', the railway stations now swarmed with a mass of small traders, exporters and commission merchants, all buying grain, hemp, hides, lard, sheepskin, down and bristles – in a word, everything bound for either the domestic or the foreign

---

* Figures quoted by Patrick O'Brien in his introduction to *Transport and Economic Development in Europe 1789–1914*. He put the same idea in economic terms 'static equilibrium analysis cannot deal effectively with the dynamic effects of railways over time.'

market. Operating with relatively little capital, aided by credit, with a small mark-up in price but with a rapid turnover of capital, these petty commercial middlemen penetrated deep into the village, constantly drawing the rural area into the orbit of cash turnover.[7]

Railroad transport costs were a fifth of those by wagon. This 'offered millions of farmers, thousands of small manufacturers, and dozens of giant trusts the opportunity to expand their sales (and profits) by moving into new markets. Some of these new markets were a hundred miles from their base. Others were located thousands of miles away in Europe and Asia . . . As a French commentator wrote, "each mile of railroad constructed in a new country is a kind of centrifugal pump, furnishing for

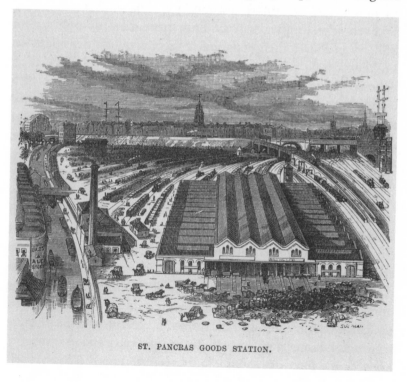

ST. PANCRAS GOODS STATION.

In Victorian times, goods stations were just as important as passenger ones.

137

exportation hundreds of tons of the products of such a country".[8]

In already settled countries the railways usually based their forecasts on the passenger traffic between the towns and cities they served, not realising the amount of new freight traffic their very presence would generate – a scepticism shown by the often remarked inadequacy of goods yards. But the people who ran them soon realised that their very existence – linked to preferential freight rates – could attract an undreamt-of variety of new customers. They also underestimated the number of passengers wanting to use them – just as twentieth-century transport planners have often been overwhelmed by unforeseen surges in demand for new roads. In France, for instance, the 'secondary effects', not felt until the end of the century, included a dramatic increase in the numbers of provincials coming to Paris to shop, encouraged by cheap fares for family travel.

Even when railways were built primarily for political or military purposes their economic effects could be considerable. In Italy, where railway tariffs were designed to reduce their deficits rather than encourage traffic, the very existence of a complete railway network greatly boosted the country's economic growth at the turn of the century, especially the development of the upper valley of the Po, and thus the port of Genoa. Moreover, numerous minor railways which did not face competition from sea-borne transport were both profitable and economically productive.

The strategic railways in Soviet Asia east of the Caspian provided an enormous boost to the production of cotton destined for western markets. Similarly in India the railways – some constructed to counteract the supposed threat from their Russian equivalents – proved crucial to economic development. The same applied in Senegal, where a line built to allow the French to police the country 'allowed the rubber, the cereals and the peanuts from a rich hinterland to reach the Senegal river and to transport towards the interior manufactures produced on the coast, such as textiles, foodstuffs and machinery.'[9]

A railway's financial viability was often irrelevant to its economic usefulness. 'For eighty years the Grand Trunk Railway

How the railways destroyed the forests: a logging train in British Colombia, circa 1910.

in Canada was subject to recurrent financial crises and was a failure as a commercial enterprise, [yet] the Railway made a significant contribution to the economic development of Canada.'[10]

In France, as elsewhere, railways reduced price discrepancies between two cities, or two regions, linked by rail. They completely eliminated the vast price differentials between South and North, the previously unconnected halves of the country. The effects could be international: the Paris markets, for example, acted as a clearing house for fruit and vegetables from all over the country, destined for export to Germany.

Railways transformed business habits, most obviously by obviating the need to invest so heavily in stocks and thus releasing cash for investment. In France the Nord railway from the coal mines of the north cut out the middlemen who had previously made their fortune buying and stocking during the summer, and then selling at enhanced prices during the winter months. In the United States 'in pre-railroad days businessmen calculated in terms of months. Inventories were replenished by semi-annual trips to wholesale markets, credit terms were six to ten months or in some rural areas from crop to crop. During the northern winters commercial activity in the interior of the country slowed nearly to a halt.'[11]

Before the railways came transit times could drag into months in winter when canals and rivers froze and roads, especially in then-undeveloped countries like Spain, became impassable rivers of mud. The shippers soon learnt the lesson. 'One night's frost locked the [Erie] Canal so as to embargo five hundred canal boats, all loaded with western products bound for New York, the value of which is five million dollars, and which has to remain unmoved for four months. [But] not one solitary boat ... moving West can be found caught in this commercial trap – it paying even the makers of stoves and heavy goods to move them west on railroads.'[12]

Even unfrozen rivers were unreliable. The Rhône was so crowded, its river-bed shifted so unpredictably, that it could take up to eighty days (more than twice the normal, leisurely month or so) to cover the four hundred miles between Lyon and the Mediterranean. Similarly iron ore from Lorraine was shipped to the Ruhr by rail because the River Moselle, a theoretically more direct route, was shallow and winding, unsuited to navigation by steam tugs and large barges. The only country where water-borne freight remained competitive was Japan, where coastal shipping retained its predominance. Elsewhere speed combined with security to ensure the railways' supremacy, for that very security reduced the cost of insuring goods in transit.

River or canal transport could never be speeded up. Libergott showed that railways required virtually the same amount of force to move goods at 2½ or 10 miles an hour, while water's inertia meant that merely increasing a barge's speed by ½ mph to 3 mph doubled the force required. 'Canal speeds were limited to 6 mph. If the boats went any faster their waves broke the mud wall of the canal; locomotive speeds increased year after year.'

Even so the railways were liberated from water only when they conquered obstacles, like the Appalachian mountains, impassable to canals. Originally, railways had been designed to be complementary to navigable waters, which, by implication, retained their supremacy. When the Stockton & Darlington was built, its rails carried London's coal for only a fraction of its journey – it took forty years for rail coal to compete with the traditional 'sea coal'. When the railway was built from Budapest to Pecs the Danube steamship company took a large shareholding and ensured that the coal traffic from Pecs remained water-borne. (In a similar spirit, the SNCF had a substantial stake in Air Inter, which provides most of France's internal air services.)

But railways invariably cost less to build than canals: as early as 1833 the Belgians established that a railway would cost an eighth less to build than a canal, would carry freight a fifth cheaper, taking a single day rather than the ten required by water transport over the same route. Nevertheless, railways still had to compete with the mass of existing canals, as well as the watery routes Nature provided free in the form of rivers, lakes and seas.

Railways could make up for Nature's deficiencies, most obviously by by-passing rapids. As early as 1824 the newspapers of 'Lower Canada' projected a railway round the rapids on the Richelieu River to improve transport between Montreal and New York, and for many years railways in Canada and New England were often conceived as links between two stretches of navigable water; between the sea and the Great Lakes, or the Niagara and the Detroit rivers.

More dramatic was the line by-passing the rapids on the Madeira and Mamore rivers in the depths of the Amazon forest, a railway which took thirty years to build, only for its *raison d'être* to disappear almost immediately with the collapse of the Brazilian rubber boom. A similar line, painfully constructed to avoid the Stanley Falls on the Congo, was crucial in unlocking that immense country's riches.

But the savings had to justify the considerable expense involved, as the projectors of the Grand Trunk Railway found in trying, unsuccessfully, to divert traffic from Canadian ports to Portland in Maine. Moreover, in contrast to Europe, most of the traffic in the New World consisted of coal and wheat, basic products whose travel times were not crucial, so water could often compete successfully with the more sophisticated, faster, but usually more expensive railways.

Railways often made it possible to exploit steamships more efficiently by maximising the mileage travelled by rail rather than sea. The long line down Italy to Brindisi, built to further the cause of Italian unity, provided a vital link in the British Imperial route to India. The opening of the rail link across the Andes in 1910 cut several days off the journey from Hamburg to Valparaiso on the West Coast – via rail to Genoa, followed by sixteen days steaming to Buenos Aires, then a further 36 hours for the 880 kilometres to Valparaiso.

In the United States the canals' supporters (and the states which had funded them) naturally tried to prevent railways competing too ferociously. Indeed the New York legislature actually passed a law requiring that any railroad which passed within 30 miles of the Erie Canal pay the Canal Board the equivalent of the canal's tolls. (This law was repealed only in 1851.)

Railways represented an obvious threat to canals and those who worked on them. A Chinese official warned blackly that 'several tens of millions, who earn their living by holding the whip or grasping the tiller, will lose their jobs. If they don't end up starving in the ditches, they will surely gather [as outlaws] in the forests.'[13] Chinese nationalism ensured that opposition to railways was more highly developed than anywhere else, yet even those lines which, in theory, offered no advantage because of existing water routes, found enormous freight potential to exploit.

Well before the end of the century the navigable waters were reduced to playing a secondary role. Before the arrival of the railways the river pilots of the Mississippi transmuted their intimate knowledge of the ever-shifting waters of Ole Muddy into a lucrative monopoly – the Pilots Association, which forced newcomers to pay ever-increasing initiation fees. In *Life on the Mississippi*, Mark Twain wrote: 'The organisation seemed indestructible. It was the tightest monopoly in the world. By the United States law, no man could become a pilot unless two duly licensed pilots signed his application; and now there was nobody outside of the association competent to sign.' But the railroads first took the passengers and then the freight, removing the pilots' monopoly.

The development of railroads competing with the Mississippi before the Civil War ensured that much of America's heart-land, which had previously looked towards New Orleans and the Gulf of Mexico, instead turned its back on the Mississippi and started to transport its grain to the Atlantic via Chicago and the Great Lakes. During the Civil War that arch-capitalist 'Commodore' Vanderbilt, who had made his fortune from steamboats, saw how Confederate control of stretches of the Mississippi had reinforced the trend. Immediately after the war he sold his steamship interests 'for what they would bring, and began buying railroads despite the fact that his friends warned him that, in his old age, he was wrecking the fruits of a hard and thrifty life'.[14]

The shrewd old Commodore also tried to exploit the idea of a rail bridge between the Atlantic and Pacific Oceans. He failed in Nicaragua, partly because of the transshipment required by his over-complicated plans, but largely because a parallel project, a railway built at immense financial and human cost across the Isthmus of Panama, made a fortune for its promoters in the fifteen years before the Transcontinental railroad was opened across the United States. But the idea has remained valid to this day. In the first years of the twentieth century the great contractor Weetman Pearson, later the first Lord Cowdray, built the Tehuantepec railway across southern Mexico, whose 'creative originality', in the words of R. S. Joby, 'foreshadowed the use of railways as container bridges between oceans in our time'.[15]

The railways could compete with water transport even in Germany, the only country to develop its waterway network at the same time as its railways. The River Rhine and its tributaries, flowing past the country's major industrial centres, provided a means of transport a mere half as expensive as rail transport – water remained the principal means for transporting Ruhr coal more than a short distance. Yet, in Rayner Fremdling's words, 'The railway deserves to be labelled the hero of Germany's industrial revolution ... it is ... extremely difficult to conceive of growth without railways because the increased use of natural waterways, and above all the construction of canals, was not a viable alternative to a railway system at the time when German economic growth gained its momentum.'[16] The two could coexist. In Russia the economic boom engendered by the railways also ensured that the waterways doubled the traffic they carried in the last quarter of the 19th century – a period in which rail freight nearly trebled.

In France political pressure favoured railway building and the canals were neglected. The turning-point came in 1857, in the midst of the railway boom, and, by no coincidence, the first year in which railways carried more freight than waterways. For in general the canals simply could not cope with the railways' implacably increasing efficiency. As the original investment was written off so speeds rose and prices fell, by almost a half in Britain and France between the 1840s and the end of the century, by three quarters in the United States. No wonder nearly half of all the 4,468 miles of canals in the United States had been abandoned by 1880 and that few if any of the remainder were profitable.

1
The Railway Regions

Even railways could not magically transform a barren region. A diamond rush into Bahia province in Brazil promoted the construction of a narrow-gauge railway. The rush subsided before the railway was completed. Nevertheless, as late as the 1960s, 'toy-like trains, belching clouds of black wood-smoke, today still creep across the seared land on the narrow rails laid without ballast directly onto dirt. The area languished in backwardness. Without a profitable crop like coffee to feed a growing international demand, no railroad could transform this region.'[17]

By contrast they were an incomparable instrument in unlocking the wealth of previously inaccessible regions rich in natural resources, agricultural or mineral; and, a natural corollary, in attracting immigrants, usually from the Old World. The lyrical observer quoted below by William Fleming, describing the effect of the Central Argentine Railway on the pampas, could have been writing about the prairies in Canada or the United States or about much of Siberia:

> I have traversed districts which three years ago were wilderness; but a spur of railway has been driven into them, and instantly farming has been started. I saw hundreds of newly-built homesteads – crude and the life harsh, but it was the beginning of great things – and alfalfa has been laid down ... cattle were feeding, and wide spaces which previously were sandy and apparently inhospitable were carpeted with the bright green of new wheat.[18]

The Central Argentine Railroad attracted thousands of settlers from Italy, the country's principal source of immigrants. Railways encouraged internal as well as external migration. In France they greatly increased seasonal migrations as well as making it far easier for peasants to escape from rural poverty; waves of Bretons, in particular, emigrated to serve Parisians, mostly as domestic servants or on the city's public transport system.

The biggest achievement by a single railway system was the creation of modern Siberia by the Trans-Siberian. Yet, as J. N. Westwood pointed out, Russian railways 'never entered the national consciousness like they did in America . . . the railways were not a spontaneous grasping for territory and prosperity as they were in the United States, but a forced growth sponsored by the Tsar and built by foreigners.'[19]

The railways' influence was not confined to Siberia, for those built in Russian Central Asia were also essential instruments of regional development. But the Trans-Siberian transformed the life of half a continent. The migration it induced was on a gigantic scale, the most concentrated in history. Between 1896 and 1913 over 4¾ million emigrants were settled in new regions from all over Russia, mostly to Western Siberia. The results were dramatic. During the first decade of the century, grain exports trebled.

This unprecedented shift of population was the result of deliberate government initiatives designed to act 'as a safety-valve to the revolutionary unrest in Russia proper, while at the same time it is establishing a Greater Russia in Siberia, it is the government that leads them out, spoon-feeds them on the way, gives them grants of land and tools to till it with, until they are finally established in their new eastern homes.'[20] The land still belonged to the Tsar – as the British journalist, Philips Price, put it, 'Siberia exhibits perhaps the most extensive scheme of land nationalization in the world.' But it also had profound social as well as economic effects. For the first time Russian peasants intermarried with those from other ethnic groups, with local Siberians, or with emigrants from other regions.

The Turkish government copied the efforts of its Russian enemies. The Sultan's agents even used religious arguments to try and persuade Muslims from all over Southern Russia as well as Anatolia in central Turkey to settle in Cilicia after the railways had enabled the region's wheat and cotton to reach the Mediterranean coast by rail.

But the most familiar tale concerns the prairies in the United States and Canada. In fact the colonisation process had started east of the Mississippi well before the Civil War when the Illinois Central, running south from Chicago, set the pattern for all subsequent regional railroad developments. The railroads relied on land grants, a major feature of federal, and sometimes state, policy between the first grant to the Illinois Central in 1850 to the last 'Pacific' charter twenty-one years later.

These looked generous – a checkerboard of alternate strips between ten and twenty miles wide along the tracks. They were naturally perceived differently by radicals, appalled at what they interpreted as the profligacy of corrupt legislative bodies, and by the railroads' supporters, who asserted that the railways needed the grants for their very existence. Radicals proclaimed that the land went mostly to already-wealthy speculators, boosters that they enabled the settlement of the West by hundreds of thousands of sturdy homesteaders, each with their 160-acre plot. (Until recently the radicals wrote most of the history books, greatly exaggerating the size and, above all, the value of the grants).

In Argentina a legal limit of 100,000 acres was easily evaded by unscrupulous speculators who cornered most of the new land on offer. But in the United States, where over 150 million acres were involved, there was plenty of room for everybody. Speculators did often exploit ordinary settlers, for everyone was acting from a variety of motives.

Although the Illinois Central set the pattern, it followed earlier grants of land for canals and war veterans. At first it was considered 'primarily a land company . . . and secondarily a railroad company. Its construction was made possible by a mortgage secured on its lands, and the interest charges were paid and the shares bought back by the proceeds from land sales.'[21] The transcontinental lines, too, required massive land grants to act as a credit base before they could start to build. The grants proved particularly useful in enticing foreign investors, lured by the supposed value of the Golden West. But shrewder locals, dubious of the value of Western land, preferred to rely on the inherent value and the managerial capacity of the railroads themselves.*

* See Thomas Cochrane in Journal of Economic History, Supplement X, 1950.

The railroads usually had to sell off the lands quickly and thus at bargain prices simply to finance construction. Moreover the grants provided only potential income; and, as the promoters of the Central Pacific up from Sacramento into the high Sierras found to their cost, the land could be so mountainous and unattractive that it was worthless. The biggest beneficiaries were the promoters of short lines designed to exploit attractive parcels of land, and the directors and managers of major lines. They bought alternate sections, combined them with the sections granted to their railroads and exploited the combined package with considerable success.

Investors' motives were often mixed. In Albert Fishlow's words, 'landowners invested in railroads not for the private return the projects earned, but for the indirect transport advantages that ultimately raised his land value. The manufacturer contributed, not for the dividends he received, but for the additional profits he would subsequently earn.'[22]

The Canadians also had a long tradition of using 'Dominion' (public) lands to encourage settlement and development. But whereas the Americans favoured checkerboard grants, the Canadian grants consisted of unified chunks, designed to provide compact groups of homesteads. As a result the Canadian Pacific Railway was endowed with 25 million acres of Dominion lands, far and away the biggest grant to any single railway in the world. This vast area, as big as England, was integrated with the homesteads occupied by individual settlers far more harmoniously than in the United States. Nevertheless the promoters had a delicate task: they had to persuade potential investors that the land was immensely valuable while at the same time reassuring the politicians and public opinion that it was virtually worthless, if only to preserve the fiction that, as the Prime Minister Sir John Macdonald put it, 'not a farthing of money will have to be paid by the people of Canada'. But inevitably, 'as in the United States, so in Canada, railway land subsidies were at first hailed with delight, had their day, served their purpose, and ultimately called forth a widespread popular disapproval.'[23]

The railroads required immigrants, as buyers of the land and as tied customers. Jim Hill, creator of the Great Northern, from Duluth to the Pacific, was a firm believer in the idea that a railway through virgin territory, provided only that it was fertile, automatically generated its own traffic. 'If we build a road across the prairie,' he said, 'we will carry every pound of supplies that the settlers want, and we will carry every pound of produce that the settlers wish to sell, so that we will have freight both ways.'

The Illinois Central began its sales campaign in New England, enticing many internal immigrants to the virgin glades of Illinois. But it ventured further, to Germany and Scandinavia, using distinguished salesmen like Francis Hoffman, a former Lieutenant-Governor of Illinois. He and his fellow-salesmen faced competition from individual states and from Canadian agents, as well as well-founded suspicions derived from unhappy experiences with earlier, unscrupulous salesmen. Moreover the Central lost many Scandinavians, who preferred colder states like Minnesota and Wisconsin. Yet the railroad did succeed in colonising over 1.5 million acres.

Earlier migrations had been prompted more by states than by railroads, but some of the newer states were largely created by the railroads and naturally relied on them for new inhabitants. They were forced to look abroad because the supply of internal émigrés dried up during the Civil War, though the Northern Pacific had some success in attracting Easterners, especially former soldiers, in the 1870s. Competing railroads deployed their agents at strategic points, in Germany and Scandinavia, at the major ports of entry, notably Boston and New York, and at key railway junctions like Topeka. The Burlington was particularly active in Britain, where its major propaganda weapon was a map showing the Burlington's lands in the very heart of the United States, lands it grandiloquently termed the 'Gulf Stream of Migration'.*

The Santa Fe accepted the challenge from wealthier railroads by the lavish distribution of percentages to a horde of agents

---

* Burlingtonia was 'said to be bounded on the north by the Aurora Borealis, and on the south by the Day of Judgment.'

backed by promotional literature in German, Dutch, Swedish, French, Danish and Russian. It faced a further problem: it disposed of three million acres in odd-numbered sections for ten miles either side of its tracks, but much of the Kansas section was already settled, so in the end the road received wider strips further west. Among the most professional operators was the Northern Pacific, a route inspired by Henry Villard, himself a German by birth. His agents had to lure immigrants to the Pacific North-West, reachable only by sea from San Francisco until the rail link was completed in 1883.

The competition was so intense that the Santa Fe made no profit at all from the 100,000 acres it sold to those ideal settlers, the Mennonites. They were Germans settled in the Crimea since the days of Catherine II, but persecuted by Tsar Alexander III and famous equally for their efficient farming and their God-fearing ways. To attract them the Santa Fe had not only to satisfy material demands but also guarantee them exemption from military service.

But it was the Canadian Pacific which went furthest in actually colonising its lands, deriving its ideas from the St Paul, Minneapolis and Manitoba, a railroad with which the founders had been connected.

> More important than the cash proceeds to the Company was the ability of the settler to buy land at moderate prices, to get it under cultivation without loss of time, and to produce that indispensable commodity for the prosperity of a pioneer economy – an export staple for world markets . . . the resources of the Company were directed from the outset, not to the manipulation of real estate on a variable market, but to the far sounder interests of settlement and transportation.[24]

By 1924, thirty years after it opened, the CPR claimed it had been responsible for the settlement of 55,000 families on thirty million acres of the prairies. A tenth of the land had been improved thanks to the biggest single irrigation project ever undertaken by a railway, or anyone else in the world up to that point, in a scheme by which the railway invested $20 million in 4,000 miles of irrigation canals and ditches.

But to film-goers the new regions are symbolised, not by irrigation projects, but by a series of images: of a handful of cowboys corralling great herds of cattle through the prairie dust, and guiding them to the railhead. The railways did not create the great cattle trails. They simply spread inexorably along existing routes. The process was set in motion just after the end of the Civil War when a pioneer livestock trader named Joseph McCoy based his entrepot at Abilene, an oasis of rich green grass and plentiful supplies of water, but one which on his arrival was a 'very small, dead place consisting of about one dozen log huts, low, small, rude affairs, four-fifths of which were covered with dirt for roofing.'[25]

Within a few months 35,000 cattle had been driven into this 'very small, dead place', and then the further hundred miles north to the railhead of the Kansas Pacific, which in the succeeding years faced considerable problems keeping up with the subsequent surge of traffic. Within a few years observers were overwhelmed, not only by the size of the bovine pilgrimage, but also by its speed, noting that the trains averaged nearly twenty miles an hour, every hour, day and night.

2

The Industries the Railways Created

Railways brought the whole universe of capitalism to previously self-contained regions. Such regions could never again be self-sufficient, could never retain the introversion characteristic of peasant cultures the world over. Nowhere was this more obvious than in rural France. Eugen Weber[26] describes how in Savoy, once the railway arrived in previously isolated valleys like that around Die:

> Buyers appeared for cattle, lavender and in due course fruit from newly developed orchards, chemical fertiliser and superphosphates could reach the narrow valleys and help meet new demands; rye gave way to wheat; comfort replaced grinding poverty. The profound transformation can be dated to the railway's coming in 1894 and the years immediately following, when the peasants became used to it and learnt how to handle the formalities involved in shipping and receiving merchandise. The outside world, which till then had little bearing on their own, now came in with a rush: skills like writing invoices and bills of lading, counting, and schooling in general acquired concrete meaning as occasions to use them multiplied. It was a story that repeated itself elsewhere.

Outside Europe many regions were actually created by the railways. As soon as it was settled, the American Mid-West supplied far-distant markets with its specialities and received in return bulk materials like fertilisers, bricks, clay, timber and other building materials.* But the leader in the specialisation process was the railway industry itself. In the words of the great economist Alfred Marshall, 'The dominant economic fact of our time is not the development of manufacturing industry, but the development of transport industries.' The railway 'sector' started

---

* By limiting his calculations to low-value, high weight agricultural commodities Professor Fogel tilted the argument against the railways.

its leadership by simply being built. At the height of the great railway boom of the 1840s four per cent of the employed male population in Britain was involved in building them.

Even in the giant American economy, railways accounted for 15 per cent of all the capital investment undertaken in the quarter of a century before the Civil War. In other countries they could account for as much as a quarter of a country's industrial investment – in France their share varied between ten and fifteen per cent for nearly half a century.

In Germany – the *locus classicus* for all types of railway-induced industrial progress – railway construction accounted for up to a quarter of industrial investment, also acting, as in other countries, as a strong counter-cyclical force in times of industrial recession. In the peak years Britain's railways consumed nearly a fifth of all the pig iron produced in the country – a proportion which reached 30 per cent, including exports. (Britain still remains the world's largest exporter of the rails themselves.)

But it was the Germans who most effectively exploited the railways to help develop their engineering industries. In 1843 only a tenth of all the rails in Prussia were home-built. Twenty years later the figure was 85 per cent, and by then all the locomotives were also made in Prussia. In Britain the locomotives were built by an already well-developed steam-engine industry, while in Prussia the locomotive came first; as late as 1875 three quarters of all the steam engines in Prussia were railway locomotives.

Railways, unlike steamships, and unlike such other major industries as cotton textiles, entailed a long tail of associated industrial structures. The maintenance required by rolling stock during its long life ensured that even a country which relied on imported equipment would develop a considerable mechanical base, and one, moreover, free from foreign competition. By 1870 railway repairing alone accounted for a fifth of all the machinery produced in the United States, and the industry as a whole absorbed forty per cent of all the rolled steel.

As the biggest industrial organisations of their kind, the railway companies' impact naturally included their industrial demands. While they were major consumers, most obviously of coal, iron and steel, their biggest impact was more qualitative than quantitative, because of the standard of performance they demanded, the pressures (literal and metaphorical) they imposed on their suppliers.

In Japan railway equipment, more particularly steam locomotives, performed as a 'leading sector' in the economy. The first mass-production locomotives came off the assembly lines as late as 1903, thirty years after railways had first been introduced into Japan. Eight years later the import of steam locomotives was virtually at an end, and the Japanese started making electric locomotives only six years after the Germans. For the Japanese, building rolling stock, like mastering the construction of the lines themselves, was a symbol of technological advance which could easily be measured against European and American standards.

The Japanese were following the examples of the Americans, the Germans and the French, all of whom had relied on British technology for their first railways but who had soon surpassed their mentors.* The railways required unprecedented numbers of bridges, for example,† and as they were built in increasingly inaccessible corners of the globe they demanded more, and more ambitious, prefabricated structures. Ernest Gouin of the Société des Batignolles developed a standard construction kit for bridges after he had received an order for 5,000 tons' worth to be erected in the then-inaccessible South of France. He went on to use the same techniques to build ships.

But under extreme conditions even French engineering proved inferior to the American. The Central Peruvian railway in the high Andes proved the ultimate test. One branch line was built at an altitude as high as Mont Blanc. The French system, in which they used their own teams to build ready-assembled prefabricated structures, proved a failure. The Americans then showed that they could erect a bridge weighing over 60 tons in a

* When Thomas Brassey built the line from Paris to Le Havre he relied for his locomotives on a works at Rouen built and owned by W. B. Buddicom, the chief engineer at Crewe.

† As John Francis pointed out in 1851, 25,000 rail bridges had been built in the first fifteen years of the railway era, or 'more than all that previously existed in the country.'

mere eight days, whereas comparable British structures weighed over twice as much and took eight weeks. The Americans' greatest triumphs came with the Verrugas bridge over a tributary of the Rimac (celebrated by a medal struck by the great Louis Tiffany), and later with the Gokteik Bridge, transported safely from the works of the Pennsylvania Bridge Company to its home in Upper Burma.

With railways inevitably came a whole series of technological challenges. Their requirements for greater strength and durability sparked off the replacement of iron by steel and the development of improved types of steel. In the twentieth century we have become used to defence industries providing the funds for technical advances. In the nineteenth the process was reversed. Alfred Krupp and, to a lesser extent, Tom Vickers, used techniques originally devised to produce strong steel wheels and rails to transform the technology of cannon-making. Krupp prospered making axles and springs for railway wagons before developing the cast steel wheel which provided the technical and financial backing for his subsequent fame. In *The Arms of Krupp* William Manchester quotes him as writing: 'It was only through the manufacture of tyres that the works were able to make enough profit to lay down the gun-making plant.'

The demand for rails and wheels alike, was not domestic – the Prussian state railways were the last to be convinced – but international. In 1874 alone Krupp shipped 175,000 tons of rails from Hamburg to the United States, and by the time the Americans had caught up with German technology, Chinese railways – and German guns based on railway technology – had filled the gap.

In Belgium, railway industries were at the heart of the country's wealth and international fame. Belgian industry had a disproportionate share of the world market in iron, steel and locomotives, and a corresponding importance in technological advances. Walschaerts invented the vital valve gear named after him, designed to regulate the flow of steam into the cylinder, Alfred Belpaire improved combustion through developing a wider firebox – and in the twentieth century two other famous

Belgian names, Flamme and Lemaitre, also improved steam locomotive technology.

The railways demanded a wide range of improved engineering tools – like the heavy steam hammers and overhead cranes directly attributable to their requirements – as well as improvements in the rails on which the whole industry depended. In the United States the price of standard T-shaped rails dropped from $200 a ton in 1850 to $28 a ton in 1914: by then they were 30 feet long – double the length and four times the weight of their predecessors, a crucial factor in enabling trains to carry heavier loads.

The first industrial revolution depended on coal, iron and steel, and railways played the crucial role in developing all three, especially the first. Coal begat the railways, which in turn consumed a substantial proportion of the coal they carried, although increasingly efficient locomotives demanded correspondingly more combustible 'steam coal'. In the 1870s the Philadelphia & Reading was described as 'less a railroad carrying coal, but more a coal company operating a railroad to carry its product'.* A hundred years later, during a decade when virtually all other traffic had deserted them, American railroads relied on coal for survival.

In Britain by 1865 the railways were transporting 1,700 million ton miles of coal, the difference in the cost alone (4.33 (old) pence per ton mile by rail, 16.3 (old) pence by alternative methods) accounting for nearly 11.5 per cent of Britain's national income. Unfortunately for Britain's railways, they retained the small, unbraked wagons suitable for working round the sharp curves in colliery sidings well into the twentieth century when they proved too slow to compete with road transport.

Britain was not the only country where the first railways were short, unambitious lines linking coal mines to the nearest market

---

* There were a few exceptions. In *The Railway Age* Michael Robbins describes how 'In the early days of railways we are told that a certain company carefully sheeted their coal trucks because they were ashamed of such a low class of traffic'. They soon learnt better.

or stretch of navigable water. The same rule applied in Belgium, France, India and China. Their traffic, and their profits, were assured, providing a good advertisement for rail transport, and a sound base for more ambitious schemes.

Coal railways had many other effects. In France, for instance, the rural economy had previously been based on wood as a fuel. In Belgium the coal mines and the railways were so important, indeed, that when they were threatened with takeover by foreign interests the whole country was galvanised into action. Even in Spain, usually such a negative example, railways resulted in the development of coalfields in regions like Leon, well away from the coast.

Since the time of Marco Polo the Chinese had used porters to carry coal, in one case for over sixty miles, and fully realised its importance. In defending his extremely expensive proposed southern network Sun Yat-Sen quoted an old proverb, 'Nobody would build a city where there is no coal underneath.' Not surprisingly, the country's first line, privately built by an English engineer, was designed to serve the Kai-ping coal mines near Tientsin. The venture was perceived as a major challenge to local traditions, showing the capability of this new, foreign, and much-feared form of transport.

The railways replaced the ironmakers' previous dependence on limited supplies of charcoal with much more dependable supplies of coal, and enabled the industry to tap distant supplies of iron ore. Both demonstrate the railways' biggest single contribution to industry: its capacity to liberate factories from the need to be on navigable water, which had previously monopolised the transport of industrial raw materials. More generally the railways provided industry with an unprecedented geographical flexibility. Industrialists could draw their raw materials from a wider range of sources, and allocate the manufacturing process (which itself could be fragmented) to the most economic location.

The railways' direct demands could overwhelm an infant iron and steel industry. The Spanish railways were forced to depend almost exclusively on imported iron and steel, and in Russia the railways themselves absorbed the majority of the pig iron produced in the last two decades of the 19th century.

But more often the railways acted as midwives to entirely new industrial centres. One of the most amazing was Birmingham, Alabama, the major industrial city improbably situated in the heart of the deep South, a success story due almost entirely to the missionary efforts of the Louisville & Nashville Railroad. The railroad invested directly, lent money, granted favourable freight rates, extended the tracks to tap the iron ore deposits at Red Mountain. The L & N's crotchety, if prescient, president, Milton H. Smith, understood that 'while higher rates would have given a better return on the capital invested, they would probably have prevented development'.[27]

But, as so often, it was the previously backward Germans who best demonstrated the railways' capacity to unlock latent industrial potential. 'Iron production had not developed much beyond the technological level of the 16th century.'[28] As late as 1835 nine tenths of all Germany's iron was still being smelted in furnaces using charcoal, a fuel long abandoned in Britain. But 'at the start of the 1850s new modern coke-using blast furnaces were erected in the Ruhr area.' As a result the iron ore traffic multiplied over forty-fold during the 1850s to reach 227,000 tons by 1860, a period which also saw the Ruhr's greatest surge in coal production, encouraged by a sharp drop in the cost of rail transport.

Inevitably railways created uprecedented strains on existing industries, existing ways of life. Switzerland, formerly over-reliant on small-scale enterprises, agricultural as well as industrial, had to switch almost overnight to the scenery which begat mass tourism and to specialised manufactures like watches and machinery which could exploit the country's excellent educational system.

Once the railways had established a base load of a heavy commodity like coal they were poised to cash in on the low marginal cost of additional, smaller scale, widely-varied freight. This was not only industrial, it included the innumerable items of baggage which accompanied nineteenth-century travellers. Trains could absorb – albeit only after the sort of muddle beloved of comic writers looking for material – the untidy parcels carried by the poor and the trunks and fine leather suitcases belonging to richer travellers. Households could move far more frequently, far more ambitiously, than ever before. But the personal freight was not solely domestic. In *Le Musicien Errant*, Hector Berlioz complains that the enormous cost of transporting music by post-coach removed all his profits from provincial concert tours in the pre-railway age.

On a larger scale, as the cost of transport dropped – and, almost as importantly, continued dropping – so efficient producers of the whole gamut of agricultural and industrial goods found that they could dominate their markets throughout a region, a country, a continent. In Britain, as Michael Robbins pointed out in *The Railway Age*, 'Specialization was the key to success. Each district ... had its particular range of products: the Victorian child's game which showed steel and ship-building at Barrow, jute at Dundee, straw hats at Luton, boots and shoes at Northampton, cutlery at Sheffield, was not seriously misrepresenting the facts.'

Symbolically the barrels of beer brewed at Burton, over a hundred miles from London, were stored in special cellars built under Saint Pancras Station in London. The specialisation continued for generations after the railways' arrival: it took forty years before the clay deposits at Whittlesea near Peterborough were exploited to produce the bricks which standardised so much of Britain's housing.

The extraordinary variety of goods pouring into London every morning was hymned by *The Railway News* as early as 1864:

In the grey mists of the morning, in the atmosphere of a hundred conflicting smells, and by the light of faintly burning gas, we see a large portion of the supply of the great London markets rapidly disgorged by these night trains: Fish, flesh and food, Aylesbury butter and dairy-fed pork, apples, cabbages, and cucumbers, alarming supplies of cats' meat, cart loads of water cresses, and we know not what else, for the daily consumption of the metropolis. No sooner do these disappear than at ten minutes' interval arrive other trains with Manchester packs and bales, Liverpool cotton, American provisions, Worcester gloves, Kidderminster carpets, Birmingham and Staffordshire hardware, crates of pottery from North Staffordshire, and cloth from Huddersfield, Leeds, Bradford, and other Yorkshire towns, which have to be delivered in the City before the hour for the general commencement of business. At a later hour of the morning these are followed by other trains with the heaviest class of traffic: stones, bricks, iron girders, iron pipes, ale (which comes in great quantities, especially from Allsopps', and the world-famous Burton breweries), coal, hay, straw, grain, flour, and salt . . .[29]

In France Rondo Cameron lists 'the concentration of the cotton and linen industries, exploitation of the coal mines of the Pas de Calais . . . the development of Languedoc vineyards, stock raising in Thierache and Charentes, fishing off Boulogne, coal, sugar, oil, iron and steel in the north and east of France and mechanical and food processing industries in and around Paris'[30] among the railways' contributions to industrial development. Production of animal-based products, from eggs to butter and the like, more than doubled in the first quarter of a century after the railway network was completed. Nevertheless, in France as in Britain, large-scale, national specialisation had a corollary, the decline and fall of hundreds of local, small scale firms historically protected from competition by transport costs.

The most spectacular world-ranging specialities bred by the railways were agricultural, most obviously grain and meat. Rail-borne grain flooded from the American and later Canadian prairies, then from the Argentine pampas, causing a major agricultural slump throughout Europe. The railways opening up the prairies thus had a direct interest in improving the quantity of wheat they could produce. The Mennonites lured by the Santa Fe brought with them the 'Turkey' strain of hard wheat which proved admirably suited to prairie conditions. Specialisation liberated land previously used for grain for more profitable crops. In Southern Russia a number of lines, culminating in the

'Turksib', brought cereals to Central Asia, freeing the land for growing cotton.

In some cases the connection was more direct. William Van Horne of the Canadian Pacific built enormous grain elevators to ensure that the reputation of Manitoba grain would not be tarnished by unsuitable storage conditions. He encouraged farmers to grow the most suitable varieties of soft wheat and he carried one variety, Red Fife, free of charge. When the CPR's profitable monopoly led to the construction of the more northerly Canadian National Railway the protagonists could not rely on existing strains of wheat. After twenty years of research, a leading agronomist, Dr Saunders, developed 'Marquis' wheat which would grow two hundred miles further north than existing varieties requiring longer summers in which to ripen. In the United States the Illinois Central went even further, awarding prizes to encourage production of a steam-driven plough, a ditching machine and a workable corn-cutter and stacker.

For arable farmers, railways meant not only wider markets, but, crucially, a far cheaper and greatly increased supply of fertiliser. In France, for instance, the railways carried 627,000 tons in 1868, and double that quantity a decade later, in a period in which wheat production rose by over a third.

Railways revolutionised distribution as well as production habits. In Hungary a whole network of local rural lines was hurriedly built in the late 1860s to carry away the contents of barns groaning with bumper grain harvests. But railways did not merely salvage local surpluses, which included oranges in Mexico as well as grain in Hungary: they greatly increased its value. Alfred Chandler showed that the price of corn and hogs, which Ohio produced in abundance, increased by fifty per cent or more once the Erie canal improved communication to the East. Between 1835–1860, years which saw the completion of the railway network 'the price of corn advanced 50 per cent and that of hogs 100 per cent'.[31]

The animals previously required to transport produce to market ate their way across country; a hunger which meant that up to a third of all the arable land in Spain could be turned over to growing wheat once railways had replaced horses and oxen. Among the hungriest animals were those being driven hundreds of miles across country before being slaughtered: with the coming of the railways they could enjoy a last restful ride. In Spain, for instance, the merino sheep no longer had to eat their way across the country but could be transported to market by train, thus ensuring that the Southern pastures were grazed the year round.

In Britain railways revolutionised the cattle trade: all the major markets gravitated to the railheads, the trade of the drover declined, the cattle reached market – and thus the consumer – in far better condition (according to contemporary figures every day's droving reduced the weight of the cattle by some 8 lbs). Whole areas could be devoted to fattening cattle rather than less specialised grazing, and the trade in dead meat flourished, because different parts of the carcase could be sold in markets with different tastes – tripe in the North of England for instance. Sheep could be bred on the hills before being sold for fattening to graziers in the lowlands.

Because there was no return traffic for wagons carrying live cattle railways encouraged another major change, the slaughter of meat before it was shipped. By the 1860s London was fed by two daily meat trains from Scotland, trains taking a mere thirty hours for a journey of over 500 miles, trains which sparked off an agrarian revolution in the Scottish Highlands, But the Scots had no monopoly. Until new animal disease legislation was passed in 1892 London welcomed meat from much further afield, from Austria, Hungary and Poland, via Rotterdam and Hamburg. The legislation was aimed at the minority of dishonest butchers who shipped diseased meat by rail, confident that the railway provided them with a shield of anonymity. 'In some cases,' wrote Richard Perren, 'the worst carcases were salted down to avoid inspection but some were so bad that they rotted in the salt tubs.'[32]

For railways had a double effect. They could provide urban populations with undreamt-of quantities of such luxuries as fresh fish: during the mackerel season London consumed 90 tons a day, much of it from Fenit, a small village in Kerry, on the West

Coast of Ireland; while two loaded trains carrying herrings arrived every day from Yarmouth during the season. But at the same time they encouraged the spread of the mass-produced, inferior 'industrial' foods which stunted the growth of the British urban proletariat for a hundred years. (In his standard work on British food Sir Jack Drummond mentions only the second role.)

Other countries exploited the railways to produce vastly increased quantities of standardised, yet wholesome, foods. The Danish bacon and Dutch butter which graced British breakfast tables depended on railway-based specialisation, while British farmers found that they could supply housewives with milk the year round if they built better barns to house the cattle in winter. Specialised agricultural railways were to be found wherever there was profit to be made. The French built lines to transport alfalfa in Algeria, palm oil and peanut oil in west Africa. The British built lines to transport cotton in Egypt, the Sudan and Uganda and lines to exploit the beef and grain in Southern Africa.

The railways could also set up pressure to find new regions to exploit. When the land in the Upper Pariba Valley in Brazil was exhausted by over-production of coffee, the growers kept having to look for new land. For with the railways, and with them industrial-scale agricultural exploitation, came the whole paraphernalia of modern capitalist production: the replacement of increasingly costly and restless labour by machines and, in many cases, some form of processing near the point of production. By 1883 Brazilian coffee arrived at the processing machinery 'hulled, sorted, polished, bagged, and weighed mechanically'.[33]

Only a few products did not require railways. Although a railway was built to Kimberley in the decades after diamonds were discovered there, the fields did not depend on them. The diamonds were light, and the needs of the 6,000 or so settlers could be met by horse transport. But diamonds were the exception to the rule that the exploitation of any major new mineral discovery relied on a railway.

Railways exploiting a known body of ore were commonplace: phosphates in Morocco, tin in Nigeria, copper in French Equatorial Africa and in the Rhodesian and Congolese Copper

Belt. The railways could also uncover undreamt-of riches. The Canadians were rewarded for their patriotic ardour in insisting that their transcontinental railway should traverse the barren tundra north of Lake Superior instead of taking an easier, southern route through the United States. Shrewd eyes examining the rocks in the hills round the construction camp half way along the line where the mining town of Sudbury stands today spotted the traces of what subsequently proved to be one of the biggest deposits of nickel in the world.

Ice: The Disappearing Traffic

For a generation or more American railroads carried loads which, quite literally, melted en route: ice. The quantities involved were astonishing. Richard Cummings has calculated that every inhabitant of a major city consumed two thirds of a ton annually, and even the benighted denizens of smaller towns used a quarter of a ton apiece.[*]

The trade was pioneered in New England, where a prime source was Walden Pond, the beloved home of Henry Thoreau. For decades its shores echoed every winter with the scraping of the ice-saws developed by Nathaniel Jarvis Wyeth, a Massachusetts man who saw the value of 'ice rights'. Not surprisingly the ice promoters compared the north's frozen riches with its coal mines and granite quarries – although the ice could be harvested only during the winter months.

A special railroad was built to tap the pond's riches and specially insulated cars were developed to transport the ice. The users were equally ingenious. A Cincinnati pork packer even 'modeled his entire packing room on the principle of a household refrigerator' and a fruitgrower in central Illinois built 'a cold-storage warehouse in the shape of a large natural ice refrigerator in which considerable quantities of fruit could be carried over from season to season'. The ever-increasing demand for the cool lager beer especially popular with German immigrants ensured

* *The American Ice Harvests*, the source of this note.

164

Cutting ice for use in the summer: a long-forgotten industry.

that the brewers were consuming over a million dollars worth of ice annually by the 1860s. At the receiving end, New York's food distributors equipped themselves with hundreds of ice chests holding meat, fruit and vegetables, fish and perishable dairy produce, its quality greatly improved by refrigeration facilities available from cow to customer.

The railroads themselves patented a dozen different types of refrigerated wagons. The industry even supported its own paper, the *Ice Trade Journal,* and its horizons were widened by the completion of the Transcontinental railroad in 1869. The Californians hacked their own ice from a number of locations, including the 'Summit' of the Sierras, where the ice was floated over the edge of a dam to end up in two icehouses holding thirty thousand tons, though the local product had to compete with ice brought by sea from Alaska. The refrigerated cars carried apples, pears, oranges and salmon eastwards and returned with cargoes of peaches, grapes and oysters – some of which were planted in San Francisco Bay.

Ice was one of the few instances in which railways actually delayed technical advances. Because so much capital had been invested in the less efficient natural technology it proved difficult to finance the development of ice machines using compressed air or ether. In the event the steamship companies, denied the same access to natural ice as the railmen, encouraged the development of mechanical refrigeration. But the natural icemen did not give up without a struggle. Even at the end of the 1880s three million tons of ice were stored on the Hudson River ice fields in normal years.

The Grapes of Rail

As railways spread so did the culture of the vine, for the wine trade, like so many others, was liberated from its dependence on access to waterways. In the pre-railway millenia no wine – or spirit for that matter – without access to a navigable waterway stood much chance in international markets.

Not that railways could always tilt the balance. The Cognaçais, with their easy access to Northern Europe via the River Charente, retained their lead over the Armagnaçais, historically handicapped by reliance on slow and expensive road transport.

The most spectacular success story was Mendoza, the great Argentine wine-growing region, where an upsurge in wine production in the late nineteenth century was intimately associated with the arrival of a whole generation of mostly Italian immigrants. The indenture system ensured that a hard-working immigrant could hope to set up on his own after only a few years and make a comfortable living from a relatively small vineyard, each hectare of vines producing 60,000 lb of grapes. They were a close-knit community who 'tenaciously defended the local economy, particularly the wine industry, against perceived threats to their individual and collective success. They formed voluntary associations, for example, to encourage and modernize wine production. These groups also served to organise opposition to taxes, wine falsification'[34] – and the railways' allegedly excessive freight rates.

But most of the development was in Europe, especially in Italy, Spain and Southern France. In Italy the railways created the international fame of the land-locked vineyards of Chianti in Tuscany, performing a similar function in helping the vineyards of central Spain against their coastal competitors. Even though domestic demand remained concentrated on locally-produced wines, export demand ensured that the vineyards in Navarre grew by a third in the thirty years after the railways arrived, while those of Albacete increased four-fold. They also improved the quality. In pre-railway days many wines tasted decidedly resinous because they had been carried on mule-back in hog-skins painted with pitch – a treatment, and a taste, which survive today only in that appalling beverage, retsina.

The quality of the wines of Rioja in Northern Spain were improved because they were near Bordeaux, a source of capital and technical expertise, and it was the rail network which allowed Spanish wines to take the opportunity offered when the dreaded phylloxera louse attacked French vineyards before their neighbours in Northern Spain.

It was the railways which covered the plains of Languedoc with even more vines – previously the growers had been forced to distil their surplus produce. At harvest-time the railway stations were a chaotic mess, besieged by cart-loads of wine night and day. Casks lay everywhere, right on the crowded platforms, in warehouses throughout the region, scattered in the fields round the stations. The surge in production of strong wines from Provence killed many vineyards, most notably those near Paris, whose only asset had been their proximity to a major market. Even the Burgundians found it difficult to sell their wines, while the Champenois had to concentrate on sparkling rather than still wines, and the Orléanais turned to the production of vinegar.*

At least one fine wine area flourished because of the railways. In the eighteenth and early nineteenth centuries the Saint Emilionais had lived rather in the shadow of their grander brethren in the Graves and Medoc round Bordeaux. The railway,

---

* The railways encouraged the long-haul traffic from the South by charging lower rates compared with the shorter haul from Burgundy to Paris. The growers in Beaujolais allegedly shipped their wines down the Rhône to Arles then back to Paris by rail.

snaking round their little town and marking the bottom of the slopes on which the best grapes were grown, served to transport their wines to Paris and thence to Belgium and Northern France, regions still faithful today to the wines of Saint Emilion and its neighbour, Pomerol. By no coincidence the region's wines first attracted notice at the Paris Universal Exhibition in 1867, a decade or so after the railway's arrival.

But Saint Emilion was an exception. Most 'railway wines' were inevitably mass-produced, and because the makers were relatively uninterested in their quality they helped conceal the potential for making fine wines in such sites as the hills of Provence.

VI

IMPERIAL RAILWAYS

1
Colonies:
Direct and Indirect

Railways were a major instrument of national, political and economic assertiveness and influence, their intrusions abroad increasingly resented as the ability to construct and operate them became a test of national development. The colonising powers built and often operated railways all over the world – and not only in their own direct possessions – bringing their own habits, their own languages, with them. The influence could be simply financial – in 1914 Bradshaw's *Railway Manual* estimated that British investors owned 113 railways in 29 countries. But it could also be much more direct. The first American the Andean peasant or the Nicaraguan labourer ever met would be connected with the railway, which thus became the single most potent symbol of the control of an alien power over their lives.

The railways are popularly envisaged as an imperial force because of their role in conquering and then controlling the empires built up during the nineteenth century. Railways enabled imperial conquerors, like the British Raj in India to police, and exploit, their conquests. In Africa, particularly, they became the supreme symbol of the way the dark continent was carved up by the European powers in a grid composed of competing railroad lines. Only railways provided putative colonialists with the technical means to exploit the conquests they had made through other symbols of technical superiority like the Gatling gun.

Railways helped protect old empires as well as developing new ones, and they enabled the Tsars of Russia, the Habsburg emperors and the Sultans who presided over the decline of the Ottoman Empire to retain power over their far-flung dominions till the advent of World War I. However, in empires old and new the role of the railway was largely technical, supportive, secondary.

By contrast they, and the train of financial and technological obligations they brought with them, played the leading role in the 'indirect imperialism' that became so prevalent in developing countries not directly subject to the colonial powers. In those countries we find far more support for Lenin's thesis that imperialism was a search for outlets for finance capitalism than we do in directly-controlled colonies. Informal, indirect, accidental imperialism, much of it engendered by the railways, paid far more handsomely, and ran far fewer risks, than the more formal imperialism which involved responsibilities as well as power. Any form of indirect colonisation, whether the investment was for mines or plantations, required railways and inevitably they became of enormous emotional and psychological significance as the outstanding symbol of the men and powers which were controlling – and, too often, cheating – developing countries.

The conquistadores of steam needed support from local politicians who were usually crooked and generally incompetent. So, permanently and irretrievably, railways, their foreign promoters and their local supporters became associated with foreign interference of the most undesirable description, power asserted, and fortunes gained, without any corresponding degree of responsibility. The inevitable popular disillusionment was the greater because of the initial fund of goodwill felt for the promoters.

The consequences, in terms of permanent and only too-justified suspicion of western finance, has bedevilled what we would now call North-South relations to this day. The railways, the first capital-intensive industry any of these countries had ever seen – one, moreover, which they needed and which only foreign capital could construct – was the first, crucial battleground which gave capitalism in general a bad name, associated as it was with foreign extortion, as any attempt to get back the money that had been invested was seen by the locals. The pattern, and the results, were global. The whole process meant that many underdeveloped countries still suffer today from the paranoia inevitable in those who have been persecuted in the past.

Naturally such schemes produced a new breed of men. Eric Hobsbawm captured their major characteristic, their overriding, global ambitions. 'Such men thought in continents and oceans, for them the world was a single unit, bound together with rails of iron and steam engines, because the horizons of business were like their dreams, world-wide. The such men human destiny, history and profit were one and the same thing.'[1]

The process they engendered time and again was graphically described in the *Rio News* in 1887:[2]

they have floated schemes which they must have known to be visionary and unpromising, and they have flattered and wheedled Brazilian officials into the belief that scores of these wretched enterprises could be made remunerative, and that the 'natural resources' of the country are incalculably great and can be developed properly only through these so-called improvements . . . Then they have turned to the confiding investor and have made him believe Brazil to be the long-sought El Dorado, and that for every shilling planted there, nothing less than a sovereign could be produced. They have traded upon the amiability and rectitude of the Emperor, the peaceableness of the Brazilian people, the fertility of the soil, the wide expanse of territory, the product of a few gold and diamond mines, and the 'splendid future' in store for the country. They have baited their hooks with many a glittering generality and have never failed to catch their fish with them.

The enormous capital requirements of this 'Imperialist conspiracy' could only be satisfied by capital markets far larger, more international, and more complex than those required by previous borrowers, a handful of European states. The new markets were initially imperfect, often downright crooked, and the debt burden they imposed on poor countries was comparable to that felt today as a result of the loans made after the oil shock of 1973. But at least the earlier lenders generally left a physical legacy. As was said of Henry Meiggs, the 'Yankee Pizarro', 'while he was in many ways a scoundrel, he built some remarkable railways', which is more, much more, than can be said for the results of the Euromarkets of the 1970s and 1980s, in many ways the natural successors to the 'railway markets' of the 19th century.

Direct Colonialism: Intermittent and Grudging

The supposed intimacy of the connection between railways and direct imperialism is rather undermined by the evidence of the men on the spot. They tell a surprisingly similar tale: they were all forced to muddle through, they all complain of being neglected, of parsimony by the home government. Even when railways were supposedly being consciously employed as an imperial instrument they were never allowed adequate funds to carry out the imperial plans. No wonder that so many remained a dream, no wonder that most relied on the hazards of private, rather than government finance.

Yet railways were so important that their ownership was sometimes more important than nominal political overlordship. In the early part of this century, for example, Mozambique was reckoned to be in the British rather than the Portuguese sphere of influence because the railways were owned by British financial interests. But these were private, not the result of some diabolical Foreign Office plot to outwit the Portuguese.

With the single major exception of the Belgian Congo, a colony virtually worthless without a railway to by-pass the cataracts of the Upper Congo River, the imperial powers in Africa proved remarkably grudging in their financial support. In France's West African colonies the authorities at home were invariably mean, and the French Parliament allowed railways to be built without ballast. The pioneers had to fend for themselves, or rely on private initiatives. As a result by the 1930s the whole of French West Africa had only 2,000 miles of track, mostly private, with only one military railway, from Kayes to the River Niger, which proved very useful in providing access for the local peanut crop to navigable stretches of the Senegal and to transport manufactures from the coast to the interior.

In Algeria it was the same: the pioneering private companies were given grants which were soon reduced to interest guarantees, while in Tunisia the most profitable line was purely commercial, carrying phosphates from Gafsa to Sfax. Even when French imperial interests were directly involved, as they were in Indochina, the Trans-Indochinois line between Hanoi and Saigon was completed only in 1936, after decades of strenuous argument, despite its strategic importance and its usefulness for planters trying to recruit workers from all over Indochina. Indirect, private-sector imperialism got things done more quickly: by 1910 the French had already extended their railway north from Hanoi to Kunming in Southern China for vague imperial purposes, and to get access to silks, minerals, leather, furs and precious stones. For a long time thereafter it was easier to go from Shanghai to Kunming in Southern China indirectly via Hanoi rather than directly.

In Africa the Germans were aroused to action only by panics, generally related to military security. The first major line in South West Africa, from Windhoek to Swakopmund, was initiated only because of fear of a native uprising, and by an outbreak of bovine flu which stopped transport by bullock cart. In the event the insurrection was soon quashed and vaccine preserved the cattle. Only then did the imperial power cast around for an economic justification. Similarly the line through what eventually became Tanganyika only just squeaked through the appropriate Reichstag committee. Indeed the Reichstag, like all its fellow European assemblies, was habitually parsimonious, refusing to provide guarantees to German financiers, who then had to rely on large grants of often barren land.

Britons generally cite India as the prime example of imperialism in action through railway construction, and indeed British rule did provide the country with a railway system, honestly, if patchily, built. But the story does look very much like another example of muddling through. In the 1840s Lord Dalhousie, fresh from his collision with Britain's railway interests at home, wrote a series of lucid minutes analysing India's requirements. In the event imperial policy wavered, for the money was never going to be available to build an adequate network. In the words of Horace Bell, the imperial government wanted 'to obtain the much-needed railways extension on terms the least burdensome to the revenues of the Empire, and in avoiding as far as possible the undue relief of the present tax-payer at the expense of his successors'.[3]

The imperial government first provided a limited if relatively generous guarantee to private companies for every mile they

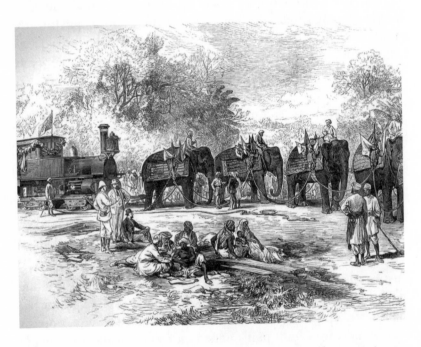

Indore, central India: elephants haul in the train that is going to replace them.

built. Then for a decade in the 1870s the Indian government built the lines itself, but the policy suffered from interference by the home government which even allowed private financial interests to build two key, and obviously profitable railways. Subsequently the government provided ungenerous assistance to private lines after continuing complaints that British capital should be available only with government guarantees: whatever Marxists may say about investment following the flag, British capitalists preferred to put their money in independent countries like the United States. The final policy was somewhat similar to that followed in France, another country anxious to try and guide railway development for national purposes, though the Raj was rather less generous than the Emperor of France.

From 1883, productive lines, in theory anyway, were leased to private enterprise while the government bore the burden of non-economic lines. Travel was cheaper in India – fares were less than two fifths those prevailing in Britain – and six passengers out of seven travelled third class, yet by 1914 the supposedly uneconomic government lines provided more revenue than customs and excise together. Nevertheless the inadequate legacy of a muddled policy was a muddled and inadequate system, with a great deal of metre-gauge track and only 10,000 miles of the broader 5½ feet gauge chosen for the main lines. The inadequacy was pointed up by a commission which reported as early as 1880 that India needed 20,000 miles of line merely to save it from the threat of famine.

The line which best exemplifies the contradictions and dilemmas inherent in imperial railways runs from Mombasa on the Indian Ocean to Lake Victoria in Uganda. The motives behind its construction were, as usual, confused: a combination of a humanitarian desire to counter the Arab slave traders operating in East Africa and an imperialistic impulse to reach the interior before the French and the Germans. The muddle and the expense were denounced by Henry Labouchère, a ferociously anti-Imperialist member of Parliament, in a famous squib:

What it will cost no words can express
What is its object no brain can suppose;
Where it will start from no one can guess;
Where it is going to nobody knows
What is the use of it none can conjecture
What it will carry there's none can define;
And in spite of George Curzon's* superior lecture,
It clearly is naught but a lunatic line.

In the event the railway proved a triumphant success, creating the new colony of Kenya on the way to Lake Victoria. It is also notable as the only imperial railway to have created a first-class political crisis in the mother country, for the line provided a convenient symbol for all the arguments between the Imperialists in both political parties and the so-called 'Little Englanders' within the Liberal party fiercely opposed to imperial expansion. Yet even the appetite of the Imperialists was limited. As we shall see, it was that arch-Imperialist the Marquis of Salisbury who, for practical reasons, doomed that great British dream, a railway on British territory from the Cape of Good Hope to Cairo.

Struggling for freedom, in Europe, Asia, Latin America

Today we think of underdeveloped countries as non-European, but during the early railway age many of the new nations struggling for freedom against a foreign domination which usually included an element of financial imperialism were in Europe. As we have seen, Belgium defined itself in relation to railways, and in Switzerland the populist agitation of the 1880s and 1890s, which led to the nationalisation of the country's railways, sprang from widespread disgust at the incompetence and greed of French and German financiers.

The Swiss rid themselves of their fear of foreigners by taking control of their own railways. In Spain, the efforts of those same

* Lord Curzon. Imperialist and 'superior person'.

financiers had more lingering effects. Some of the foreign promoters were casually Imperialist – to the Pereires the northern Spanish line appeared as merely an extension of those they were financing in the South-West of France, while American financiers showed a similar insensitivity when they prolonged their lines into Mexican territory. But the revulsion in Spain was profound enough to persuade a whole school of modern Spanish historians that foreign control of their railways prevented the creation of a rail system better adapted to the country's real needs. Moreover, they claimed the network imposed by foreign investors in league with a corrupt court and government should at least have been built with native iron and steel.

In fact,[4] Spain lacked the economic, technical and financial infrastructure required to take greater advantage of the arrival of the railways than she did: they added 11.8 per cent immediately and 18 per cent in the long run to the country's GNP (even by the restrictive 'Social Savings' criteria analysed above). There was simply not enough local capital available. Even the native investors in Catalonia, Spain's most developed province, had to be bought out by the French-controlled Norte company.

The complex relations between Spain and its railway-builders were as nothing to the tangled web created in Eastern Europe. Men have gone mad trying to understand Balkan politics in the latter half of the nineteenth century. Disentangling the crucial role played by railways, the outstanding physical symbol of the interrelationships involved, is an even surer path to the asylum.* The on-off love-hate relationship between the Austro-Hungarian Empire, Russia and the Ottoman Empire was complicated by the hostility between the Austrians and the newly and proudly independent Kingdom of Serbia. Hence the Austrians' eternal quest for a route from Vienna to the Black Sea and Constantinople which did not involve going through Serbia.

At first the Serbs welcomed the French as a means of escaping

---

* The route to Constantinople passed through Hungary, Roumania, Serbia, Bulgaria, Greece and Turkey. Eventually the Austrians found a way via Ouvatz and Mitrovitza. Not that Balkan railways were ever direct. To travel to Bulgaria from Russia or Bucharest you had to go round via Hungary.

from Austrian financial imperialism, but the French presence itself bred resentment. In 1883 the Serbians took the opportunity to nationalise their lines after the scandal-ridden collapse of their principal French bank, the Union Générale, led by the flamboyant Eugène Bontoux.

The 1870s had been dominated by another row, that between the Germans and the Roumanians. The latter were naturally interested in railway development. So was the German Chancellor, Otto von Bismarck. Some of the locals were dubious at the idea of any foreign infiltration, doubts encouraged by the Roumanian press which screamed that foreigners were mulcting their country, even though the journalists involved were waiting, palms outstretched, to be bought up by the same foreigners. To complicate matters the promoter, Bethel Henry Strousberg, was using railway money to shore up other shady enterprises.[5] The upshot was an international incident with Germans being beaten up by a Roumanian mob. Bismarck had to support either Strousberg or the Roumanians, whom he held in a profound contempt. 'Such degenerate people cannot be held in check through good dinners but through a few strong battalions,' was his verdict.

Bismarck was under pressure, not only from German bond-holders, but also from his Jewish friend and banker, Gerson Bleichroder, who wanted to use the Roumanians' indebtedness to force them to stop persecuting their Jewish citizens. In the end Bismarck showed himself keener to help German investors than Roumanian Jews, though his decision was not without its opponents – one German prince objected to the way Bismarck had committed his government's prestige merely because 'some capitalists had thrown their money into an industrial speculation'. In 1880 the Roumanians were forced to accept the original convention and to allow the Austrians to complete the system, a surrender much resented as state action on behalf of private bondholders.

But the tangle continued. The Treaty of Berlin in 1878 included an attempt to complete the railway to Constantinople, but it took another five years to reach an agreement for the three other countries involved, the Austro-Hungarian Empire, Serbia and Bulgaria, to finance their national sections.

The Ottoman Empire provides the classic proof that railway development, especially when financed and organised from abroad, did not necessarily produce any sort of economic, let alone political revolution.

The Sultans tried to promote commercially viable railways themselves – the first stretched just over 200 miles from fertile inland valleys to Smyrna on the Mediterranean – but the principle of independence was soon lost in the politico-financial morass which marked all Ottoman relations with foreigners in the last half of the nineteenth century. They were exploited by the likes of Baron Hirsch, and were forced to surrender a great deal of their financial independence to the foreign commissioners of the Ottoman debt. It was the Germans in their pursuit of the Berlin – Bagdad dream who showed that only what amounted to direct colonialism could provide the empire with an efficient network.

The Russians, tougher, less bankrupt than the Turks, nevertheless had an unhappy early experience with the 'Main company', a monopoly theoretically subject to Russian government supervision. In fact it was controlled by the French who wasted a lot of money – the chairman built himself a lavish house at the company's expense while his company tried to take over the state-run line from Saint Petersburg to Moscow, even though it was making only slow progress on building its own line to Warsaw. Having annoyed its influential Russian noble shareholders, it then defaulted on its obligation to build railways south of Moscow. The foreigners had sparked off strong nationalist opposition (the line from Odessa to Balta was so Germanic that even the tickets were printed in German), and by the mid-1860s the Russian government was resigned to the need to build its own railways.

Everywhere financiers and contractors left a trail of mistrust. The misdeeds of the notorious Irish swindler John Sadleir led the Swedes to rely purely on their own resources and the Portuguese suffered from the depredations of three British contractors, the Waring Brothers. Charles Waring was the worst. When he stood for Parliament for the port of Poole his Conservative opponent confidently declared that 'If there is one name in Portugal which is a byword and a reproach, it is the name of Waring . . . associate Mr Waring's name with Poole and no Portuguese or Spanish merchant will consign a cask of wine to your port.'[6] The opponent was being a trifle unfair. The Spanish banker and promoter José de Salamanca did more to exploit the Portuguese than the Warings. Having secured the privilege of building the railways he managed to postpone the most crucial single project, a bridge across the River Douro at Oporto.

But one of the earliest and most spectacular clashes engendered by railway imperialism was not in Europe but over the Grand Trunk Railway in Canada. At first British finance and expertise were welcomed by the port of Portland in Maine, which was trying to upstage Boston and, within Canada itself, by the powerful interests in the lowlands round the Saint Lawrence River who wanted closer ties with Britain. Moreover the timing was propitious. That year, 1852, marked the completion of the British main-line network, so British contractors were hungry for work and fielded their first team, Brassey and Peto, for what was projected as the world's longest line, 1,100 miles. However the bankers, Baring and Glyn, got cold feet before they had issued the necessary bonds, and although they could not stop the project the line was saddled with a considerable burden of debt and unpopularity in Canada as a 'colonial' railway. The patriotic feelings were reinforced by the fact that the railway's Board was based in London until it was finally nationalised after World War I to become part of the Canadian National Railway network.

Even the Americans had to buy their independence. Early British financial involvement often consisted merely of export finance to help the sale of British rails – in the 1850s this totalled over 1.5 million tons, a third of all British exports of iron and steel. Previous foreign portfolio investment had been largely in the bonds of individual American states, many of which had defaulted, as had many of the loans issued in the 1830s to finance public works like canals.

Not surprisingly the first issues of railway capital in the 1850s appealed mainly to the more adventurous investors. They were looking 'first for shares, later for convertible bonds, and then for land-grant bonds issued in conjunction with shares'.[7] The Americans soon became equal partners in the financial game, and the legacy of mistrust left by the railways was directed not so much against foreign capital but against the middle-men, the 'Eastern financiers' of Wall Street.

However, in Latin America, the locals could not shield the foreigners. British bankers had originally been interested in protecting and encouraging the export of British rails to Argentina in the 1860s. But the impact of foreign capital was bound to be much greater in Argentina, where most of the pampas had been totally unoccupied before the railways, or in Mexico where, as Bernard Moses points out, the railway 'came as a rival of the half-starved donkey and the not-overfed Indian'.[8] The railways had another, psychological, impact. Previously the landowning classes had lived in a state of not caring if 'a large part of their lands are not under cultivation, and produce little or nothing'.

But before the pampas were settled or the Indian fed came the race to find a railway route across Central America. This became urgent after 1849 with the discovery of gold in California, formerly reachable only by sailing round Cape Horn. The winner was the railway across the Isthmus of Panama, but only after every country had competed for the route. The Hondurans[9] offered promoters 1,000 square miles of land as well as a 400-yard stretch each side of the tracks, plus options to buy a further 800,000 acres cheaply. The offer was taken up by one Ephraim George Squier, a dubious promoter who doubled as American consul. Unable to raise the necessary funds in the United States he sold the concession to the British who in 1857 launched the Honduras Inter-Oceanic Railway Company. Originally it was estimated that the route, which would be quicker than its rivals through Nicaragua or Panama, would cost a mere $7 million to yield a net profit of $2 million a year. But by 1873 the country – and the railway – were both bust, though the latter did bring some prosperity to the northern part of the country.

Foreign capitalists bred their own client regimes, served by Western-educated technocrats similar to those who have flourished since the oil crisis of 1973. Typically in Mexico President Porfirio Diaz leaned on the much respected José Limantour, his principal economic adviser. Like his successors in the 1970s, Limantour hoped to attract but control foreign capital. Like a majority of his fellow-countrymen he and his colleagues, the 'Cientificos' as they called themselves, were humiliated by the rough treatment brought about by lack of *'mejoras materiales'*. They wanted concrete, physical progress at almost any cost, and the railway was the prime symbol of such progress.

Unfortunately the first line from Mexico City to the port of Vera Cruz was not finished by its European promoters, which set off a reaction in favour of American companies. This was also short-lived, largely because the likes of Jay Gould and Thomas Scott treated Mexico as merely an extension of the American battlefields on which they waged their interminable and costly wars.

As we have seen, Argentina was the classic case of railways determining the very nature of the country. They were foreign-controlled because 'Argentine interests were not concerned either to invest in or gain control of such undertakings, no matter how freely they might criticise their activities in their newspapers and in the halls of the Congress . . . it was easier to kick the companies through the agency of the government and more profitable to speculate in land, sell cattle and wool, and institute share-cropping, all of which railways greatly stimulated by opening a way to the markets first of Buenos Aires and then the world . . . in 1885 a million pounds invested in railway plant in Argentina contributed to the production of more saleable commodities than a million pounds invested anywhere else in the world at that moment in history'.[10]

The railways into the pampas brought prosperity by supplying Europe with meat and grain. On the return journey up country trains carried cheap manufactured goods imported through Buenos Aires, products which have helped prevent the Argentines from developing efficient manufacturing industries ever since.

Another cause of complaint came from the crops they encouraged. In the inland sugar province of Tucuman the only work was seasonal, ill-paid, cutting cane. As James Scobie wrote (in *Argentina*), 'The concentration of economic and political power in a few hands, the seasonal aspect of sugar growing, and the masses of transient Indian labourers turned Tucuman into a backwash of poverty and a source of future political discontent'.

Single crop economies dependent on sugar or coffee, or other tropical products whose development was much favoured by the railways, virtually precluded balanced development. The railway map of Honduras showed a fine network of lines serving the banana-growing districts at a time when the capital and other important centres were still miles from the nearest lines. The same applied throughout Central America. In the words of a recent history:[11]

> Railroads were vital to the banana enterprise. If the banana interests had not provided them, railway service for the scantily populated lowlands in Central America would have been delayed for many decades. But the banana did not provide any network ideally suited to serve the overall economic needs of the several national economies. That was not their business. Nevertheless historically railroads and bananas have been so closely associated in the minds of the people of the area, that the banana companies more often have been censured for their failure to provide fully for all railway needs than credited for their considerable contributions to this important field.

The railways did not invent the idea of a single-crop economy (in the eighteenth century the 'sugar islands' of the Caribbean were reckoned as valuable as Canada) and a single crop was better than nothing, though you wouldn't believe the fact if you read some Argentine nationalist commentators: but dependence bred resentment, with fatal long-term consequences for the foreign investors whose biggest, and most visible asset were the railway companies.

Rail conquers the Andes.

Not that the foreigners had done too badly in their time. They had taken a considerable initial profit because bonds were almost invariably issued at a considerable discount. Developing countries therefore never received anything like the amount they nominally borrowed. The Turks received only three-fifths of the £200 million they borrowed between 1845 and 1875, while the Costa Ricans, whose credit was reckoned to be above the average, received only 72 per cent of the proceeds of an issue in the early 1870s. Naturally dissatisfied, they tried more direct negotiations with another firm of bankers.[12] In the ensuing disaster the bankers had to take up most of the issue and the Costa Ricans were left owing £2.4 million from an issue from which they received only £700,000, although the president received another £71,000 from the grateful bankers. Borrowers could also suffer when exchange rates moved against them. In 1878 the Companhia Paulista, one of the best-run Brazilian railway companies, took out a twenty-year £150,000 loan. By the time it came to repay, the milreis had halved in value against sterling.

It took nearly a hundred years for the Argentines to grasp the nettle and nationalise their railways fully – with disastrous results. In China – where the conflict between national pride and financial imperialism found its fiercest battleground – the reaction against foreign investment was immediate. At the end of the nineteenth century China was increasingly being carved up into spheres of influence including 'concessions' in which individual Western powers held sway over the inhabitants of the oldest civilisation in the world as if they were total savages. All the imperial powers of both the nineteenth and twentieth centuries were involved: Britain, France, Belgium and Germany represented the old imperial order; Russia, the United States and Japan the new.

The occupiers were a force for disunity. They set themselves up against the Chinese, in Han Suyin's words 'they were not all racketeers but they all thrived on China's disunity'. In *Riding the Iron Rooster*, Paul Theroux, writing in the 1980s, explains why two stretches of line had not been connected because it was not in the interest of the Japanese and the Germans who had built them. Nevertheless each of the European powers thought that it, unlike the others, was loved by the Chinese.

To the sceptical Han Suyin, 'the truth is, they were all the

The opening of the first railway in China from Shanghai to Woosung Port, 1876

same', although filial pride* led her to point out (in *The Crippled Tree*) that the Belgians were different: 'Their engineers and technicians in China were hard-working, honest and what they promised they did, in record time. They were also exacting towards themselves. The Chinese were not afraid of small, hard-working Belgium.' In fact, the Belgians needed China as a market for the rails and locomotives on which their economy depended, and in the end even little Belgium proved dangerous: King Leopold II dreamed of a Belgian Empire in the heart of China.

Inevitably the occupying powers in China disagreed, with the loudest rows involving the longest lines, north and south connecting Peking and Hankow. These lines were naturally perceived by the Chinese as instruments of imperial policy, and in 1898 one Chang Chih-tung wrote that 'the interest rates on

---

* Ms Suyin's father was a Chinese railway engineer, educated in Belgium, where he had married a local girl. So Suyin was a well-placed, if obviously partisan, witness.

British loans are low, but their injury is great. By using railways above Hankow, and gunboats below, the British will make the entire Yangtze an English possession and overnight the twelve provinces south of the river will be cut off.' It did not much help when the Belgians gained the coveted contract for the major east-west railways after considerable intrigue, and a wave of anti-Belgian sentiment in Britain. The Chinese paid dear: the Belgians made a substantial profit at the time, and another in 1908 when the Chinese bought back the lines on onerous terms.

All the Chinese contracts were agreed in a squalid atmosphere. The railways' only native allies, who naturally acquired a bad name as collaborators, followed the traditional pattern, involving nepotism, tax farming, 'squeeze', automatic corruption. Not surprisingly the foreigners were faced with an explosive mixture of historic Chinese pride and hatred of foreigners – and thus of the modern techniques they brought with them: the mixture found allies in precisely those groups which in other countries were the promoters' greatest allies, the modernisers. In China they were totally unprepared to accept outside help – or the outsiders themselves – because of the burgeoning Chinese desire for independence. The pattern became plain when the locals tore up the nine miles of narrow-gauge track which constituted the country's first railway and threw the rails, carriages and locomotives into the nearest river.

Foreigners believed that only ignorant peasants and self-serving old-time officials opposed the railways, but in fact even the most enlightened would accept them only if they were Chinese-built: phrases like 'self-built railways' were key political terms in the Chinese struggle for independence. Unfortunately the Chinese needed the foreigners, and in what was termed the 'self-reliance period' between 1881 and 1895 only an average of eighteen miles of track were built each year. As soon as the foreigners were allowed back the figure increased to 345 miles annually between 1895 and the revolutionary year of 1911. But even then less than 6,000 miles of track had been built in all – half the figure for India, smaller and itself not over-supplied with railways.

It was not surprising that the leader of the 1911 revolution, Sun Yat-Sen, was obsessed with railways, nor that the first signs of the upheaval were centred on a railway line. When he was shunted aside after the revolution he was given a nominal job planning them, a task dear to his heart. He envisaged an enormous network, which was considered totally fanciful by his contemporaries, although most of the routes he sketched out have been built since the Communist takeover in 1949. His planned railway network was the heart of an imaginative international aid programme which, if realised, would have anticipated the World Bank by a quarter of a century. He envisaged an international organisation 'to formulate plans and standardize materials' which would gain the confidence of the Chinese people. As he pointed out, Manchuria, previously considered a desert, had already been transformed by its railway into the world's prime source of soya. 'As Argentina has superseded the United States in supplying the world with meat', so with the help of 7,000 miles of new railway for this 'vast and fertile region . . . the Mongolian pasture will some day take the place of Argentina'.

Naturally the Chinese have always poor-mouthed the foreign-built railways' contribution to their economic well-being, the denigration helped by the unreliability of the figures. As R. H. Huenemann put it recently: 'the difficulties involved in gauging the impact of railroads on Chinese incomes are so complex and intractable that we will never have a satisfactory measure of that impact.'[13] Nevertheless – and contrary to decades of Chinese orthodoxy – he concluded that 'Imperial' railways contributed a net half per cent annually to China's GNP by 1933, a total less relevant than the fact that 'it was brought about by investment that the Chinese did not have to finance.'

But, whatever the economic benefits, to the Chinese foreign-built railways represented national humiliation. In Han Suyin's words, 'After 1900 the demand that Chinese railways must belong to the Chinese was also a claim to real independence, an end to subjugation. For true independence is not only political, but also economic.'

188

China was not the only country where the Empire-builders clashed. Conflict, between rival empire-builders as well as between natives and imperialists, was endemic wherever outside finance was involved in railway-building.

'Imperial' influence depended on the availability of funds from the imperial country and markets to handle the vast sums involved. And, throughout the nineteenth century, only Britain, France and, much later and to a much lesser extent, Germany, had the spare capital and organisation required. The British investing public was avid for the good 'stories' behind any successful financial promotion from anywhere in the world. Most of these involved railways. It was only in the 1880s and 1890s that they were partly replaced as speculative instruments by 'Kaffirs', shares in South African mines.

The flows were enormous. By 1914 British investors had £1.6 billion in foreign railways.* Of this £440 million were in 'Colonial' railways, while £617 million had been invested in the United States where railroads accounted for four-fifths of the British financial presence. Even today a few 'foreign railway' stocks and bonds are still quoted, while names like 'Antefegasta' stir memories of former speculative favourites.

The relationship between British investors and banks and most of the recipients of their money was strictly 'Colonial'. But relations with the United States, the biggest recipient of British capital, was far more complex. As early as the 1830s foreign investors were attracted by railroads radiating from New York or Philadelphia, but even in 1853 foreigners controlled only $52 million out of the $400 million already owed by railroad companies.

The subsequent surge was greatly helped by technical changes, notably the regular steamship services introduced in the 1850s,† and the first Atlantic cable laid in 1866, which linked London and New York into one international financial market. The move was timely: investors had made large gains from buying up

---

* The details can be found in Herbert Feis *Europe, the World's Banker.*

† One of the most dramatic moments of the Erie Affair (see pages 126–30) involved the arrival of a steamship from London bearing masses of Erie stock which, it was assumed, would be dumped on the market.

federal and railroad paper at depressed prices during the darker hours of the Civil War – a process that had already first been seen during the panic of 1854 and which would be repeated in subsequent crises.

In the decade before and during the Civil War foreign holdings of American railroad paper barely changed, but quadrupled to reach $243 million by 1870, a mere five years after the end of the Civil War. By the 1880s any fall in these securities had a considerable knock-on effect on the whole London market. This is not surprising. In 1867 only ten American railroad companies were quoted in London, their capital a mere £78 million. By 1888 there were 82 companies quoted with £450 million of capital. Already by the 1870s railroads were steadily replacing federal and state borrowers – the federal government was able to repay most of its debts thanks to the balance of payment surpluses generated by ever-increasing exports of railborne grain from the Mid-West.

At the same time American banks were steadily strengthening their position. Before the Civil War the London banks were the senior partners: but the failed 1848 revolution in Germany, like Hitler's rise to power eighty-five years later, led to a wave of emigration by a mass of largely Jewish financial talent, and this encouraged existing German-born settlers to look to investment in their new country rather than their birthplace. By the 1880s American banks had achieved parity, although the London branch of some houses, like Rothschild, Baring and Morgan, remained the senior. More typical were Siamese-twin relationships, like the houses of Morton Bliss in New York and Morton Rose in London. Together they mobilised funds, sponsored new railroads, acted as the reputable middleman required not only to back long-term loands but also provide working capital.

By 1890, when London was shaken by the Baring crisis, caused by that house's over-involvement in Argentine railways, the Americans themselves were becoming major capital exporters. The Dutch had been early on the scene, but rather lost their nerve in the mid-1870s after a spate of railway defaults at home and abroad. But their ill wind blew favourably towards the promoters of the Canadian Pacific, who were able to buy up masses of bonds from the disgusted Dutch, who thus bore the brunt of the early losses inevitable in any major project.

By contrast the French were an ever-increasing force in the markets, the only other investors with capital to spare on the same scale as the British. By the 1850s they had somehow found enough finance and organising capacity not only to build their own network but other people's as well, so that by 1860 there were very few railways in the rest of Europe not dominated by French capital. The flows accelerated again once the French had recovered their nerve following their country's defeat in the Franco-Prussian war of 1870. By 1914 it had trebled from its 1880 level of 15 billion francs, with the money still overwhelmingly invested in Europe, above all in Russia, where the French accounted for a third of total investment.[14] They had 11.3 billion francs in Russia, an increase of over four billion since 1900; and the complete loss of this investment, the single biggest item in the country's foreign portfolio,* in the Russian Revolution, not only destroyed the Paris international capital market and deterred French investors from foreign adventures for generations, but it also obscured the fact that Paris's position had been near-equal to London's before 1914.

Paris housed the most powerful branch of the Rothschild clan, a veritable one-firm international Jewish conspiracy, with family members in five countries, giving an enormous advantage over even the Barings, outgunned in both Spain and Russia. In Northern Italy the Rothschilds controlled the Lombardy–Venetian line, the only profitable major route in the country, and their dominance extended into Austria, including the crucial line over the Semmering pass from Vienna to Trieste on the Adriatic. Indeed, until the opening of the Saint Gotthard tunnel in 1882, the Rothschilds controlled the only two direct routes between Italy and Germany.

The degree to which trade followed the financial flag varied. In the last half of the century the British financial flow became

---

* In *La Position Internationale de la France* Maurice Levy-Leboyer reckoned that the losses between 1917 and 1921 amounted to between 15 and 16 billion gold francs, about five months of France's national output.

increasingly detached from the British exports which had provided the initial spark. In France engineers and equipment continued to flow with the money. But the link was much more direct with the Germans. In 1914 the Austro-Hungarian Empire accounted for nearly a third of the $6 billion (five times the 1883 figure) they had invested abroad, a clear case of politically-inspired investment.

As the sums involved grew bankers and financiers had to cast their net ever wider. This in itself produced major changes in the banking world. In the last decades before 1914 bankers without national branch networks could not mobilise the vast sums required. As a result even the most powerful investment bankers like the Rothschilds could not compete with broader-based commercial banks like the Crédit Lyonnais and the Société Générale, which could distribute endless issues of Russian bonds through their thousands of branches.

Fortunately for the banks, railway investments offered something for every temperament. Most were in bonds, but enough were in stocks of individual railways to appeal to the more adventurous – like those dreaming of the wonders of the American West in the two decades after the Civil War. As always the promoters were selling dreams, dreams in which they often believed themselves. 'What George Bliss called a "young American spirit" conditioned his firm's investment criteria,' wrote Dolores Greenberg in *Financiers & Railroads 1869–1889*.

Bliss, working in a 'mid-Atlantic' environment, was one of the few participants who understood the considerable culture gap between the two sides of the ocean. Following the Granger agitation against the railroad companies he wrote how 'throughout Europe the opinion prevailed that capital invested in American railroads – in new western railroads especially – was at the mercy of a reckless and unprincipled democracy.' But the investors soon returned, and with them their dreams and their nightmares; the bankers all knew that dewy-eyed foreigners could be attracted to stocks rather shunned by the locals. By 1891 they owned almost as many shares in the perpetually-troubled Union Pacific as did investment institutions based in

New York, while they had only small stakes in such solid lines as the New York Central and the Pennsylvania Railroad.

But these idealistic 'punters' were often joined by more conservative investors. In E. M. Forster's *Howards End* Margaret Schlegel showed her independence by putting her money into 'Foreign Things which always smash' as against the supposedly safer home rails like the Nottingham & Derby. Irritatingly 'the Foreign Things' did admirably and the Nottingham & Derby declined with the steady dignity of which only Home rails are capable. As so often, reality confirms the novelist's insight, at least into the composition of the investing class, if not into its choice of investment. In an analysis of the 411 original shareholders in the Central Argentine '83 were gentlemen, 14 were widows or spinsters, 40 were professional men, civil servants, officers of the armed forces, and members of parliament, and the rest were merchants, tailors, farmers, upholsterers, glass manufacturers, and so on.'[15]

Nevertheless as soon as money was invested the shareholders needed protection. By the 1850s Barings were involved with the Illinois Central. They didn't want to be; for the state, if not the railroad, was already in default, but their clients were in the securities anyway. The greater the flow of funds, the more reputable the institutions involved had to be.

The need for protection had some odd results. Henry Villard, the father of the Northern Pacific, the second railroad across the western United States, first became involved with railways on a visit to his native Germany for the sake of his health when he was approached by an unhappy investor anxious for his advice. Villard found himself on a committee set up in Frankfurt to help such investors, and found that one line in Oregon, saddled with $3 million in 7 per cent bonds, had never been built. According to his autobiography his subsequent battles on both sides of the Atlantic generated a passionate belief in the future of Western Oregon. His vision was shared by sober German bankers, including the mighty Deutsche Bank, and enabled him to promote the Northern Pacific, the second railroad to the West Coast of the United States. This had considerable financial problems, but Villard had once been a journalist, and he retained a flair for publicity which enabled him to cover them up, not least with spectacular special visits. Guests on one such jaunt included an ex-Lord Chief Justice of England, a handful of peers, ex-President Grant as well as Dr Georg Siemens of the Deutsche Bank.

As investment soared protection became institutionalised. By the 1880s there were regular London committees designed to protect bondholders in individual stocks and bonds. Otherwise unscrupulous promoters would, for instance, offer repayment of bonds within fifteen days, a period deliberately chosen as too short to enable foreign holders to take the opportunity. In 1884 the English Association of American Stock and Bondholders was formed to act as proxy, to insist that it get 'full statements, clean balance-sheets and ordinary honesty' from railroads and 'Proportional Representation of Investors in the Control of the various Roads'. The association did have some success in its difficult task, it even managed to force the Chicago, Milwaukee and St Paul Railroad to stop its financially reckless pricing policy.

Scottish investors, basically more interested in ranching, became fearfully entangled in the affairs of Oregon's railroads. The ensuing law-suit went to the US Supreme Court, which ruled in favour of the Scots' rivals, a bankrupt line in the Villard sphere of influence. This cost the Scots $1¼ million, a loss for which they never forgave William Reid, previously the uncrowned King of the Scottish investment community. Yet – and this applies to tens of thousands of foreign investors of every nationality – the Scots did not lose their appetite for railroad stocks, a final proof of the universal spell they cast throughout the century.

Don Enrique – and his Dynasty

The story of imperial railway-building is epitomised in the life-stories of Henry Meiggs and his nephew, C. Minor Keith. Meiggs, the 'Yankee Pizarro'[16], was a handsome, charming, larger-than-

Henry Meiggs, conquerer of the Andes

life character, universally known in Chile and Peru as 'Don Enrique', so popular that at his death he was accorded the grandest funeral ever seen in Peru. He lived and died a gambler: indeed he arrived in Chile in 1854 as a fugitive after the failure of a property deal in San Francisco, where he had been a town councillor. (Meiggs later repaid his debts, largely by buying up the paper at a discount, thus enabling him, rather disingenuously, to claim that he had settled all his accounts.)

In Chile he swiftly found his true vocation. Like all great contractors he had only to travel once over a projected route to compute the real costs of building a railway over it. After completing two relatively small, if troublesome, contracts he bid successfully for the crucial route from Santiago to Valparaiso. The contract made his fortune and his reputation, not only as a railway builder but also as a liberal influence because he treated his workers, the Chilean rotos, as men rather than slaves.

But his greatest fame came from his work in Peru, a country suddenly rich, thanks to its rich deposits of guano, the bird droppings which were then essential fertiliser the world over. The Peruvians believed they could use their new-found wealth to create a new national unity through a network of railways. The people welcomed Meiggs with open arms; their rulers with outstretched palms – so much so that he had to build the necessary massive bribes into his costs. The first line was to run from the coast to Arequipa, birthplace of most of the politicians then in power in Peru. The cost was reckoned at 10 million *soles*. The government was told the line could not be built for less than 15 million. Meiggs completed the contract, early, for 12 million.

Unfortunately in 1868 the Peruvians elected as President Colonel Jose Balta, a typically unbalanced military revolutionary. In the next three years he and Meiggs agreed six contracts to build just over a thousand miles of railways, on terms highly favourable to Meiggs. The railways, especially the Central Peruvian, were amongst the wonders of the world, but they were built against a background of a steadily deteriorating financial situation for Peru, as the guano started to run out, and thus for Meiggs himself: he was even forced to use his own bills of exchange, the so-called '*Billetes de Meiggs*'. In a last desperate effort he offered to build a railway to the fabled mines of Cerro de Pasco but died in 1877 at the age of 66 before it was completed.

Typically, he, not Peru's rulers, was blamed for Peru's troubles: 'the ruin of Peru', wrote a local opponent just after his death, 'is the monument of Henry Meiggs'. His legacy included: some wonderful railways and an ambitious, and financially more successful nephew, C. Minor Keith, who carried the particular Meiggs brand of swashbuckling piracy through Central America.

Keith arrived in Central America in 1871 to help his uncle on a contract Don Enrique had taken on and left to his nephew to complete. Minor Keith soon realised that bananas, heavy, much in demand, and the major cash crop for the countries concerned, formed ideal freight traffic. And in Central America only railways could carry them to the coast: the roads were terrible, the topography difficult and the climate worse (254 inches of rain were recorded one year on the Caribbean coast of Costa Rica).

His eventual success was built on a notorious agreement he signed with President Soto of Costa Rica in 1884. This enabled the country to refund its foreign debt, and allowed Keith to build fifty-two miles of railway in which the government would have a one-third interest. In return he received a grant of 800,000 acres and freedom from tax for twenty years.

By 1899 Keith had built seventy-one miles of line inland from the Caribbean coast at a cost of nearly 8 million (and 4,000 lives) and 61,000 acres of banana trees were in production. That year Keith's desire for an integrated monopoly (combined with the failure of the firm handling his bananas in New Orleans) led to the formation of the United Fruit Company, its position based not so much on its vast banana plantations – for anyone could buy land and plant trees – but on its position as owner of the crucial railways, in Honduras and Guatemala as well as in Costa Rica.

This archetypal 'indirect imperialist', 'the E. H. Harriman and J. Pierpont Morgan of Central America',[17] was in many ways a sympathetic figure, described by even an unsympathetic observer (Henry Stimson) as 'the perfect type of Anglo-Saxon man'. Notably unlike later imperialists, he integrated into the local society, marrying the daughter of a former President of Costa Rica, and formed a valuable collection of local antiquities which he later presented to the American Museum of Natural History. Keith himself survived until the 1920s, while his creation remained the prime symbol of American imperialism for a further half-century.

'Without our railway, there is no Szechuan left'

Szechuan, deep in the heart of China, is one of the country's most enclosed, least westernised provinces, with a fierce local patriotism. It was naturally determined to have its own railway, parallel to the Great (Yellow) River from the capital, Chengtu, through Chungking to Ichang. In 1903 the locals set up the Szechuan Provincial Railway Company, modelled on the old salt and iron monopolies, as a private concern under the aegis of the provincial government, although such was the opposition of the central government that it was officially recognised only four years later. The shares were issued in two denominations, 100 and ten silver ounces – much later one of Han Suyin's uncles showed her some of them, 'a small trunk full of useless printed paper. He kept them as a souvenir'.*

The company determined to start on the most difficult, eastern, section to make it easier to ferry supplies later to the rather easier western section. But progress was slow, by 1911 a mere fifty miles, less than a thirtieth of the total, had been built. The locals were confronted by a plot by the evil Sheng Hsinsun, the director of railway building and chief broker in dealing with Europeans. On May 9th 1911 he promulgated a nationalisation decree which removed the rights previously granted to provincial companies to finance and build their own railways. As the locals rightly suspected at the time, the decree was the result of a deal to hand the railway over to the foreigners.

As Hsinsun knew full well, the decree put the board in a difficult position because so many of them had been involved in defrauding the shareholders. But no one was prepared for the spontaneous uprising which brought together over a thousand shareholders in a 'Save the Railway League', an organisation which included every class, not just the natural revolutionary leaders, the students who had returned from studying abroad, but also many officials – including those from the railway itself who simply didn't want anyone to inspect the accounts.

* This note is based on Han Suyin's account in *The Crippled Tree*. Suyin was told the story by an eyewitness, Li Chiehjen, a writer known as 'the Maupassant of China' who was there at the time.

The Leaguers pleaded to the central government that they were not rebels but merely opposing a treacherous minister who was betraying his country's interests. Peking's reply was to cut off Szechuan and send in a hard man to restore order, Chao Erfang, warlord of the borders, who had showed his mettle by ousting the British and the Russians from Lhasa. He was opposed by a general strike. Many of the official leaders wanted to surrender but, as the student leader Lung Mingchien put it, 'without our own railway there is no Szechuan left'.

On 7th September, the Chinese All Souls day, the two assembly-men representing the railway company were arrested, and several people were killed in the subsequent riots. Their crucial allies were the Kelao Brotherhood, an anti-Manchu Mafia, in the original sense of that much-abused term, a group of people banding together to defend their local interests against a centrally-imposed despotism. The Brotherhood organised key groups like the manure collectors, the boatmen, the water carriers and the small shopkeepers. Although the leaders of the rebellion felt they had to accept any help on offer, there were natural culture clashes between the students and their hardened Kelao allies.

The three Changs, or leaders of the Brotherhood, were tough, practical men who would fight only if they were sure of winning. The improbable alliance mobilised the whole province into a mass movement, with massive arms smuggling. Chao Erfang kept winning battles but 'it was like cutting water with a sword', for in the five months between the nationalisation decree and the official start of the 1911 revolution on 10th October, 'the people of Szechuan in one way or another fought nearly every day'.

Three weeks before the revolution the Kelao Brotherhood, 'their gangster methods under control' took Junghsien, and on 22nd December a young officer beheaded Chao Erfang and held up the severed head by its pigtail in front of a delighted crowd. But that was not the end of the story. In 1952 one of the old engineers, blind with age, was told that the dream had come true, that the railway had been completed under Chinese ownership. He 'bent down to stroke and kiss the rails, not only because it was a railway, but because it was built by the Chinese, for the Chinese'.

Hirsch: Railway King Extraordinaire

Baron Maurice de Hirsch was the single most startling example of the small band of cosmopolitan Jewish financiers who dominated the popular imagination at the turn of the century. He was the third generation of a family of Munich bankers, distinguished enough to have acquired a title. But before his death in 1896 at the age of 65 Hirsch had acquired an enormous fortune of something between £14m and £30m – and that after giving much the same amount to charity. In today's terms he was a billionaire.

Hirsch had grasped the fortunes to be made from the kilometric guarantee, the sums given for constructing a given length of railway line. These did not necessarily have to join two towns, the lines could be built through the easiest countryside. Hirsch's nick-name 'Turkenhirsch' explains how the bulk of his fortune was made through exploiting the desire of the Turkish Empire to acquire a proper network. During the 1840s and 1850s a number of promoters had sketched a line from Belgrade to Constantinople. Progress was slow and in 1869 Hirsch got his first opportunity because the Turkish government wanted to demonstrate its independence from French financiers, the Rothschilds and the Pereires.

All Hirsch's many and varied sources of profits depended on his crucial role as an individual middleman between great institutional powers: the Sultan, the bankers like Rothschild and Pereire, who wanted to finance or operate railways, and banks prepared to sell the bonds he had acquired. His first deal was over an issue of three per cent lottery bonds with a nominal value of 792 million francs. They were credited to him at a price of 32 per cent: he promptly sold them to a syndicate led by the Société Générale at a profit of 40 million francs. They were then resold to the general public at 45 per cent – giving the bank a further profit of 50 million francs.

Hirsch never wanted to run the railways he financed, and in 1869 nearly got the Rothschilds to take on the obligation – with an advance which would prevent Hirsch from having to use his

Baron von Hirsch, rischest and most devious of all railway promoters.

own money to build the line. After some misunderstandings Hirsch had to create his own operating company,[18] but was able to use external funds, often from individual Turks, to avoid investing any of his own money. After ten years of wars (and the onset of the great slump in 1873) he had built only two thirds of the desired tracks, some 1,275 kilometres, in seven separate sections, and these were so badly constructed that they needed an extra 27,000 francs per kilometre to be usable. Not surprisingly his chief engineer, the Prussian genius Wilhelm von Pressel, died cursing Hirsch's name.

Hirsch repeated his selling techniques with later issues, blatantly puffing his shares in newspapers paid for the purpose, and when his activities aroused opposition – especially because of his habit of building isolated stretches of line – he simply transformed his French company into an Austrian one, thus ridding himself of troublesome French directors.

Not surprisingly no-one quite knows how much money he made. His receipts included his 'turn' on sales of the bonds, profits from the construction contracts (estimated at 100 million francs), operating profits of another 50 million and the substantial sums from unclaimed winning lottery bonds. He even won the law suit brought by disgruntled bondholders when the bonds he had issued suspended interest payments.

Disreputable Hirsch undoubtedly was. Disagreeable he wasn't. He was a tall, healthy, bustling fellow, a sportsman who found it natural to buy his way to prominence on the English turf, and thus to the attention of the Prince of Wales. Nevertheless he was not welcome in Society either in Paris or Vienna. As Sir Philip Magnus wrote in *King Edward VII*, 'He was richer than the Rothschilds, but unlike them never assimilated himself socially. He was excluded from the Jockey Club, cold-shouldered, or treated, at best, with a mortifying condescension by most archdukes and great magnates and never received at Court.'

Probably Hirsch did not mind, for his all-embracing cynicism included a disarming lack of any sense of self-importance. In *La France Juive* that notorious anti-semite Edouard Drumont treats him as a cheerful *arriviste* less ridiculous than his fellow Jewish bankers, his arrogance mitigated by his bad jokes and his bonhomie. 'Whereas the Rothschilds believe they belong to the aristocracy, he believes the aristocracy belongs to him.'

Margot Tennant, who later married Herbert Asquith, the future British Prime Minister, has left an hilarious account of a dinner in which he asked her to marry his son Lucien. When she objected that Lucien was ill he replied simply, 'But no one would die if they married Margot Tennant.' Unfortunately Lucien died in 1887 at the age of thirty-one, though after Hirsch's own death his widow graciously accepted as his heir Hirsch's illegitimate son, Count Arnold de Bendern, who became a British Member of Parliament and a well-known figure in British society.

After Lucien's death Hirsch was clearly at something of a loss. He sold off his investments. According to Kurt Grunwald in *Turkenhirsch*, he had only three passions, 'hunting, law suits and the evasion of income and inheritance taxes, which he considered unjust.' But these activities did not satisfy Hirsch's energy. To Grunwald, 'restlessness was Hirsch's basic characteristic. The need for work, for activity . . . a footloose migrant, restless himself, who, possibly subconsciously aware of this inner restlessness, advocates rooting in the soil for the wandering Jew.' Although Hirsch was an absolute anti-intellectual who hated the hypocrisy which he saw in religion, he was a generous supporter of Jewish causes, giving $4 million to the Alliance Israelite Universelle for the relief of Jews in Russia, as well as substantial sums to help his fellow-religionists in New York.

His restlessness led him to back the idea of a Jewish homeland on the pampas, giving £2 million to Jewish immigrants in Argentina. Unfortunately they were more like Hirsch than he might have wished. In Grunwald's words 'many of the settlers and their children eventually moved to the towns, 4,000 in all.' The year before Hirsch's death Theodore Herzl presented him with the idea of a homeland in Palestine. Herzl claimed that Hirsch received the idea with some favour. Which leaves one unanswered question: was Hirsch too cynical, too practical a man to give his backing to an idea which seemed a mere dream at the time?

2
Dreams of Empire

All major railway projects started as dreams, and many remained in the field of fantasy. Their number and variety is a reminder that railway building was a fundamental element in the dreams of a whole century – no country, no statesman, no businessman, no political scientist, it seems, was without his own locomotive vision. So they can tell us more about the nineteenth century's collective subconscious than more practical projects. Railways liberated the imagination.

Three of the most seemingly impractical dream railways – across the United States, Canada and Siberia – all came true. The most ballyhoo attached to the American Transcontinental: yet the Trans-Siberian was twice as long and the Canadians, by insisting on an all-Canadian route, handicapped themselves by having to tackle hundreds of miles of barren rock north of Lake Superior, terrain far more daunting than anything faced by the Americans east of the Rockies.

As we saw in Chapter III, the Canadians built the railway to complete their country, and to retain British Columbia within the federation. The Russians were anxious to use the Trans-Siberian to open up Siberia as the Americans had opened up the Prairies. But the primary impetus behind the American desire for a transcontinental railroad was to reach the Pacific and thus the Orient. Walt Whitman's railroad 'from sea to shining sea' was merely a means of reaching the ultimate dream ocean. The Pacific dream merged with the more practical desire to reach California after the discovery of gold there in 1849, and with the feeling that a railroad was an essential symbol of national unity, but the 'Pacific' element in the idea lingered on, and it was not until the mid-1870s that a best-selling guide-book (George A. Crofutt's *Great Transcontinental Rail Guide*) finally fixed the word 'transcontinental' in the public consciousness.

All three projects succeeded in girding their countries with hoops of iron. But the mere existence of a railway connection, however daring in conception, however exciting in construction, could not counteract underlying political, economic and social forces. In 1857, for example, the first six miles of the Western Railroad out of Buenos Aires were greeted with the cry 'On to Chile'; and just over half a century later the dream was achieved, after a tunnel had been dug through the Andes at an altitude of 10,500 feet. But it did not generate much traffic; indeed the service was suspended for a number of years in the 1930s, when a stretch of line was washed away, and it has never been profitable. The mere existence of a railway couldn't help fulfil the politicians' dream of a Greater Argentina linked to, and thus dominating, Chile and Peru.

There were many other dreams of railway empire that never even achieved their physical destination. They varied, but can broadly be divided into three categories: the individual projects; the globe-girdlers; and the lines which were inherent parts of a country's imperial dreams.

The most obvious and economically sensible individual project was a rail tunnel under the English Channel. But even this has been a century in the making* since it was first seriously promoted in the 1880s. At that point it was defeated by the objections of the British military, and even when it was finally transformed into reality a century later it has had to face the hysterical objections of sundry British citizens who have camouflaged their deeply ingrained fears of losing their island status through a fixed link with Europe behind absurd claims that the British way of life would be threatened by terrorists, rabid dogs, drug dealers and the like.

The next most obvious idea, a tunnel linking Europe and Africa under the Straits of Gibraltar, faces the problem that the Straits are too deep for a tunnel at their narrowest point. Nevertheless it has surfaced at times, and formed an essential link in the French dream of a railway from Paris to French West Africa via the Sahara. But we are now seeing the gradual realisation of a number of other longstanding dreams for tunnels

---

* This is a record, although the railway across Swaziland to the Indian Ocean, first projected in the 1880s, was finally built eighty years later.

or bridges, usually carrying road as well as rail traffic, like those linking Sweden with the European mainland and Japan's northern and southern islands, Hokkaido and Honshu, with Kyushu, the mainland.

Global railways have an even longer history than more practical, more limited schemes. The first proposal for a transcontinental railway was put forward by Angus B. Reach in a *Comic Bradshaw*, published in 1839. His fantasy provided details of Bradshaw's timetable a hundred years in the future. Its authenticity, he assured his readers, 'can be entirely relied on'. There would be trains from Shoreditch in London to Pekin, via Constantinople, Jericho ('where Babylon used to was . . . omnibuses meet the trains at the Jericho Terminus') Bagdad and Canton ('Return tickets for Pekin available for three days'). He was followed by the entirely serious Saint-Simonian, Michel Chevalier, whose 'Mediterranean system' envisaged a railway from the English Channel to the Persian Gulf.

It was the opening of the Suez Canal in 1869 which liberated the world's imagination as to the true possibilities of modern transport systems. It was natural for Ferdinand de Lesseps, the visionary French diplomat who had guided the canal to its triumphant completion, to turn his attention to even more ambitious rail projects. 'As early as 1873', wrote Charles Beatty, 'Ferdinand had sent [his son] Victor, now a foreign service officer in the family tradition, to explore the possibility of a railway joining Paris with Moscow, Pekin and Bombay. At first the Russians gave encouragement to the idea . . . but before he could report the scheme was dropped for political reasons. England and Russia were coming into conflict over Afghanistan and also in Northern China.'[19]

A largely railway route round the world moved from the realm of the ridiculous to the merely fantastic once trains were running across the United States and the Trans-Siberian was under construction. By the end of the century that eminently practical railroad magnate E. H. Harriman had a perfectly clear plan for a 'round-the-world transportation line, under unified American control.'[20] Harriman planned to secure access to the Pacific by buying the railway through Manchuria, and acquiring trackage rights over the Trans-Siberian itself. Since Harriman owned the Pacific Steamship company and controlled major networks in the United States he required only a fleet of ships ploughing across the Atlantic to achieve his goal.

Unfortunately the Japanese were unwilling to share control of the Manchurian railways they had acquired following their war with Russia, but that did not deter Harriman, although an alternative 1,200-mile line across the Gobi Desert proved too ambitious even for him. Another attempt to build a new line through Manchuria, well away from the existing tracks, was foiled by the death of the Empress of China and by the financial crash of 1907, and Harriman died before he could find alternative routes.

The Pacific dream did not die. The Americans have always hankered after a major role in the Far East, especially in China, a mission which clearly necessitated railways from the Mid-West to ports in Mexico as a more convenient route to the Pacific than through California. In this instance a novelist anticipated the promoters. Anthony Trollope's novel *The Way We Live Now* revolves round a projected – and clearly fraudulent – 'South Central Pacific and Mexican Railway'. The line 'was to run from the [sic] Salt Lake City, thus branching off from the San Francisco and Chicago line, and pass down through the fertile lands of New Mexico and Arizona, into the territory of the Mexican republic, run by the City of Mexico, and come out on the gulf at the port of Vera Cruz'.

A few years later Nature duly copied Art when a number of schemes followed Trollope's routes. Most notably the American promoter Arthur E. Stilwell, who had already made Kansas City the hub of a railroad network with access to the Gulf of Mexico, came up with the idea of a trunk line to the little Mexican port of Topolobampo, one of the many such attempts to transform Mexico into an extension of what became the Sunbelt and to transform Topolobampo into the gateway to the Orient. Unfortunately his grandiosely-named Kansas City, Mexico and Orient Railway met the same fate as Trollope's fictional line, though, unlike Trollope's August Melmotte, Stilwell did not commit suicide after his scheme had collapsed.

Even Stilwell's scheme was less grandiose than the notion of a Pan-American railway extending from a convenient point on the Southern Pacific through Mexico, Central and South America. Since the time of President Monroe the Americans have believed in their civilising mission in Central and Latin America, and the mission clearly demanded a railway. This was first proposed in 1879 by an American diplomat 'the famous abolitionist Hinton Rowan Helper ... [who] published a book advocating the construction of what he termed the "New World Longitudinal Double-Track Steel Railway".'[21] This would be a conscious attempt, designed, like many other such schemes, to assure even firmer American control over the western hemisphere, not, they felt, as colonialists but as liberators, as part of what the French would call their *mission civilisatrice*.

Helper's railway would have run from 'the westerly shores of Hudson Bay to the midway margin of the Strait of Magellan: the two terminal points, measured along the line contemplated, being nearly, if not quite, eight thousand miles apart ... in justice and fairness, and in conformity with the highest attributes of republican justice & fairness' the line 'should avoid, and thus isolate, the iniquitous dictatorship of Brazil'.

Ten years later the First International American Congress created a 'Committee on Railway Communication' which in turn mapped out a possible route for a Pan-American Railroad. Over the next forty years progress was spotty. The Banana King C. Minor Keith contributed to the idea through his proposed 'International railways of Central America', but little progress had been made before the idea was overtaken by an alternative dream, that of a Pan-American Highway.

The Americans liked to think that such schemes were not imperial. Other similar dreams were more nakedly so in spirit – and far less practicable. Every imperial power had its own pet projects. The dream which most nearly came to fruition was the German plan for a railway from Berlin to Bagdad. This was not merely an imperial dream, but also a way of unlocking the real riches in oil and agricultural produce of Mesopotamia, as well as providing a way of transporting troops to quash disaffected

Bedouin tribesmen and of carrying pilgrims to Mecca, one of the few objectives actually achieved. None the less it was a dream, for it involved the resuscitation of the medieval land routes across Central Asia. The railway would 'bring back to Anatolia, Syria and Mesopotamia some of the prosperity and prestige they had enjoyed before the explorations of the Portuguese and Spaniards had opened the new sea routes to the Indies'.[22]

In the first years of the present century the project became deeply embedded in the German psyche as a means of carrying the German language, allied to German finance, trade, industry and engineering, to the very cradle of civilisation. 'Here was a country which had been the much-sought-after empire of the great nations of antiquity, Assyria, Chaldea, Babylon, Persia, Greece, Rome. Here had risen and fallen the great cities of Nineveh, Babylon and Hit. To these regions had turned the longing of the great conquerors, Sargon, Sennacherib, Nebuchadnezzar, Alexander, Saladin.'[23]

But the cultural sell concealed the line's two eminently practical objectives: to reinforce the German military alliance with the Ottoman Empire and to capture the massive oil reserves just being uncovered in the Mesopotamian valley. The route had been surveyed by an unsung engineering genius, Wilhelm von Pressel, although he was forced to take an inland route through the Amanus mountains because the easier route along the Mediterranean would have made it vulnerable to attacks by hostile warships.

Building began a few years before 1914, and although construction continued throughout the war, the through service to Aleppo was inaugurated only in October, 1918, a month before the Armistice. Inevitably the line was sequestrated by the Allies. Afterwards an American syndicate proposed to reach Bagdad with the help of a 25-mile wide land grant along its whole length. But the fragmentation of the Ottoman Empire has prevented any real progress from that day to this.

Yet even in the 1920s, enthusiastic Syrians dreamt that the ancient entrepot of Aleppo would 'become the crossroads of the world – a junction point for rail communication between Berlin

209

Rhodes the Colossus inspires the Cape-to-Cario dream.

and Bagdad, Calais and Calcutta, Bordeaux and Bombay, Constantinople and Cairo and Cape Town'.*

* Earle op cit. The Aleppans were not alone in devising such a grandiose plan. Sun Yat-Sen envisaged that one of his projected lines would connect 'with the future Indo-European line and through Bagdad, Damascus and Cairo, will link up also with the future African system' – thus connecting Peking directly with Cape Town.

The Berlin-to-Bagdad suffered very little domestic political interference within Germany. By contrast the British equivalent, the Cape-to-Cairo, was sabotaged by domestic politics, and was finally scuppered because it most influential supporter, Cecil Rhodes, was too practical a man to undertake himself a project of such dubious commercial viability. Despite its fame and the romantic aura which surrounds it, the Cape-to-Cairo was never a unified project, the only unifying factor was the name. As Lois Raphael wrote in *The Cape-to-Cairo Dream* (New York, 1936), 'the railway followed mineral discoveries northwards'. Rhodes 'wanted his Cape-to-Cairo railway to pay its way through Africa'. As a result the route was diverted hundreds of miles west of its most direct route to serve the coal deposits at Wankie in what is now Zimbabwe and the copper belt in Zambia.*

The idea did not lack supporters. 'I can conceive of no more civilizing influence that could be brought to bear than the laying down of a railway throughout that great continent,' declared a British politician. An active group of 'Little Englanders' was always at hand, determined to scotch such Imperial dreams but the biggest blow was struck by an Imperialist Prime Minister, the Marquess of Salisbury when he allowed the Germans sway over Tanganyika as far west as the Belgian Congo, thus interposing a foreign power directly in the path of the all-red dream.† Indeed the Germans took the idea more seriously than the British themselves. 'The placing of British South Africa in communication with the Sudan by a railway would be equivalent to the premeditated ruin of our colonial empire in Africa,' declared the *Taglische Rundschau.*

The Cape-to-Cairo dream evaporated because its supporters were too hard-headed. The French equivalent, the Trans-Saharian, though long lived and never without powerful supporters, could never be accused of excess practicality. Yet this manifestly absurd idea was taken seriously from the 1880s until

* See also Leo Weinthal, *Cape to Cairo* (London 1923).

† In the words of an 1887 agreement, 'where one power occupies the coast another power may not, without consent, occupy unclaimed regions in its rear.'

1943, when the Vichy government actually started to build it. No other project illustrates so clearly the power of the Saharan dream in French public life – although, ironically, the money lent by French investors to build that more practical dream, the Trans-Siberian, was lost just as surely as if it had been poured into the sands of the Sahara.

Although French generals proposed the idea in the middle of the century as they forged France's African empire, the idea first entered the political arena at the end of the 1870s as part of the Freycinet plan for vastly expanding the French railway network, a plan naturally attacked as politically rather than economically motivated. The Trans-Saharan idea erupted sporadically over the next sixty-five years – first in 1898 when the French had to retreat in ignominy from Fashoda in the Sudan. Unfortunately its supporters could never decide whether it was primarily strategic, or could provide the key to unlocking the supposedly vast riches of the great plains surrounding the River Niger. A third argument employed the Trans-Saharan as part of grandiose schemes to rely on colonisation to counter the demographic advantages possessed by France's enemies – most obviously the Germans.[*]

Assuming that a tunnel was built under the Straits of Gibraltar the Trans-Saharan, said its proponents, was the only line able to bring the capital of a great imperial power within a week's journey of its rich tropical colonies, a mere third of the time required to traverse Siberia. Supporters like the economist Paul Leroy-Beaulieu (*Le Sahara, le Soudan et les Chemins de fer transsahariens*) poured scorn on the prevailing wisdom that the Sahara could never be developed, arguing that its very real subterranean water resources provided it with considerable potential.

Opponents relied on extending the existing network of railways in French West Africa to bring tropical produce to the Atlantic, while protagonists made much of the endemic fevers, and the sandbars blocking the harbours of French West Africa. Not surprisingly successive governments temporised, afraid of

[*] See Commandant ECV Roumens, *L'Imperialisme Francais et les Chemins de fer Transafricains.*

accusations that they were betraying a railway so vital to France's eternal and ubiquitous *mission civilisatrice*. In the late 1920s they even set up an 'Office du Transsaharien' to study the projected route, but the dream evaporated after the downfall of the Vichy government.

Every Imperial power, however small, felt entitled to its own dream. Leopold II of Belgium, not content with the personal ownership of the Congo, dreamt of a new Belgian-controlled Eldorado in the heart of China, Kansu province on the old Silk Road. This involved Belgian control over the railway to the China Sea, an ambition he tried to conceal by pretending that the Belgian emissaries in fact came from the 'Independent State of the Congo'. The Chinese viceroy Li Hungchang punctured the pretence with the simple question: 'You are supposed to represent an African state. How is it then that you are not at all black?' In the event the Belgians did indeed build the railway to Kansu, but Leopold's death and the First World War ended any further ambitions.

Curiously and ironically the most useful dream was a Japanese plan designed to bridge an island-studded strait over a hundred miles wide between their Southern island of Kyushu and Pusan on the southern tip of Korea, a country then (in the 1930s) part of the Japanese Empire. The crossing formed an essential element in an Axis dream to link Tokyo and Berlin via Moscow. In anticipation, the authorities bought land to enable the line to run from Tokyo to Kyushu. The dream died in 1945 but the preparations ensured that nearly a third of the land required for the New Tokkaido line, the first high-speed railway in the world, already belonged to the Japanese authorities when it was built in the early 1960s.

VII

THE ARMIES OF STEAM – AND
THEIR BATTLEFIELDS

1
The Great Captains – and their Mercenaries

The construction of the world's railway systems presented an almost superhuman challenge. It was eagerly taken up, for railways were a *carrière ouverte aux talents* in even the most hierarchical of societies. Building, and then running, railway systems required the capacity to organise and control industrial armies of unprecedented size, sometimes dispersed along thousands of miles of track, and this gift was not related to an individual's social standing.

The military simile came naturally to observers, like the Peruvian journalist describing the building of a railway through the Andes in 1872:[1]

> The army (distributed along the line in eleven camps), consisting of Don Enrique's* engineers and labourers, was attacking the Andes. The scouts went ahead to determine the best and least costly route; the advance guard followed in their tracks, staking out the exact course to be followed; next came the main body, leveling the barriers, making fills and cuts and piercing tunnels; lastly there was the rear guard, putting down ties and laying rails.'

* The Peruvian name for Henry Meiggs.

214

The men in charge obviously possessed that indefinable capacity for command found in all successful generals. More specifically they shared with their military equivalent a degree of daring – knowing what was truly impossible and what was merely unprecedented – a knowledge they combined with a scrupulous attention to detail. But railway generals waged campaigns which lasted years, decades even, which brought into play another of their characteristics, patience and resilience. When Thomas Brassey was told that an expensively-built line in Spain was being washed away by a succession of floods, he said simply, 'I think I shall wait till the rain has entirely ceased; then we'll go over and find out what is left of the works, and I shall thus be saved some useless journeys.'

Robert Stephenson was one of the few members of this select band to harbour inner doubts as to his own capacities, but not even he ever dared express them, for one of their major assets was a reputation for overcoming obstacles, including – and especially – those deemed insurmountable by their contemporaries.

Navvies: the unsung heroes of the world's railways.

This outward confidence was combined, as with the best generals, with an extraordinary eye for the landscape through which they were to build their railways, an equally extraordinary intuitive awareness of the best possible route – and a prodigious reservoir of energy, which they all drained with heroic recklessness. As a result, most of the greatest engineers died from prolonged and unremitting overwork from 20-hour days, seven-day weeks, the wear and tear of constant travel on primitive, bumpy, roads, often frozen or soaked to the skin.

The death rate was most obvious among the heroic band which built the tunnels under the Alps. Many of them were from Italy, a country which depends on tunnels to provide routes between many of its major cities. But the work also represented a challenge to the Italians' powers of improvisation under stress: 'In life the best system is not to be too systematic,' in the words of Giorgio Lanino. The words came from his bitter experience on the Cristina tunnel, one of the six under the Apennines between Naples and Foggia. The tunnel has lived in the nightmares of tunnellers ever since because of the clay through which it was dug: clay that lacked any cohesion, clay that entailed the excavation of a deep trench filled with masonry before the timbers supporting the tunnel could be erected.

The pioneer of Alpine tunnelling, Germain Someiller, provided a model for his successors. He was charged with building what we now call the Mont Cenis* tunnel within twenty years. In the event he achieved his aim in a mere fourteen, dying after the eight-and-a-half-mile tunnel was finished, but before the first train had run through it.

Quite apart from proving that the Alps were not invincible, he left both a technical and a human legacy – technical in the new rock drills and drilling methods he devised, human in the care he took of his workers. The precedents, as far as the latter was concerned, were not encouraging. The excavation of the Woodhead Tunnel between Manchester and Sheffield ten years

---

* The tunnel actually passes under the Col de Fréjus. It acquired its present name because it replaced the old carriage road near Mont Cenis, fifteen miles away.

Louis Favre, instigator and victim of the St Gotthard tunnel under the Alps.

earlier had been marked by scandalous neglect of the workforce, and Someiller was working in a far bleaker and more deserted area. Someiller rebuilt the hovels in the village nearest the entrance to the tunnel and then created a new, modern town on the site for the 4,000 men he employed.

Someiller lived to see his work completed, a satisfaction denied to poor Louis Favre, the Genevan contractor who accepted the awesome task of excavating the tunnel under the St Gotthard pass. Inevitably, by 'the summer of 1879 Favre was broken by the combination of evil forces – seven years of incessant struggles with the mountain, during which he had spent days on end submerged in water up to his waist personally supervising the work, the shocks and frustrations, his long persecution by the railway management, and, lately, his deteriorating economic conditions'.[2]

Favre was buried with the rest of the tunnel's victims in an ever-expanding cemetery. He was not its only distinguished victim. Alfred Escher, the banker whose vision had seen the project through endless obstacles, died seven months before it

Navvies in Arizona, crossing the American desert.

was opened, and his second-in-command had died before him. Favre, a rich man before he embarked on his last contract, died bankrupt. The railway company honoured his memory by granting an annuity of a mere hundred francs a month to his only surviving daughter. Such ingratitude was not uncommon.

As the single biggest challenge available in the nineteenth century, and one, moreover, open to men of a wide variety of talents, railway building naturally attracted more than its fair share of the world's chancers, many lines resembling playgrounds for adventurers rather than rational enterprises. Their leaders' habits were echoed, on a smaller scale, by thousands of suppliers who overcharged, sold short, bribed the purchasing clerks.

The 'soldiers' the builders commanded had enlisted for reasons which were many, various, generally unsurprising, and often comparable to those found in recruits to more orthodox armies: a need to earn a living; a sense of adventure; a desire to prove themselves; greed; wanderlust; a means of escape from domestic problems – or from the police. Frederick Talbott, himself a former surveyor, admitted that at first sight the work appeared to be an unappealing combination of danger and discomfort. Nevertheless, he said, he would not exchange the virgin country, with its invigorating air and life of exciting adventure, for a smoke-begrimed centre of activity for any consideration. He quotes another surveyor, 'if it is not the natural difficulties or the hostility of the natives which lend variety to the work, the chances are a hundred to one that a revolution will fill the gap, especially in China or the South Americas'.[3]

In developed countries most railway lines were defined by the towns and cities they were connecting, so the routes were pretty obvious, the builders were working within relatively narrow parameters. It was very different in the Wild West, or the Andes, or Siberia. Someone had to find a route, often through mountains which had proved impassable even for the surest-footed mule. The job could not be done by legislators or financiers – the entrepreneurs building the Canadian Pacific Railway, for example, surveyed a better route through the Rockies in half the time it had taken their bureaucratic predecessors.

The politicians were at the mercy of the men on the spot, who could be engineers, surveyors, contractors – the labels were applied haphazardly in an age which lacked precise professional or functional demarcation marks – everyone connected with railway building aspired to be the sort of 'Renaissance engineer'

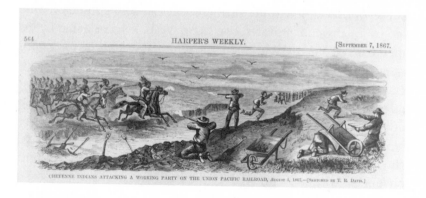

The Cheyenne do their best to halt the railroad.

typified by George Stephenson. The transition from known to unknown country was not always easy however. The railway across the Isthmus of Panama destroyed the reputation of Minor C. Story. He used the same materials on the Panama railway as he had, successfully, in New England. His wooden bridges collapsed within a few months and he fled 'bankrupt financially, tarnished in reputation and broken in spirit'.[4]

Daring was often rewarded. Finding a route from the Peruvian coast up to Arequipa, Peru's second city, over 7,500 feet up in the Andes, was left to two self-styled 'engineers':

'Echegaray knew nothing about railway surveying but happened to possess an old and very inaccurate theodolite, which was the party's sole instrumental equipment. Blume, for his part, was presumably gifted in some subtle way – not that it mattered; the Government knew nothing of surveys and in any case were not willing to spend any money on it.' (Brian Fawcett, *Railways of the Andes*).

Yet theirs was the route chosen, and built.

The surveyors were the advance guard and naturally took the brunt of local opposition. In civilised countries this was mainly verbal: elsewhere it was physical. In the Rockies dozens of surveying parties were ambushed by local Indians, killed or, if they were lucky, merely scalped – and this despite the best efforts of an army commanded by General Sherman in person.

Employers could be as dangerous as Red Indians. The surveyors seeking a route through the Canadian Rockies were led by an absolute monster, one Major A. B. Rogers, hated by his men who frequently starved on the minimal rations he took with them. Rogers 'resembled many of the other railway surveyors, each of whom embraced the cause of a piece of real estate almost as if he were married to it'.[5] After several years of hair-raising adventures, Rogers finally found the watershed at which the streams flowed in different directions. It was named Rogers Pass, the only reward he was seeking – he merely framed the $5,000 cheque he was given for finding the pass.

The influence of the 'experts' was personal, dependent on their character rather than any formal qualifications they might possess. One man, William Dargan, 'built, promoted, financed and guided the Irish railway system for three decades' from the 1840s to the 1870s. More daring and far-sighted was 'Crazy' Judah, the brilliant engineer who earned his nickname from his fanatical belief that a railroad across the United States was a practical proposition. He turned out to be right, for he was one of the many visionaries whose apparently impractical ideas became triumphant reality within a few years. Before he died, while on a visit to New York to try and interest Wall Street in the idea, he had surveyed a practicable route east from Sacramento; although it was a pharmacist from the little town of Dutch Flat, anxious to promote his town, who first found a route through the High Sierras, a discovery which Judah then exploited.

Some of the century's greatest heroes are to be found in the ranks of the engineers. Yet, with the notable exception of the British pioneers, few of their names are remembered today. This is partly because engineers' lives have not attracted the attention of historians, partly because they were overshadowed, even in their own lifetime, by the promoters and financiers who exploited their talents. On the biggest projects like the Union Pacific even the most powerful engineers like Grenville Dodge needed the help of General Grant, a future president, to gain the upper hand over an incompetent rival backed by Dr Durant, trickiest of promoters. Poor Peter Dey, Dodge's predecessor, who resigned in the face of Durant's dishonesty, was immediately forgotten.[6]

Not surprisingly the engineers, the 'coolest' of men, ranked worldly honours well below the esteem of their professional colleagues. Thomas Brassey, in character more an engineer than a contractor, spoke for all of them when he thanked Louis Napoleon for one of the numerous decorations he was awarded with the words, 'Mrs Brassey will be pleased to have it.' He followed the example of the great canal engineer, Thomas Telford, and the Stephensons, father and son. They accepted awards from foreign monarchs out of politeness and certainly without attempting to ingratiate themselves, while scorning British titles. It was Brassey's worthy but far less distinguished son who acquired a peerage. The great captains of the armies of steam felt they needed no formal recognition. Their memorials were the lines they built.

Mutual esteem was another matter. Brunel and Robert Stephenson were the most bitter of professional rivals, yet they were personal friends and Brunel was on hand to support his friend during the nerve-wracking week when he hoisted his prefabricated bridge high above the Menai Straits separating the Welsh mainland from the Island of Anglesey. Their successors are often equally appreciative. Russian engineers still celebrate the achievements of Constantine Ya Mikhailovski, who built much of the Trans-Siberian railway at a rate of over two miles a day. Although much of his track had to be rebuilt (like his American counterparts, his first priority was to get some sort of track laid, knowing that improvements could come later when it was earning some revenue) yet many of the steel bridges he built remained in use for over half a century.

Even his achievements were surpassed by Alexander Yugovich, the 'stout and deceptively dull-eyed engineer' who built the Chinese Eastern railway through Manchuria.

Other engineers throughout the world have contended with deserts and mountain ranges, arctic cold, rampaging floods, pestilence, bandits, saboteurs and obstructive officials, but Yugovich and his associates were perhaps unique in that they coped with all of these formidable impediments simultaneously . . . the few roads were fantastically rough, and, during the rainy season, remained impassable quagmires until tediously filled in with brush and innumerable logs . . . In parts of the eastern section, there was wood but no stone; in the western, stone but no wood for upwards of six hundred miles. Fourteen major water-ways – icebound for at least four months annually – would require spans of anywhere from eight hundred feet to a half-mile in diameter . . . Along the entire northern route of 927 miles, there were no utilizable laborers and fewer than six towns, each the periodic prey of Manchurian outlaws.[7]

222

Navvies on the Trans-Siberian, the world's longest railway.

Then the workers were struck by bubonic plague which claimed 1,400 victims.

Originally engineers like Joseph Locke were the dominant force, employing, and trusting, contractors like Thomas Brassey. For a time, as we saw in Chapter IV, the contractors moved to the front of the stage as the movers and shakers of the railway business. But their dominance was confined to Britain, and lasted only until the Overend Gurney crash of 1866 put paid to their independence. They remained formidable characters – as the sketch below of George Pauling's work in Africa makes clear – but even he was an agent, relying on British bankers. Similarly a powerful American banking syndicate backed Andrew Onderdonk, the most successful contractor on the Canadian Pacific Railway, who built the appallingly difficult section over the Rockies to the Pacific.

Onderdonk, the dignified, reticent scion of a distinguished New York family, was less typical of the breed than the men who supervised the building of the first railroad across the United States. The western half was built by the Big Four themselves (partly because no one would have trusted them to pay), led by the bull-headed Charlie Crocker, who employed a notoriously foul-mouthed slave driver of Irish extraction, James Harvey Strow-bridge. A teetotaller, who habitually carried a pickaxe as a 'persuader', Strowbridge successfully controlled the largest labour force ever assembled in the United States (in peacetime). The eastern half was farmed out to two equally formidable characters, iron-hard, red-bearded brothers, Jack and Dan Casement. Jack dominated thousands of navvies through sheer force of character, reinforced by the bullwhip he habitually carried, while Dan kept the books and organised the flow of material to his brother in the field.

Their achievements bordered on the fantastic. To get a desperately-needed steam engine to help haul material for Summit Tunnel, Crocker and Strowbridge enlisted the help of a legendary mule driver called Missouri Bill. But it took even him seven weeks to haul the twelve-ton engine, nicknamed the 'Black Goose', the seventy-five miles to the top of Mount Summit. Some years ago a film company tried to duplicate the feat, using modern machinery and a smaller engine. After five hundred yards they gave up.

As the century wore on, the pace of building quickened – partly because railway builders became increasingly obsessed with the need for their line to earn revenue as quickly as possible, even if this meant that the track was laid directly onto the earth. Three, four, and even six-mile days became possible.

The acceleration bred a spirit of competitiveness. In one famous bet[8] Charles Crocker of the Central Pacific won $10,000 from that infamous financier Dr Durant of the Union Pacific when his men laid ten miles and fifty-six feet of track in a single day, track which Crocker immediately tested by driving a locomotive along the line at forty miles an hour.

Chinese workmen loaded each handcar with sixteen rails, bolts, spikes and fishplates, which they doled out at the right intervals. The advance guard were the tie crews, followed by the eight aptly-named iron men who picked up the six-hundred rails with tongs, followed by the straightenders, the levellers, twenty spikers (each hammering only one blow on this assembly line in the desert) and the fishplate men. Finally came hundreds of tampers smashing home the ballast.

The unquestioned heroes of the operation were eight Irish track layers. They had lifted over two million pounds of iron that day, over a hundred tons each. Their 850 colleagues placed over 25,000 ties, laid over 3,500 rails, hammered home 28,000 spikes and turned 14,000 large bolts in establishing a record which has proved unbeatable by even the most sophisticated machinery.

A few engineers, like Louis Favre, or George Totten, the American who built the railway across the isthmus of Panama, were commemorated with modest plaques or statues. More typical was the story of Wilhelm von Pressel. He had started work on railways in his native Wurtemberg, had constructed much of the network in North-East Switzerland for the Pereires, then spent eight years building the Sudbahn lines from Vienna to the Adriatic. He believed that the Ottoman Empire could be saved by a proper railway network which would recreate the medieval caravan routes from Europe to Central Asia. As adviser to the Sultan he naturally became a passionate enthusiast for the railway from Berlin to Bagdad and sketched most of the route. Nevertheless he died alone, impoverished and forgotten, in Constantinople in 1902.

His fate was characteristic of that of the many engineers who worked in foreign countries whose politicians were anxious to believe that their railways were all their own handiwork. Major George Washington Whistler, who built the line between Moscow and Saint Petersburg, then as now Russia's pride and joy, is forgotten, whereas his wife was immortalised by their painter son, James Macneill Whistler. But then the Russians, like most other nations which had relied on foreign expertise to build their first railways, later naturally played down the foreigners' contribution.

The French seized on the fact that it was an English engineer, Joseph Locke, and an English contractor, Brassey, who had built a viaduct at Barentin, twelve miles from Rouen, which collapsed even before the line had opened. Brassey took on the responsibility for rebuilding the viaduct before the question of blame could be apportioned – in the end it was found to be due to defective mortar from local lime. Nevertheless the French naturally blamed the British, as well as the French directors, 'for employing foreigners, who swallowed up the money of the country in return for scamped-up works, which jeopardised the lives of their fellow-subjects'. In fact the line was opened on time and the viaduct survives today in all its Victorian splendour.

There was endless room for misunderstanding. The Brazilians had established their own company to build an important railway from Rio de Janeiro over the coastal escarpment, the *serra*. They admitted they lacked the knowhow and hired a British contractor, Edward Price. The equally British engineer, Christopher Lane, insisted that Price improve the line by reducing the gradients and replacing wooden bridges with iron ones. Nevertheless the Brazilians got it into their head that the two were in collusion and replaced them with Americans after the first thirty miles of track had been built. Soon afterwards the company went broke.

A few of the foreigners were treated as heroes, as the standard bearers of the new age. William Wilson, who arrived with the engine used on Germany's first railway, from Nuremberg to Furth, was paid more than the director, and remained a local hero during his twenty-year service. Japan's first railways owed a great deal to two British engineers, both grandsons of the great Richard Trevithick. The first trains in Japan were driven by English drivers, and for a long time an Englishman was always called upon to drive any train used by the Emperor Meiji. But the Japanese learned quickly. In 1877, 120 British advisers were working for the Japanese Railway Administration: by 1880 only three remained. The learning period was short enough for the Japanese not to feel any hang-ups about the help they had received. Joseph U. Crawford, a distinguished American engineer sent to Japan by President Hayes at Japanese request, was decorated by the Emperor after building the first line in the island of Hokkaido and planning a number of others. Even after he had retired to Philadelphia Japanese engineers continued to consult him.

Most of the 'mercenaries' or other ranks in the armies of steam were those anonymous heroes, those simple workmen, the navvies. The 'navigators', the Irish in Britain, the Irish or the Chinese in the United States and Canada, have contributed most of the more spicy, sordid, picturesque folklore connected with the building of railways. To Marx they were 'the light cavalry of capitalism', to Eric Hobsbawm, 'the shock troops of indus-trialization'. To the inhabitants of the countryside they invaded they were the devil's own army. To objective observers they were miracle-workers. Samuel Smiles reckoned that in building the London to Birmingham Railway twenty thousand of them had shifted more rock, earth and stones in five years than the hundred thousand Egyptian slaves who spent twenty years building the Great Pyramid.

They were aware of being a race apart. In conversation with a parson, one of them compared navvies with the Israelites: 'We goes about from place to place, we pitches our tents here and there, and then goes on.' The average working man worked in factories and sweat shops, but the navvy was different. 'His life', wrote Terry Coleman, 'was a strange one, isolated and free, quite different from that of his fellow-countrymen, and unknown to them' (*The Railway Navvies*).

The work required not only a capacity for grindingly hard labour, but also the willingness to leave their homes, and usually their homeland, for long periods at a time. The motive was sometimes merely the availability of the work, as it was for the Chilean *rotos*, though they worked only in their home country and in Peru. The Irish, their ranks swelled by thousands fleeing from the potato famine of 1845–46, worked the world over and, not unfairly, dominate the popular image of the breed as a whole.

Then contractors in the New World, notably the builders of the California end of the Transcontinental Railroad, found that the Chinese, especially those from round Canton, made even more admirable recruits. In the 1840s and 1850s their homeland was devastated by civil wars in addition to the normal cycle of flood, drought and famine. Fugitives were the more welcome because they were highly disciplined, kept to their traditional healthy diet and bathed frequently. Unlike the Irish with their noisy drinking, their favourite vice was a quiet one, gambling, and their drug, opium, made them soporific rather than aggressive.

Opium did lead to one major tragedy. The company building the Panama Railway was legally registered in New York, a state which banned drug trafficking. In the absence through fever of the railway's chief engineer, George Totten, an officious clerk cancelled the Chinese's regular allowance of the drug. By the time Totten recovered he found a scene of total despair and carnage, for hundreds of the 'Orientals' had hanged themselves from the trees, and hundreds more had drowned. He was forced to ship the remainder to Jamaica, hoping that their compatriots there had sufficient supplies of the life-saving drug.

In East Africa Indian coolies did most of the work and although many of them, unlike the Chinese and most of the Irish, eventually settled in their new country, this was only after they had served a hard apprenticeship on the railways.

Southern Africa, then as now, was a special case. Whatever the financial inducement, the Afrikaners would not desert their farms. In Cape Colony the authorities tried to encourage white immigrant labour to avoid giving the natives ideas (and wages) above their station. The policy proved counter-productive – in the 1870s the blacks were simply not prepared to work for the wages the builders were prepared to offer. Immigrants proved little better. The railway commissioner in Cape Colony complained that 'your continental agents [mainly in Belgium] appear to be mere tools in the hands of the police, who have palmed off the scum and refuse of the large towns'.[9]

The same problem confronted C. Minor Keith when he was building a railway in Honduras. The police chief in New Orleans used the opportunity to rid the town of nearly seven hundred undesirables. When they arrived in Honduras most of them had fever, for which their only remedy appeared to be whiskey. In the end only nine of the twenty real railroad men survived, but they kept the work going, supervising the Jamaican Negroes. They alone could work in the climate and were so loyal that they worked for nine months without pay when Keith was short of cash. The Jamaican Negroes also replaced the two hundred Italians he imported to help build his railway across Costa Rica. Half of the Italians had promptly bolted into the jungle, hoping to avoid the work and thus avoid paying for their passage, and sixty died before they could be induced to return.

Italians generally had a bad reputation. In South-West Africa their German masters found them sullen and often rebellious and soon replaced them with the local Ovambos, ill-nourished though they were. The only exception I can find is that Italian stone-masons were responsible for most of the stoutly-built bridges on the Trans-Siberian. An American civil engineer recounted how 'they agreed pretty well with the severe climate, but missed the good, pure cheap wine of their own country, which was a sore trial to them, and the Russian gin (fodka) they wisely avoided'.

In many countries, especially in autocratic societies, local rather than immigrant labour was the norm. In the first sixty years of the century the Russians had an unlimited supply of serfs to help build their railway system. Just as old Bolsheviks refused to hold Stalin responsible for their unjust fate, so the serfs on the railways refused to believe that the Tsar of all the Russias knew about their working conditions. In the summer of 1844 they ran towards the Tsar's summer palace, begging to tell him of their wormy bread, their broken shoes, their inadequate wages. The soldiers' swords soon put an end to their delusions.

The term 'navvy' covered a variety of skills. John Hoyt Williams described the make-up of the Union Pacific's assault force: '3,500 graders – some working as far as two hundred miles in advance of track – 450 trackmen, 350 of the "train force", and another 400 or so masons and bridge builders, plus 100 surveyors. To that force in the field must be added . . . several thousand tie cutters and lumberjacks, some floating their products hundreds of miles from the distant Black Hills, and as many as a thousand shopmen and uniformed personnel.'

The main contractors employed hundreds of sub-contractors, many merely the foremen of a gang of a dozen men. Samuel Smiles describes how 'ten or twelve of these men would take a contract to cut out and remove so much "dirt" (as they denominated earth-cutting) fixing their price according to the character of the "stuff" and the distance to which it had to be wheeled and tipped. The contract taken, every man put himself to his mettle, if any was found skulking or not putting forth his full working power, he was ejected from the gang.'

In the Rockies, on the Canadian National Railway to Prince Rupert, 'station men', in charge of their own gangs would get through two or three times as much work as normal employees. The most famous was led by 'Swansie the Tireless Swede',[10] described by a sub-contractor as,

> The greatest raw-meat man of them all and in every respect the most uncooked specimen that I have ever seen. Swansie's men would work right through the hours of daylight, which in summer meant from three in the morning to nine or ten at night. 'Got to work,' Swansie told the sub-contractor, who went on, 'no time to boil porridge or make bread. No time to suck water with a carrot or tomato flavour, which is all a vegetable is. Give him meat, every ounce the solid right stuff. Dried meat, brined meat, smoked meat, canned meat, and if it comes fresh and raw, just gulp it like a dog. Total elapsed time preparing dinner, three minutes. Total elapsed time eating, nothing. Eat it while driving the stone boat.' [The boat carrying the stone for the railway].
>
> 'Got to work,' says Swansie. Inevitably the gang got scurvy; the sub-contractor sent them a barrel of lime juice, threatening to take the job away from them if they didn't drink it. Some of the gang used the $2,400 they earned to buy 160 acres each of good Saskatchewan farmland. 'Fixed for life', recounted the subcontractor, 'but not the rest of them. And particularly not Swansie. He is a railway builder. Got to work'.

Railways got people that way.

Inevitably the navvies were blamed for any havoc, riot, malefactions of any kind which occurred in their passage through a district. Sometimes, one suspects, English gentlefolk rather enjoyed the thought of these hordes of hulking evil-doers being let loose on their once-tranquil countryside. A classic picture of depravity – in contrast to Samuel Smiles's romanticised vision quoted on page 209 – was provided by the *Carlisle Patriot* in February 1846, when describing a navvy accused of wounding one of his fellows. Apparently, 'for nine years he has never slept in a bed, or worn a hat; that his custom was to put on his boots when new, and never remove them until they fell to pieces, and his clothes were treated very much in the same way, except that his shirt was changed once a week.'[11]

The supposedly unexampled scenes of horror at the navvies' camps were matched every night in the slums of Britain's industrial towns, but railway-building did bring an, admittedly rather exaggerated, version of working-class reality into forcible contact with the respectable classes, who would never have gone near, say, Whitechapel. (The British rural middle-class underwent a similar culture-shock a century later when they received lice-ridden, ill-nourished evacuees from those same slums).

The first British navvies who ventured abroad were respected, rather than feared. 'My God, how they work', was the French comment on the 5,000 British navvies brought over to France by Thomas Brassey to work on the railway from Paris to Rouen. The other 5,000 navvies on the line spoke twelve other languages, from Erse and Gaelic to Polish. A *lingua franca* soon evolved, a third English, a third French, the rest made up from half a dozen different languages, flexible enough to be understood wherever railways were being built throughout Europe.

Further afield the refusal of many of the supervisors, especially the Irish and the Americans, to learn any foreign language could result in sheer farce. An observer watched Sam Norris, an American surveyor, trying to retain control of his local navvies in Costa Rica:

As I watched [old Sam] whistled, untied a huge red bandana handkerchief which he wore around his neck, waved it frantically a few times and then threw it on the ground with considerable violence along with his Stetson. Then he stamped on the handkerchief and hat, grinding them both into the dirt. I asked what was wrong.

He said, 'Oh there's nothing really wrong. I was just signaling my foreman. I don't understand any Spanish and he only speaks a little English, so we have arranged a signal code. One long whistle means cut to the right, two means cut to the left, three means that the line is all right and four long blasts is to tell the gang to come to dinner.'

'That's all very well, but it doesn't explain your removing your hat and handkerchief and stamping all over them.'

'Oh, that's a supplementary signal,' Sam explained, 'when I go through those motions it means that everything has all gone to hell, the work is all wrong, and that Cinforiano is to bring in the gang to get their time checks.'[12]

Everywhere the locals were afraid for the same reasons as the British, afraid for their womenfolk, afraid for their property values. The navvies on the line running north from Cape Town to Worcester drank deeply of Cape Smoke (the local firewater); they obtained it from wagons travelling north, which they would stone if they had run out of cash. They would then raid[13] 'Coloured and Hottentot locations . . . The aboriginals fought fiercely to retain their native brews and their womenfolk,' and

Chinese manpower conquers the Sierra Nevada mountains for the Central Pacific Railroad.

one poor Boer farmer complained that his property had fallen thirty per cent in value.

On the railway across the desert to Delagoa Bay in Mozambique, the navvies organised themselves in racially separate gangs. The Irish brigade, not surprisingly, were the most feared, though no individual Irishman on the line was as ferocious as another navvy, the legendary 'Kentish Jim' who, it was said, had once brained a man with a single blow of his fist. The gangs fought each other, and quite overwhelmed the wretched Portuguese police. The Irish brigade even hi-jacked the official train bringing the Portuguese governor and his retinue to the frontier with the Transvaal. By the time it arrived only broken chicken bones and empty bottles remained of the official banquet. At the coast the police kept the navvies' usual haunt, 'an inn of ill-repute', under surveillance, but the navvies slipped out one by one and ransacked a gun-boat the Portuguese had sent to keep order. This last episode was unusual enough to be treated as an international incident.

Similar, unreported, fracas were equally frequent wherever railways were built, for railway camps made indifferent melting pots. Racial problems had dogged railway construction from the very beginning, since British navvies, not unfairly, believed that the Irish were undercutting them. But outside Britain the most frequent clashes were between the two very different races, the Chinese and the Irish.

The Chinese were suspect everywhere they went. Leland Stanford, the politician among the 'Big Four' who controlled California's railways, had actively campaigned against what he called the 'dregs of Asia' and 'that degraded race'. He forgot such epithets when he found how hard the 'Celestials' worked, much harder, indeed, even than Cornish miners on his Central Pacific Railroad. But the prejudice remained. In 1870 only two whites in the whole state were convicted, although ninety Chinese had been murdered that year.

The Central Pacific had to rely on immigrants because there was a desperate labour shortage in California. By contrast the Union Pacific, builders of the eastern half of the Transcontinental railroad, which also employed many Irishmen, could also choose from amongst a 'crowd of ex-Confederates and Federal soldiers, mule skinners, Mexicans, New York Irish, bushwackers and ex-convicts, tens of thousands of Civil War Veterans and newly-liberated Negroes'.

The weirdest of all culture clashes occurred when a gang of French labourers on the Panama Railway suddenly stopped work one day, hoisted the tricolor, sang the *Marseillaise* and refused to discuss their grievances except in their native tongue, which foxed the Irish foreman. The company's chairman, who could speak French, refused to negotiate except in English. The stalemate was resolved when he cut off their rations for a couple of days and the men went back to work, their grievance unknown and unresolved to this day.

The racial tensions were merely light relief from the danger inherent in the work itself. Samuel Smiles had noted how the labourers, 'seemed to disregard peril. Indeed the most dangerous sort of labour – such as working horse-barrow runs, in which accidents are of constant occurrence – has always been most in request amongst them, the danger seeming to be one of its chief recommendations.' Even in peaceful New England Henry Thoreau lamented how 'every sleeper marks the death of an Irishman who died that the road might be built'.

In the mountains, when the line, often unapproachable even on foot, was being blasted from the solid rock, no one needed to exaggerate the dangers. Deaths from gunpowder, or rock falls, were routine, unreported. On the Erie Railroad:[14]

> the pick of the Irish drilling crews were lowered in great wicker baskets from the high ledges and there suspended in mid-air while the tarriers drilled like devils, then tamped their powder into the holes, lighted the fuses, and yelled for the boys above to haul them up before the blasts let go. Lives depended both on the ropes and on quick response, and sometimes the ropes broke, again the windlass was slow. And then there was sure to be another wake . . .

> On the Central Pacific the death rate was artificially increased by the unamiable Irish habit of exploding their blasts

234

while the Chinese were still working in the cuttings beneath.

Tunnels were more dangerous than the steepest hillsides. Even today, with the most modern machinery, the most rigorous safety precautions, a dozen or more deaths can be expected on a major tunnel like that under the English Channel. In the nineteenth century the accidents were inevitably more frequent and deadly. Twenty-four workers died in a single accident on the Simplon tunnel, but the grimmest record was accumulated during the fifteen-year agony of building the Saint Gotthard:[15]

> Some twenty five deaths and hundreds of casualties were reported each year due to accidental explosions from unignited cartridges, rock falls, train accidents, burst air-pipes etc. More serious, however, were the diseases induced by the wretched working conditions. Rock dust, explosive fumes, exhalations from men and animals, temperatures that at times rose to 122°F caused numerous ailments, and an untold number of men died from 'miner's anaemia'. A man became incapable of working after three or four months; if he persisted, he died or became incapacitated for life. The tolls among animals was just as bad, about thirty horses and mules dying each month.

In the tropics natural conditions in the days before quinine were enough to produce an even more frightening death rate. In South West Africa, 'it was said that there was a dead man under every sleeper from Komatipoort to Nelspruit'. Fever was routine – indeed the contractor George Pauling's doctor made a game of it, organising a daily pool in which every patient bet a shilling, the winner being the one with the highest temperature. It seems to have helped morale. As Pauling put it, 'frequently several of the patients with temperatures of from 105 degrees to 107 or 108 were off their heads when their temperatures were taken, but with a falling temperature the first indication of incipient consciousness was an enquiry as to the result of the previous pool'.

The record for fatalities was probably set by the Panama

Railway – at one point one worker in five was dying every month. They were a veritable foreign legion, known only by their nicknames or their number on a payroll. As a result the railway's doctor, J. A. Totten, brother of the line's engineer, found it difficult to dispose of the bodies. During the five years the railway was under construction he, 'pickled the bodies in large barrels, kept them for a decent interval to be claimed and then sold them in wholesale lots to medical schools all over the world . . . the bodies brought high prices, and the profits from the sale of the cadavers made the railway hospital self-sustaining during the construction years'.[16]

The navvies' only preventive medicine was hard liquor. 'It could almost be said,' wrote one observer, 'that the Union Pacific was built on whiskey.' In the famous song of Pat, 'who worked upon the railway,'

> In eighteen hundred and forty eight,
> I learned to take my whisky straight,
> 'Tis an illegant drink and can't be bate,
> For working on the railway.

Pat was also typical in having a more or less faithful female follower:

> In eighteen hundred and forty three,
> 'Twas then I met Miss Billy Macghee
> An' an illegant wife she's been to me,
> While working on the railway.
>
> *
>
> In eighteen hundred and forty-seven,
> Sweet Billy Macghee she went to heaven,
> If she left me one child she left eleven,
> To work upon the railway.

Navvies even devised their own wedding ceremony. According to Terry Coleman, 'At Woodhead [tunnel] in 1845, where 1,100 men were camped in shanty huts, they even had their own marriage ceremony which consisted in the couple jumping over a broomstick, in the presence of a roomful of men, assembled to drink upon the occasion, and the couple were put to bed at once, in the same room.'

Most railway sex, however, was casual. Generations of historians have dwelt with considerable relish on the 'hells on wheels', the mobile groups of saloons, whore-houses (and the occasional chapel) which housed the camp-followers of the armies of steam across the American prairies. Unfortunately for the prurient, the surviving photographs of these clusters of dens of iniquity show merely a few dusty shacks. Standing in front are a handful of unremarkable, if cross-looking, ladies, totally indistinguishable from their respectable contemporaries.

In East Africa the Indian coolies happily harnessed natives of both sexes for their sexual purposes, while British observers huffed and puffed about 'dens of iniquity' and 'unnatural vices'. 'Some tribes', wrote Charles Miller, 'were able to view the Indians' sexual habits with a certain amused detachment . . . the Nandi, on the other hand, were not amused, and sought redress of their wrongs with the time-honoured tribal penalties of pillage and murder.' (*The Lunatic Express*).

Inevitably, in a religious age, clergymen were obsessed by the need to bring the word of God to these obvious heathens. It was not easy. According to Samuel Smiles, 'Robert Stephenson used to tell a story of the clergyman of the parish waiting upon the foreman of one of the gangs to expostulate with him as to the shocking impropriety of his men working on Sunday. But the head navvy merely hitched up his trowsers, and said, "Why, Soondays haint cropt out here yet."' Nevertheless one contractor, Sir Samuel Morton Peto, ensured that these 'savages' were given Christian instruction, books and lessons, gifts which did actually moderate their behaviour.

Peto was always an exception. Unlike most of his brethren he would not allow a company store to increase the contractor's profits by monopolising the supply of food and, more especially, drink. In Britain there were a number of rather perfunctory efforts to outlaw the practice. The better employers, like Peto and

Brassey, frowned on the practice, partly through benevolence, but also through enlightened self-interest. Their navvies were noticeably more loyal than the average, so they had the pick of the best men. But most of their fellow-contractors could not resist the chance of extra profit. As Pat complained,

> Our boss's name it was Tom King
> He kept the store to rob the men,
> A yankee clerk with ink and pen,
> To cheat Pat on the railroad.

The bosses almost invariably had the upper hand, although the navvies' wages never fell as low as those of unskilled factory workers. Migrant labour is notoriously difficult to organise, and the few recorded strikes seem to have ended within days – usually with the dismissal of the strikers – though the Chinese on the Central Pacific did get a pay rise on the one recorded occasion when they went on strike, a stoppage conducted with their habitual impeccable politeness. In general, though, protest was confined to songs. The last two verses of a famous railway song, 'Drill, ye tarriers*, drill', summed up the feeling of generations of navvies:

> The new foreman is Dan McCann,
> I'll tell you sure he's a blame mean man,
> Last week a premature blast went off,
> And a mile in the air went big Jim Goff.

> When pay day next it come around,
> Poor Jim's pay a dollar short he found,
> 'What for?' says he, then came this reply,
> 'You were docked for the time you were up in the sky.'

In the United States, where local labour was always expensive, it was the steam shovel, rather than the worker, which was given

---

* The origin of the word is unknown. By the end of the 19th century it had come to mean the labourers who drilled and blasted their way through the hardest of rocks.

the name of navvy. But the human navvies' work rate, their reliability, and the contractors' perpetual shortage of capital ensured that they competed successfully with machinery. Even in Canada – where men had to be brought expensively from Britain and paid the, higher, local rates – the Grand Trunk used steam excavators only because labour was so short, and then only when faced with very hard material. In Britain the navvies retained their monopoly for a generation after technocrats would have used machinery, a tribute to their legendary qualities, which have never been surpassed. For the builders, like the monuments they left behind, were incomparable.

Samuel Smiles's Navigators

In his *Lives of the Engineers* Samuel Smiles traces the navvies back to the canals – hence the term 'navigators' – to the Durham railways, and to the fen districts of Lincoln and Cambridge, where they had been trained to execute works of excavation and embankment.

'Their expertness in all sorts of earthwork, in embanking, boring and well-sinking – their practical knowledge of the nature of soils and rocks, the tenacity of clays, and the porosity of certain stratifications – were very great; and, rough-looking though they were, many of them were as important in their own department as the contractor or the engineer.

'During the railway-making period the navvy wandered about from one public work to another – apparently belonging to no country and having no home. He usually wore a white felt hat with the brim turned up, a velveteen or jean square-tailed coat, a scarlet plush waistcoat with little black spots, and a bright-coloured kerchief round his herculean neck, when, as often happened, it was not left entirely bare. His corduroy breeches were retained in position by a leathern strap round the waist, and retied and buttoned at the knee, displaying beneath a solid calf and foot encased in strong high-laced boots . . . their powers of endurance were extraordinary.

'In times of emergency they would work for twelve and even sixteen hours, with only short intervals for meals. The quantity of flesh-meat which they consumed was something enormous; but it was to their bones and muscles what coke is to the locomotive – the means of keeping up steam.

'Working together, eating, drinking, and sleeping together, and daily exposed to the same influences, these railway labourers soon presented a distinct and well-defined character, strongly marking them from the population of the districts in which they laboured. Reckless alike of their lives as of their earnings, the navvies worked hard and lived hard. For their lodging, a hut of turf would content them; and in their hours of leisure, the meanest public-house would serve for their parlour.

'Unburdened, as they usually were, by domestic ties, unsoftened by family affection, and without much moral or religious training, the navvies came to be distinguished by a sort of savage manners, which contrasted strangely with those of the surrounding population. Yet, ignorant and violent though they might be, they were usually good-hearted fellows in the main – frank and open with their comrades, and ready to share their last penny with those in distress. Their pay-nights were often a saturnalia of riot and disorder, dreaded by the inhabitants of the villages along the line of works.'

George Pauling

George Pauling, a throwback to the heroic days of railway contracting, flourished in Southern Africa in the last years of the nineteenth century. His regular backer and banker, Emile d'Erlanger, described how he was, 'endowed with a physique that made light of any feat of strength and enabled him to defy fatigue or illness' – even though Pauling admitted that in conditions of over 100 degrees heat he 'was never able to reduce my weight below sixteen stone.' (*Rhodesiana* July, 1968).

This is not surprising. In his autobiography *Chronicle of a Contractor*, he states bluntly that, 'there is much virtue in a good appetite, as long as one is able to foot the bill', although 'my appetite, both for liquids and solids, has always been a source of amusement, and sometimes of concern, to my friends'. This was something of an understatement. With the help of two friends he consumed three hundred bottles of 'this excellent refreshment', German beer, while stuck for 48 hours on the Beira railway. On another occasion he and two other friends consumed a thousand oysters at a sitting – apparently they were 'small, but of very delicate flavour'.

He was very much a self-made engineer, who had started work in a contractor's office at the age of 15, his only asset a family connection to that eccentric contractor, Joseph Firbank. Pauling would go anywhere there was work to be found. While in Jordan he formed the idea of selling a ready-made mixture of whisky and Jordan water. He also surveyed part of the projected Berlin-to-Bagdad railway, losing the contract, he claimed, after his partner had failed to bribe that crucial intermediary, the Sultan's barber.

Like so many British nineteenth-century adventurers he drifted to South Africa where he was involved in hotels, in gold and diamond mining, floating a number of companies (including the 'Big Golden Quarry'), but his schemes mostly centred round railways. While supervising work on Waai Nek tunnel near Grahamstown he realised that there was more money in contracting, and persuaded a firm of merchants in Grahamstown to finance him, getting their profit from the company store they would establish – on which he took a third of the profits.

The first contract was so profitable that 'the contracting fever took hold of me'. This was not surprising. In rough country where absolute accuracy was not crucial 'he was a genius at railway contracting,' wrote Erlanger, 'he would ride over a projected route, and without consulting the surveys, forecast to his associates the construction costs of the railway per mile; and he was almost invariably within a fraction of the actual figures.' He would insist on being paid according to the line specified by the engineers, but 'reserved the right to make any deviations calculated to shorten the line without increasing the gradient. He made his profits from the mileage he saved by these deviations while, at the same time, he improved the layout of the railway.'

His work, like the man himself, was rough and ready. On his 'pioneer' lines he didn't wait for bridges to be built, he would run the tracks across the beds of rivers, and though in the wet season there might be occasional delays, a few hours' work would repair any damage done by floods. He knew his work was reliable and durable and was confident enough to promise Cecil Rhodes, who chose him to build the line from Mafeking to Bulawayo, that he would build a 400-mile line at the rate of a mile a day.

Pauling worked hard, and played harder. Up at four o'clock for a tour of the line, after a fourteen hour day he still found the energy 'to go into Grahamstown to the Masonic Hotel, enjoy a good dinner, drink freely with congenial spirits, and play billiards till the hotel closed. Riding back to camp I usually arrived there before midnight.'

Like all contractors he inevitably faced cash-flow problems. Once these led to a declaration of bankruptcy, incited by a malevolent railway inspector. Pauling was 'mad with rage, I went up to him, and after a few brief but incisive words I knocked him down. He refused to get up. I gave him one or two gentle kicks, just to help him up, when his wife appeared on the scene. I was so enraged that I picked him off the ground, and although he weighed over twelve stone. I threw him against his wife and both of them fell into the doorway of the cottage. It all seems very funny now, after the lapse of years, but I saw no amusement in it at the time.'

Fortunately Pauling was always protected by his friends – on one occasion in South Africa a High Sheriff warned him to stay at home during the hours of daylight to avoid arrest. One particularly useful contact was the fearsome President Kruger. When they met 'Oom Paul' remarked that someone called Pauling had given him and two companions a bed for the night when they were stranded in a small town overnight. The Good Samaritan turned out to be Pauling's brother, and Oom Paul promptly entrusted George Pauling with the construction of the line from Pretoria to the frontier with Angola, which was making indifferent progress in the hands of another contractor.

During the Boer War Pauling took the opportunity to tour the United States. He was not impressed. All he could get in his hotel room was iced water, 'never a favourite beverage of mine'. Lynching proved that 'you have not even got sufficient confidence in your justice to see that your laws are carried out'. And the transcontinental railways, as he pointed out to his American fellow-travellers, were slower than those running from Cape Town to Johannesburg ('on a three foot six-inch gauge line – which they would probably consider a toy railway'). Eventually Pauling retired with a fortune and his memories to a palatial home at Effingham in Norfolk.

Lion Fighting with Station

Tsavo, a small riverside camp on the line from Dar es Salaam through Kenya to Uganda, was the unlikely scene of one of the most famous railway mortalities. The aggressors were two lions, immortalised as *The Man Eaters of Tsavo*, in a best-selling book of that name written by Lt Colonel J. H. Patterson, the man who eventually shot them.

Apart from Mount Kilima N'Jaro in the distance, the River Tsavo, 'always cool and always running' was the only relief in the 'interminable nyika, or wilderness of whiteish and leafless dwarf trees' which confronted Patterson, an experienced railway engineer sent from India to supervise the railway from Dar es Salaam to Lake Victoria through what became Kenya.

Even without lions, life at Tsavo was never dull. If the Indian workers weren't all pretending to be stone-masons in order to get higher wages then Nature would take a hand. 'When the camp was not being attacked by man-eating lions, it was visited by leopards, hyenas, wild dogs, wild cats, and other inhabitants of the jungle around us.'

The lions kept at a respectful distance while Tsavo was a large scattered camp housing hundreds of workers. They moved in for the kill after the railhead had moved on, ignoring the all-night fires and a stout thorn fence round the encampment. The workmen believed that it was useless to try and shoot them because the lions 'were the angry spirits of two departed native chiefs who had taken this form in order to protest against a railway being made through their country.'

Before Patterson finally shot them the two lions – each nine and a half feet long – had bagged between them no fewer than twenty-eight Indian coolies, in addition to scores of unfortunate African natives of whom no official record was kept. Patterson kept watch in an old closed wagon, but missed the first one by a foot. The lion then 'swerved off in his spring, probably blinded by the flash and frightened by the noise of the double report which was increased a hundred-fold by the reverberation of the hollow iron roof of the truck in the absolute silence of the African jungle'.

After the first had been shot Patterson 'sat in my eyrie like a statue, every nerve tense with excitement . . . very soon, however, all doubt as to the presence of the lion was dispelled. A deep long-drawn sigh – sure sign of hunger – came up from the bushes.' The rustling started again as Patterson cautiously descended. 'In a moment a sudden stop, followed by an angry growl, told me that my presence had been noticed.' It took six bullets to kill the second monster.

But that was not the end of the menace. Another man-eater killed a road engineer called O'Hara, and a wretched Indian clerk sat shivering in Kina station while a lion prowled over the roof, bleeding copiously from the wounds it had inflicted on itself trying to tear up the iron sheeting. The incident evoked what must surely have been the most extraordinary message ever transmitted over a railway telegraph line: 'Lion fighting with station. Send urgent succour.'

2

The Railway Community

The completed railway systems brought together unprecedented numbers of workers into individual enterprises. These in turn produced an unparalleled community consciousness. Railways were – and to an astonishing extent still are – worlds of their own, in-bred, complete with their own systems of law and order. 'I've heard of the call of the wild,' wrote one railwayman, 'the call of the law, the call of the Church. There is also the call of the railroads.'

'Thus was created', wrote Frank Mckenna, 'a new form of industrial anthropology, a tribalistic grouping of men based on an elaborate division of labour, a hierarchy of groups and a ritualistic adherence to territory, myth, symbolism and insignia unknown outside the specified boundaries . . . From the earliest days, the railway companies sought a new type of loyalist, nothing less than a prototype, an "organisation man".' Mckenna was referring to British railwaymen, but his analysis rings true world-wide.[17]

Moreover, and notably unlike virtually every other nineteenth-century industrial organisation, major railway companies were not family businesses. Even when they were the creation of one dominant personality, the sons rarely took over, so the companies very soon became impersonal organisms, requiring a vast range of skills to build and operate. As such they were the prototype of the modern industrial corporation.

'Railwaymen are cut of the same cloth everywhere. The calling moulds a type, just as the ocean does,' wrote Brian Fawcett.[18] The variations were between trades, not between countries. 'Maintenance-of-the-way crews,' wrote Walter Licht[19], 'lived together out on the road, often in the homes of their section bosses, they comprised a strange mixture of young immigrants, farm boys, and college men seeking respite from the boredom of study in the romance of hard labor. Trackmen were invariably bachelors who lived, worked, drank and caroused together in the absence of other company.'

Even the most militant railwaymen were intensely proud of their line. For a century after Brunel's time the Great Western was known, only half jokingly, as God's Wonderful Railway – it was the top regiment, employees of other companies were 'foreigners'. More narrowly, drivers identified with their engine, signalmen with their signal box. This loyalty was of enormous benefit to the railway companies in controlling their workers, a control made the easier because of the habit of family loyalty to railway work.

The most obvious example of the railway community was the railway town.* The name could be loosely applied to existing towns like York and Derby, 'railway towns' only in the broadest sense that the railways were the biggest employers there. But the British also created complete new towns devoted exclusively to railways, like Crewe, Horwich, Swindon and Wolverton – the last two conjured up from nothing because they happened to be half-way between the termini of the lines they served.

The railway towns developed into medium-sized towns rather than major cities, which demand a greater flow and variety of employment than even the railways could provide. By the 1850s, a mere decade after its foundation, Frank Mckenna quotes a distinguished visitor (Sir Francis Head) as noting that Crewe had '514 houses, one church, three schools and one town hall . . . the new houses at Crewe were originally built solely for railway servants, yet it was soon found necessary to construct a 'considerable number for the many shopkeepers and others who were desirous to join the new settlement, and accordingly, of the present population of 8,000, about one half are strangers.'

There were few such towns outside Britain, although the German engineers building the railway across what is now Turkey transformed the little village of Eskishshir into one of the busiest places in Anatolia.[20] The biggest in India was – and is – at Jamalpur, nearly three hundred miles west of Calcutta. It is near a deep-water port and was thus convenient to help importing locomotives. By the end of the nineteenth century it employed 250 Europeans and 10,000 Indians. Its isolation ensured 'that its

* For the best discussion of the whole subject see Jack Simmons's *The Railway in Town and Country 1830–1914*.

workers would not be enticed by the bright lights and vices of the metropolis. In this Jamalpur proved to be an excellent choice, for it still remains inhospitable and God forsaken.'[21]

Jamalpur had all the attributes of a company town.[22] 'The company had supplied houses for all its employees, and in addition there was a church, a club, a Masonic lodge, and several schools.' Most of these facilities, more especially the sporting ones, were reserved for Europeans. Indian railways, with their infinite variety of rank, were divided by the minute gradations of a thoroughly stratified society. As the *Railway Magazine* put it, 'the wife of the general traffic manager may refuse to patronise the club because forsooth! she may meet there the assistant store-keeper's sister – a person whom she considers her social inferior.'

Jamalpur had been chosen because it was well away from metropolitan temptations. For the same reason American companies chose small, isolated towns as the site for their workshops, trying especially hard to isolate the mechanics from those independent-minded aristocrats, the engine drivers, whose status was enhanced by the American description 'engineers'.

The most famous railway town in the United States was Pullman, the pride and joy of George Mortimer Pullman. Unlike its utilitarian English equivalents, built up haphazard by speculative builders, it was created by an individual who could permit himself the expensive whims not permissible to railway managers elsewhere answerable to directors and shareholders. So Pullman was much praised for its flowers, its elegance, its magnificent site on Lake Michigan. Pullman resembled other model industrial settlements, like Saltaire, also created by a single employer.

But an iron hand was visible under the flowerbeds. 'The blacklist was used against employees who found fault with Pullman the town, or Pullman the company, or the preachers and teachers employed in Pullman schools and churches.'[23] In 1894 wages were cut while rents remained the same. Driven to desperation the inhabitants of this model town began a strike and thus set off a major national dispute in which they became the most obvious victims and martyrs of labour mythology.

The railway industry took time to develop. By 1850 most of Britain's main-line network was already complete; nevertheless railwaymen were only the country's 33rd largest single occupation, totalling a mere one per cent of the working population. Twenty years later the percentage had trebled and the railways were the sixth largest employers. And by then most of the workers were employed by a few major companies.

In many countries, most obviously in Prussia, but also in France, the railway companies imposed standards of discipline familiar to us now in any major industrial organisation, but then confined to the armed forces. In Prussia, indeed, stationmasters, signalmen, and lower ranks used to stand to attention when trains passed, as if the trains housed a senior inspecting officer. But everywhere the stationmaster, with his shiny top hat, was a highly visible symbol of authority, and the railway director at the very peak of the industrial hierarchy.*

The type of organisation the railways required was different from even the biggest of individual factories. The building and running of the networks demanded industrial discipline as strict as those found in an army, but exercised over an ever-expanding sprawl, perhaps extending over thousands of miles of track. Even in Britain, least militaristic of societies, many of the leading early railway managers were former army officers who retained their ranks in civilian life.†

These militaristic tendencies were inevitable, not only because of the nature of the work, but also because, initially, army officers were the only people with the necessary experience of disciplining and controlling large bodies of men scattered over a wide area. 'Such men,' wrote O. S. Nock,[24] 'were experienced in establishing chains of command, and the setting up of posts and outposts at which all the men concerned were required to act in a disciplined

---

* In her novel *The Railway Children* E. Nesbit employs the director as a deus ex machina saving the children's father from the unjust prison sentence to which he has been sentenced.

† The boys of Wellington College, founded at the beginning of the railway age, originally wore German-style officer cadet uniforms. These were rapidly replaced after Lord Derby, the Prime Minister, handed one of them his ticket, mistaking him for a uniformed railway employee.

manner according to a clear set of rules.'

The organisational structure, hierarchical, regimental, remained much the same for a hundred years. It proved immensely effective in organising the armies of steam, but it led to an institutionalised rigidity which has proved fatal since World War II in trying to compete with those supremely flexible means of transport, the car, the coach and the lorry.

From the very beginning, every 'regiment' had to trade with dozens of others. In Britain this led to the establishment, as early as 1842, of the Railways Clearing House, which devised exceedingly sophisticated criteria for apportioning the costs incurred by the different companies in handling any business which involved more than one of them. The costs were divided between an allowance for handling at the terminals, and a rate per mile, the sort of division between fixed and marginal costs familiar to all modern businesses.

Even more complex were the negotiations between the railways and its biggest customer, the Post Office. The success of the British Post Office after the invention of the penny post in 1840 was very largely due to the speed and reliability of the service it received from the railways. Nevertheless it still expected to pay only the marginal cost involved in handling the additional freight, while the companies naturally asked for their fixed costs to be taken into account, and generally won their case when the disagreement reached the courts. The arguments continue. Today British Rail incurs a penalty if mail trains are more than ten minutes late.

To cope with their sheer size, the railways inevitably became innovators in industrial management. In Britain the pioneer was Captain Mark Huish, general manager from 1846 to 1858 of Britain's largest industrial enterprise, the London & North Western Railway, which controlled all the traffic from Euston through Birmingham to the North West and Scotland.

In Frank Mckenna's words he 'devised methods of management and control necessary to the conduct of his employer's business'. He also proved an excellent 'political' manager, scheming, combining, making secret treaties – one of his most successful campaigns restricted the spread of Brunel's broad gauge lines. But even Huish was never made a director of the company he served so faithfully, for the railways provided an early example of that most socially divisive of British managerial structures, in which the board of directors was composed exclusively of generally well-born amateurs, while the organisation was actually run by the equivalent of non-commissioned officers, although Huish was invariably referred to under his military rank of captain.

In the United States the railways thoroughly deserved their title of 'the nation's first big business'.* By the middle of the 19th century three quarters of the railroad workers in the United States worked for organisations which were large by any standards. 'Every day, railroad managers had to make decisions controlling the activities of many men to whom they rarely talked or even ever saw ... both the short-term operating decisions ... and the long-term policy decisions – involving expansion by construction or purchase of tracks, equipment, terminal and other facilities and the methods used to finance such expansion were unprecedented in their intricacies.'

American railroads matured in the decades before and after the Civil War. There was need. The first lines were usually mere sketches, tracks hastily laid on the ground. It took decades for the picture to be completed. The process was, in fact, started by some of the 'robber barons'. It was Commodore Vanderbilt, more famous as a financier than as an improver of railways, who double-tracked and then quadrupled, some major routes, like that from Albany to Buffalo, and E. H. Harriman was famous for the improvements he effected on the Union Pacific.

But it was the tycoons' successor, the usually anonymous managers, who rebuilt the majority of the major routes, spending vast sums on doubling and quadrupling lines, boring new tunnels, eliminating gradients, straightening curves, laying heavier rails, transforming them into the finest piece of infrastructure the world had ever seen.

The managers were working within an increasingly modern

* The title of a study by Alfred P. Chandler from which the quotations are taken.

managerial environment. The Baltimore and Ohio's managers 'were the first to separate the management of financial and accounting activities from those of moving trains and traffic'. As general superintendent of the New York and Erie, Daniel C. McCallum, later the hero of Civil War railroading, 'was the first to define clearly the duties and responsibilities of the several executive or administrative officers on a large railroad and to spell out the lines of authority and communication between them'.

J. Edgar Thomson of the Pennsylvania, lordliest of them all, took McCallum's ideas one stage further with a widely-copied divisional structure. Thomson established a holding company to manage the Pennsy's interests in leased lines or those to the west of its main routes. He then introduced a traffic department which marketed and organised the railroad's traffic, while a central office concentrated on broader issues. In 1869 Albert Fink, known as the 'Teutonic Giant' (he was 6 ft 7 ins tall) a distinguished engineer and inventor of the Fink Bridge Truss, became chairman of the Louisville and Nashville and introduced the modern idea of 'control through statistics', separating fixed from marginal costs. Since fixed costs accounted for two thirds of the total, there was a considerable incentive to increase business at almost any price.

Some of the bigger railroads introduced systems of operational decentralisation very similar to those supposedly invented by General Motors in the 1920s. With them came an increasing formalisation of internal relationships. American railroads issued rulebooks of a hundred pages or more: that issued by the Pennsylvania in 1875 included 410 regulations, 'which in minute detail outlined the expected activities of every grade of operative from foreman to road repairmen,' wrote Walter Licht.

In Britain the first railway workers had come largely from the armed services, domestic service, and other occupations marked by the habit of obedience – unlike employees in other industries the workers were called 'servants', a status recognised even in the name of one of their unions. In the lower grades, both in Britain and the United States,* agricultural labourers predominated, largely because railways were the biggest industry in rural areas otherwise largely untouched by industrialisation; indeed, in many countries it was the railways which first brought an extreme and specialised form of industrial discipline into the countryside. In Britain the workers from agricultural backgrounds were resented by their urban colleagues because it was thought that they were more docile, and accustomed to lower wages than urban recruits.

Except for a minority of workers on the fringe, like part-time porters or men employed on the permanent way, railwaymen enjoyed a greater degree of security, a greater regularity of payment, than in other industries at the time, so the jobs were much sought-after. Even the almighty directors did not neglect their powers of patronage – in one company, for instance, the chairman was allowed to nominate twelve clerks. Nevertheless by the 1870s the companies did face competition from the police, another body where obedience was a key requirement.

The quasi-military atmosphere in the railway world extended to an obsession with rank. In Britain there were over a hundred grades by 1870. 'The goods porter was looked on as an inferior animal by the shunter,' wrote P. W. Kingsford, in *Victorian Railwaymen*; 'the shunter was tolerated as a necessary evil by the goods guard, who had wild hopes that some time he would be able to look a passenger guard squarely in the eyes as a man and brother of equal rank.' More fundamental was the strict distinction, drawn the world over, between mere 'workers', paid weekly or even daily, and the monthly-paid salaried employees.

In France the hierarchy was even more formal. By 1900 the mighty Northern Railway included seventeen grades, each with a formal minimum and maximum salary, with carefully graded equivalent ranks in each branch: administrative, operational, permanent way, and mechanical engineering. Lowest paid were female employees (whatever their work, it seems), taking home a

---

* In the North George Pullman was the first to employ negro workers in any number, although before the Civil War most of the work on Southern railroads was done by negroes. Some even rose to drive the trains.

few hundred francs annually, even if they were full-time employees, while Grade I, the chief engineers and their brethren, earned up to 35,000 francs a year (the equivalent of £1,400, an immense salary for the period).[25]

Nevertheless most railway systems included a clearly visible promotion ladder, itself a considerable innovation in industrial practice. As Kingsford remarks, there was 'much more freedom of movement between the manual worker, unskilled as well as skilled, and the clerical and supervisory worker than there was in the twentieth century', when the railways' managerial arteries had seized up. Most senior British railwaymen, remarks Michael Robbins in *The Railway Age*, 'began their careers straight from school. It was not often a public school; and a university man was very rare indeed in the railway service.' Sir George Findlay, for thirteen years general manager of the London & North Western, was the son of a railwayman. His career was typical in that 'the father had a railway connexion; that it began early; and that it owned nothing to any influence except the man's own work and the impression that it made on his superiors. There were no examinations passed, no careful training courses.' He was transferred so often that 'the railway service engrossed all his interest; it was his community, much more so than the place where he happened to be living'. The same pattern – of fast internal promotion of likely lads – applied in the United States where one in every six railwaymen received some form of promotion every couple of years.

Outside Europe, and not only in colonies like India, the hierarchy was openly racial. In *Railways of the Andes*, published in 1963, Brian Fawcett, a veteran railwayman, shows how late and how grudgingly the natives were trusted to run their own railways. The replacement of expatriate experts 'was gradual, nationals taking over when the foreign incumbents retired, died or drank themselves out of a job ... and so it went on until virtually the only foreigners remaining were the officers. It stopped there. As long as British companies operated South American railroads they kept a majority of British officials.'

Fawcett's book is redolent of his obviously genuine affection for native Andean railwaymen. But he dismisses the 'young men of Spanish ancestry', refusing to sully their hands with hard work, and whose tradition 'militates against the donkey work that goes into the making of a good operating official' – an accusation he could have levelled with equal validity against the well-brought-up young English exiles, who sometimes found themselves in charge of some far-away railways.

The distinctions were not merely between expatriates and natives. The *Cholos*, the mountain Indians, did the dirty work in the engine sheds and on the track, while the *mestizos*, men of mixed blood, could aspire to higher ranks; although, Fawcett warns, 'the *mestizo* of the coast is generally at the bottom of labour disputes'.

The same divisions were found in the Indian railways, then the largest single employers of labour in the railway world. Naturally the officer class was exclusively British, and even the expatriate engine-drivers considered themselves a cut above those recruited locally. But the mass of middle-rank jobs, operational and clerical, in India, as in the Andean countries or Malaya, were filled by men of mixed parentage. This may have been because, despite the obvious cut-off point at managerial level, railways provided a career ladder higher than any other occupation, and one where intelligence and a variety of skills brought their appropriate rewards.

The social distinctions 'were reflected in the residential patterns of workers associated with the stations. At the bottom of the scale, some "third-class" stations, which were expected to be used only by Indian travellers, were staffed entirely by Indians. The Anglo-Indians . . . were always accommodated in their own railway settlements not far from the larger stations.'[26]

As railway systems grew throughout the world, so their operational requirements grew more complex. Typical was the 'chief despatcher', responsible for operational complexities today handled by a computer. In Fawcett's words, 'His knowledge of the whole system must be encyclopedic; he must know the traits of every engine, every engineer and every conductor . . . he must be capable of concentrating for hours at a time on the train-

sheets without letting his mind wander a degree off course . . . he must be a diplomat by nature; and of course he must be an authority on train movements and "the book" in general.'

But the most romantic post was that of engine-driver, or engineer. Even Freud dreamt of being an engine driver: the two most popular American railway ballads, 'Casey Jones' and 'The Wreck of the Old 97', both concerned the fate of engineers. Neither song dealt with a major crash and both the engineers were painted as heroic figures, even though both were driving with extreme recklessness and Casey Jones had been reprimanded for the same offence on nine or ten occasions before his fatal crash.

'Pioneer drivers,' noted Walter Licht, 'guarded their machines as prized and personal possessions. The engines were painted a variety of colours, that is until Commodore Vanderbilt clamped down on personal exuberance by insisting that all the locomotives on the New York Central should be painted a funereal black.' Nevertheless some drivers retained their status. Photographs of Russian engine-drivers show them as 'proper middle-class gentlemen, complete with starched collars'.

But for all the romance, all their pride in their job, their engine, their status, all their insistence on representation by a separate union, the job was limited, more so even than the modern equivalent, the driver of a long-distance lorry. In Wolfgang Schievelbusch's words, 'Because a train runs on a predetermined line, an engine-driver can never aspire to the social role of a "captain on dry land".' Even at the time there was a fundamental status conflict between the engineers and the conductors, the 'hogheads' and the 'brains'. 'An engineer', it was said, 'is a fireman with his brains baked out.'

The very specialised corps of railway policemen played a major role in the lives, and the folklore, of the railway community. By 1905 the Russian railways employed 8,000 policemen, more than one for every hundred workers. In Fawcett's Andean railways the key figure was the 'Comisario', a highly special type of chief of police. 'His methods are his own business; they are not questioned by wise management. He enjoys a large measure of independence, his official reward is good and his unofficial rewards remain his own secret.'

He and his equivalents elsewhere had plenty to occupy them. Workshops were used for private jobs, and a superintendent on the Pennsylvania, quoted by Licht, complained that 'most of the brass is carried off and taken by workmen in their dinner buckets or else wrapped up in their overalls.' On the Baltimore and Ohio trainmen would throw coal overboard to be collected by their families.

Institutionalised crime centred around the railways' procurement departments, where even the top officials might well be involved, and, operationally, on the sale and checking of tickets. In 1866 the Northern Argentine Railway discovered that a group of their employees had set up a ticket office of their own outside the northern station in Buenos Aires where they sold tickets a third cheaper than the standard fares. Once on the train things were worse. Whether they were called guards, as in Britain, conductors, as in the United States, or inspectors, as in Russia, the scams were much the same. American conductors, it was said, practised the art of 'knocking-down'. They would throw the cash they had collected in the air: any that stuck to the roof of the carriage belonged to their employers; the rest they kept for themselves. In 1865 things got so bad that one railroad discharged its whole corps of conductors.

In Russia the inspectors would let passengers travel without a ticket or in a better class of carriage than they were entitled to, and if the inspector asked for your *biletchik* and not for your *bilet*, it meant that he might cut up nasty if no tip was forthcoming. But the passengers – and the authorities who issued over-many free passes – were just as much to blame. In 1908 an official enquiry[27] discovered that nearly 33,000 passengers travelled without tickets from Moscow to St Petersburg. Most had passes: few were entitled to them; only 716 transgressors were fined, and a mere seventeen railway officials dismissed.

Working on the railways was more dangerous even than in a traditionally high-risk industry like mining. Not surprisingly the companies tried to keep this damning fact quiet, especially as they had an appalling record in introducing even the simplest of safety devices. In Britain railway companies managed to disguise the figures for accidents until 1871. It then emerged that every year one in 167 of their workers was killed or injured. In the United States in the late 1880s three men in every hundred were injured every year.* In France 43 per cent of a sample of retired railwaymen surveyed in 1900 had suffered at least one accident while working for the railways – not surprisingly, since the Nord network alone was averaging an injury a day at the time.

In the half century before corridor trains became standard in the last decades of the century even the guard on a passenger train had a dangerous job. In *The Uncommercial Traveller* Dickens recounts how the guard came 'clambering round to mark the tickets while we are at full speed (a really horrible performance in an express train, though he holds on to the open window by his elbows in the most deliberate manner), he stands in such a whirlwind that I grip him fast by the collar, and feel it next to manslaughter to let him go.'

The worst danger, accounting for a third of all the injuries suffered by American railwaymen in 1889, came from the links between the coaches or wagons, a primitive link-and-pin coupling device. The switchmen (also known as 'fielders') had to work at the ends of the cars to drop the coupling pins into the hooks just as the cars came together. Veteran fielders could be distinguished by their missing fingers. If the buffers ('drumheads') at the end of the cars failed to withstand the impact the fielder was smashed to death or knocked down between the cars to be run over by the wheels.

The automatic coupler was perfected in 1873, but human life was cheap, railway companies mean, and it was introduced only slowly into service. Even in 1912, couplings were responsible for 2,300 deaths among railroad employees in the United States, nearly four fifths of the total. But accidents only hit the headlines when passengers were involved. The sufferings of ordinary railway workers were so commonplace that the phrase 'only a

---

* The American figures became public only in 1888, when it was revealed that over 2,000 railway workers had been killed that year.

brakeman was killed' became commonplace, familiar enough to be immortalised in yet another bitter railway ballad.

'Twas only a poor dying brakeman,
Simply a hard lab 'ring man . . .
'Twas only a poor mangled being,
Nobody knew 'What's his name' . . .

Railway companies did make some attempts to improve their employees' lot. 'The picture which emerged from the evidence of railway servants,' wrote Geoffrey Alderman in The Railway Interest about a report from a Royal Commission of the mid-1870s, 'was of a benevolent despotism exercised by the companies over the men for the latter's own good.' Moreover and crucially, 'higher wage packets meant much more to them than longer hours'. Many companies provided blocks of flats or houses at railway centres like Glasgow, Manchester, Stratford in east London and at Peterborough, where the estate was known as 'The Barracks'. Some even provided schools: the mighty London & North Western had twenty. But most benefits, like free passes and clothes, were confined to the superior grades, and, at lower levels, proved useful to divide militants from more peaceable workers.

In Britain the companies also ran the only savings institutions then available to employees. As a commission of enquiry noted in 1874, the Friendly Society 'as a means of thrift existed only for a minority, and that minority was the better-paid . . . many disputes between workers and servants in which the existence of a [Friendly] Society enables a company by dismissing a servant to inflict a heavy fine as well', the former 'servant' could not reclaim the money the company had paid into the society on his behalf.

Not unexpectedly, the railways had their own, highly structured, disciplinary systems. If fines, cautions and reprimands went unheeded, the next inevitable step was dismissal. In Britain five workers out of a hundred were sacked every year, mostly for drink or neglect of duty, though over a tenth of the sackings were due to 'misconduct and unsubordination'. In the United States discipline centred round 'trainmen', the engineers and conductors:

one in eight of all the trainmen employed by the Chicago Burlington & Quincy were dismissed. Prussian railway employees were, legally, military reservists. If they struck, an official told Samuel Dunn[28] 'they would be ordered to their colours. They would then be directed to return to their work. If they refused they would be shot for mutiny.'*

In Japan self-discipline seems to have been the order of the day. A legendary, much-quoted story (which, however, lacks any verifiable source) tells how a Japanese stationmaster felt obliged to commit suicide because the Emperor had been delayed by a signalman at the station for which he was responsible. In Britain, the operating rules of the railways had the force of law once they had been approved by the Board of Trade, whereas in the United States the individual worker enjoyed greater freedom – in theory at least.

The very idea that the workers were combining together to improve their lot was anathema. In 1866 the general managers of three leading Scottish companies, 'desirous of meeting the legitimate demands of their employees . . . will most firmly withstand all dictation by the men'. 'Dictation' was firmly defined as 'combination, or joining any union for the avowed purpose of dictating to their employers'. And that was that.

In 1871, the Amalgamated Society of Railway Servants was founded to cater for all grades of railwaymen, although, then as now, British engine drivers remained sturdily independent. The general anti-union bias remained intact. In the 1890s one British general manager remarked how 'you might as well have a trades union or an "Amalgamated Society" in the army . . . as have it on the railways'. In Russia, as one pamphleteer put it, 'In the railroad world, the director is Tsar and God', and behaved appropriately. When the train greasemen petitioned a director for redress of their grievances he said simply, 'Do greasemen have rights? What kind of rights could they have?'

* In 1911 the French government took a leaf out of the Prussian book. They had had enough. Before the strike of that year, over half the men in some grades in the French state railways were on sick leave at any one time. They called up strikers for three weeks' military training. The next day the trains were running again.

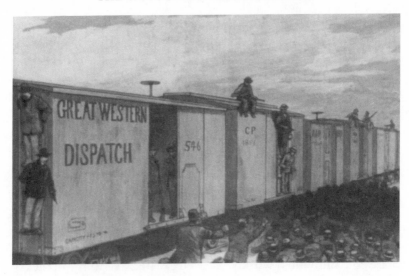

Calling in the US Marshals to end the 1886 Great Railroad strike American-style

The tradition of militancy was established early. In 1832 the enginemen on the Stockton & Darlington had forced their employers to agree that they should complete only one round trip every day. But until the 1870s the bosses remained on top. There were only eleven recorded strikes in Britain during the first railway generation, mostly caused by companies' attempts to reduce wages in bad times. One of the few losers was George Hudson, the railway king, who sacked a number of protesting drivers and firemen on Christmas Eve. They were reinstated when their replacements turned out to be both drunk and dangerous.

Working hours were incredibly long – a petition to the French National Assembly in 1871 revealed that drivers often went for twelve hours without food and worked forty hours at a stretch – hours which naturally contributed to the appalling accident rate. In Latin America, in Meiggs's day, firemen slept on their engines, helped maintain them, and worked for up to eighteen hours, as did the engineers and conductors, although they 'came ashore' in Fawcett's expressive phrase, every week or so.

Even before unions had been founded conditions everywhere had slowly improved. At first railwaymen worked a seven-day week, but by the 1870s the norm had become a ten-hour day and a six-day week, a trend led by the enginemen, helped by engineering workers in railway towns. By then two fifths of British railway workers were on duty ten hours or less, though some were still on twelve-hour shifts.

In France unionism got off to an even slower start than in Britain. Even in the last decades of the nineteenth century the unions concentrated on welfare issues like the provision of sickness benefits, pensions and mortgages. The unions' impotence was shown when they tried a major strike in 1911, but they, like their brothers in Russia, Britain and the United States, were hampered by the refusal of the status-conscious engine-drivers to unite with lesser breeds.

Only in the United States and Russia did railway unionism have a broader impact. In 1877 the railwaymen united American capitalism in the face of the first, and thus the most serious, threat it had ever received from an organised body of workers. Twenty-eight years later the Russian railwaymen triggered an abortive revolution.

In the spring of 1877 the American railroads were in a parlous state. After four years of depression the companies were unable even to agree on pooling arrangements to prop up freight rates. But they could and did agree that wages, already greatly reduced, should be cut by a further ten per cent. They were naturally not prepared for the resulting strike, which affected virtually all the major Eastern lines and cities.

The strike started in the yards of the Baltimore & Ohio in Buffalo and quickly spread to Chicago, where it was immediately transformed into something like a general strike. In Chicago, as elsewhere, the normal instrument of control, the National Guard, proved useless – since the Civil War it had degenerated into little more than a fancy-dress parading society. The railroad magnates needed more protection directly from the federal government. Although the police killed a score of strikers, several companies of regular soldiers were required to suppress the Chicago disturbances.

The strikes marked the end of an age of innocence, in which

the bosses genuinely believed they were appreciated by their employees. It marked, too, the emergence of the fear of foreign Communism springing from the Paris Commune of 1871, which played a role very similar to the Bolshevik revolution in Russia forty-six years later. The Commune infected railway bosses in Britain as well. That same year three leading Scottish companies, while expressing themselves as 'desirous of meeting the legitimate demands of their employees they will most firmly withstand agitators influenced by the Parisian Communards'.

The most popular of the dozen or more novels based on the year's upheavals was *The Bread Winner*, a fiercely anti-labour work by John Hay, formerly President Lincoln's secretary. Another who profited from the situation was Allan Pinkerton, founder of the famous detective agency. Before 1860 he had been the fiercest of anti-slavery radicals, running an 'underground railroad' to help fugitive slaves. By the 1870s he was famous as the most ruthless of policemen, employing *agents provocateurs* against union activists. This fear of foreign agitators was to provide a rich seam for demagogues for generations to come.

The factual basis for the fears was pretty minimal. In Chicago and in St Louis the 1877 strike was taken over by an allegedly radical group, the Workingmen's Party, while in San Francisco the workers took the opportunity to stage a race riot against the wretched Chinese. In Gabriel Kolko's words in *Railroads and Regulation*: 'The Great Strike focused attention on . . . the growth of a working class capable of subverting and destroying by political, or even more direct means, the existing power structure.'

The strike provided the railway magnates with the shock of their lives. 'I confess that I felt like a Doctor dealing with a new and unknown malady,' wrote Charles Eliot Perkins of the Chicago Burlington & Quincy. For the first time (if not for long) they abandoned their own normal internecine warfare to fight the strikers, assuming, as they would for the next generation, that the state would automatically rally to their cause. The strike profoundly affected their previous allegiance to democracy. It would wither, said one commentator, 'if the thousands who pay taxes get no protection from the millions who govern.'

The authorities were by no means as virulent as the bosses. Before 1877 state legislators were often hostile to railroads, and executives used to look longingly to the situation in Britain where politicians, it was fondly imagined, were loyal supporters of the railway campanies. By contrast even President Hayes, supposedly the creature of Tom Scott of the Pennsylvania Railroad, confided in his diary on August 5th, in the midst of the 1877 upheavals: 'The railroad strikers, as a rule, are good men, sober, intelligent and industrious.' A few days later he wrote to a friend, 'If anything can be done to remove the distress which afflicts laborers, and to stimulate enterprise, I am ready and not afraid to do my share towards it.'[29]

After the failure of the strikes the workers started to transform their Brotherhoods, previously more akin to friendly societies than unions, into increasingly effective instruments of union power. The bosses had to speed up the formalisation of their management structures because the strikes had revealed the local tyrannies created by many of their far-flung subordinates. After 1877 the more enlightened managers gradually started to negotiate contracts with the Brotherhoods. This normalisation, however, was concealed by the explosive growth of the romantically-named 'Knights of Labour', who aimed to transform the railways into cooperatives. But by 1893 their rather muddled idealism had been superseded by a more orthodox, if democratic, American Railway Union, led by the charismatic Eugene Debs.

In the end hierarchical pride triumphed over worker solidarity. 'The common experience of being employees failed to dissolve the divisions of skill and status that materialized among railwaymen,' wrote Walter Licht. The brotherhoods stayed aloof when the Pullman workers started a major strike in 1894. Like many such spontaneous uprisings it was doomed, for it was ill-planned, fragmented, faced with overwhelming governmental force.

In the short term the ARU was destroyed by the Pullman strike and Debs was transformed into a major Socialist hero, while thousands of workers were black-listed.* In the long term the strike marked the final triumph of the brotherhoods, craft unions whose interests were – and are – narrowly confined to the protection of one particular class of worker. Even today American railway managers have to deal with eleven brotherhoods, and they have greatly impeded the efforts of railroad management to run their systems economically.

In the United States the revolutionary menace existed mainly in the fevered minds of the bosses. Even in Russia in 1905 it was slow to emerge. Previously only two strikes there had had anything like even partial success. But early in 1905 strikes broke out all over Russia – with the provinces as militant or more so, than Moscow and St Petersburg. Moreover, the protest involved white-collar workers previously thought of as loyal. 'Nevertheless the demands of January and February', wrote Henry Reichman, 'were with few exceptions still explicitly economic and professional'[30] – higher wages, shorter hours, pensions and other fringe benefits. Initially even the Bolsheviks were sceptical, distrusting amorphous strike movements.

However, in the course of the year the strikers, loosely grouped in a single, quarrelsome, under-organised union, began looking to political solutions, a constitution, freedom – though, even then, political agitators found that the mass of unskilled railwaymen were still more interested in direct benefits than vague political ideas. Indeed, 'Some railwaymen sought in different ways to preserve or restore the status that railroading had seemed to enjoy in the 19th century,' while others sought support from other industrial groups.

In the end the Tsar did concede a few of the railwaymen's demands, but only under duress and only until he had rallied the forces required to suppress them – as he did with the help of two military trains which moved in opposite directions along the Trans-Siberian, crushing strikers along the way.

---

* Managers gave strikers and non-strikers apparently similar letters saying that the worker 'had left our service of his own accord'. The paper was watermarked with a crane. If the man was of 'good character' then the crane was erect; but if he had been an 'agitator' then the crane was broken-necked.

After 1905 the Bolsheviks lost their influence in the Railwaymen's Union, which by 1917 was powerful enough to pose a serious problem. The railwaymen took the idea of giving power to the workers altogether too seriously for Lenin's liking and it took him nearly two years to impose his will. Railwaymen have always remained a potentially subversive force in centralised Communist societies – during the Cultural Revolution in China they formed a sort of bush telegraph at a time when no real news was available to anyone in the country.

Some of the 'revolutionaries' in the United States were not railwaymen, they were hoboes, many of whom used to carry cards proclaiming their membership of the IWW, the much-feared revolutionary Industrial Workers of the World, the 'Wobblies'. As such they felt entitled to lenient treatment by their fellow proletarians, the trainmen. The civil police were not too bothered about them, merely requiring them to leave town on the next train, which is precisely what most of them wanted to do anyway. The railroad police ('bulls') were more brutal, beating them up and firing warning shots, which often hit home.

There was a whole hierarchy of illegal passengers. 'Hoboes worked and wandered, tramps dreamt and wandered and as for the bums, well, they just drank and wandered'.[31] They had in common their sadness, their poverty, lives which were squalid in reality and hopelessly romanticised in myth and legend. They multiplied with the trains – in times of depression up to a million rode the rails annually. The tycoons naturally fought against them. Jay Gould went so far as to remove the platforms from the mail and baggage cars of the Missouri Pacific, thus removing a comfortable means of transport for hoboes – and providing the opportunity for another song:

Old Jay Gould said, before he died:
I'll fix the blind so the 'boes can't ride.
If they ride, they will ride a rod,
And place their life in the hands of God.

An Extraordinary General Manager

A number of relatively humble American railwaymen left detailed accounts of their lives, but the most extraordinary is *The General Manager's Story*, written by a man calling himself 'Herbert Hamblen'. I am not sure who he was and whether he is recounting his own experiences or blending stories he had picked over a lifetime. He provides a bleak picture of capitalist oppression, yet it is also infused with a uniquely American optimism, a feeling that the best man will win in the end and that every railroad worker, however humble, has the general manager's baton in his pocket: 'the general manager, if not the president, started in just where he is now' – a humble railroad employee.

Hamblen was a rail-struck lad. 'The sound of the switch engines as they puffed to and fro, and the bang and rattle of the cars as they were rammed together, was music to me, and served to strengthen my resolution to become a railroad man.' He soon learnt the grim reality. His story is of chaos, of appalling overwork, of periods of 52 hours on duty, of repeated, systematic exploitation and injustice, and, above all, of accidents. On almost his first day at work he met an old fellow who

> had only one eye, and a terrible scar ran diagonally across his face from eyebrow to chin. This had crushed and distorted his nose, drawn one corner of his eye down, and the opposite corner of his mouth up, thereby showing a couple of filthy, tobacco-stained tusks, and giving him the most repulsive appearance of any human being I ever saw ... His overalls were black with dirt, and so shiny with grease that when the sun shone on him he glistened like a crow. His left arm was cut off just below the elbow, and finished out with a three-pronged iron hook, in which he carried a great iron pail filled with colored cotton waste soaked in oil.

One worker 'believed that accidents were largely due to the recklessness of the men themselves ... he hoped to escape the almost universal fate by being careful. Poor fellow! He was blown from the top of his train a few months afterwards, and found by the section gang, frozen stiff.'

Another victim of 'the insatiate maw of the railway' had been impaled on the drawhead of a car. 'He was a poor man with the usual poor man's blessing, a large family, so we made up a purse to bury him, and the company gave his wife and two oldest children employment in the car-cleaning gang.'

The stars in Hamblen's story are not the managers, for they were too remote, but the engineers. They were expected to display 'instant judgment' and even to wreck their engines 'to avoid greater damage'.

'He is expected to have and to exercise better judgment than the other employees; and as they have no orders to submit to his will, friction arises, he is d . . . d for a crank, and when an accident occurs conductors, brakemen and switchmen all unite to swear the blame on the unfortunate engineer, who, being in the minority, is lucky indeed if he escape discharge.'

In one case the engineer 'was sacrificed to save the despatcher, who was a son-in-law of the president of the road'.

Hamblen soon learnt that 'every day that he remains in the company's employ he is one day nearer to a better job; for promotion is the rule on all railroads . . . if he is discharged, he becomes almost absolutely ineligible in the railroad business . . . the average railroader had never known anything but railroading.' Anyone who complained was automatically branded as an agitator. Hamblen himself was sacked because he wouldn't perjure himself to help the railroad escape responsibility for a crash – although in the event the railroad could not pin the blame on the train crew, and it was bankrupted by the resulting law suits.

Following a strike, when Hamblen and his colleagues knew 'the vicinity of Chicago would be anything but a sanitorium for us for a long time to come', they went on the run, were flung in jail for ten days, started as labourers on a new line, and were gulled out of their money by a crooked contractor, before being rescued by a kindly old general manager who had rescued him once before. Then the manager himself was expelled as a result of a 'stock jobbing scheme inaugurated by the eastern syndicate which had secured control' – and who had incited the strike and thus wrecked the road.

On one road a new management, installed because dividends had been unsatisfactory, instituted a policy of systematic meanness. Workshop crews were put on short time, with a consequent lack of engines, 'brake-shoes were never renewed while a vestige remained, several wrecks were caused by inability to stop trains . . . cheap oil that would not lubricate cut out journals and crankpins . . . waste was no longer issued, so that the engines became coated with grease and dirt, making it next to impossible to detect a fracture in any of the parts . . . the quality of the fuel became so depreciated that it was impossible to make time, the first result of which was that the engineers and firemen were suspended, and the result, that business fell off, for people would neither ship their goods nor travel on a road where the service was so unreliable.'

Pay was cut by ten per cent, and Hamblen eventually roused the workers to protest, claiming that while the pay cut 'would impoverish us greatly, it would not add to the already luxurious living of the stockholders a single case of champagne, or a new suit of liveries for their flunkies'.

Hamblen and the others were finally admitted to the spacious private office of the president, 'the highest railroad functionary that any of us had ever seen. We firmly believed his power to be greater than that of any Tzar.' They found him 'with an extremely fragrant cigar cocked at an angle forty five towards his left eye.' He soon disposed of their arguments, claiming that if he met their demands for 'the exorbitant wages you men have been receiving' the railroad would be placed in the hands of a receiver 'and then we should be paid in scrip, which we would have to sell for what anybody chose to give for it'. In the end Hamblen led an, inevitably unsuccessful, strike and he was sacked once more.

He ends up running his own line . . . and calling in strike-breakers when the workers want more money. The final touch is his remark, 'I flatter myself that today our stock compares favourably with the best in the market.'

VIII

SOCIETY ON THE MOVE

1
Social Changes – and Social Relationships

Railways were not built for the purpose of social change. As a result they do not seem to have been a revolutionary force in social relationships. In most cases they reflected society as it existed and did not often initiate change themselves. Nevertheless they permeated life so thoroughly that only the first generation could remember social behaviour as it had been before the railway revolution. In *Mr Facey Romford's Hounds* R. S. Surtees was characteristically cheery about their influence:

> Among the great advantages afforded by railways has been that of opening out the great matrimonial market, whereby people can pick and choose wives all the world over, instead of having to pursue the old Pelion on Ossa or Pig upon Bacon system of always marrying a neighbour's child. So we now have an amalgamation of countries and counties, and a consequent improvement in society – improvement in wit, improvement in wine, improvement in 'wittles'*, improvement in everything . . . each fresh dinner was only a repetition of the last, and people got tired of the same thing over and over again. That is the case in most counties. Railways have gone far to annihilate that sort of society.

* Wittles = victuals = food.

In the same book Surtees went even further, opining that 'all people are put so much upon a par by the levelling influence of the rail, that a versatile man may pass for almost anybody he likes – a duke, a count, a viscount.' He was exaggerating, but the artificial, temporary confinement with perfect strangers in a railway compartment was a godsend to novelists anxious to bring characters together.

The railway carriage was also a boon to fortune-hunters, as witness the famous music-hall song which starts:

'Oh Mr Porter, what shall I do,
I want to go to Birmingham and they're taking me to Crewe,
Send me back to London as quickly as you can
Oh! Mr Porter what a silly girl I am.'

The 'silly girl' nearly overbalances in her agitation, but was saved by an old boy:

nearly fainting with the fright I sank into his arms . . .
On his clean old shirt front I laid my trembling head
'Do take it easy, rest-a-while', the dear old chappie said,
'If you make a fuss of me and on me do not frown,
You shall have my mansion dear, away in London town'

However railway travel, especially outside one's own country, could merely narrow the mind, confirm existing prejudices. Travel on foreign railways provided the English, in particular, with a new opportunity to dilate on the general undesirability of foreigners, especially those encountered on long night journeys. According to Martin Page in *Lost Pleasures of the Great Trains*:

Lord Russell shared a compartment with a foreigner who 'proceeded to open his carpet-bag, take out a pair of slippers and untie the laces of his shoes'. 'If you do that sir', proclaimed the great Victorian jurist, 'I shall throw your

Plenty of room for first-class US passengers travelling between New York and Chicago, circa 1890.

shoes out of the window'. The foreigner remarked that he had a right to do as he wished in his own country, so long as he did not inconvenience others. Lord Russell demurred. The man took off his shoes, and Lord Russell threw them out of the window.

Railways could also reinforce, rather than transform, class structures. In India only the British invariably travelled first class, in their own time and space capsules, their first-class accommodation totally separated from the life of the country, whereas before the railways they had perforce to mingle with the natives on the roads. Among the Indians themselves it was feared that higher castes would be reluctant to share any kind of space with the lower orders, a reluctance which would have impeded the spread of rail travel. Quite the contrary. As the philosopher Herbert Spencer pointed out (in *The Quarterly Review* 1868), in India 'when it was seen that the different classes of carriages were not intended, as the natives expected, to accommodate different castes . . . the Brahmin manifested no reluctance to travel in the cheapest class'. In England, by contrast, 'the quality travelled first-class to save their caste, and in India they went third-class to save their money, regardless of caste'. But both caste systems, British and Indian, survived intact.

The class structure of the trains themselves showed the railways as social reflectors, rather than innovators. From the start British and, following them, most Continental European trains were divided into three classes (The Prussians had four, plus a fifth special 'military' class). More democratic countries, like the United States, Norway and Switzerland, did not divide their trains so markedly, indeed the democratic Norwegians never had more than one class.

American trains were different. While European passengers travelled in separate compartments*, in the United States the whole carriage was open, in a deliberate contrast to less democratic European societies. Nominally, at least, the Americans did not have class distinctions although immigrants travelled in huddled masses in cars which, as Robert Louis Stevenson put it, 'are only remarkable for their extreme plainness, nothing but wood entering into any part of their constitution' (see note on page 264). Inevitably, too, railways echoed racial distinctions. Railways – and stations – in the South at least were so organised that the races did not meet on the station or on the train.

In practice the Americans also divided their coaches into two types, the first-class 'parlor car' and the 'day coach', which was roughly equivalent to European second class. As R. S. Surtees pointed out in his *Hints to Railway Travellers*, even Second Class, the equivalent of the 'outside' or inferior class, was infinitely better than the inside of the old stage-coaches, supposedly the same as First Class railway travel – although Second Class

---

* Originally the compartments were locked, which greatly increased the loss of life in the famous accident of 1842 at Meudon.

coaches were originally exposed to the weather and devoid of upholstery*.

First class passengers naturally travelled on upholstered seats. The Japanese, used to tatami rush matting, found them puzzling†. The rich also travelled as far as possible from the engine, to minimise the risk of dirt, smoke and dust. Little care or expense was wasted on the luckless proles in the third class. Until the 1840s their accommodation consisted of open boxcars attached to freight trains. In 1844 the *Railway Times* argued that 'we do not feel disposed to attach too much weight to the argument in favour of third class carriages with seats on a short line. Little physical inconvenience can result from their absence'.

In Britain Gladstone's 1844 Regulating Act required even third class coaches to be covered but they still resembled boxcars with roofs rather than true passenger carriages – by then the first class coaches looked like exactly that, coaches on wheels. But even the cheapest seats were expensive by working-class standards. Even the cheap night rate for the first French train between Paris and Le Havre represented the weekly pay of an agricultural labourer. In most of Europe rail travel remained a middle-class prerogative until the very end of the nineteenth century.

Continental railways retained the true third class until relatively recently, its seats wooden or covered with a mere apology for upholstery. Yet in 1874 the Midland Railway had moved to a two-class system, improving its third class accommodation to the level previously associated with second class, with six people to a compartment, compared with four for first class and eight or ten for third on other lines. This was brilliant marketing 'based on the realization that the three-class system was uneconomical and that larger returns were to be derived from stimulating than from discouraging third-class travel.

* In Surtees's words, Second Class 'only needed cushions to be as comfortable as First Class . . . in the summer there was less dust from the cushions so it was more comfortable even in open 3rd class'.

† At first the Japanese removed their shoes before getting into a carriage, a natural gesture since they were going indoors (hence numerous, probably apocryphal, stories about how shoes were left strewn all over stations).

Though unconvinced and indignant, the other companies had no alternative but to follow the example set by the Midland . . . Soon third-class accommodation equalled the old second; soon it was much better'.[1]

The distinctions in the atmosphere in the various classes' social atmosphere was largely imaginary, the supposed frostiness in first class was matched by an equally mythical jollity in third. Perhaps the neatest definition was made by an Englishman ignored by two ladies in a Prussian second-class carriage. According to Martin Page he remarked 'that in first class, the passengers insult the railway staff, whereas in the third class the railway staff insult the passengers. Now I learn that in second class, the passengers insult each other.'[2]

Class divisions extended from the trains into the stations where waiting rooms were separated by class as well as by sex. The waiting rooms played a particularly important role in Continental European stations, where they housed the passengers until a few minutes before a train's departure. Some early stations even had separate entrances for different classes. In India in the 1980s Paul Theroux noticed some delightful distinctions, including 'Third-class Exit, Second-class Ladies' Waiting room, First-class toilet, Sweepers Only.'

A few great landowners ensured that railways crossing their estates provided them with their own stations. The Duke of Beaufort had his own station at Badminton in Gloucestershire, originally with the right to stop express trains to suit his convenience. Even grander was the Duke of Westminster, who built a three-mile railway, albeit of a mere 15" gauge, to his mansion at Eaton Hall in Cheshire. This was a working railway, required for the vast quantity of goods the hall consumed, including forty tons of coal a week. The Duke of Sutherland, himself a railway fanatic, had helped to finance the railway through the Highlands from Wick to Thurso. In return he was allowed a private station to serve Dunrobin Castle where he kept his private coach.

For most passengers speed was the greatest luxury. The differences between various passenger services could be considerable. At the end of the nineteenth century the fast night trains between Kiev and Odessa covered the 654 km in just over twelve hours, at an overall average of 33 mph including eleven stops. The daily mixed train for third-class passengers took over 26 hours. Mark Twain cautioned travellers in New Zealand to ensure that they took the twice weekly express between Auckland and Wellington. On any of the five 'wrong days . . . you will get a train that can't overtake its own shadow'.

The speed of trains, or, more usually, the lack of it, bred many a joke. Man offers guard a child's ticket. 'But you're not a child.' 'I was when I boarded this train.' On the Southwold line in Suffolk the passengers, it was said, would leave the train, pick a few mushrooms, and then rejoin it a few minutes later. (The line was narrow-gauge, with locomotives and coaches originally destined for use in China.)

The desire for a special style of travel gradually evolved into special, named trains of which the most famous was the Orient Express (see page 261). Its success spawned numerous imitators, mostly run by the same company, the *Compagnie Internationale des Wagons-Lits*. Most of these were designed to whisk the affluent from northern capital cities, usually Paris or London, to Mediterranean sunshine and specially-built railway hotels.

In Europe those in a hurry could charter a special train – Sherlock Holmes was for ever doing so. It was not necessarily the done thing, however – when Winston Churchill hired a special during an election campaign it was cited as typical of his general flashiness. Royalty, needless to say, had its own trains. The first was commissioned by the Dowager Queen Adelaide, widow of William IV. Queen Victoria was not to be outdone by her predecessor's widow, and other royalty followed her example. In Japan the Emperor owned the country's first special, built to allow him to celebrate the opening of the line between Kobe and the ancient capital of Kyoto in appropriate style, complete with a traditional flower painting on the panel of the Imperial door.

The more autocratic the country, the more insecure the monarch, the more outrageously luxurious the ruler's train. In 1857 the Emperor Napoleon III commissioned a splendid train

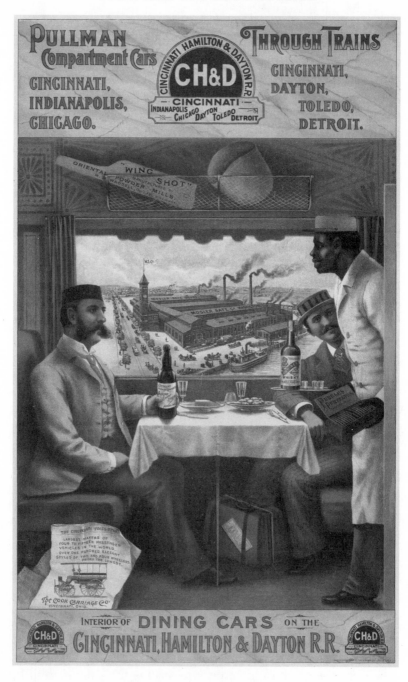

George Pulman's idea of rail travel.

much envied by his fellow-monarchs. The Tsar went one further. His train was painted the same sky-blue colour used for his gendarmerie's uniforms. It included:

a sleeping car, a dining car, a kitchen car with an icebox and a wine cellar; and a number of cars for the Imperial entourage . . . There were fireplaces . . . In the ante-room the ceiling was padded with white satin, the walls were softened with quilted silk stuffs, the doors had mosaic work as their master feature . . . A most prominent piece in this car was a combined clock-chandelier of bronze and Sèvres porcelain. In the sleeping car, walls were done in crimson, with a few mirrors and rose-coloured draperies for contrast. On a rich rug stood boudoir chests and chairs of rosewood.'[3]

To most monarchs trains were simply a convenient means of travel. But to two successive kings of Bulgaria, Ferdinand and his son Boris, they were a passion. Boris, in particular, gained a reputation for royal eccentricity by his love of train-driving, and there was a minor scandal when his insistence on speed resulted in an inferno which killed a fireman. But Boris had the last laugh: thanks to his informed interest his country's trains became a byword for efficiency.

By contrast in the United States luxury was democratised, thanks largely to George Pullman. He did not actually invent the modern sleeping or restaurant cars, but during the 1860s he manufactured and publicised them so effectively that they spread round the world within a decade.

As Siegfried Giedeon put it in *Mechanisation Takes Command*, 'Pullman's strength was not in mechanical devices: here he availed himself of anything appropriate to his purposes' – a rival had invented the crucial idea of folding the bed into the wall. 'His strength lay in quite another sphere, not the technological but the sociological. His invention was luxury in travel,' but his version of luxury was not confined to royalty or their American equivalents; it could be purchased for a relatively modest supplement on the normal price of a ticket.

His biggest gamble was the Pioneer, a sleeping car he built in 1865 at four times the cost of any previous vehicle. Pullman, like the Boeing company a hundred years later, assumed that the infrastructure would be improved sufficiently to permit his product to be used. The Boeing 707 required stronger and longer runways, and in Giedeon's words 'Pullman's sleeping car could not be used in normal traffic, as it was too wide for the bridges and fouled the platform roofs. However, things happened as Pullman foresaw: the bridges were widened and the platform roofs were adjusted to the size of car he believed necessary for comfort.'

Within a few years he had developed a restaurant car to match the sleeping car, and in 1873 his triumph was crowned when he shipped eighteen sleeping cars to Britain. His name soon became synonymous with comfort. In fast Russian trains the saloon cars, says J. N. Westwood, in his *History of Russian Railways*, 'were modelled on American parlor cars, with eighteen revolving armchairs, large mirrors and windows, electric lighting, separate toilets for ladies and gentlemen, a smoking room, carpets and wall paper . . . the railway took even greater pride in its "Pul 'manovskii'" sleeping cars, with their two-berth compartments, side corridor, hot water in the toilets, and covered gangways between each vehicle.'

In the United States, Pullman parlor cars were mundane. Every millionaire of any consequence felt entitled to his own special, the more luxurious the better, and Pullman was only too happy to oblige. There were hundreds of 'business cars', aptly described by their loving chronicler, Lucius Beebe, in *The Big Spenders*, as 'mansions on rails' symbolising the Golden Age from which naturally emerged the concept of 'conspicuous consumption'. The owners vied with each other with their marble bathtubs, Venetian glass, the luxuries of three continents. The wife of a Morgan partner averred that the only economical feature in her private car was the gold taps: 'It saves polishing, you know.' Gold dinner services were relatively commonplace. The financier Salamanca, the first commoner to own a private railway carriage in Spain, served his guests off gold plate. In the end Carlist revolutionaries burnt the coach as a symbol of corruption and privilege.

Even the richest millionaires had problems with their bathing arrangements. According to Beebe, the soprano Adelina Patti had a sunken marble bathtub aboard her appropriately named 'Adelina Patti' which, when the car was finally dismantled, turned out to be painted metal. Fritzi Scheff, another singer, had a bathtub neither sunken nor allegedly marble, but the water splashed so that she could only take a bath when her train paused for at least twenty minutes. Sometimes this was at three in the morning, an inconvenient hour.' Sleeping arrangements were easier to manage. According to Beebe, Pullman built one car in which the division between two staterooms could be made to disappear, allowing the two separate beds to move together.

Private cars were highly visible instruments displaying not only wealth but also power of a very special kind, for it assumed that the owner was a member of America's equivalent of royalty, and possessed the power to control the tracks on which the coach was to run. James J. Hill of the Great Northern deliberately used the modesty of his own specials as an advertisement for the general simplicity of his life-style: for him they were a combination of inspection vehicle and symbol of power. By contrast William D. Mann, an early Pullman rival, designed the coach in which Lillie Langtry toured the West to be a temple of luxury. In Cheyenne the awe-struck local paper noted that 'the drawing room is a perfect bower, fitted up with sofas, antique chairs, an upright piano, little tables, elaborate desks and escritoires with a wealth of steel engravings and photographs scattered everywhere, which would do honour to an art gallery.' She named it 'Lalee' which, she said, was the East Indian word for flirt. It was painted Jersey Blue to match her eyes.

In 1876 Henry C. Jarrett, the manager of Booth's Theatre in New York, organised one of the most famous of the early transcontinental specials to carry his actors to San Francisco to appear in Shakespeare's *Henry V*. The excursion was suitably theatrical – as the train passed Reno Mr Jarrett prepared a mass of Roman candles and set them off. Flames rolled out of the smokestack, an immense red fire blazed on the tender and hundreds of fire balls belched out of the Roman candles. The townsfolk responded with bonfires and the thunder of cannon.

Jarrett's special crossed the continent at about 40 mph, the same speed as in the journey made by Harvey Cheyne, the tycoon in Kipling's *Captain Courageous*, when he heard that the son he had thought drowned was in fact alive and well in Boston. Kipling instinctively grasped that the mere possession of a private railroad carriage was less significant than the power it symbolised, the fear created by its owner's movements. From the Pacific to Chicago Cheyne's special car, the *Constance* 'ran special'.* The journey is a bravura hymn to the power of the railroads and the men who controlled them.

As messages rippled across half a continent so did the unease:

> we want to know why-why-why? General uneasiness developed and spreading' . . . Cheyne smiled grimly at the consternation of his enemies when the telegrams were laid before him. 'They think we're on the warpath. Tell 'em we don't feel like fighting just now . . . tell 'em the truth – for once . . . let them have peace,' and in boardrooms two 'thousand miles away the representatives of sixty-three million dollars' worth of variously manipulated railroad interests breathed more freely.

Kipling's art was reflecting nature. Twenty years before Harvey Cheyne's fictional journey Judge Roy Bean flagged down the 'special' carrying the great Jay Gould as it passed Langtry, the small town where he held sway. 'As the train jarred to a halt several men on each side of the train poked out their heads and sawed-off shotguns'[4]. After an initial moment of tension the two got on famously. When Gould's train finally left the telegraphist received an agitated message querying why it had been delayed. 'Reported New York Gould killed in wreck. Stock Exchange

---

* From Chicago eastwards not even the most special train could compete with the Twentieth Century Limited. But only a tycoon of Cheyne's eminence could hitch his private car to such a train.

280

wild. Trains piled up all over division. Answer quick.' To which the telegraphist replied: 'Jay Gould been visiting friend Judge Roy Bean and me. Been eating ladyfingers* and drinking champagne. Special just left.' Not even Kipling's imagination stretched that far.

Magnates often made more leisurely tours, like emperors touring their kingdoms to assert their authority. They did not hurry – typically Charles Eliot Perkins of the Burlington averaged a mere 216 miles a day on a tour he took with six companions in May 1892. We forget the continuing precariousness of life in the West.

'The party – with frank fascination – skirted the edge of a murderous war between cattlemen and rustlers; visited Hot Springs when the water was 95 degrees and there was snow on the ground outside; inspected a coal mine; made an excursion to the Garden of the Gods (with a stop at the Broadmoor's casino on the way back) and finally survived a long detour on the return trip to Burlington because of badly-flooded track.' (An account of the journey appeared in *Railroad History*, 1978).

Pullman's restaurant cars only served a minority of hungry travellers. Before their introduction passengers dined at stations and two contradictory traditions of railway catering had developed: in Britain, of unmitigated horrors, celebrated in innumerable jokes; by contrast in France and the United States the food at stations was often something to be celebrated.

British railway caterers have never recovered from the assaults of those two otherwise dissimilar geniuses, Charles Dickens and Isambard Kingdom Brunel, on the licensees of British refreshment rooms. The great engineer's crushing remark to a certain Mr Griffiths, who leased the station buffet at Swindon (known to railwaymen as 'Swindleum'), deserves its continuing fame: 'I assure you, Mr Player was wrong in supposing that I thought you purchased inferior coffee. I thought I said to him that I was surprised you should buy such

---

* One of the few delicacies permitted by the fragile state of the tycoon's digestion. His doctors also allowed him the milk from the cow which travelled in a special baggage car attached to the train.

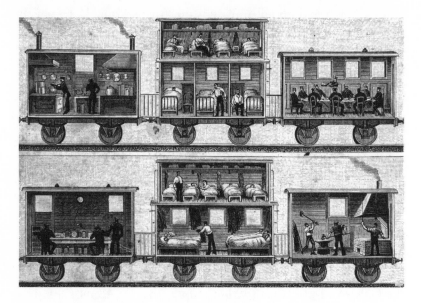

Life aboard the Trans-Caspian railway, circa 1888.

bad roasted corn. I did not believe you had such a thing as coffee in the place: I am certain that I never tasted any. I have long ceased to make complaints at Swindon – I avoid taking anything there when I can help it.'

At 'Mugby Junction'* in Dickens's story of the same name, 'There is a refreshment room,' the Lampsman tells the traveller, 'but it's a blessed circumstance for you that it's not open.' Later on the 'Boy at Mugby' describes with great glee the 'stale pastry', the 'sawdust sandwiches', the 'ha, ha, ha, – the sherry', the appalling offhandedness of the barmaids, and the magnificent, deliberate incompetence of Mrs Sniff who 'did hold the public in check most beautiful! In all my time, I never see half so many cups of tea given without milk to people as wanted it with.' Then 'the Missus' returns from a short trip to France with the appalling news of 'eatable things to eat, but also drinkable things to drink' and life at Mugby was never the same again.

In 'A Flight' Dickens had already expressed his approval of the arrangements in a French refreshment room. 'Large hall, long

* Allegedly based on Wolverton, half way between London and Birmingham.

counter, long strips of dining-table, bottles of wine, plate of meat, roast chickens, little loaves of bread, basins of soup, little caraffes of brandy, cakes and fruit.' In the United States the railways played a positive role in spreading civilised dining, most famously through the efforts of Fred Harvey (see page 297).

Elsewhere government-owned railways, in particular, were susceptible to dishonest deals – in 1893 the Minister of Railways in the Cape Government had to resign because he awarded a contract to a friend without any form of tender. Not all government-run refreshment rooms were poor, however. In Australia Mark Twain found the breakfast good, 'apart from the coffee' and most of the girls . . . 'would attract attention at any royal *levée* in Europe.'

Many otherwise obscure stops became famous or infamous for their dining facilities. At Voi in the middle of Kenya, weary travellers from Mombasa to Nairobi dined in a bungalow described by Charles Miller, in *Lunatic Express*, as 'the Howard Johnson's of East Africa and looked every bit the oasis with its wine stewards, white-jacketed waiters and barmen'. The main course, which 'almost invariably consisted of iron boiled beef, rubber mashed potatoes and something that the menu called cabbage', the whole 'garnished with insects', was consumed in a garlic-sodden atmosphere.

But primitive lines did not necessarily involve poor eating. On the Trans-Caspian line that most pernickety of travellers, George Curzon, thoroughly approved of 'first-rate tea at id a glass' and equally cheap fresh grapes and melons. Sometimes it was the restaurant stops' associations, rather than the food, which mattered. Trains from Wellington to Auckland always stopped half way at Kaitape, so that travellers could eat,* and this one-horse junction is fondly remembered by many New Zealanders as an integral part of holiday weekends.

In Japan each station prided itself on its own special lunch-boxes. A lady living at the otherwise obscure station of Yokokawa invented 'Kamameshi', a combination of rice packed with boiled

---

* The narrow-gauge New Zealand railways have never had room for dining cars.

prawns, mushrooms and a local sauce, gingko doy, which tasted just as good hot, tepid or cold. It remains famous, people still make special trips to buy it, there's a book about it – and even the pottery bowl in which it is packed is treasured as a souvenir.

*

'One of the peculiarities of modern travel,' wrote R. S. Surtees in *Plain or Ringlets?* 'is the great demand there is for books, a book to prevent people seeing the country being quite as essential as a bun to prevent their being hungry.' He was not joking. At a congress of French physicians held in 1880 the minutes stated that 'practically everybody passes the time reading while travelling on the train. This is so common that one rarely sees members of a certain social class embark on a railway journey without first purchasing the means by which they can enjoy this pastime.' (Quoted by Schievelbusch).

This ubiquitous 'pastime' provided numerous entrepreneurial opportunities. In the United States the American News Distribution Company, founded in 1863, employed 'news butchers', sprightly lads who travelled on the trains selling anything and everything. Generations of aspiring young Americans were supposedly uplifted by the story of the young Thomas Edison taking a chance on ordering a thousand papers with the latest news of the Battle of Shiloh – papers which he sold at steadily increasing prices in line with demand. He had instinctively understood the way railway speed encouraged the purchase of newspapers.

In Britain national newspapers were whisked to major provincial centres within a few hours* and special journeys were marked by the delivery of papers in record times. In 1844 George Hudson, the Railway King, celebrated the completion of the line from London to the Tyne with a special 'Flying Train' carrying a copy of the day's papers 303 miles in nine hours. The Jarrett

---

* The newspaper boom was triggered by the abolition of stamp duty, not by the spread of the railways, however. Indeed, far from bringing greater centralisation, the two forces heralded the great age of the British provincial press.

special enabled Fort Wayne, Indiana, to receive the same day's *New York Herald* a mere eighteen hours after it had left the presses.

Special editions recording important news were also hustled across country – in February, 1848, news of a major speech by the Chancellor of the Exchequer reached Glasgow (a distance of 472 miles) in less than 10½ hours, and a year later the Paris Bourse received its copy of *The Times* 6½ hours after it had left London.

The railways merely helped newspapers, but they created a totally new market for books, mostly sold at bookstalls on the stations themselves. Originally these were mere trays or stands, manned by crippled railwaymen or their widows, and purveyed slush and tosh. But soon a number of publishers tried to improve the public's taste. As a result novels, usually by famous names like Dickens and Trollope, either in their entirety, or as part works, became staple fare and the demand from railway readers clearly had a considerable impact on the form and content of 19th century fiction. They increased the demand for novels and even more so for short stories, and not only in Britain: most of Kipling's earliest stories appeared in a magazine devoted to railway reading in India.

Routledge launched a Railway Library with novels by well-known authors like Nathaniel Hawthorne and Fenimore Cooper, while John Murray advertised his 'Literature for the rail – works of sound information and innocent amusement.' Most obeyed Paul Theroux's injunction in *The Old Patagonian Express*: 'For railway reading, the best book is the plottiest, a way of endowing the haphazardness of the journey with order.' The biggest single influence on railway reading in Britain was W. H. Smith II. He did not become a publisher, though he encouraged the publication of the cheap reprints which came to be known as 'yellowbacks'. He bought the reprint rights for novels by a number of popular authors and went into partnership with Chapman and Hall, the publishers, to produce the Select Library of Fiction.

But railway reading was not confined to fiction. The great Lord Macaulay encouraged Longman's to introduce a cheap and popular series called the Travellers Library, which included a range of improving literature, while a lesser-known publisher, Wheales, did a good trade selling its practical scientific works to 'the mechanics, engine-drivers and other employed upon the line.'[5]

W. H. Smith I had become a major newspaper wholesaler. His son negotiated special terms with the major lines as soon as they were built, but went further by acquiring the bookstall concessions at the majority of Britain's main line stations. He had not held the first concession, a stall which opened at Fenchurch Street Station in London in 1841, but, in conjunction with a friend and neighbour, the redoubtable Captain Mark Huish of the London & North Western, he cleared the previous vendors and their trays of dubious reading from major stations. Smith's efforts, and the respectability of the literature he sold, reflected and then became a symbol of the growing prudishness of the British middle classes.

On a visit to London to see the Great Exhibition the French publisher Louis Hachette observed Smith's success and pointed out to the French railway companies that in Britain[6] bad books are sold by their thousands in stations 'to relieve the monotony . . . the boredom . . . the impatience' of the journey. He proposed a partnership in which he would publish the books and run the bookstalls and the railway companies would find work for railway widows. Within two years Hachette had created his Bibliothèque des Chemins de Fer, an ambitious venture including travel guides, texts on agriculture and industry, illustrated children's books (these became the celebrated *Bibliothèque Rose*) as well as ancient and modern literature from all over the world – Hachette was Dickens's publisher, for instance.

By 1854 he had opened sixty bookstalls. At first sales were slow but by the mid-1860s newspapers were outselling books and bringing in a handsome profit. Unfortunately for Hachette the concessions were put out to tender in the 1890s and he lost most of them. But by then Hachette's publishing house could take the strain, and he made up some of the losses by moving into Smith's original business, newspaper wholesaling.

Publishers and newspaper proprietors soon found a lucrative

sub-market in accounts of crimes committed on the railways. In late 1860 every paper in Paris provided its readers with a massive dose of the shivers following the murder of Chief Justice Poinsot. When a train from Mulhouse arrived in Paris he was found dead in a compartment he had shared with only one other person, his murderer. To increase passengers' concerns, travellers in the next compartment had not heard a shot, although 'they thought they had heard a shout, but only one'. Within a few weeks *Le Figaro* was proposing that, as well as carriages reserved for ladies or nonsmokers, there ought to be one 'reserved for assassins'. (Quoted by Schievelbusch).

Four years later it was the turn of the English press to lick its collective chops following a gruesome compartment murder. An official report described a panic amongst first-class passengers afraid of each other. They were also scared stiff of travelling 'singly with a stranger of the weaker sex, under the belief that it is only common prudence to avoid in this manner all risk of being accused, for purposes of extortion, or insult, or assault'.[7]

Most of the crimes were less bloodthirsty. One ingenious female fraudster was celebrated in a splendid music-hall song as the 'charming Young Widow I met on the train'. She was naturally attired in deepest black, and suitably equipped with a baby:

'When I think of my child I am well nigh distracted,
Its father, my Husband! Oh my heart breaks with pain!'
She, choking with sobs lean'd her head on my waistcoat,
Did the charming young widow I met on the train.'

Inevitably, she gets off, leaving the 'baby' with the dupe, who soon discovers that it is a dummy and that his watch, purse and valuables have all been removed. But the long-term best-sellers were accounts of Great Train Robberies. The first was in 1855, when a substantial quantity of gold bullion was stolen from a train between London and Folkestone in the normally tranquil county of Kent, though systematic train robbery was largely confined to the wide open spaces of the Wild West and Siberia.

Such was popular hatred of the railroads in the American West that thousands of otherwise law-abiding folk took to their heart a whole breed of railroad desperadoes, who were mostly murderous psychopaths. They were recalled as romantic heroes in many a story, many a ballad, and the myth was later perpetuated in hundreds of films. Even in the 1970s, film-goers were expected to side with Butch Cassidy and the Sundance Kid when they were being pursued by a highly professional group hired by the great E. H. Harriman. The tone was set by the very first train robbers, the Reno brothers, defended by the inhabitants of Jackson County, Indiana against the detectives employed by Allan Pinkerton.

The tradition of popular support was maintained in the 1870s when Frank and Jesse James ranged the Mid-West for several years with apparent impunity. Stewart Holbrook[8] explains how 'Farmers who felt they had been cheated . . . other men who had lost their savings in wild-cat railroad stocks and bonds . . . laboring men [who] felt the railroads were grinding them down were not going to help the strike-breaking "Pinkertons" to hunt them down'.

The most famous such incident was the so-called 'Battle of Mussel Slough', when five farmers and two agents were killed when trying to arrest two train robbers, Christopher Evans and John Sontag. Evans, a former warehouse manager for the Bank of California and Sontag, a former railroader crippled while a brakeman on the Southern Pacific, systematically robbed five trains. Eventually two detectives turned up at Evans's home. He lost his temper and opened fire. As a result he and Sontag became the objects of the biggest manhunt California had ever seen. Yet they holed up happily in the hills for nearly two years, living very well and 'eating at logging camps, where no questions were asked.' In the end they were caught in an ambush. Sontag was killed, but Evans managed to travel six miles with 'his clothing soaked with blood, both arms hanging by his sides, one of them mere strips of flesh and bone, and with three shots embedded in his head.' He was caught, tried and given a life sentence. His wife and daughter raised funds by appearing as themselves in a melodrama, *Evans and Sontag*. Eventually he was pardoned by an anti-railroad governor and spent his retirement writing a book envisaging a

Utopia in which prisons were genuine reformatories.

Surprisingly, 'Train robberies were perhaps as frequent in Russia as they were in America,' wrote J. N. Westwood (*A History of Russian Railways*). But the Russians did not hate their railway tycoons, so did not glorify their train robbers, who consequently remain anonymous figures compared with the anti-heroes of American folklore. This is a pity. One would like to know more about them. 'The robbers were sometimes professionals, like those who terrorized the Tashkent Railway until troops were sent to dislodge them, or amateurs like those peasants in Tula province who in 1913 had the idea of bettering their lot by loosening the rails of a local main line, causing a train to derail and fall down an embankment, where its injured passengers could be robbed at leisure.'

Trains, like ocean liners, also became notorious as the haunts of fraudsters and conmen of every description. In the United States a pack of cards became known as a 'railroad bible'. Some 300 card sharps operated the Union Pacific, including George Devol, who was supposed to have pocketed some $2 million of travellers' cash, and the lovely 'Poker Alice' Invers, a fair haired, blue-eyed wisp of a girl who retired to run a brothel in Deadwood, South Dakota.

Stations were even more crime-ridden than trains. They were favourite haunts of pickpockets, and notorious for the sort of steady, if petty pilfering associated with any major staging point, the sort which gave rise to the famous soubriquet 'Thiefrow' for London Heathrow airport. As early as 1853 the managers of the London & North Western 'were at our wits' end to find out the blackguards. Not a night passes without wine hampers, silk parcels, drapers' boxes or provisions being robbed; and if the articles are not valuable enough they leave them about the station. A roll of chintz was found on the station this morning; of course mistaken at first for silk, but on tearing the paper the plunderer discovered it to be chintz and threw it away in disgust.'[9]

Accidents were as regular a feature of rail travel as crimes. But, as with railway murders, only a select few permeated the public consciousness. The most famous of all was the very first:

Charles Dickens's accident at Staplehurst.

the death of the eminent statesman, William Huskisson, under the wheels of the engine at the opening of the Liverpool & Manchester Railway. One of the few famous nineteenth-century figures to be involved in an accident was Charles Dickens, injured in a terrible crash at Staplehurst in Kent in which ten people were killed. He recorded his impressions in a vivid letter, recalling how he 'was not in the least fluttered at the time. I instantly remembered that I had the MS of a number with me and clambered back into the carriage for it. But in writing these scanty words of recollection I feel the shakes and am obliged to stop.' He wrote nothing publicly about the accident and avoided the inquest not, as he claimed in the letter, for reasons of modesty, but because he was accompanied by a girl friend.

In 1866, the year after Dickens's accident, a number of medical reports analysed the fact that 'There is something in the crash, the shock, and the violence of a railway collision, which would seem to produce effects upon the nervous system quite beyond those of any ordinary injury.'[10] Other authors wrote about the 'emotional or hysterical state' peculiar to railway accidents, a state previously dismissed as purely physical, as 'railway spine'.

'Mechanical shock' was a direct result of the revolutionary nature of the railways as the first means of transport unrelated to nature and their effect on the human psyche as well as the human frame. It was naturally of considerable medical – and more especially psychological – importance in leading 'alienists', as psychiatrists were then called, away from purely physical explanations of human ills. It also had a demonstrable follow-on effect on legal settlements compensating those victims of accidents who, like Dickens, were physically unharmed but shaken up.

But this interest was confined to the victims themselves and to relatively narrow legal and medical circles. The public was more interested in blood.* Sometimes a major accident produced repercussions which lasted for years. One such was the famous accident on a train from Paris to Versailles in 1842. This delayed the spread of railways in France, and in Britain affected the public's attitudes to travelling on the Sabbath and the locking of individual compartments.

There was no necessary correlation between the numbers killed in an accident and its long-term fame. This often depended largely on the quality of the works – generally the ballad – it generated. In Norm Cohen's words[11] 'The big takers of human life have not been immortalized in song, as if strength of numbers conferred silent anonymity to the victims ... The wreck ballads of the 1890s and later were built upon an already traditional verse style that was used in early poems, if not songs.'

In a century which liked some of its amusements to be bloody the American public lapped up simulated accidents. In the 1890s collisions involving two locomotives were featured at almost 150 fairs in the United States. But these were sideshows: more importantly the railway freed one major form of entertainment, the circus, from previous restraints imposed by the size, speed and range of horse-drawn wagons. The older type of 'wagon show' gave way to the railway circus only as the rails connected enough cities to form an adequate touring base. By 1854 Dr

* In 1860 a book, *The Railway Accident*, was published in a series of 'Tales for the young men and women of England'.

A single train could carry a whole circus.

Gilbert Spalding, 'perhaps the most innovative circus manager of all'[12], was master-minding such revolutionary new shows as the Great Western Railroad Circus – which had none of the wagons required to stage the parade a circus traditionally used to announce its arrival in a new town.

By the mid-1860s the ingenious doctor was ordering special circus wagons, adaptable for different gauges. But even he was upstaged by William Cameron Coup, the brains behind the great showman, P. T. Barnum. It was Coup who created the modern circus, mounted on uniform platform cars, which could 'travel 100 miles a night and still have time to put up tents and seats, give a street parade and present two, even three, performances per day.' These new giant shows played only in major towns, where, in another Coup touch, circus agents working in advance arranged for special trains from outlying towns and villages on circus days.

When Coup sold out, fed up with Barnum's habit of franchising his name, he bequeathed a system which lasted until lorries took over from railway wagons, a system in which the size

292

of a circus was measured by the number of rail cars it took to transport. By 1911 there were thirty-two shows roaming the United States by rail, ranging from Ringling Bros and Barnum & Bailey, each with 84 cars, to the humble Bulgar & Cheney outfit with a mere five cars.

Railways also enabled theatrical troupes and individual artists and singers to wander fast, far and frequently, thus opening the way to the truly international star, not only on the stage but, perhaps more importantly, as prima donnas of the opera house and concert hall, very much the creatures of the railway age, complete with their own private cars.

Playwrights and stage designers could not resist the challenge involved in presenting a train, particularly one in motion. As early as 1844 the desire to exploit its dramatic possibilities led to the first 'railway play', *London by Night*, in which the heroine, peering through a convenient grating, sees a man lying across the rails whom she saves at the last minute. The cardboard train used for the play was speedily replaced, but even at the end of the century 'a bundle of steel umbrella ribs, beaten vigourously against a piece of sheet iron, still proves the best method of imitating the clattering of the wheels', wrote W. J. Lawrence in *The Railway Magazine*.

The most successful of all the sets portraying a proper, substantially-built train was originally built in London for an unsuccessful play about George Stephenson. The set was salvaged and adapted for another, successful, play, *The London Arab*, as well as for quite different plays in Paris and New York: result one set, four plays, three cities. Twenty years later they were upstaged by Hanlon Lees in his farce *La voyage en Suisse*, featuring a Pullman car with four compartments full of unlucky honey-mooners, customs men etc etc.

Cheaper and easier to present were slide shows on railway themes, which grew steadily more complicated as photography and the projection of images became increasingly elaborate and life-like. As early as 1833 the Bazaar in Portman Square in the West End of London showed the Disyntrechon, 'a mechanical-graphicoramic view of the Liverpool Railroad'. By the 1870s a former school-teacher who called himself 'Professor' Stephen James Sedgwick made a handsome living taking 'lantern shows' round the New York suburbs. His glass slides were so skilfully arranged that by the time he had finished his audience felt they really had travelled by rail to the Western Sea.

But these displays were merely a foretaste of the motion picture, an art form seemingly devised with the railways in mind. Not surprisingly the very first truly moving picture was Louis Lumière's *Arrival of a Train at a Country Station* and the first box-office hit was Edwin S. Porter's *Great Train Robbery*. Of all the railways' 'secondary' 'delayed' effects, that on motion pictures was as strong as any. Regrettably no writer seems to have tackled the way the cinema exploited the railway itself, its stations, its locomotives and trains, the landscape it ran through, not to mention the heroes, villains and comedians it transported and the dramas, the laughs and tears film-makers have wrung out of the trains and their passengers.

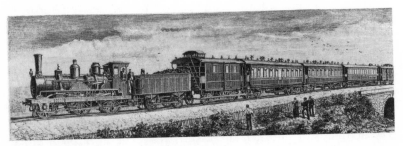

Dream train: the first Orient Express.

Expresses to the Orient

No train could compare with the Orient Express. Thanks to the novelists (Graham Greene with *Stamboul Train*, Maurice Dekobra with the world-wide best-seller, *La Madonne des Sleepings*, Agatha Christie with *Murder on the Orient Express*) and the film-makers (Alfred Hitchcock's *The Lady Vanishes*, was based on *The Wheel Spins* by Ethel Lina White, a spy story set on the train) the name still conveys an aura of glamour and international intrigue. Which was just what the train's promoters intended.

The Orient Express first ran in 1883, making its way from Paris via Vienna and Budapest to the Black Sea. Passengers reached Constantinople itself by ship, first from Varna in Bulgaria, then from Constanta in Roumania, a day's steaming from Constantinople. It was, and remained, a by-word for glamour, an element built into the train by George Nagelmackers. This young Belgian created the whole network of international sleeping-car expresses, using German-built sleeping cars running on bogies, which provided a far smoother ride than traditional coaches with fixed axles.

The first train marked 'Compagnie Internationale de WagonsLits' had reached Vienna in 1882, but its extension to Constantinople required negotiations with eight different countries. These were concluded in May 1883, and on Sunday 4th October that same year the first Exprès d'Orient left the Gare de L'Est, accompanied by the head-shaking of pessimistic wiseacres. The train held only forty people, two of whom provided an eagerly waiting public with full accounts of the journey which ensured its lasting fame as the epitome of glamorous travel. The well-known Parisian man of letters, Edmond About, wrote a whole book about his journey. But *The Times*' special correspondent, the extraordinary Henri Stefan Opper de Blowitz, 'The Prince of Journalists', transformed the journey into a major international news event when he secured interviews with the King of Roumania and, for the first time, with the Sultan of Turkey, Abdul Hamid.

The train immediately became news, although for a long time it remained basically a daily service from Paris to Vienna, running into the deep, sinister Balkans only twice a week. But it was this venture into the unknown which gave the train much of its glamour. 'Once off the great international route, but whilst still within a few days from London, he might just as well be in the heart of some unexplored continent. Many parts of the Balkan Peninsula are stranger to the ordinary Englishman than are the wilds of Central Africa,' wrote H. Charles Wood (in the

Geographical Journal, 1916). The dangers were real enough. In 1891 the train had been held up sixty miles from Constantinople by a gang headed by one Anasthatos, a bearded German-speaking giant, creating an international incident, with the Kaiser threatening to send troops.

The train's limited capacity endowed it with the same sort of clubby atmosphere found today on Concorde, and for the same reason – the passengers were interested above all in money, and, more especially, in international loans. The Orient Express was the quickest route to Constantinople, destination of all the world's shadiest financiers because of the Sultan's unquenchable thirst for funds.

Unlike Concorde, however, the Orient Express was a hot-bed of sex, mostly of the simple, straightforward paid-for variety. The conductors would telegraph their customers' requirements to the next stop where the girls would board the train. One bishop, known to the train's staff as the Archimandrite Cyril, travelled on the Orient Express between Sofia and Belgrade for purely sexual purposes for several years, free from the prying eyes of his co-religionists. One romantic exception was the encounter of Basil Zaharoff, most sinister of arms-dealers, with a lovely lady, the Duchess Maria, distraught at the attacks of her homicidal husband, the Duke of Marchena. By the time the train reached Vienna Zaharoff, the ultimate cynic, had fallen firmly in love with her and she remained the only love of his life.

After World War I the Orient Express itself was only one of a number of luxury expresses which headed through Europe to Constantinople. The most glamorous was probably the Simplon Orient from Paris through Northern Italy to Belgrade and Sofia; but after 1945 all these trains decayed until they ended up transporting mainly impecunious students until they were discontinued in the 1960s and 1970s.

Fred Harvey – The Man and the Movie

In 1875 Fred Harvey, a former freight agent, persuaded the Santa Fe railroad to let him manage a small restaurant in Topeka. He called it Harvey House, a name which became famous for civilised eating throughout the whole sprawling Santa Fe system from Topeka to Los Angeles. From the beginning Harvey determined to maintain only the highest standards of food, drink and delicacy of presentation, and his first step was to hire a chef from the Palmer House in Chicago, supposedly America's finest hotel.

Harvey's brilliance showed itself, not only in the food, but in the meticulous preparation which enabled travellers to feel they had plenty of time in which to eat, since their orders had been telegraphed through in advance. He even ensured that menus were rotated so that travellers could not complain of monotony – although he imposed standard menus, ignoring the local delicacies which had previously brightened buffet menus.

Harvey encouraged local arts and crafts, and his restaurants were carefully designed in accordance with local tradition. The formula was carried through to a number of resort hotels which were famous in their time; alas, only one – at El Tovar on the rim of the Grand Canyon – still remains. In its day the most famous was at Montezuma Hot Springs six miles from Las Vegas, New Mexico, renowned for the fact that none of the food served there was canned. Harvey even had a contract with an Indian tribe on the Gulf of California to supply green turtles for transformation into soup for his restaurants.

Harvey was immortalised by the Harvey Girls, the highly respectable and presentable waitresses he employed, most of whom stayed only a few months before marrying, generally very well. The label became so desirable that a great many girls got jobs by pretending to have been Harvey Girls. A generation later they, and he, were accorded the greatest of accolades, a musical named *The Harvey Girls*, starring Judy Garland – with a song which remains a show-stopper, 'The Atchison Topeka and the Santa Fe'.

The Reluctant Emigrant

In 1879 the poet and novelist Robert Louis Stevenson, looking for experiences to provide raw material for his books, travelled by emigrant train across the United States and recorded his experiences in *The Amateur Emigrant*. Even in that democratic country immigrants were treated as inferior citizens, travelling in separate trains, eating and sleeping apart. At the stations they huddled in separate waiting rooms, labelled 'second-class'. Such separate facilities were not confined to the United States. The Paragon Station in Hull, the port of entry for Eastern European immigrants travelling through Britain to Liverpool and the United States, had a separate waiting room especially for them. The photograph I saw is dated 1887, the year my paternal grandfather entered Britain through Hull. He intended to emigrate to the United States, but in Liverpool his ticket was stolen and he was forced to settle in Britain.

Once R.L.S.'s inferior status had been established he found he

was to be branded once more and put apart with my fellows. It was about two in the afternoon of Friday that I found myself in front of Emigrant House, with more than a hundred others, to be sorted and boxed for the journey. A white-haired official, with a stick under one arm and a list in the other hand, stood apart in front of us and called name after name in the tone of a command. At each name you would see a family gather up its brats and bundles and run for the hindmost of the three cars that stood awaiting us, and I soon concluded that this was to be set apart for the women and children. The second, or central car, it turned out, was devoted to men travelling alone, and the third to the Chinese.

The conditions were spartan. The emigrants' railroad cars were 'only remarkable for their extreme plainness, nothing but wood entering into any part of their constitution'. And the train was slow. 'Haste is not the foible of an emigrant train. It gets through on sufferance, running the gauntlet among its more considerable brethren; should there be a block, it is unhesitatingly sacrificed; and they cannot, in consequence, predict the length of the passage within a day or so.' The trip was a trial, the nights worse than the days. Stepping over the ranks of groaning, snoring, restless bodies 'gave me a measure of the worthlessness of rest in that unresting vehicle . . . they that long for morning have never longed for it more earnestly than I.'

Most of R.L.S.'s fellow-travellers were not travelling directly from Europe, but moving from the East to try their luck in the West. He found them 'mostly lumpish fellows, silent and noisy, a common combination; somewhat sad I should say, with an extraordinary poor taste in humour and little interest in their fellow-creatures beyond that of a cheap and merely external curiosity.' But the last days' travel over the high Sierras made up for the weariness. 'All the passengers on board threw off their sense of dirt and heat and weariness, and bawled like schoolboys, and thronged with shiny eyes upon the platform, and became new creatures within and without . . . At every turn we could see further into the land and our own happy futures . . . this was the "good country" we had been going to so long.'

Paradise was awaiting them when 'the city of San Francisco, and the bay of gold and corn, were lit from end to end with summer daylight'.

2
The Habits the Railways Changed

The railways may not have transformed society, but they did change a lot of habits, broaden people's horizons in a dozen different ways, and impose their own 'industrial' discipline by standardising time itself. Before the coming of the railways, time had been an indefinite concept related to the movements of the sun. Towns even a few miles apart kept different times. The railways' need for regularity inevitably led to something of a revolution.

According to Michael Robbins in *The Railway Age*, early time-sheets have footnotes converting Greenwich time to local times; and the general adoption of a standard 'railway time', even in Britain, had to wait until 1852, when the railways' partner, the Whetstone telegraph, had spread throughout the country. Nevertheless a handful of towns retained their own time until Greenwich Mean Time was officially adopted in 1880. Even then a few older habits persisted. For another half a century a specially-regulated watch was sent daily from Euston to Holyhead to time the departure of the mail boat to Ireland, and the clock at Christ Church, Oxford, remained on local time for over a century.

It never occurred to the British that other people might have different ideas about the time. On a journey to Paris Charles Dickens found that one of his fellow-travellers was 'a compatriot in an obsolete cravat, who thinks it a quite unaccountable thing that they don't keep "London Time" on a French railway, and who is made angry by my modestly suggesting the possibility of Paris time being more in their way.'

Dickens's journey, in 1851, could be checked by that new-fangled idea, the railway timetable. In 1839 William Bradshaw had published his first timetable covering all the passenger services in Britain. Eight years later he provided a similar volume for the railways on the continent of Europe. After he died of cholera in Norway in 1853, his name lived on as a symbol of reliability and devilish complication.

Standardisation was a slow process. Miller's *Wintering on the Riviera*, published in 1879, complains that 'in Menton no two clocks were alike. By common consent they all differed. On going south to Avignon, the time is nearly a quarter of an hour in advance of Paris time; at Menton it is twenty minutes.' Not surprisingly 'one of the first inquiries on first reaching a hotel is, "What is the time of your town?" and to note the difference between that and railway time.' Fortunately 'the complex and extraordinary mode of measuring time formerly in use in Italy, by counting twenty-four hours from the varying time of vespers, seems to be now wholly abandoned.'

The Americans learnt from others' errors. Although their continent could not be linked in a single time zone, the railroads performed a major act of unification, or, rather, had it thrust upon them. Until the adoption of Standard Time on 18th November, 1883, Americans ran their lives by 'sun time' which varied by about one minute for every thirteen miles.

The first suggestion for a system of time zones came from an unlikely source, Professor C. F. Dowd, principal of the Temple Grove Seminary for Young Ladies at Saratoga Springs. He had found that the clocks in the station at Buffalo showed three separate times. Further investigation revealed a total of eight thousand in the country as a whole, a total he proposed to reduce to four time zones. Although he was only an amateur he developed the necessary intellectual framework including time zones and linkage to the Greenwich meridian. His ideas were ignored by the railroads, since he was presenting the passengers' viewpoint, not that of the operators. In standardising their times – an eleven-year process – the railroads developed their own trade organisation. A 'Time-Table convention' met in 1872 to arrange passenger train schedules. The convention changed its name several times as its role broadened, until it became the still-flourishing Association of American Railroads.

Under the guidance of William F. Allen, editor of the *Railroad Guide* and the Association's founding secretary, the railroads adopted the General Time Convention on 11th October, 1883. It came into force a mere five weeks later, on 18th November – a

301

Sunday because there was less traffic. The 'day of two noons' passed off quietly, though some towns on the boundary between zones, like Pittsburgh, found it difficult to decide what time they should adopt; and one town, Bangor, Maine resolutely refused to accept the power of the railroads to dictate people's lives, declaring that no one had the power 'to change one of the immutable laws of God'. Moreover, the council had touched a raw nerve: the railroads had acted quite independently of the federal government, and as a result Congress only ratified their decision in March, 1918.

'Railway time' remained a symbol of national unity: in Russia all the clocks on the immense journey across Siberia remained on Saint Petersburg time; and the British imposed standard – railway – time in South Africa after the Boer War. Nevertheless pockets of anarchy remained. In 1900, the *Railway Magazine* reported from Portugal that 'town time', especially in the country's second city, Oporto, remained between eight and twelve minutes ahead of railway time, which was supposedly derived from the Lisbon Observatory.

*

The railways may have imposed their own time, but they could not guarantee that countries would take the opportunity they offered to organise their food supplies more rationally. Famine relief was a leit-motif in discussing railway-building in China or India, where bullocks consumed more food than they transported in the carts they pulled. By 1880 the British in India had found that railways had their limitations, most obviously that railheads in such a vast country were often far from the seat of the famine. Nevertheless railways could bring dramatic relief. In China an estimated thirteen million people died from starvation in the great northern drought of the 1870s, against a 'mere' half million in a comparable drought in 1920–21, after the construction of a railway through the affected regions.

Railways were needed to prevent famines even in apparently well-provided countries, including France. As late as 1846–47 there had been desperate food shortages in much of rural France, with their usual accompaniment of profiteering. In Roger Price's words,* 'The existence of the railway helped to establish a climate of confidence, so that a poor harvest no longer resulted in a panic rush to buy up foodstuffs ... after 1856 there were no more cases of wheat prices doubling at times of shortage, and after 1867 no more increases of 50 per cent or more.' In the process the previous substantial regional differences were ironed out. In the early 19th century wheat cost four times as much on the Côte d'Azur as it did round Paris: by the 1860s the difference was merely the few francs required to transport the wheat across the country by rail. The same theme is found in Germany and Eastern Europe. Even before the arrival of cheap American grain, agrarian societies used railways to balance the local shortages, which were far more common than any general threat of famine.

Even where famine was not a threat, railways served to regulate the price of basic foods. In the 1830s Bostonians had advocated the construction of railways westwards to provide cheap food for the workers, and after the Western Railroad was completed in 1841 it became known as the 'regulator to the bread market of Boston', wrote R. O. Cummings in *The American and his Food*. The effect could be even more fundamental. It was the railways which transformed the whole of Japan into a rice-eating country. Previously the potato had been the staple food in quite a number of rural areas.

Railways altered the balance between foods available at a price, and those affordable by the mass of the population. In Zurich, Switzerland's first railway became known as the *Brötlibahn* because it brought delicious bread rolls from Baden in time for the breakfast tables of most of Zurich's population. By contrast the boxes of Japanese tea whisked across the United States in the first transcontinental freight train were destined exclusively for the better-off.

Railways provided the mass of urban populations with supplies of healthy milk for the first time. Before the construction of the first stage of the Erie Railroad in 1842–43 New Yorkers

* *The Modernisation of Rural France.*

drank almost exclusively thin, sour skimmed milk, usually of dubious cleanliness. By 1849 the Erie was delivering nine million quarts of milk to the city, and in the post-Erie decade average consumption had multiplied several times.

Even before the railways London was self-sufficient in milk. Somehow the Metropolis supported enough cows to provide milk – of a sort. In 1852 *Punch* said that a clean glass of milk would be one of the seven wonders of London, and asked if the capital would have to wait for it until 1922 – the next year when there would be a February with five Saturdays in it.

In the event Londoners had to wait less than fifteen years. In 1865 a major outbreak of cattle plague led to a court order to destroy all the cattle in London. 'Within a week there was not a cow left legally alive within the boundaries of London and the inner home counties. And the capital faced a milk famine', according to Bryan Morgan in *Express Journey*. An enterprising dairyman, George Barham, took the opportunity to bring in supplies of milk by rail from round London, emphasising its freshness by calling his company – which still supplies London with much of its milk – Express Dairies.

Barham had greatly expanded the radius from which London drew its supplies – the Great Western's lines from Berkshire and Wiltshire became known in time as the 'Milky Way'. Paris's 'zone of provisioning' for every type of fresh foodstuff expanded five-fold to over 150 miles in the quarter of a century after 1830. In Russia the distances were even more spectacular. By 1911 half the meat eaten in Moscow and Saint Petersburg came from Siberia.

The most obvious 'railway foods' were naturally perishable items like fresh fish. 'Those who came from Boston,' declared Daniel Webster at the opening of the Northern Railroad in 1847, might have brought along 'fish taken out of the sea at sunrise'. He was being rhetorical, but speaking truer than perhaps he realised. Oysters were probably the first new delight to be introduced to the tables of both New Yorkers and Parisians by the railways, and there was great excitement in Chicago in 1842 at the arrival of the first lobster. Twenty years later the

Chicagoans were eating fish from Boston as a matter of routine. The benefits were universal. Live fish was brought from Scandinavia to Germany, and one of the first cargoes carried by Japanese railways was live carp for gourmets in Tokyo. Forty years earlier, in 1848, Londoners were already eating over 70 tons of fresh fish a week brought by rail from Yarmouth and Lowestoft, thus reducing their previous dependence on smoked or dried fish.

Londoners' fish came courtesy of the Eastern Counties Railway and it was not unusual, especially in the United States, for the increased supply of a particular commodity to be associated with an individual railway. The Erie not only improved the New Yorkers' supply of milk. It was also responsible for ensuring that more strawberries were consumed in New York than in any other city in the world. Previously New Yorkers had to pay twelve times the price paid by the inhabitants of Baltimore, who were much nearer the strawberry fields. Another railroad, the Camden & Amboy, became known as the 'Pea Line' after the vegetables it brought from New Jersey, although it could just as well have been called the 'Peach Line' after another major speciality.

Urban catchment areas could be enormous. By 1852 Chicagoans were able to buy fresh green peas brought by express freight from New Orleans, a thousand miles away. The opening of the transcontinental railroad provided another surge: not just Japanese tea but, in much greater quantities, deciduous fruit, apples and pears from California.

Railways not only broadened urban menus: they also lengthened the season for previously short-lived delicacies. New Yorkers could enjoy strawberries for four months because the railroads enabled them to bring in supplies from such a wide area, while tomatoes became available the whole year round. By the late 1860s the Parisians could indulge in one of their favourite snobberies, the consumption of expensive *primeurs*, early fruit and vegetables brought from far and wide for the delectation of jaded metropolitan palates, sometimes more interested in the earliness than the taste. The fruits came from all over France: tomatoes grown at Perpignan, near the Spanish border, grapes from the south, and other specialities from every corner of 'l'Hexagone'.

Transporting such perishables demanded increasing quantities of ice (see Chapter V). By the 1850s fresh strawberries from Southern Illinois were being transported in refrigerated cars to Chicago, and even stored through the year. The first refrigerated beef was shipped from Chicago in 1857, and within a couple of decades the railroads had perfected proper mobile refrigerated cars in time for the first oranges to be shipped from Florida in 1886. Florida's great rival, California, followed a year later.

By then the world market for meat and for tropical fruits, especially bananas, had been revolutionised by the development of refrigerated ships, but these would have been useless without proper railway links at both ends – across the pampas of Argentina and the jungles of central America, and into the heart of the consuming countries.

Most of these foods were destined for a mass public. In times of relative economic progress and constantly increasing competition among railways, there was a considerable 'trickle-down' effect, above all in the biggest cities, where the diet of the poor had been appallingly narrow. Everywhere railways introduced fresh produce from far and wide onto urban menus for the first time. The majority of the population in the United States and Western Europe seem to have benefited from the increased availability of fresh meat – average consumption in Germany doubled between the 1830s and the 1870s, and rose another thirty per cent in the 1880s and 1890s.

In France the choice widened in the fifty years after the late 1830s. Bread consumption rose by only a fifth, while that of potatoes and root vegetables rose by a half, meat by over three quarters, fruit and fresh vegetables doubled and the consumption of sugar quadrupled. Thanks to reduced prices bread accounted for only two fifths of the total cost of food – itself relatively stable as a proportion of average wages – against nearly three fifths before the arrival of the railways. By the end of the century protein in the form of meat, eggs and fish, formed nearly a third of the average Frenchman's food intake, against a mere fifth fifty years earlier.[13]

In Paris these trends could be seen in extreme form. By the end of the century Parisian consumption of such basic commodities as wine and wheat was static and expenditure was increasingly concentrated on relatively optional 'secondary' foods, like meat and vegetables, fruit and fish. By the end of the century, even the poor of Paris could afford butter and apples from Normandy, oranges from the South of France, and vegetables from all over France. By then the French were eating far more meat than ever before, half a century after the American working classes had been able to increase their consumption of railway-hauled meat.

The diet of even poor New Yorkers in the 1860s included tomatoes, string beans and turnip greens in addition to the potatoes which had been the only vegetable they could afford as late as 1851. Urban workers often spent more on food once a better variety became available, a little-mentioned factor in the relative fall in alcoholism in the late nineteenth century – although precisely the opposite happened in France, because wine was one of the agricultural products whose production and consumption was most increased by the spread of the railways.

Even in France the flow was not confined to the capital. Inland provinces learnt to savour for the first time the joys of eating fish, and such previously exotic products as coffee. Everywhere rustics ceased to be entirely self-sufficient, preferring to buy basic foods like bread rather than bake their own, to the chagrin of self-appointed custodians of rural values but to the great relief of overburdened rural housewives.

*

The food the railways carried was not only physical. It was also spiritual, enabling pilgrims to travel far more easily. But there were natural hesitations before God-fearing folk were prepared to use such an obviously secular phenomenon. The Russian bishops, for instance, were afraid that 'pilgrims would come to the monastery [Sergiev Posad (now Zagorsk), site of the sacred Troitsk monastery] in railway cars, in which all sorts of tales can be heard, and often dirty stories, whereas now they come on foot and each step is a feat pleasing to God'. Despite this reluctance the Metropolitan himself opened the line from Moscow to the holy spot, and by the time the Trans-Siberian was opened, the church was happy to commission a splendid 'church car' to minister to the congregations en route.[14]

The pattern was repeated with different religions throughout the world. The first railway in what was then called Persia was a narrow-gauge line which ran six miles from Tehran to a shrine in the village of Shah Abdul Azim. In Japan at least two railways served important shrines, at Ise and a special line from Oji to the temples at Nara. By the 1890s there was a convenient stop for pilgrims to pay their homage to Mount Fuji.

Some of the promoters of the first railways in India had hoped to spread Christianity, others were afraid that pilgrims would not use them to travel to their sacred shrines. According to Herbert Spencer, Robert Stephenson referred the matter 'to the Dhurma Subha of Calcutta, the great sanhedrin of orthodox Hindoos, who, after consulting the sacred texts and the learned pundits, delivered it as their opinion that the devotee might ride in a railway carriage to the various shrines without diminishing the merit of the pilgrimage.' The result was an amazing growth in pilgrimages, to the mutual advantage of the 'Hindoos' and the railway companies. (*Quarterly Review*, 1868).

Railways could also be used for secular worhsip. As late as 1968 the pious Chinese built a railway sixty miles from Hangsha, the capital of Hunan province, to Shao-sha, the birthplace of Mao-Tse-Tung. Over the next decade, before the cult of Mao's personality waned, three million passengers took the leisurely four-hour journey every year.

Railways were obviously most suitable for mass religious movements and so concentrated attention on a small number of famous shrines, leading to the neglect of older sites. The most obvious beneficiary was Lourdes, which can truthfully be described as The Shrine the Railway Made.

Bernadette Soubirous' visions had started in the late 1850s, before the route of the line from Bayonne to Toulouse had been decided. So the town council seized with both hands the opportunity to ensure that the line passed by Lourdes.

In October 1862, the council agreed to compensate any landowners who suffered, even from the railways' surveys. In May 1863 councillors asked the railway to site its station as close as possible to the centre of town and complied with every one of the company's requests. They admitted the navvies and railway workers to the local hospital and ignored their riotous behaviour.

Their reward came in 1866 with the simultaneous opening of the grotto and the railway from Tarbes, which connected with trains to Bordeaux and far-off Paris. Between 1870 and 1878 a total of 958 pilgrimages to Bernadette's shrine brought 661,000 pilgrims to Lourdes, 100,000 of them on a single day, 3rd July, 1876, to rejoice in the newly-proclaimed doctrine of the Immaculate Conception and affirm the idea of *la France Catholique*.

At much the same time similar ideas were being spread throughout France by another railway-based religious order, the Assumptionists, who exploited the railways to assemble mass rallies, largely of the most humble of folk. The Assumptionists were a strange, and in their time highly important, sect, founded by the scion of a rich land-owning family, who acquired considerable political influence through their ability to mount mass rallies.

*

But the railway's most dramatic influence was not on Christianity, but on Islam. Throughout the 19th century increasing numbers of pilgrims had made the difficult and dangerous journey to Mecca. In September, 1900, Sultan Abdul Hamid proposed to build a railway to Mecca as a pious gesture on the twenty-fifth anniversary of his accession to the Ottoman throne. The idea was immediately greeted as an important affirmation of Muslim values.

The Sultan naturally insisted on building a purely Muslim railway. He decreed that[15], 'only Muslim workers and Muslim materials ought to be employed; timber from the vast forests of Anatolia and Macedonia; ballast from the country being crossed, rails and wagons from the Imperial workshops; engineering regiments would provide the workforce, the schools of Constantinople the engineers and the foremen.'

In the event much of the material had to be bought in Europe, together with some skilled labour, supervised by the German engineer who had built most of the railways in the Levant. The combination of ferocious piety, the Sultan's will-power and German organising ability ensured that this railway, nearly a thousand miles in length, was built within eight years.

Meissner Pasha, the German chief engineer, was simply given the two terminals, Damascus and Mecca, and told to connect them by rail as best he could. He was a genius. He had to handle a huge construction force composed of a dozen nationalities. The line was built across some of the bleakest, hottest, most implacable terrain in the world, without natural resources of any kind. His worst problem was with the Bedouin, furious at being deprived of the pilgrims who had been their prey, ruffians eventually hunted down by an implacably efficient Turkish general, Kaisim Pasha.

Meissner was not allowed to complete his work. Neither he, nor any other infidel, was allowed to venture beyond Medina Saleh, the 587th mile-post on the line. Fortunately he had trained up a highly-accomplished Turkish engineer, Muktar Bey, who brought the line into Medina in August, 1908. But then the Bedouin took their revenge, wiping out a whole construction camp, and thus scotching any idea of building the railway the final 300 miles to Mecca itself. Unfortunately the line ran for a mere eight years until T. E. Lawrence blew it up. Since then it has lain abandoned, the break-up of the Ottoman Empire signalling the end of any hope of cooperation between the peoples along the lines.

In Anglo-Saxon countries deep religious faith produced, not railways, but strong hostility to the very idea of running them on the Sabbath, as a serious challenge to the fundamental Sabbatarianism which was as much a feature of the age as the railways themselves. The famous Versailles accident of 1842 was naturally

Versailles, 1842: 52 people perished in the worst rail disaster in the world at the time.

exploited by the Sabbatarians as an awful lesson meted out to the Godless foreign travellers who had dared desecrate the day. After an equally appalling accident in Clayton tunnel just outside Brighton twenty years later[16] 'plenty of people rushed about proclaiming the accidents as a judgment of God.' In between times the railways' Sunday excursions were denounced as 'trips to Hell at 7s 6d.'

But it was not the excursionists (who included such devout souls as Thomas Cook) who forced the railway companies to break the Sabbath. According to Michael Robbins in *The Railway Age* it was the absolute need for mail trains to run on a Sunday which broke the resistance of the Sabbatarians in both Scotland and Wales. They were never as powerful as was made out, and most clerics probably reacted like Dr Grantley in Trollope's *Barchester Towers*: 'If you can withdraw all the passengers the company I dare say will withdraw the trains. It is merely a question of dividends.'

Nevertheless the argument rumbled on. In 1883 the inhabitants of a small Highland village managed to prevent a load of fish from leaving on the Sabbath and were greeted as heroes when they returned from serving the jail sentence to which they were sentenced. Six years later 'the anti-Sunday Travel Union' had 58 branches with some 8,000 adherents. Partly owing to its activities, trains on suburban lines normally ceased running on Sundays during the hours of Divine service.

Similar battles were fought in the United States. In Galesburg, the railroad was the blunt instrument which broke the power of the Sabbatarians. The first Sunday train was boarded by the impressive figure of President Blanchard of Knox College, who was told to go to Hell when he ordered the engineer to take the engine back to the roundhouse. And that, wrote Ernest Elmo Calkins,[17] was the end of the power of 'the little group of pious men who had founded Galesburg to be a Christian town after their own ideal'.

In South Africa the Reverend Van Lingen managed to prevent any Sunday trains from desecrating the Sabbath at the settlement of Paarl. After denouncing the railway from the pulpit he founded a Sunday stage coach service for passengers from Cape Town which successfully kept the railway at bay for half a century.

There was, and remains, a strong counter-current, a positive railway-worship among clergymen of the Church of England. Bishop Eric Treacy and Canon Roger Lloyd were famous railway writers; Canon Reginald Fellows wrote a history of Bradshaw, founding father of railway timetables (which Archbishop William Temple was reputed to know by heart); and more recently the Reverend Wilbert Awdry made a fortune by recounting the adventures of Thomas the Tank Engine and his friends.

3

The Leisure the Railways Stretched

Railways could not create leisure time. Deeper social forces gradually reduced the working day and the working week, thus creating the 'English weekend' and giving many workers Saturday afternoon off. Longer holidays for the mass of the working class depended on legislation, like the 1871 Bank Holidays Act in Britain and the work of the Popular Front in France in the 1930s.

However, railways could enable everyone to take far fuller advantage of such leisure time as they had. Indeed, the mere idea of 'leisure' was new. In J. A. R. Pimlott's words in *The Englishman's Holiday*, 'The idea that a holiday was a waste of time meant by God or natural law to be devoted to the increase of wealth died hard; but, as *The Times* said in 1871, with reference to the Bank Holiday Act, there has been "an increasing tendency of late years among all classes to find excuses for Holy Days".'

Railways provided a means of escape at a time when towns were expanding at an unprecedented rate. At first the novelty of rail travel was enough; the destination mattered less than the mere fact of travel. But soon the railways became bolder, went further, created and defined mass tourism: the workers enjoyed their Sunday excursions, the middle classes longer holidays at far-flung seaside resorts, or in the hills, or, in the case of the British, abroad as well. They spread such tastes downward: a mass of middle-class tourists could visit the Alps, or Italy, delights previously confined to a tiny upper-class minority. By the end of the century the middle-class family, in particular, cemented its solidarity through the annual seaside holiday, almost invariably by train, holidays which became increasingly child-centred.

The combination of railways and holidays is indissolubly associated with one man: Thomas Cook (see note on page 323). He enticed the British middle classes abroad; and he made it safe and respectable for women to travel by themselves to dangerous foreign parts. He was helped by 'his almost infinite capacity for taking pains, his acute sense of the needs of his clients, and the

Paddington Station, as seen by William Powell Frith.

powers of invention and the bold imagination which made him the greatest of all travel agents. But he was also an idealist: before he began to campaign for cheaper holidays he had been active in the fight for cheaper food. He was a 'natural missionary . . . the cheap bread missionary',[18] and a temperance enthusiast who edited a magazine devoted to the cause and owned a temperance hotel run by his wife.

At the same time he (and the railways) created the biggest single dilemma of modern travel: by increasing the accessibility of desirable destinations and thus the sheer numbers visiting them, they destroyed, not only the character of the places

themselves, overrun by gaping hordes, but also the effect on the sensibility of the individual visitor for whom the experience becomes just another item in an impersonal itinerary.

Despite Cook's efforts railways could not entirely democratise holidays: once the railways had popularised a resort, the upper classes simply abandoned it. Queen Victoria never went near the former royal resort of Brighton, partly because she found its inhabitants 'very indiscreet and troublesome'. Thanks to the railways, 'persons of distinction' could flee to remote, sporting regions – by 1865 the great eye-surgeon Sir William Wilde could suggest to his London patients the recreational value of a jaunt across the Irish Sea for a weekend's fishing in Connemara.

The railways provided the average worker with his first ever opportunity for travelling outside his home town. As a Board of Trade report put it, the 'benefits to the operative classes' included those 'for keeping up family ties by visits to parents and relatives . . . for moving in search of employment . . . excursions for innocent and healthy recreation on Sundays.' And an 1849 guide book rejoiced that the excursion ticket was 'a boon to those whose duties confine them during the greater part of the year to the close atmosphere of our overgrown city.'

Middle-class reformers approved of these jaunts because they removed the working classes from the temptations, and above all the drunkenness, associated with the traditional urban holiday entertainments, the fairs and the race meetings – although in the event the railways merely transferred the rowdiness to the seaside.

Excursion trains originated, not in London, but in the industrial areas of the north, where communal organisations were strong – even the manufacturers themselves organised works outings. The tickets were much cheaper, often a mere quarter of the price of ordinary trains, so excursions immediately acquired the same reputation as charter planes have today, and for the same reasons. As M. Vivian Hughes put it in *A London Child of the 'Seventies*, they meant 'all that was horrible: long and unearthly hours, packed carriages, queer company, continual shunting aside and waiting for regular trains to go by, and worst of all the contempt of decent travellers'.

The discomfort was common to all 'tourist' travel. 'On Sundays, during the holiday season, passengers sweat blood and water to acquire their tickets' warned one journalist to intending excursionists between Bordeaux and the new resort of Arcachon. On the train itself 'The coaches are packed like prison cells.' Unlucky passengers unable to find a place clung precariously to the running-boards hoping to find room inside once passengers got off at an intermediate station.

The tickets needed to be cheap.* Ordinary tickets were out of the reach of most working men and longer holidays did not necessarily imply higher pay. Indeed it was often ill-paid clerks rather than manual workers who were best able to take advantage of the days off provided by the 1871 Bank Holidays Act.

Railway outings were not confined to the seaside. London was ringed by favourite picnic spots, in woods or by the Thames, and by 1880, 'there was no sizeable riverside place that was not served by train,' wrote Jack Simmons in *Railway in Town and Country*. In South Africa the Wynberg line out of Cape Town was famous for the Sunday outings and picnickers it carried. And the railway was ideal for special occasions – in 1848, a crowd of 15,000 people travelled to Coventry to see a revival of Lady Godiva's ride through the streets.

Three years later the railways transported millions of excursionists to see the Great Exhibition in Hyde Park. This proved a magnificent tribute to the railways' universal power and influence, technical and financial, as well as in their capacity to transport millions of passengers. Henry Cole, secretary to the exhibition's commissioners, had been unable to find a financier who would provide a first guarantee for the investment required. Then he happened to meet Sir Samuel Morton Peto, the great railway promoter. Peto marched Cole into the Reform Club and signed his personal note for the first £50,000. He was followed by other contractors and the exhibition was on its triumphal way.

Technically, Mr Barlow, the 'eminent engineer' of the Midland Railway, helped Joseph Paxton with his plans for the Crystal Palace[19] in which the Exhibition was held, and 'calculated the strength of the columns and girders.' Paxton secured the support of Robert Stephenson, chance-met on a train, who admired his plans and presented them to the exhibition commissioners, a powerful recommendation for a revolutionary design. And in due course the locomotives and rolling stock were an important

---

* Though they could be useful for the wealthier, and mean, classes. During the Great Exhibition of 1862 six county families from Lancashire were caught transferring their whole households to London using excursion tickets.

part of the show. But the railways really came into their own after the exhibition actually opened by transporting most of the six million visitors it attracted. On one day alone, 16th June, twenty excursion trains arrived at Euston alone, many organised by the ubiquitous Thomas Cook.

The railway companies did more to encourage holiday traffic than merely selling cheap seats on Sunday trains which would otherwise have been half-empty. Even in the 1830s a number of railways issued tourist guides, which steadily expanded in number and coverage. In 1859 W. H. Smith published a 384-page official guide to a number of Scottish lines, the most systematic of a number of volumes devoted to British railways. And in the United States the opening of the Transcontinental railroad set off a veritable gold rush of guides. 'Bill Dadd the Scribe', author of *The Great Trans-Continental Railroad Guide*, was the best-seller; issued by Crufitt's, a publisher which claimed it had sold over half a million guidebooks during the 1870s.

In 1887 the Cambrian Railway, which already published a book called *Picturesque Wales*, broke new ground with a specialist pamphlet for tourists, *What to See and Where to Stay in Wild Wales*, an idea followed by a score of other companies. By the end of the century, the North Eastern, 'who have the exclusive run of the most romantic coast and inland scenery in the North of England' was issuing not only a 'unique Tourist Programme and a smaller illustrated pamphlet' but also 'a capital series of pocket-guides'. (S. Kirkwood, *Railway Magazine* vol. vi).

Apart from the Belgians and the Swiss – always ready to publicise the Alps – Continental railways were slow to exploit the tourist potential, but virtually every line in the United States had its own guides. The leader was the New York Central, which published a dozen or more. It almost certainly held the world record with its ambitious *Health and Pleasure on America's Greatest Railroad*, which weighed in at over 2 lb and contained 532 pages, 400 pictures and 12 maps.

It took several generations to harness artistic talent to help the sales efforts, but by the last decades of the century any newly-built railway would advertise its charms as soon as (or even before) it was built.

Railway companies created excursions deliberately. Resorts sometimes took them by surprise. The promoters of the Stockton & Darlington never imagined that the little town of Saltburn would be transformed into a seaside resort. Seventy years later the Quebec and Lake St John Railroad tried to attract settlers, but soon became best-known as the route to the Laurentian National Park, 4,000 square miles of wilderness much favoured by sportsmen canoeing and fishing in its rivers.

Resorts had originally developed from ports, but once the railway arrived the smallest seaside village could aspire to tourist-led prosperity, and the most remote fishing villages could add a 'tourist element' to their usually precarious economic base. The little villages offered peace in a picturesque setting: elsewhere attractions varied according to the social class of the visitors. Resorts like Blackpool and Southend developed exciting funfairs and seaside shows for their working-class visitors, while Eastbourne, Bournemouth and Torquay worked equally hard to preserve their reputation for exclusiveness.

The developers were a varied bunch. Sir Samuel Morton Peto exploited his dominance in East Anglia with the encouragement of Lowestoft, and he saw the tourist potential of the little North Wales town of Llandudno, although neither was a 'pure' resort. The pattern varied, however. At Folkestone and Eastbourne a great local landowner created a resort, while in other cases the crowds the railways brought dictated the pattern of development. But none of the resorts were large. By 1881 only Brighton had more than 100,000 inhabitants.[20] The next biggest pure resort was Hastings with 42,000 and only a handful of others had more than 20,000 permanent residents. And, like Brighton, largely a resort for Londoners, most of the others remained regional in their appeal, especially in the North of England. So they did in the United States, with Atlantic City playing Brighton's role for New Yorkers. Both had excellent rail services. Indeed at the end of the nineteenth century, the trains between New York and Atlantic City were the fastest regular services in the world.

Across the sea: from Miami to Key West.

select, health resort. In the words of a certain Dr Bennett, before
the railway Menton was 'a quiet little Italian town on the sunny
shore of the Riviera with two or three small hotels, principally
used by passing travellers, and half a dozen recently-erected
villas.'[21] Fourteen years later it had become 'a well-known and
frequented winter resort, with thirty hotels, four times the number
of villas, and a mixed foreign population of about sixteen hundred'
– as at Nice, invalid foreigners would settle for the winter.

The rise of Monte Carlo was even more spectacular. In 1861
Prince Charles III of Monaco had signed a treaty with the French
government which provided him with more independence than
funds. The railway, in Howarth's words, was destined to be
'almost literally his lifeline'. The Prince had already tried to
exploit his freedom from the ban on casinos on French soil, but
the first concessionaires were forced to abandon their franchises
for lack of customers. In 1863, however, a far-sighted operator
called François Blanc acquired the concession, confident that the
railway would reach Monte Carlo within a few years. He was

duly rewarded. Between 1868 and 1914 Monte Carlo was synonymous with high-stakes gambling. In the February following the railway's arrival 'the Prince announced that rates and taxes in the Principality had been abolished . . . in 1868 there were two hotels in the Principality; thirty years later there were forty-eight. In 1878 there were three jewellers; twenty years later there were fifteen.'[22]

In the United States one man, Henry Flagler (see note on page 290), did more than Blanc and the Prince of Monaco combined. He built railways which opened up a whole string of resorts along the east coast of Florida, from Georgia south through what became Miami to the island chain ending at Key West. Not all resorts were at the seaside. In hot climates (including many parts of the United States) they were in the hills. The most famous, like Poona and Simla, had existed before the trains somehow managed to climb the heights to bring even more sahibs escaping from the torrid Indian plains. Other resorts were simply watering-places. A dozen or more, like Baden-Baden and Marienbad, became the summer retreats of an international 'railway set' which gossiped, took the waters, and discussed the fate of nations. At Saratoga Springs, the American equivalent, they discussed money rather than politics. This resort, up the Hudson from New York, was already such a favourite that the railway arrived as early as 1833, replacing the tiresome journey up river and then by stage-coach. By the mid-century most of Wall Street's finest could be observed on the long verandah of the Grand Union Hotel.

Railways not only broadened the geographical range of holidays, they also widened the sports played on them. Yet, ironically, the sport initially most fundamentally affected by the railways was that most traditional of English pastimes, fox-hunting. It was already being professionalised, with 'subscription packs' taking over from older, more casual arrangements, but railways completed the revolution. 'Railways have made sportsmen very ubiquitous,' wrote Surtees in *Mr Facey Romford's Hounds*: an author who instantly grasped the transformation the railways were effecting. The historians agree. 'The first-class carriage and the rail horsebox with the stud groom in his miniature compartment . . . transformed hunting by extending its range both socially and geographically,' wrote Raymond Carr[23] – so far, indeed, that the Royal buckhounds once made a kill in the goods yard at Paddington.

At first fox hunters were firmly convinced that the railways would be the death of the English countryside, and thus of all country sports, especially fox hunting, which demanded large stretches of fields unencumbered by railway lines. But the ever-adaptable British aristocracy soon grasped the opportunities the railways offered to hunt with a wide variety of packs. Railways virtually created a new hunting centre in the New Forest in Hampshire, while it became quite the done thing to return from a day out in the prime hunting country of Leicestershire to vote in the House of Commons that night. (In the House Lord George Bentinck would conceal his riding habit with a 'light coloured zephyr paletot'). Later in the century blending hunting and politics became a fine art. One junior Minister, Squire Chaplin, says Raymond Carr, would 'hire a private train and draw up on the track at a point near the meet where his stud groom would have his horses waiting for him'.

In Britain the sport most affected was soccer. Obviously the very idea of a national league in any sport anywhere depended on a proper rail network. But there were closer connections. London football clubs had an incestuous relationship with railway companies anxious for special excursions on a Saturday. Similarly, eight racecourses within thirty miles of London were served by special stations. The railways even mounted special excursions to prize fights, and when these were banned the promoters merely sold tickets marked, simply and mysteriously, 'there and back'.

Later in the century the Scottish railway companies, in particular, ensured that their tourist guides contained a full description of all the golf courses on their lines, but every company with trains running to thinly-populated coastal regions off season had an interest in encouraging the sport – a regular train took golfers over a hundred miles to Hunstanton on the Norfolk coast every Sunday. The list could be indefinitely prolonged, as games and their supporters multiplied the world over.

Thomas Cook the Social Revolutionary

Thomas Cook's first excursion in 1840 was for a temperance organisation. As he himself wrote, he carried his customers:

> the enormous distance of eleven miles and back for a shilling, children half price. We carried music with us, and music met us at the Loughborough station. The people crowded the streets, filled windows, covered housetops and cheered us all along the line with the heartiest welcome . . . All went off in the best style and in perfect safety we returned to Leicester; and thus was struck the keynote of my excursions, and the social idea grew on me.[24]

He had already found his formula: plenty of publicity in the form of handbills; added attractions – he induced a rich patron of temperance causes, one Mr Paget, to open his park; and a good commercial deal – the Midland Railway needed additional traffic on a newly-completed line and sold him the seats cheaply enough for Cook to charge a mere one shilling for the whole outing.

It was this same railway which forced him to expand his business. In 1851 everyone in the travel business saw the Great Exhibition as a golden opportunity. Cook, still based in Leicester (he opened his first London office only in 1865) had already agreed a price with the Midland railway when the Great Northern slashed its fares to London. The Midland wouldn't budge, so Cook had to increase business vastly to survive. He did, conveying 165,000 visitors, and from then on could survive the periodical assaults of the railway companies, who, like the airlines today, went into direct competition with specialist tour operators. (The railways were particularly active in competing for the business generated by the 1862 Great Exhibition which attracted more visitors than its more famous predecessor.)

The pressure from British railway companies was one of the factors which drove him abroad, where their writ did not run. He took thousands of visitors to the 1855 Paris Exhibition. By 1863 he had initiated tours to Geneva and Mont Blanc, and in 1878, at the height of his powers, he transported 75,000 British visitors to the Paris Exhibition – so many that he had to provide special hostel accommodation for many of them.

Cook clearly expected his tourists to be a good deal more adventurous than their modern equivalents. At a time when there was sporadic warfare and endemic banditry throughout the Ottoman Empire he thought nothing of offering a tour 'With Constantinople for a centre may be visited the principal battlefields of the Russo-Turkish War, the Dardanelles, and the reputed site of Troy'.

Inevitably the customers attracted by the first and greatest of package tour operators became a target for ferocious social scorn and condescension from those who had hoped for exclusivity. One Charles Lever, who wrote under the name of Cornelius O'Dowd, initiated a style of criticism which has been familiar ever since. 'These people, from the hour they set out, regard all foreign countries and their inhabitants as something in which they have a vested right . . . they have paid for the Continent . . . and they *will* have the worth of their money. They mean to eat it, drink it and junket it to the uttermost farthing . . . Europe in their eyes, is a great spectacle, like a show piece at Covent Garden; it is theirs to criticise the performance and laugh at the performers at will.'

Cook shrewdly noted that the author was no aristocrat but 'of the precise class who honoured me by accepting my escort to Italy last year'. Cook asked another critic why his 'susceptibilities should be outraged, and his refinement trampled on, because thirty or forty Englishmen and Englishwomen find it convenient to travel in the same train, to coalesce for mutual benefit, to sojurn for a like time in the same cities?'

Arcachon

The British were enthusiastic sea-bathers long before other races, so it is not surprising that the first enthusiasts for the then-deserted beaches round the Bassin d'Arcachon, thirty miles west of Bordeaux, should have been the Chartronnais, the Anglo-Saxon merchants of the Quai des Chartrons who dominated the Bordeaux wine world from the eighteenth century until the wine crisis of the mid-1970s.

However, it took a railway and two Franco-Jewish financiers, helped by an eccentric priest and an ambitious architect, to transform the whole area into a major seaside resort. The financiers were Emile and Isaac Pereire, working, as they often did, as the indirect instruments of the Emperor Napoleon III. He had insisted that the railway to the Spanish frontier should serve the then-deserted Landes by going directly from Bordeaux to Bayonne, and encouraged attempts to harness the shifting sands of the Landes by planting massive pine forests. Moreover an initially unsuccessful railway had been built from Bordeaux to la Teste on the Bassin d'Arcachon, as the only means of transport over the bogs and marshes which separated Bordeaux from the ocean. That railway link remained the key to the success of Arcachon; a resort which could not be reached by road.

An ambitious, worldly, witty *curé*, Xavier Mouls, persuaded Emile Pereire that the soft piney air of the Bassin d'Arcachon would bring relief for the bronchial problems of asthmatics like himself. He fell in love with the site, which, like the whole Atlantic coast, combines pure sand and the peculiarly seductive aromas emanating from sand and pine. The site was blessed by a visit by the Pereires' Imperial friend, unfortunately in appalling weather, and the brothers set about developing it at a time when the sort of cures Arcachon could offer were growing increasingly fashionable. But Emile Pereire was determined to lengthen the season by building a '*ville d'hiver*' for invalids like himself.

To realise his dream he hired Paul Regnauld, who had already designed the splendid Gare St Jean and the railway bridge across the Garonne at Bordeaux. They decided that the key to the new resort should be curves, so different from the straight lines practised by other Imperial favourites like Haussmann. The result was a whole area of winding streets dotted with an original architectural form, the Arcachon villa, the sort of Victorian monstrosity decried for generations and now cherished as a deeply human and charming architectural style. His young assistant, Gustave Eiffel, designed a steel footbridge linking two of the dunes.

Inevitably the splendid new resort irritated earlier visitors, like Gounod, who had loved Arcachon as a haven of tranquillity. As he wrote to a friend,[25] 'You told me I would see only gulls, larks, squirrels, nightingales and pine cones, and here I am with Parisians who are going to talk about the Opera, the Conservatory, the Academy, politics.' But he stayed – he even conducted Masses and composed a canticle for the church and a tune for its carillon.

Flagler Beach

He could have been as famous and as rich as John D. Rockefeller. Instead he chose to build a railway – and Florida. He was Henry Flagler, Rockefeller's partner in the creation of Standard Oil. Flagler's biographer, David Chandler states that Rockefeller himself always admitted that Flagler 'was an inspiration to me'.[26] He had contributed more than Rockefeller to the organisation of 'The Standard', and was wholly responsible for its brilliant legal structure, but a combination of restlessness and unfulfilled creativity took him away from its management after the death of his first wife. Flagler's Floridan adventure sprang partly from a feeling of guilt that her health would have improved had he been prepared to spend more time with her in the sunny south. But it was also an outlet for his colossal creative and intellectual energies.

Florida had been a state only since 1845, and was still desperately poor, desperately eager to sell the federal land grants which were its major asset in 1883 when Flagler started investing in the state. Thirty years later, when he died at the age of eighty-three, the railway he had financed reached from Jacksonville on the border with Georgia down through the resorts he had developed – St Augustine, Daytona, Palm Beach, the new city of Miami – and continued island-hopping over the Florida Keys to Key West, far out in the Gulf of Mexico.

Flagler began as he meant to go on: in Saint Augustine, the old Spanish town which was the oldest European settlement in the United States, he built a magnificent resort hotel, the Ponce de Leon, designed in the Spanish style by Hastings and Carrère, architects of the old Metropolitan Opera House and the New York Public Library, and adorned with stained glass designed by Louis Tiffany. But Flagler knew that the only way to attract rich men like himself to Florida was a direct rail link to New York. The existing railroads down the East Coast of Florida were primitive, involving numerous changes of gauge. Using his persuasive powers – and as much money as was required – Flagler persuaded the state legislature to grant him the right to construct the line to Key West. (He also arranged a bill making insanity grounds for divorce. This enabled him to get rid of the second Mrs Flagler.)

The first stop along the line was Palm Beach, an idyllic peninsula Flagler had already visited in his yacht in the late 1880s. At Palm Beach he built the Royal Poinciana, 'the largest resort hotel in the world . . . equipped and staffed in the most luxurious fashion imaginable' – and built in a mere nine months. The guests did full justice to the luxury, with a hundred private railway cars arriving each winter at the station on the hotel's doorstep, their occupants prepared to spend fortunes for the Washington Birthday Ball held every 22nd February – a ball famous for the way the country's most powerful men (including Flagler) would attend in the most elaborate drag costumes, complete with fishnet stockings, powdered wigs and strings of diamonds. He also built West Palm Beach for those who could not afford the Royal Poinciana.

Flagler did not want Florida to be a purely service economy. He established a 'Model Land Company' which, in Chandler's words 'did more perhaps towards actually building up the

Florida East Coast than any of his other undertakings'. He encouraged the planting of vegetables, citrus fruit and pineapples, and when an unprecedented snowstorm wiped out the fledgling industry in the winter of 1884–85 he secretly spent a lot of money supporting the unlucky farmers. He even arranged a link-up with the weather forecasters. When a drop in temperature was forecast his engineers would sound six long blasts of their whistles as they passed through the orange groves, and the owners could then hurry out with their smudge pots.

The next stop was Biscayne Bay, protected from the Atlantic by another barrier island, and watered by the little Miami River. Flagler brought his railroad to the site and promptly set about building another luxury hotel, the Royal Palm. The barrier island, unlike Palm Beach, was no paradise. In Chandler's words, the thin strip which subsequently became famous as Miami Beach was originally 'mostly swamp, and was filled with mosquitoes, snakes, mangrove thickets and Spanish Bayonet' – a nasty type of cactus.

The locals wanted to name the town after Flagler but he insisted on naming it after the Miami river. Miami was not his final destination, however. 'There is an impelling force within me,' he told a friend; and the force drove him to Key West. The move made better financial sense than his other, purely speculative, Florida ventures. By the time his plans were ready President Theodore Roosevelt had authorised the building of the Panama Canal, and Key West was 300 miles nearer the canal than any other deep-water anchorage in the country.

As with all his other ventures in Florida, Flagler simply found the best man for the job and told him to get on with it. The chosen engineer, Joseph Carroll Meredith, had to cope with problems undreamt of elsewhere in the United States: bottomless swamps, a lake a mile long unmarked on any map, snakes, alligators, mosquitoes, a dearth of fresh water – and a terrible hurricane which delayed construction for a year. But Flagler lived long enough to ride in triumph on the railroad he had financed, a road to the very edge of the United States. The next year he died, leaving a state bound by his creation.

The 1935 Labour Day Hurricane washed away 40 miles of the Middle Keys section of Flagler's railway.

Unfortunately the dream railroad lasted less than a quarter of a century: the track across the Keys was destroyed on Labour Day, 1935, in the worst storm for a century, a storm in which the barometer dropped to the lowest level ever recorded in the Northern Hemisphere. But Flagler had built well. The highway which replaced the railroad is built on the roadbed he had financed.

IX

RAILWAY IN TOWN AND CITY

1
Growth and Creation

In theory railways could override all previous natural, social or geographical reasons why people should congregate in a particular locality. Yet in fact they tended to reinforce, rather than disturb, existing patterns. To attract traffic, and to minimise construction costs, they tended to follow the routes pioneered by roads and canals, routes which already connected a country's major centres of population. In *Technics and Civilisation* Lewis Mumford pointed out that:

> the poor performance of the railroad on grades of over two per cent caused the new lines to follow the watercourses and valley bottoms. This tended to drain the population out of the back country . . . with the integration of railroad systems population tended to heap up in the great terminal cities, the junctions, the port towns . . . steam power thus increased the area of cities; it also increased the tendency of the new urban communities to coalesce along the main line of transportation and travel.

These main lines included many historic trade routes, like the Old Silk Road to China. In R. N. Taaffe's prosaic words: 'The Kazalinsk route also reinforced the position of Tashkent as the gateway for the overland commerce of Central Asia. Even today,

Ludgate viaduct: rail in the heart of London.

all the interregional rail freight of this region, with the exception
of northern Kighiziya, must be channeled through the Tashkent
Junction.'[1] Similarly the railway through Anatolia enabled
Smyrna to regain its role as the most important Mediterranean
outlet for the whole of Asia Minor.

Everywhere railways gave profound, immeasurable,
permanent encouragement to centralisation, reinforcing the

331

Euston arch: London's first monument to steam

supremacy of capital cities the world over – in Uruguay every
station had a sign giving the distance from Montevideo. Yet their
effects have often been exaggerated and distorted. To the British
reader the idea of the railway in the city is at once cosy and
dramatic. The cosiness derives from the mental pictures of the
many suburbs it is popularly supposed to have spawned. The
drama derives from vague memories of Dickens's description, in
Dombey and Son, of the havoc wrought as the railway crashed
through London, how:

> the first shock of a great earthquake had . . . rent the whole
> neighbourhood to its centre. Traces of its course were visible

on every side. Houses were knocked down; streets broken through and stopped; deep pits and trenches dug in the ground; enormous heaps of earth and clay thrown up; buildings that were undermined and shaking, propped by great beams of wood ... Everywhere were bridges that led nowhere; thoroughfares that were wholly impassable; Babel towers of chimneys, wanting half their height; temporary wooden houses and enclosures, in the most unlikely situations; carcasses of ragged tenements and fragments of unfinished walls and arches, and piles of scaffolding, and wildernesses of bricks, and giant forms of cranes, and tripods straddling above nothing.

Building the greatest steam shed of its day at St Pancras.

Both images, the cosy and the dramatic, were true. Both were misleading. The railways created surprisingly few suburbs in the generation after they were built. And for every sort of reason – communal, financial, technical – railways found the greatest difficulty in penetrating into the heart of major cities like London, Paris and Berlin. It was said of the first line into Rome that 'the train does not leave Rome and never arrives at Frascati.' At the time they were built stations like the Gare de Lyon or Euston were on the outskirts of the cities they served, an idea difficult to grasp now because Paris and London expanded so quickly in the decades following the railways' arrival. In both cities the idea of a single central station inevitably foundered on simple economics. The Pereires never succeeded in their dream of building a station in the Place de la Madeleine and in Britain no one took seriously the idea of 'the Great Victorian way' to connect the main railway stations.*

The actual intrusions into city centres made the point even more dramatically. The final mile of track from Shoreditch to Liverpool Street on the eastern edge of the City of London cost the Great Eastern £2 million – a hundred times that figure in today's money. Not surprisingly the station was described as a 'white elephant of the largest magnitude'.† One scheme in Glasgow cost the same, another in Liverpool £1 million, while the last four miles of track into Charing Cross in the West End and Blackfriars in the City cost £4 million and triggered off the Overend Gurney crisis, the biggest financial panic to hit the City of London during the whole century.

It was soon clear that only underground or elevated railways could provide access into the heart of major cities at anything like reasonable social or economic cost. In 1863 the Metropolitan Railway made the point by opening the first underground railway in the world, from Paddington Station to the City of London. The mass of underground railways, metros, subways and the like built in the succeeding half-century merely confirms the surface railways' defeat, and for this reason alone the enormous effects of underground systems do not belong in this book.

By the 1860s all the main lines into London had been completed, yet only a tenth of the 600,000 people who worked there travelled by train. Most lived close enough to their place of work to walk or use horse omnibuses. Even at the turn of the century not more than 250,000 commuters travelled by train. Although most of today's suburban lines had been built they were not heavily travelled until London exploded, and the railways south of the Thames were electrified, between the wars.

In provincial cities the figures were much smaller. For a long time most major British cities remained very compact, with the merchant class living within a couple of miles of the centre of the

---

* The concept of the 'Way', complete with a glassed-in arcade and eight railway lines, was that of Joseph Paxton, the architect of the Crystal Palace.

† Quoted by John Kellett, *The Impact of Railways on Victorian Cities*. In recent years this railway-owned property has been of enormous financial benefit to British Rail.

city, which also housed huddled masses of workers. In Birmingham and Manchester, for instance, only a few thousand commuters travelled by train; though in Glasgow there was a considerable counter-flow, with thousands of workers making the daily trip from the inner city to the factories along the Clyde.

Most major railway companies were not unduly interested in promoting commuter traffic; quite the contrary. In the early part of this century the Great Northern was highly embarrassed by the growth of London's northern suburbs as the passing trains interfered with the company's most profitable source of income, its main-line goods traffic. The company's lack of interest was natural because only the Metropolitan Railway was legally allowed to speculate in land or promote new developments.

The beneficiaries of the spread of railways near London were the individual managers, directors, and above all, their solicitors, many of whom made fortunes from profitable land speculation. Nor was there a mass of customers waiting to be served. Even clerical workers were operating on a tight budget, as an official report at the end of the century makes clear. It pointed out that these commuters, by the nature of their employment 'are compelled to preserve a respectable appearance. If they fail to do so they may lose their employment, and very seriously impair their prospect of advancement. To such persons the payment of a daily fare constitutes an appreciable pecuniary burden.' Although the companies were forced to provide cheaper 'workmen's fares' these had a limited impact.

In London the great exception was the poor Great Eastern which desperately needed the money to pay for Liverpool Street Station. So it encouraged the development of the working-class suburbs which still extend far into the north-eastern edge of London, suburbs far denser than those in other directions. Nevertheless, as F. M. L. Thompson points out in *The Rise of Suburbia* even before the arrival of the underground railway, horse trams 'had a much more widespread effect than workmen's trains and fares in enabling the lower middle-class and the artisans to push out into suburbia'.

For the progress of suburban development was slow and irregular, depending more on the break-up of major estates through death and the introduction of death duties in 1894 than on the railways. In Thompson's words 'a railway should be regarded as a necessary, although not a sufficient, condition for outer suburban growth'. Nevertheless, in Britain as elsewhere, according to Kellett, the railways 'profoundly influenced the internal flows of traffic, the choices of site and patterns of land use, the residential densities and development prospects of the central and inner districts of the Victorian city.'

Inevitably the first urban railways traversed working-class districts where the inhabitants, living in rented housing, could simply be turfed out into already overcrowded streets without any compensation. These 'improvements' merely increased the rents of the inhabitants by up to a quarter, making a mockery of the claim that they 'ventilated' the city, that in Kellett's words 'they let in light and air by providing open spaces and air courses through densely crowded and noisome areas of working class housing, and that they improved the drainage.'

In their brutal progress the railways occupied nearly a tenth of all the land in Britain's five biggest cities. They also intruded into the earlier grid of city planning in which the landed estate had been the basic unit. Not surprisingly, they were no respecters of persons. The intrusion so graphically described by Dickens in *Dombey and Son* was caused by the London & Birmingham Railway as it made its way into Euston. Altogether, the three major lines into Euston, King's Cross and Saint Pancras uprooted around 150,000 people.

Even Dickens never suggested that the wretched inhabitants should have been compensated in some way. This idea was a rather later by-product of the Victorian social conscience to which the railways contributed, if only by creating so much disturbance and misery. Within a couple of decades successive commissions of enquiry had established sophisticated methods of measuring the density and flow of traffic and the railways' economic effects, and had started to examine the social costs of new forms of transport.

Brighton Station: an early masterpiece.

Slowly but surely, however, a pattern emerged: a commercial and above all financial core devoid of residential life, surrounded by a ring of inner-city decay, and outer rings of housing moving steadily up the social scale the further you moved from the centre – a logical progression at a time when only the wealthy could afford to commute more than a few miles. It was they who occupied the small groups of detached houses built within easy reach of railway stations in Surrey. As early as 1845 a first-class season ticket was introduced at the then enormous annual cost of £50 for those wanting to live in Brighton and work in London, fifty-five miles away. Three years later an observer quoted by Simmons noted that 'merchants who formerly made Dulwich or Dalston the boundaries of their suburban residences now have got their mansions on the south coast and still get in less time, by a less expensive conveyance, to their counting-houses in the City.'

By the 1870s a Manchester observer quoted by Kellett was complaining how 'a large portion of the middle-class, the clerks, warehousemen and others seize upon the new suburbs, vacating their houses in town, which are most frequently absorbed for shop and business purposes, or sub-divided and sublet, until the dwelling which has served for one household contains as many families as it did persons.'

Outside Britain the railways played an even less important role in the growth of major cities. In the United States, however, the railways often defined your status: when a settlement was first established along the tracks the saloons and other disreputable buildings were on one side 'the wrong side of the tracks', and avoided by all right-thinking people.*

Most American cities remained 'walking cities' while continental European cities grew upwards rather than outwards, with the inhabitants preferring apartments to houses. Nevertheless, scattered round New York and London, as well as a few other major British and American cities are a host of 'railway suburbs', and very pleasant they were too. As Lewis Mumford pointed out, they 'had a special advantage that could be fully appreciated only after they had disappeared. These suburbs, strung along a railway line, were discontinuous and properly spaced . . . The size and scale of the suburb, that of a neighbourhood unit. Being served by a railroad line, with station stops some three to five miles apart, meant that there was a natural limit to the spread of any particular community'.

Before the days of the motor car the houses, themselves well spaced out, had to be sited 'within easy walking distance of the railroad station'. Among Mumford's examples of what were cosy villages, rather than impersonal dormitory towns, were Bronxville near New York, with fewer than 7,000 inhabitants, while Riverside, Illinois housed only just over 9,000. 'They were natural pedestrian communities with natural greenbelts. It was the car which destroyed the pedestrian scale of the suburb.' In Britain the pattern is still recognisable in Cheshire and in Surrey, where Surbiton (see page xxx) was the prototype. Such suburbs are now scorned: in fact they were agreeable but not major contributors to the urban scene. It was the horse-bus, and above all the electric tramway and the underground railway which formed today's cities to a far greater extent than the steam railway.

* Railways also established the idea of the 'red light district'. According to Frank P. Donovan in *The Railroad in Literature*, one of the rowdiest saloons in Dodge City had a red light in the window and trainmen advised respectable citizens to stay clear of the 'red light district'.

In settled countries as much as new regions, there was intense competition for a town's access to a railway. In many countries it became the first duty of politicians to ensure that their constituencies possessed the vital lifeline to the outside world – in 1861 they rang the bells in the little town of Saint-Girons in the Ariège in the foothills of the Pyrenees when they heard that a railway serving the town had been approved. And there were few, in Saint-Girons or anywhere else, who dared lament (in public anyway) the passing of older ways of life and the destruction involved. The problem continues: Amiens town council warned that if the town were left off the route of the new TGV Nord from Paris to Brussels it would mean the gradual erosion of the town in years to come.

In Britain the argument as to whether the railway was an essential component of a town's growth or survival soon became academic. By 1852 the largest towns without a railway were relatively unimportant – Weymouth, Hereford and Yeovil – none of which seem to have suffered from their belated arrival. For the railways were not omnipotent, they tended to sharpen existing identities, confirm existing social and economic trends. In Britain many railways were financed locally, so Norwich, a declining city which could not afford to finance its own link with London, lost further ground compared with Bristol, another historic regional centre, which could. In Simmons's words the decline of many small towns 'was part of a general trend, the movement from rural England and Wales . . . the towns that shrank were not only those that were unfortunate in their railway communication. They include a fair number that were well placed on the system quite early.'

If the town were important or dynamic enough then it could afford initial neglect. Being by-passed by the original line from London to Birmingham did not hurt Northampton, a growing centre which soon acquired its own link with London. In the United States neither Denver nor Salt Lake City declined in importance although they were over a hundred miles from the original Trans-continental railroad. The railroads were forced to provide a proper service to major centres, but smaller settlements were in no position to dictate to the promoters, and the history of the American West is littered with the sad stories of small communities which had to pay considerable sums in ransom money to the railroad builders to ensure that they were not left out of its magic circle.

In autocratic countries without any tradition of civic initiative, individual communities were helpless. With a simple wave of a ruler the Tsar had dictated the straight route the railway would take from his capital at Saint Petersburg to Moscow. He thus orphaned three historic towns: Novgorod, Valdai, and Torzhok. Even Novgorod, once the centre of an independent city-state, was condemned to everlasting stagnation.

The concentration process was not confined to Britain: there are examples as far afield as Mexico and South Africa, although, as so often, Surtees' description in *Mr Facey Romford's Hounds* is incomparably the best description of the trend:

> Before the introduction of steam, Pickering Nook was one of the quietest little places in the kingdom: one doctor, no lawyer, two milliners, and an occasional pedlar with the latest London fashions. The inhabitants were chiefly elderly ladies who loved retirement and the musical note of the nightingale. Now it is hiss, screech, whistle – hiss screech whistle – morning noon and night. Five railways run right into the very heart of the little town, severing it like a starfish. It has become a perfect anthill of industrious locomotion. People seem to go to Pickering Nook in order to pass to every other place.

But, he continued, 'Railways, which make some places, ruin others, and Dirlingfold has suffered the latter fate. The railway seemed to have sucked all the life out of it – taken it all up to Pickering Nook.'

In France, a far larger and more thinly-populated country than Britain, it took several generations for the railways to reach into the heart of the countryside. Much of rural France remained deprived of contact with the outside world because at first the railways connected only the major towns and cities. Moreover, the railways' enormous hunger for capital deprived rural roads of the investment they required. So, until the largely politically-inspired 'Freycinet lines' of the 1880s and 1890s French railways 'crossed rather than irrigated' many rural departments. 'Between 1866 and 1936 rural communes without a railway station in a zone fifteen kilometres on either side of the Paris-Lyon-Mediterranée line lost almost one-quarter of their population, while those with a station (excluding Paris) gained 1,645,373 inhabitants'.[2]

Snobbery of one sort or another led a select group of towns to reject the railways, or at least ensure that they were kept at a proper distance. Oxford refused the chance to be a major railway centre, while genteel seaside resorts were naturally afraid of social dilution. At Harrogate, smartest of Yorkshire spas, the railway created its own new centre away from the historic heart. Bournemouth, then more a town for retired gentlefolk than a mere seaside resort, felt that its heart was threatened by a railway projected by some highly disreputable contractors. The local MP expressed his constituents' concern at 'the suicidal policy of allowing one of the most beautiful portions of Bournemouth to be cut up by a railway'.[3] So the railway was kept at a discreet distance, a blessing achievable, it was said, 'only where there is money and influence'. Subsequent growth has ensured that the old station is now at the heart of a greatly expanded resort, and ironically, a new by-pass was built along the route which the townsfolk had rejected a hundred years earlier as too destructive of their peace.

The railways' biggest single effect was to change the historic balance in favour of towns and cities on navigable waters. Marcel Blanchard pointed out in *Geographie des chemins de fer* that before the railway age four ports were among the ten French towns with more than 50,000 inhabitants. By 1870, thanks largely to the railway, there were thirty such towns and cities, of which only seven were ports, and two of those, Toulon and Brest, were military encampments.

Nevertheless, in France, as elsewhere, towns where the railway met a major navigable stretch of water had a head start when the railways arrived. In the generation before the railways Orleans had largely lost its role as an entrepot, because of the increasing importance of the River Seine between Paris and Le Havre, but recaptured some of its historic commercial importance when the railway companies sited their depots on the waterfront – though even Orleans lost out to the great Parisian octopus which monopolised the profitable wine trade, itself a result of the railways.

But railways could also be powerful weapons against navigable waterways, weapons perceived as heaven-sent by a number of American cities threatened by major canals. The great Erie Canal, which linked the upper Hudson River with Lake Erie, had been half a century in the making when it was opened in 1825. Its immediate success confirmed New York's pre-eminent status as the country's biggest port. No turnpike could compete with the Erie. On a mountain road six draft horses could pull only perhaps a four ton load, whereas on a canal a single horse could pull the equivalent of several wagonloads.

Inevitably New York's major rivals, Baltimore, Boston and Philadelphia, seized on the new-fangled railroad to provide a technological leap ahead of the canals. But railroads could not achieve miracles. The Grand Trunk railroad south from Canada to Portland in Maine attracted considerable English capital but its promoters were 'trying to make water run uphill'.[4] The railroad shortened the transatlantic journey by two hundred miles, but this saving was hopelessly inadequate to challenge New York's commanding lead.

Within the United States the biggest battleground between rail and water was the huge basin of the Mississippi. The river lost its monopoly as the railroads steadily diverted the ever-growing traffic, particularly of grain, away from the long, meandering route down the river to New Orleans and the Gulf of Mexico, and towards the ports on the Great Lakes, which provided direct access to the Atlantic. The first city to be threatened was St Louis on the Mississippi. Railways were not destined to remain mere feeders to even the mightiest river systems for long, and by the time the city had woken up to the fact that railroads could act as independent forces, it had lost its primacy to Chicago.

By the middle of the century half a dozen towns along the Missouri River were fighting for pre-eminence. Before the Civil War the favourite was Saint Joseph, 'the outfitting point for much of the emigration westward', while, said one booster, Leavenworth 'can't help what seems to be its destiny, becoming the metropolis of Kansas and the West'. At the time both towns were bigger than the eventual winner, Kansas City. But this was an economically-unified community, a new town without the vested interests relying on the wagon trade which sabotaged St Jo's efforts. In the words of Charles Glaab,[5] 'political negotiation, corporate intrigue and local manoeuvring – not the logic of geography or location . . . ensured that Kansas City was the eastern terminus of one of the branches of the Transcontinental railroad. Once the river had been bridged in 1869, Kansas City was firmly on its way to superiority over former rivals as the centre for shipping cattle and beef eastwards.'

The fighting was general. Louisville had become the great entrepôt on the Mississippi, but was threatened when Cincinnati provided access for produce from the upper Ohio Valley. The Louisville & Nashville Railroad enabled Louisville to open up an alternative hinterland, the Middle South. Louisville emphasised its southern affinities by dispatching ex-Confederate salesmen into the South and sending relief to victims of Sherman's march through Georgia.

A similar change of direction greatly boosted the twin cities of Minneapolis and Saint Paul. Established as fur trading posts on the upper Mississippi, they had been relatively slow-growing: although the first steamboat reached them in 1823 a regular service was not established until 1847, and as late as 1865 there were only 210 miles of railway in the whole state of Minnesota. Yet ten years later, thanks largely to the demands of the grain trade, the figure had risen nine-fold, providing mid-Western farmers with access to Chicago, the inescapable metropolis of late nineteenth-century America, the perfect example of the all-powerful combination of rail and water, and one, moreover, with access to the Atlantic and thus to Europe, and not, like the Mississippi, merely to the Gulf of Mexico.

Chicago remains incomparable as a case of explosive expansion where railroads met an important navigable stretch of water. Ironically the town's burghers had not originally welcomed them,

GREAT RAILWAY STATION AT CHICAGO—DEPARTURE OF A TRAIN.

Chicago Station: the cross-roads of American life.

preferring to rely on the combination of plank roads and the shipping on the Great Lakes. It took the genius of one man, William Butler Ogden, to enable the town to fulfil its manifest destiny. In the early 1840s he persuaded farmers to invest in a small railroad west into the wheatlands. The idea caught on, not only among the locals, but among the financiers of New England. One of them, John Murray Forbes – the only railroad magnate of whom no-one spoke ill – made the vital connection by linking Chicago (and thus the Great Lakes) with the Mississippi at two points, Quincy, Illinois and Burlington, Iowa and thus establishing the foundation of the famous Chicago, Burlington and Quincy Railroad.

By 1856 Chicago was the focus of ten trunk railroads with almost 3,000 miles of track between them, running nearly a hundred trains a day into the world's fastest growing metropolis, and, by no coincidence, its fastest-growing railroad centre. Not surprisingly:

each new railroad that came into the city helped fashion its future . . . within a decade the Illinois Central altered the face of the lake front and stimulated suburban development along its tracks . . . Wherever the tracks ran, the use of the land was

345

affected. The yards and depots dominated surrounding neighbourhoods, and rail facilities became the nuclei of industrial and commercial growth. This crucial development was unplanned and only remotely governed by public policy ... the early railroad decisions were written on the map in lines of iron and for more than a century have constituted fixed features of the Chicago scene.[6]

There were so many railroads – no fewer than twenty-three eventually included the city's name in their title – and the city was so large that they did not exercise the same political dominance as did the Central Pacific through its monopoly of rail access to Northern California, or the Pennsylvania in its home state. Yet their presence transformed Chicago into the wonder city of the last half of the century.

Chicago typified the importance towns attached to not allowing through traffic, thus ensuring that their lucrative entrepôt trade was not disturbed. In China, Canton managed to ensure a break so that Kowloon, on the mainland opposite Hong Kong Island, did not link directly with the main line to Hankow, while in France the Lyonnais fought to prevent a through railway to ensure that all freight would have to be unloaded and then reloaded in their city. But in the end the only French city able to maintain its role as an entrepôt was Paris, not only because of its size, but because its stations were not linked.

Nevertheless early railway development had inescapably been linked to access to navigable waters. Even Atlanta, with Denver and Indianapolis the only major nineteenth-century American city not on a major waterway, owes its origin to a region's need to be connected to a navigable one. In the 1830s Georgia created three separate railway companies, each designed to placate some of the state's quarrelling communities. The three were threatened by a number of lines from out of state, so they cooperated in promoting a single route to provide access to the Tennessee River at Ross's Landing, subsequently better known as Chatanooga.

Originally the lines were to meet on a less important river, the Chattahoochee, but the river banks proved unsuitable and a junction originally called simply 'Terminus' was built eight miles away. Terminus soon blossomed into Atlanta, but proved remarkably ungrateful to the railroads which had called it into being. As the inhabitants well knew, their town was 'the incidental result of the building of [rail] roads intended exclusively for the benefit of other towns', and the railroad managers showed no inclination to invest in their accidental offspring.[7]

Before the Civil War the Atlantans had felt, in the words of the city's historian, that they were living in a 'besieged city, assailed by economic agencies subservient to older cities in the "unprogressive" plantation districts'. It was only after the Civil War that its unique position at the hub of the region's railroad network enabled Atlanta – a mass of ruins after Sherman's visit – to develop into the greatest entrepôt city in the South.

Railways could also link twin towns, one an historically important inland centre, the other (often originally less important) on the nearest coast. The twinning was particularly noticeable in Latin America: in Chile Santiago and Valparaiso; in Colombia Bogota and Cartagena; in Venezuela Caracas and La Guayra; in Brazil Sao Paolo and Santos; in Ecuador Quito and Gayaquil, happily prospered as Siamese twins.

For all the importance of a watery link, many towns without such connections flourished as never before thanks purely to their position on the railway network. In Switzerland Olten became the turntable of the whole Swiss railway system. In Italy Bologna assumed a new importance because of its position on the railway map. In France Dijon, in Burgundy, the meeting point for main lines from north, south and east, flourished for the same reason, depriving such riverside towns as Gray and Chalons-sur-Marne of their former importance. But the changes were relative: Bologna had been famous for a thousand years before the railways; Olten is still not a major city; and Dijon always was, and remains, noted not so much as a railway town but as the centre of the trade in the region's fine wines.

The true 'railway towns' were those created by the great trans-continental railways. Few were as important as their archetype, Cheyenne (see page 350) and many are now forgotten,

347

relics of long-lost speculations. More remain as inconspicuous today as they were when the railway brought them into being.

The Canadian Pacific did more than any other single railway to create new settlements. In Pierre Berton's words in *The Impossible Railway*, it 'dictated both the shape and the location of the cities of the new Canada' as it swept past Regina, Calgary, Chapeau and Cartier, Stephen and Donald (two of the railroad's organisers); as well as towns named after milords Dunmore (who had tried and failed to win the original contract) and Revelstoke (the member of the Baring family who had come to the company's rescue by underwriting a bond issue). 'With a scratch of the pen the company could, and did, decide which communities would grow and which would stagnate; the placing of divisional points made all the difference.'

In all the CPR fostered some eight hundred towns and cities in the three prairie provinces. The later, and more northerly, Canadian National route spawned 132 settlements, with a mere 60,000 inhabitants, yet their relative smallness did not discourage speculators, despite the CPR's best efforts. Typically, at Mirror, Alberta* 577 lots were sold for nearly a quarter of a million dollars in just eleven hours after the town sites were put on the market, a rate of almost one a minute. 'Before the town was a month old, it had two banks, five stores, three lumberyards, a hotel, three restaurants, two pool rooms, a sash and door factory, and a newspaper.'[8]

Inevitably a link with navigable water provided the greatest opportunity of all. The CPR rejected the existing town of Port Moody as its western terminus, because there wasn't enough flat land for expansion. William Van Home, the CPR's general manager, preferred a site closer to the Pacific near the mouth of Burard Inlet. Not surprisingly Van Home was not happy with the existing name, Coal Harbour, and preferred to name the terminus after Captain Vancouver, who had explored the coast nearly a century earlier.

The same pattern applied in Siberia as the Trans-Siberian pushed through: the biggest centres grew where the railway

* Named after the London daily newspaper.

crossed major rivers. One of the most exotic new cities was in Manchuria. Harbin was a mere fishing village on the Songhua River until the Russians bullied the Chinese emperor into running a short cut for the Trans-Siberian Railway through Manchuria to Vladivostock. The Manchurians were never fond of the Russians – they called them 'second-class light-hairs' – but thanks to them, Harbin became the Manchurian equivalent of Paris, the centre of every sin, every luxury. It was only nine days by train from Paris, so it got the fashions and the music and the latest papers long before Shanghai. The striptease and the Charleston and Dixieland jazz were introduced to China in Harbin in the nineteen-twenties because of the Trans-Siberian link with Paris.'[9]

Any railway crossing uncharted lands inevitably created its own settlements. The Atchison, Topeka & Santa Fe challenged its Canadian rivals in the number of cities it spawned. Some of the names – Presidio, El Paso, San Diego – were Spanish. Others – Pasadena, Yosemite, Palcentia – sounded vaguely Spanish but were, in fact, Indian or merely invented.[10] Bakingly hot settlements were called Siberia or Klondike, while immigrants named their towns Exeter or Moscow. But the majority of the settlements, an astonishing two hundred in all, were named after the railroad's officials, employees, their wives and children, ranging from Mr Arntz the trainmaster to Mr Conrad the despatcher.

The only railway which compared with the great transcontinentals was the 'Lunatic Line' from Mombasa to Lake Victoria, which, as we have seen, created a whole new country – Kenya. Previously the territory boasted only one town, Mombasa on the coast. Kenya's other three major urban centres – Nairobi, Nakuru and Kisumu – were pure railway creations. Nairobi's site was uninviting, described by Charles Miller as 'a bleak, swampy stretch of soppy landscape, devoid of human habitation of any sort, the resort of thousands of wild animals of every species'. But its site was strategically obvious, the last stretch of level ground before the track rose two thousand feet up the eastern wall of the Rift valley. Like many another frontier town it grew fast but haphazardly. Two years after it was founded Sir Charles Eliot remarked that 'the beauty of a view in Nairobi depends on the more or less thorough elimination of the town from the landscape'. It was only in the 1920s that its fame as a centre of East African high life gave it a glamorous veneer.

Cheyenne

Originally Cheyenne on Crow Creek, some 150 miles west of the then-significant city of Julesburg, was just another 'hell on wheels', a camp like hundreds of others famous only for sex, drink, gambling – and impermanence.

Early in June 1867 white troops and Pawnee scouts saw off the Sioux warriors who had infested the creek, leaving room for the railroad and a settlement. The next six months saw enough activity to last a lifetime. On the 19th June the Union Pacific engineers arrived and staked off a site for the city, a task which took them a mere two days. According to the *History and Business Directory of Cheyenne,* there were soon 'a large number of saloons in tents where whiskey and other poisonous compounds were retailed at fabulous prices, and coarse provisions commanded prices according to the size of the hungry individual's purse.'

In August the first building with a shingle roof was laid – previously roofs were made of 'boards placed on each other which enabled the inhabitants to get shower baths occasionally free of expense'. By then the pace was hotting up. Two gentlemen arrived in town on 15th August, and in forty-eight hours had built a substantial 'out-fitting house'. On 16th September a well-known journalist, Mr N. A. Baker, arrived in town: by the 19th he had produced the first issue of the *Leader*, 'the Pioneer paper of the future Wyoming'. It was a robust sheet, featuring a column entitled 'last night's shootings'. On the 25th, a Mr H. J. Rogers opened the town's first bank. Two days later a mass meeting laid the foundations of local government. And on the 30th 'oil springs' were discovered eighteen miles west of the town.

October started badly with 'a terrible affray' which killed Pat Mallaly 'and a man known as Limber Jim'. The affair 'caused great

* First published February 1868, facsimile edition Yale 1975.

excitement, and but for the ability and firmness of the city government would have resulted in a reign of terror'. So all was quiet for the arrival on the 13th of a party of 'Editorial excursionists' – both railroads and journalists were partial to such editorial freebies. By then the town was getting too popular. It took a battalion of troops to disperse a party of squatters from Julesburg.

November was even more eventful. A public school was established on the 9th, a day remarkable for a prize fight over 126 rounds, lasting in all one hour and forty-three minutes. On the 11th that remarkable entrepreneur, George Francis Train, hit town, and within six hours he had formed a company to organise the building of a large hotel. But all these were mere preliminaries to the real foundation day, the 13th, when the Union Pacific's tracks reached Cheyenne.

Two months later the Dakota legislature granted Cheyenne its city charter. Nevertheless the new metropolis was forced to rely on rough and ready measures to keep the peace. On 19th January three men were arrested for stealing $900. Because the court was busy the men were released. The next day they were found walking together festooned with a large canvas sheet announcing that only $500 had been restored, that 'City authorities please not interfere until 10 o'clock am, next case goes up a tree. Beware of the Vigilance Committee'. According to the authors of the *Business Directory* this case of rough people's justice gave 'an assurance of safety to the honest man who desires to make this region his home'.

The vigilantes had plenty of work. On the 20th they 'relieved the county' of three men, Jack Hays, Kief and Shorty, whose very presence had caused 'many an honest man to grasp the butt of his revolver'. Not only the policing was amateur. The city had no money. Elected officials paid many of the expenses out of their own pockets. City employees had to be paid in scrip, redeemed at a mere 50 cents to the dollar.

Cheyenne swiftly emerged as an early centre of feminism. The legislature was anxious for female immigrants and gave them the vote and the right to sit on juries. Even so the town was no place for wimps. The town's first Congregational minister, a Civil War

351

veteran, had asked to be sent to 'the toughest town west of the Mississippi'. After a few weeks he remarked that 'it needed more courage to plant the Gospel here than it did to hold up the old flag in battle'.

Within a couple of years Cheyenne had found its *raison d'être* as a centre for shipping livestock, some sheep, but mainly cattle, alive or dead in their thousands east, to Omaha and Chicago, well deserving its name of 'cattle capital of the plains'.

Surbiton for Smugness

Ever since it was built, Surbiton, fifteen miles south-west of London on the line from Waterloo to Southampton, has been a by-word for suburban smugness. A more kindly and accurate description would be that it was the forerunner of an agreeable way of life, the result of an accident of railway history.

The London & South Western Railway served the ancient market town of Kingston-upon-Thames with a station a mile away. This provided the opportunity for a speculator called Thomas Pooley. In 1838 he bought a farm and began using the land to lay out an estate between the railway and the town – which probably didn't want too close an association with the railway in the first place.

Pooley's speculation soon failed. The place 'looked almost like a mass of ruins' and Coutts' bank foreclosed on the mortgages. The bank, making the best of a bad job, hired Philip Hardwick, who had designed Euston Station, and with the bank's backing, he designed and built a substantial settlement. The guide-books emphasised the railway link by calling it 'Kingston-upon-Railway'.

The name seemed rather bald, so the locals took an old name 'South Barton' and shortened it to Surbiton. In 1855 they declared their independence from Kingston and within thirty years the town was substantial enough to justify a service of sixty trains a day to London. 'Surbiton used to be the butt of jokes,' wrote Jack Simmons in *Railway in Town and Country*, 'as a symbol of dowdy suburbia. To anyone with half an eye it was – it still is – an interesting place, in which the original plan and later accretions can be discerned, much as they can in a medieval town like Boston or Carlisle. And Surbiton can fairly claim its place in history: for it is the oldest suburb in Europe, perhaps in the world, that was called into being by a railway.'

2

The Monuments of Steam

Building the railways stretched man's capacity to master his environment. The impetus they provided, the optimism they symbolised, combined with the prospect of monetary gain, managed to force the bridging of the unbridgeable, the flinging of rails across deserts, mountains, marshes, no matter how grim, how inaccessible, how inhospitable they were. Every aspect of these monuments, the bridges, the stations, the hotels, have been the subject of innumerable books and articles, popular and learned. But they echoed the contrast, present throughout this book, between areas where the railways were genuinely pioneers, where they forced the technical and imaginative pace, and the majority of cases where they merely allowed fashion its fullest expression.

It was in the engineering of the lines themselves that the railways showed their greatest boldness, their fearless contempt for previous conventions and assumptions of the limits of the practical. Appropriately George Stephenson had shown the way with his triumph over the supposedly impassable Chat Moss (Chapter I). But engineers outside Britain were soon conquering far more difficult terrain, from the Andes to the Rockies, from Kenya to deepest Burma. Only the railways could command the funds required to tunnel through the Alps, or up the Rockies and Andes. There are dozens of such lines, many of which naturally gave rise to magnificent descriptive passages. Curiously many of the best of these accounts are those by modern travellers – older generations cannot improve on the works of Colin Thubron or Paul Theroux, for, as rail travel becomes less ordinary, less run-of-the-mill, the effects on the writer become more vivid.

These travellers remain excited by the other great thrill of railway travel: the magnificent bridges and viaducts to which they gave rise. The sense of excitement or insecurity is inevitably heightened if the bridge, or the line itself, is above the cloud line, as it so often is in the Andes or the Himalayas.

Locomotives were the ultimate symbol of man's control over nature. The first locomotives, their designers, builders and drivers, were natural stars. The Stephensons set the vogue, but the early railway age produced many others: the first locomotive made in France by the British engineer W. B. Buddicom was familiarly known as *La petite Budie*. Thomas Crampton, another expatriate engineer was so renowned that 'Prendre le Crampton' became slang for taking a train – and William Wilson, the first driver on Germany's first line, became a local hero.

All too soon the general public accepted them as simply part of the railway landscape, though they remained fascinated by the noise, the smell of engines, their perky hoots, the melancholy whistles, all the sensations they conjured up. Not surprisingly they could easily become deeply anthropomorphised, as witness Archibald MacLeish:

> Still sweating from the deep ravines
> Where rot within the buried wood
> The bones of time that are their food,
> Graze the great machines

But it was an earlier American poet, Emily Dickinson, who best distilled the universal human feeling that these were friendly, domesticated beasts:

> I like to see it lap the miles,
> And lick the valley up,
> And stop to feed itself at tanks;
> And then, prodigious, step
>
> Around a pile of mountains,
> And, supercilious, peer
> In shanties by the sides of roads;
> And then a quarry pare
>
> To fit its sides, and crawl between,
> Complaining all the while

In horrid, hooting stanza;
Then chase itself down hill

And neigh like Boanerges;
Then, punctual as a star,
Stop – docile and omnipotent –
At its own stable door.

Dickinson was certainly not interested in the technicalities of her 'docile and omnipotent' beasts. Nor, in fact, was Walt Whitman in his all-embracing *Ode to a Locomotive in Winter*, in which he provides the most complete set of outsider's responses to the great machine. He was obviously fascinated by the moving parts:

Thy black cylindric body, golden brass and silvery steel,
Thy ponderous side-bars, parallel and connecting rods,
   gyrating, shuttling at thy sides . . .
Thy knitted frame, thy springs and valves, the tremulous
   twinkle of thy wheels

But these were a small part of the whole phenomenon, 'Thy train of cars . . . thy swinging lamps at night'. His 'fierce-throated

Bombay's Victoria Station: imperialism at its most splendid.

beauty . . . in thy panoply, thy measur'd dual throbbing and thy beat convulsive' was the

'Type of the modern – emblem of motion and power – pulse
   of the continent . . .
Launched o'er the prairies wide, across the lakes,
To the free skies unpent and glad and strong.

Most of the public, like the poets, was interested only in the overall effect the locomotives created, perhaps, occasionally, in the engineers if they created a record.* But they left the details to the engineers, the spotters, the small boy in all of us who wrote thousands of books on every one of them. But they – and I am one of their number – were and are emphatically not interested in the design of the fireboxes or the names of their makers, matters of limited, specialist interest outside the scope of this book.

But it is the great railway stations, the temples of steam, the lavishly embellished secular equivalents of the great medieval cathedrals, which remain the most appropriate symbol of the railways' importance in men's lives, for they illustrated the way every country interpreted the railway dream. As we saw in Chapter I, the form of the station, and indeed of the offices and hotels which grew up as part of them, found its definite shape within the first decade of the railways' existence, and it is difficult to see any fundamental development since 1840, apart from the regrettable modern tendency to drive the trains underground to leave room for more profitable offices in the air space above.

Yet, despite their importance, their grandeur, their beauty, as architecture they usually merely distilled, reflected a country's styles at a given time. For, although they provided the opportunity (and the funds) for the century's architects to express themselves in the fullest and most lavish manner, they tended not to innovate, architecturally. Their lack of originality was, perhaps deliberate.

---

* In Britain the name of Sir Nigel Gresly, chief engineer of the LNER, and designer of Mallard, which created the world speed record for steam trains, was known to many people who would never have heard of his equally distinguished fellow-engineer on the LMS, Sir William Stanier.

As J. M. Richards[11] points out, their promoters and architects were often trying to reassure the public that this novel creature, the railways, was not as frightening as it appeared at first sight.

Although there are innumerable books and paintings celebrating the stations, their architecture, the life that bustled there[12], yet somehow, their architecture represents a marvellous opportunity missed: perhaps, as Richards says, because the promoters were trying to defuse the shock of the new represented by the railways, perhaps because the promoters, like all holders of financial power throughout the ages, were conservative creatures. For whatever reason, stations were not allowed to remain as original as they could have been and for a short period were.

Only at Paddington Station in London did the station succeed in blending the new technology, the new strength of iron and steel, with orthodox architecture. It took the combination of Isambard Kingdom Brunel and the architect Sir Matthew Digby Wyatt, who had worked together on the Great Exhibition, to conduct what *Builder Magazine* described as the attempt to 'avoid any recurrence to existing styles, and to try the experiment of designing everything in accordance with the structural purposes, or nature of the materials employed, iron & cement.' In Christian Barman's words 'the whole of the train hall structure is treated as a single design . . . artist and engineer were never to work together in quite the same lively and imaginative way again.'

The truth of Barman's remark can be seen a couple of miles to the east. King's Cross is a purely engineering solution, and very fine and integrated it is too; while its neighbour, St Pancras, represents an admission of failure, with two equally splendid edifices, the arching train shed and the arrogantly Gothic Hotel placed together with no attempt to harmonise the two totally opposing styles. The same pattern was repeated, often on an even grander scale, throughout Europe, most obviously at Amsterdam. But after King's Cross, no other stations became simply a 'machine for keeping trains in' until Eero Saarinen designed the station at Helsinki in 1910.

For stations soon became an opportunity for grandiose

displays of railway *macho* rather than an opportunity to experiment. The railway promoters, like *nouveaux riches* throughout the ages, were looking for respectability combined with grandiosity. At Lime Street, in Liverpool, in Gordon Biddle's words in *Great Railway Stations of Britain*, 'the whole purpose of the facade was to create a symbolic gateway to the railway, using the Roman triumphal arch as its theme. It was quite deliberately expressed in the classical terms of the Renaissance because contemporary thought still saw in the buildings of ancient Greece and Rome the representation of great and noble concepts which was exactly how the railways were represented.' At Nimes the idea was taken to its logical, ridiculous conclusion. The station there was a small-scale model of the town's most famous Roman monument, the Maison Carré.

The theme of triumphal grandiosity was not confined to the British. They were soon outdone, by the French at the Gare de l'Est in Paris, the very model of the Imperial architecture which symbolises the reign of Napoleon III, and by the Germans with half a dozen stations, notably at Munich and Hamburg, symbolising the pride of individual states, while in the United States no major city was complete without its splendid, usually Roman-style, Union Station.

Grandeur spread to the colonies where it often became heavily symbolic. Paul Theroux considered Kuala Lumpur Station 'the grandest in South-East Asia, with onion-shaped cupolas, minarets, and the general appearance of the Brighton Pavilion, but twenty times larger. As a monument to Islamic influence it is much more persuasive than the million-dollar National Mosque down the road, which gets all the tourists.' In Vancouver the Canadian Pacific obviously perceived its terminus, linking with the steamships across the Pacific, as a symbol, emphasised through its position blocking the view and by its style, an extravagant combination of the French and the Scottish baronial.

India was large enough to absorb all aspects of the Raj-as-station builder. At Lahore the station was a fort, that proposed for Delhi was truly Imperial in scale and style, while at Victoria Station in Bombay, built at a time 'when most of the world reverted to the classical forms, the British in India set about rediscovering and reinterpreting Indian architectural styles, symbol of a grandiose (and architecturally unhappy) mixture of west and east.'

Grandeur was internal as well as external: the finest feature of the old Euston station had been its Great Hall, its second most remarkable the directors' offices. By the end of the century the booking office of a station like the Paragon at Hull, with its twelve elaborate ticket windows, was bank-like in its grandeur, while at Glasgow Central even the indicator boards were rich, decorative – and highly practical.

As early as 1840 railway promoters had realised that travellers appreciated having somewhere to stay when they arrived. The first hotel was at Euston in 1838, leased by a Corsican hotelier, Zenon Vantini. At Paddington, according to Gordon Biddle, Brunel saw the Great Western Hotel 'as a fitting commencement to a journey from London to New York via the railway to Bristol and thence across the Atlantic on his new steamships.' Carroll Meeks[13] saw how the hotel, far grander than any of its predecessors, 'pointed the way to increased grandeur' and noted typical Brunel innovations, 'electric clocks, private lavatories and hotwater pipes in linen cupboards'.

The association of railway accommodation with conspicuous consumption spread world-wide, to the carriages, to 'the Pullmans that are like rushing hotels and the hotels that are like stationary Pullmans', in Henry James's words (*The American Scene*) and then to entire trains, most notably the Orient Express. Writers, most obviously Lucius Beebe, made it their whole life's work to hymn the special trains and carriages discussed above.

In Edinburgh the gigantic hotel built by the railways became the most prominent feature of Princes Street, and from the very beginning cities were very conscious of the impact of these new steam elephants. In Liverpool, states Barman, 'the city insisted that the station [Lime Street] harmonize with St George's Hall. The church of Saint Simon & Jude at the end of the cutting into the station was taken down, moved and rebuilt three times as the station was enlarged.'

But Liverpool proved rather an exception. As we saw in the previous chapter, financial restraints ensured that most stations were built on what were then the outskirts of major cities. In theory this provided a major opportunity for grand urban renewal or development. But nineteenth-century urban development was usually totally unplanned, and stations throughout the world have become infamous as the centre of piece-meal, squalid developments of no urban or architectural interest. Even one of the apparent exceptions, the Bahnhofstrasse in Zurich, a delightful boulevard, with the banks for which it is famous kept well out of sight, was originally at the centre of a crowded hot-bed of urban squalor and radical unrest. Stations, even in Switzerland, could not spread their aura of grandeur and luxury round them.

X

WAR ON THE RAILS

Railway promoters quickly exploited threats from internal subversion or external enemies to reinforce their cause. In 1829 the railroad lobby played on the fears of the Baltimoreans that the British would repeat their invasion of a mere seventeen years earlier. Three years later a Dr Caldwell echoed their ideas when he told a Boston audience that 'with the expedition of magic . . . all the military engineering of a nation might be brought to bear on any single point, to discomfit and destroy an approaching enemy.'

The argument was universal, self-generating. An 1833 pamphlet argued that a proposed line from Minden to Cologne would enable Prussia to reinforce its isolated provinces on the Rhine in the event of a surprise attack by the French. Nine years later it was France's turn to be concerned at the threat posed to their eastern frontier by that very same railway.

Nevertheless, economic, financial, and commercial arguments soon banished military justifications in most developed countries. Even in Prussia the military, anxious that the state railway network should fit in with their strategic plans, soon found that railways followed the same routes as they themselves would have wished – fairly obviously, since both promoters and soldiers had the same object, to join the country's major towns and cities together and to link them to the country's frontiers.

No-one else seems to have followed the example of the Argentinians in the 1850s, when they diverted money raised for railway construction to build warships. For the nineteenth-century 'military-industrial complex' was different from its twentieth-century equivalent. Governments might help

362

railways: but armaments followed, rather than led, other industries, financially as well as technologically. Both Alfred Krupp and Tom Vickers invested the fortunes they had amassed supplying the world's railways in devising new and deadlier weapons – products of the same technology which had provided stronger rails and wheels – which they then sold to the world's generals.

Nevertheless the security argument remained a trump card: the Canadian Pacific was saved at a low point in its fortunes when it helped quell a rebellion led by the half-Indian Louis Riel, and a powerful argument for promoters faced by autocratic rulers concerned that railways were instruments of democracy. At the end of the century the Chinese authorities, normally deeply suspicious of railways as foreign intrusions, were finally convinced of their value by the Boxer Rebellion.

Seventy years earlier the Austrian promoter Gerstner had tried to interest the Tsar in proposals for a network of lines throughout European Russia, to be run by a company which would enjoy a twenty-year monopoly. Gerstner told the Tsar[1] 'Your Majesty, at a notice of but twenty-four hours the railroad will be able to transport five thousand infantry and five hundred cavalry with all their horses, cannons and wagons. Permit me to recall England's experience. There, during the recent Irish troubles, the government within two hours brought troops over the rail from Manchester to Liverpool, thence to be embarked for Dublin.' At that point the Tsar, apparently, started to take a lively interest in the project.

In the early 1840s the Chartists used the railways to bring masses of their supporters to London and other major cities for peaceful demonstrations in favour of political reform. They were countered by the British military who used the same lines to 'pour troops into the disturbed districts', in Charles Greville's words. As the railways spread, so did their use to suppress internal unrest. In 1846 the Prussians moved 12,000 troops to suppress the 'Free Republic of Cracow'.

But the final confirmation of the railways' crucial security role came in 1848 when much of Europe rose against its masters. Troops were despatched all over Germany to act as mobile fire brigades to fight the revolutionaries, who themselves made very effective use of the tracks. 'Unable to stand against regular troops in the open field,' wrote Dennis Showalter[2], 'outmanoeuvred and outfought at every turn, the revolutionaries persisted in removing themselves from the jaws of disaster – and out of pursuit – by rail. As Albrecht von Roon, a Prussian staff officer, wrote to his wife, "This frustrating war will only end when the entire railway is in our hands." '

Governments could use railways to suppress, not only their own rebelling populace, but those of their allies as well. In 1849 the Russians sent 30,000 troops by rail to help the Austrians overcome the rebellious Hungarians. The Russians, the biggest Imperial power in Europe, made ever-increasing use of the railways. After moving troops by rail to quell the 1863 Polish uprising, they found a new argument: that rapid rail communications would allow a reduction in the standing army, which was mainly immobilised in frontier garrisons. As the War Minister told Alexander III, 'Railways are now the strongest and most decisive element of war. Therefore regardless even of financial difficulties, it is exceedingly desirable to make our railway network equal to that of our enemies.'

By that time the military were in a position to exercise a veto on Russia's railway plans. In the 1890s Count Witte was under severe pressure to build lines like that to Central Asia in pursuit of the 'Great Game' and to help future mobilisation against Germany. 'I tried to develop the railway network as best I could,' Count Witte told the Tsar, 'but military considerations, on whose side Your Majesty naturally was for the most part, significantly hindered the building of the railways.'

Rail construction often depended on the authorities' perception of which enemies were the most dangerous at any one time. During the 1890s the Russians were obsessed with the possibility of war in Europe and their lines were developed in that direction. Almost inevitably, their first war was with Japan; and at that point their strategic thinking shifted eastwards. The next war was with Germany – though by 1914 the Russians had prepared facilities like double-tracking and plans for mobilisation as elaborate and as universal (though not nearly as efficiently implemented) as the Germans.*

But it was in the Balkans, that cauldron of imperial ambitions, that railways became most obviously a military weapon, the outward sign of otherwise secret diplomatic manoeuvrings. The Sultan included much of the railway building in the Ottoman Empire in the defence budget. The result, as Noel Buxton wrote in 1908, was that, 'Over a large area the few railways that exist are built for strategy alone.' The use of railways as a major weapon in the convoluted geo-political chess game played by Austria, Russia, France, Germany – as well as the home teams, the Turks, the Serbs, the Roumanians and the Bulgarians – continued until the outbreak of war in 1914.

Once war had actually broken out railways enabled generals and the armies they commanded to escape – for the first time in recorded history – from the limitations imposed by the speed and endurance of men and horses. In theory the railways' capacity to transport soldiers and their equipment with unprecedented speed transformed the possibilities open to military strategists. In practice the railways' inflexibility and their vulnerability to sabotage limited their revolutionary potential.

In fact, throughout the century, troops and supplies alike remained dependent on horse-drawn transport once they had arrived at the railhead. This exposed what Martin van Creveld has called[3] 'the inherent limitations of a system of supply based on the unfortunate combination of the technical means of one age – the railways – with those of an earlier one.' Moreover the increase in mobility permitted by the railways imposed strains on the decision-making powers of statesmen and generals which proved too great in 1914, and helped make the First World War inevitable because the machine, once put in motion, proved mightier than its human controllers.

'Ask of me anything but time,' said Napoleon; but, thanks to

---

* In the Second World War – to the Russians the Great Patriotic War – their railways saved Mother Russia. Their existing network enabled them to move their whole armaments industry hundreds of miles east of Moscow, and two newly-built lines enabled them to supply Stalingrad and their forces in the Caucasus when the Germans had cut the direct lines from Moscow.

During the American Civil War, even seige guns travelled by rail.

the railways, 'Space and time, two of the key factors in the strategists' equation, meant something far different to Moltke than to Napoleon or Frederick the Great,' as Dennis Showalter put it. But the revolution went deeper. Railways gave a new meaning to the phrase 'a nation at war' by multiplying the number of men who could be mobilised in the first few days or weeks after the outbreak of hostilities.

They also radically transformed the balance between logistics and strategy. To Napoleon *l'Intendance suit*, the army's logistical tail was inevitably subordinate to the will of the commanding general. Allowing the railways to spread meant that the generals had to follow the imperatives dictated by the *intendance*.

At the same time the railways, and the telegraph, widened the gulf between the reality of the front line and the dreams of a High Command – behind the lines – itself a concept possible only in the railway-cum-telegraph age. No wonder that accounts of most nineteenth-century military campaigns are full of tales of troop trains arriving at the wrong time, the wrong place, not at all, or without the soldiers' equipment and supplies. The railways imposed their own industrial disciplines, alien to autocratic regimes: for instance, by commandeering trains sundry Grand Dukes greatly reduced the Russian army's mobility when war broke out against Japan in 1904.

Railways were used against foreign enemies well after they had been employed against native troublemakers. In the so-called 'Olmutz' crisis in 1850 the Austrians transported 750,000 troops to the trouble-spot in what is now northern Czechoslovakia quickly and efficiently. By contrast the Prussian armies wandered aimlessly between stations, bereft of orders, let alone transport. The Prussians were slow to learn their lesson. When they mobilised against the Danes nine years later there was still chaos. In the meantime the British had proved the utility of railways in the Crimea: the makeshift line built by Peto's navvies proved capable of handling up to 700 tons of supplies a day.

The French railways demonstrated their capacities in 1859. In the last ten days of April that year the Paris–Lyon railway carried a daily average of 8,421 men and 512 horses to the Piedmontese frontier to fight against the Austrians in Italy, an impressive performance helped by the way the French allowed railwaymen, not generals, to organise the mobilisation. The French did not take advantage of the time gained to change their military strategy, though. Moreover the supplies did not move at the same rate as the troops, who had nothing to eat except some mouldy biscuits in the twenty-four hours after they had defeated the Austrians at the battle of Solferino – a story of lack of coordination which was to be repeated time and again.

The lesson was learnt, not in Europe, but by bitter experience in the United States, where the Civil War proved to be the

Scorched earth in the railway age: General Sherman dismantles Atlanta's railroads.

supreme railway war, strategically, tactically, logistically. Without the railways the conflict would have been confined to the Eastern seaboard and the country's river systems, notably the Mississippi. Railways transformed the war into an almost continental conflict. The North's triumph was based on the fact that it had a better rail network, three times as long as that available to the Confederates, and had the industrial and managerial skills to exploit its supremacy.

Railways were the supreme symbol of the gap between the industrial North and the largely agrarian South. The Southerners knew this: before 1860 they had blocked progress on plans for a transcontinental railroad by insisting that it pass through the South. In their absence after Secession Congress easily passed the 1862 Act, providing for the building of a direct route from Omaha to San Francisco, well away from the South. During the war the North harnessed the managerial skills already available within the railroads to provide a transport and construction service far more professional than any in Europe. The managers and generals were backed up by the industrial infrastructure required to build and repair rails, locomotives and rolling-stock while the South had to rely on an inevitably dwindling supply of rails torn up from minor lines.

By the end of the war the Northern railroads were in far better shape than they had been in 1860. The previously separate lines serving major towns had been linked up, steel rails had replaced iron rails, coal had replaced wood as fuel, gauges standardised, many lines double-tracked, and both road-beds and the tracks themselves strengthened. The longer the conflict lasted, the greater the contrast with the South. For by the spring of 1864 the fastest train on the crucial line between Wilmington and the Confederate capital, Richmond, averaged a mere 10¼ mph.

At the outbreak of the war it was the North which was on the defensive, and their capital, Washington, was only saved by the Baltimore & Ohio. The pattern for the whole war was set by the shiftiest of the Union's many 'political' generals, Ben Butler. Unable to transport his troops through Baltimore, where the bridges had been burnt, he shipped his troops down the Potomac to Annapolis, where he found the rails torn up and the rolling stock destroyed. He found a rusting old locomotive and called for volunteers to repair it. Up stepped a private claiming, 'That engine was made in our shop; I guess I can fit her up and run her.' He did, and Butler's regiments arrived in time to save Washington. The Baltimore & Ohio remained crucial when the Union went onto the offensive because of its direct links west from Washington to the Mississippi river system.

Within eighteen months the Union had organised its railways on an integrated war footing, despite the railroad companies' objections – it took the threat of building an entirely new competing line between New York and Washington to persuade the existing lines to provide a through service. In peacetime the railroads, the country's biggest industry, had employed its best and brightest executives, and these naturally gravitated to the top of the Union government.

Thomas A. Scott, the Assistant Secretary of War, had been the general superintendent of the mighty Pennsylvania Railroad – a background which led him to create a separate corps to build and to run the railroads. In April 1862 he chose Daniel C. McCallum, a Scottish immigrant, poet and architect, and general superintendent of the rival Erie Railroad, to take control of the Union's railroads, first on the eastern front and then, for the last year of the war, over the entire country. Crucially, McCallum was given full authority over the generals whose troops and supplies he was transporting. By contrast in the South 'the so-called director of railroad transportation was pretty much a nullity', wrote Allan Nevins in *The War for the Union*.

For a time McCallum was overshadowed by the extraordinary Herman Haupt, the greatest single talent ever employed on military railroads. Haupt was a West Point graduate, a professor of mathematics and engineering, the author of a standard work on *The General Theory of Bridge Construction*, and, even more relevantly, a friend of Scott's. He was originally employed only to repair bridges, but, for a turbulent and creative year until he resigned in a huff, he also built railroads. Haupt was a towering, dominating presence – 'Mac took the office and I took the field,' he said grandiloquently – with a genius for problem solving in the best American tradition.

In the words of Thomas Weber,[4] 'Haupt took pleasure in surmounting difficulties and was delighted to find a badly tangled situation which he could clear up with his magic touch . . . this humourless man was responsible for developing not only the general principles of railway supply operation, but also detailed methods of construction and destruction of railroad equipment. Moreover he not only built, he organised. On one line, on which three or four trains a day had taken five hours to cover thirty miles, he organised five daily convoys each way, each consisting of five or six trains.' It was said that the specially-equipped ambulance trains he organised were worth an extra 100,000 men to the Union armies.

The strains were appalling. In McCallum's words, 'It was by no means unusual for men to be out with their trains from five to ten days, without sleep, except what could be snatched upon their engines and cars while the same were standing to be unloaded, with but scanty food, or perhaps no food at all, for days together, while continually occupied to keep each faculty strained to its upmost.'

Haupt – and McCallum's – most spectacular achievements, though, lay in the railroads they built. By the end of the war the Unionists had built 2,165 miles of military railroads. They also learnt how to rebuild with astonishing speed the bridges and track destroyed by the roving Confederate cavalry. Haupt's fame was made by one such incident, when he rebuilt a 400-foot bridge 80 feet above the River Potomac in nine days, in bad weather, without enough men or equipment. The feat inspired Lincoln's famous remark to his cabinet, 'That man Haupt has built a bridge across Potomac Creek . . . over which loaded trains are running every hour, and, upon my word, gentlemen, there is nothing in it but beanpoles and cornstalks.'

Haupt left a tradition of such achievements behind him. After he had resigned, a 780-foot bridge over the Chatahoocee River was rebuilt in four and a half days. According to the chief engineer, 'The work of reconstruction commenced while the old bridge was still burning, and was somewhat delayed because the iron rods were so hot that the men could not handle them to remove the wreck.' The Union forces' legendary powers of reconstruction inspired the famous cry of despair from a Confederate soldier asked to help blow up a tunnel: 'There isn't any use 'cause Sherman carries 'long duplicates of all tunnels.'

Sherman was Haupt's spiritual successor. In Weber's words, 'It was Haupt, more than any other single man, who laid down the principles and practices which enabled Sherman to carry through his brilliant campaigns in the South in the last two years of the war,' campaigns in which Sherman proved himself the supreme railway general, with a unique understanding of their possibilities – and their limitations.

Sherman was no neophyte. In 1849, as a lieutenant, he had been in charge of protecting the surveyors pioneering a railroad route across the Rockies. During the Civil War he relied greatly on Lewis Parsons, McCallum's deputy and successor, a regular army quartermaster with a unique understanding of the potential capacities available if both rail and river were used for mass transport. Parsons had shown his ability before Sherman's arrival on the western front when he had conveyed 10,000 men from central Kentucky in a mere four days to reinforce Grant at Vicksburg, an unprecedented demonstration of the railways' capacity to influence a distant operation.

Railways, more specifically the line round the southern end of the Appalachian mountains from Chatanooga to Atlanta, were the key weapon in Sherman's indirect approach to the conquest of the South; a strategy so revolutionary that it was properly analysed only sixty years later when Basil Liddell Hart published his book *Sherman, soldier, realist, American.*

In the summer of 1864, while the main Union army was bogged down in Virginia, Sherman, backed by his superior, General Grant, who understood railway warfare almost as well as he did, first swept along the tracks to Atlanta before swinging north to wreak havoc behind the lines of the South's army. 'The Atlanta campaign,' he wrote in his memoirs, 'would surely have been impossible without the use of the railroads from Chatanooga to Atlanta . . . that single stem of railroad supplied an army of 100,000 men and 35,000 horses for the period of 196 days.'

Sherman also understood the railways' limitations. As Liddell Hart put it, 'Sherman was a master strategist because he was a born quartermaster . . . he showed more joy of a small increase in car-loads than over a large reinforcement of troops.' He was fully aware that General Maclellan had had to use half of his 20,000 men in Virginia to guard the Baltimore & Ohio. He abandoned the railroad line for his famous march through Georgia because he understood the superiority of river transport in hostile territory: 'They can't stop the Tennessee River and each boat can make its own game.' By contrast any 'railroad running through a country where every house is a nest of secret, bitter enemies' would inevitably suffer – 'bridges and watertanks burned, trains fired into, track torn up . . . engines run off and badly damaged'.

The American Civil War ended just as the great Helmuth von Moltke became Chief of the Prussian Great General Staff. He was a career soldier with a strong belief in railways. He had invested his life savings in them, and was a director of one of the many German railway companies whose promoters looked for well-placed friends, supporters and directors in the closed ranks of the Prussian aristocracy. Moltke had a clear idea of railways' importance. Like many other Germans, he hoped, in Dennis Showalter's words, 'that the industrial, economic and technical progress made possible by the railways would bring Germany together'. As far as it was necessary he also hoped to shape the Prussian railway system to military purposes. Above all, as he told the Reichstag, 'Our Great General Staff is so much persuaded of the advantages to be derived from obtaining the initiative at the outset of war that it prefers to construct railways rather than forts.'

Like most European observers, Moltke had dismissed the American Civil War as a war conducted by amateurs. Although he had McCallum's reports translated into German, he does not seem to have absorbed the lessons they contained. For this much-vaunted master of the use of railways in warfare did not understand their limitations as well as Sherman, and had none of McCallum's capacity for organising lengthy supply lines.

Moltke shared Napoleon's obsession with time and speed, an obsession which naturally led him to appreciate the railways' potential. To him, wrote Dennis Showalter, 'Victory in war was not merely a function of numbers; it depended at least as much on the time needed to bring these numbers into action . . . railways were thus an enormous help in buying time for a state without significant natural frontiers, yet surrounded by potential enemies' – the French to the West, the Russians and Austrians to the east and south.

A wrecked German ammunition train, destroyed by shell fire in World War I

He faced one basic problem: Germany's railways were owned by a dozen different companies, and until 1872 he could not rely on any central controlling mechanism. But this diversity could be an advantage. In the 1866 campaign against the Austrians he could claim that, 'We have the inestimable advantage of being able to carry our field army of 285,000 men over five railway lines, and of virtually concentrating them in five days on the frontiers of Saxony and Bohemia. Austria has only one line of rail, and it will take her forty-five days to assemble 210,000 men.'[5]

The railways enabled him to disperse his troops in three widely-separated armies along the four-hundred-mile Prussian frontier with Bohemia. In doing so, as Martin van Crefeld has pointed out, Moltke was making a virtue out of a necessity. He had to use all five lines because the Prussians had started mobilising well after the Austrians. Not surprisingly, the Kaiser was worried that the Austrians could, in theory, attack any one of the armies separately. In the end Moltke was able to bring overwhelming force to bear at the crucial point and gain a correspondingly overwhelming victory. Nevertheless he and his staff clearly expected too much from the railways. In Denis Showalter's words, they were regarded 'as a sort of magic carpet. Most of the regimental bakers, for example, were retained at the depots in order to make maximum use of the permanent facilities there. As a result inedible loaves of bread arrived in the theatre of war from as far afield as Cologne.'

The Franco-Prussian war of 1870 has often been hailed as a masterpiece of railway warfare. In fact it demonstrated the same limitations as the war with the Austrians four years earlier. After the 1866 campaign Moltke had instituted a special lines of communication department within the General Staff, to enable mobilisation to be centralised and thus speeded up. It was. Before 1870 individual corps had assembled at their headquarters, then separated into trainloads before being transported to the concentration areas at the frontier. In 1870 they assembled only once, at the frontier. Using all six railway lines at his disposal he could have 360,000 men available in three weeks, 430,000 in four. His success in transporting the troops to the frontier, and the subsequent crushing German triumph, created the legend that railways were indeed a magic carpet which could waft troops to victory. This was far from the truth. The war certainly proved that they were an incomparable means of mobilising the largest of armies at the most distant of frontiers: but that was most definitely that.

The Prussian General Staff may have been better prepared for war than the French, but their railways were not. French trains were faster, their networks better co-ordinated, more of their

Special narrow gauge railway transports British troops towards the front line.

lines double-tracked, their stations were bigger, they had more rolling-stock. Finally, French organisation was sufficiently superior to enable them to run half as many trains again with the same facilities as the Prussians. Moreover – and this is the very reverse of the myth – their network was more suited to the war than the Prussian. Although most French railways led to Paris, there was amply sufficient mileage along their Eastern frontier to enable the French to mobilise at least as fast as their enemies.

The French failure was not logistical but political. In the late 1860s the Emperor Napoleon III was growing steadily more unpopular. 'Because of the fear of revolution,' observes William McElwee, in *The Art of War*, 'regiments were normally quartered in garrisons as far removed as possible from their depots and recruiting areas lest the troops be contaminated by local political feeling. The double journey which every regiment had to make, first to the depot to embody reserves and draw war equipment and then to the Concentration Area, placed an intolerable burden on an already overstrained railway system ... cross-country journeys were often virtually impossible, and troops and material piled up in indescribable congestion and confusion in the Paris stations and at the large junctions.'

As a result the troops arrived at the front usually without supplies, often without their officers, and, more often than not, drunk and disorderly from the liquid refreshment required to alleviate their long ordeal by train. When on 6th August, 1870, the twenty-third day after mobilisation, the French army fought its first defensive battles at Spliechen and Worth it numbered only 270,000 men against 462,000 German. Half the reserves were not yet in: and the whole army lacked most of its equipment and supplies.

After delivering troops to the frontiers, the railways played only a minor, supporting role in the famous, crushing German victory, and during the fighting after the main campaign they proved more nuisance than they were worth. The German railway staffs, drawn from a dozen different systems, worked badly together and the Prussians still lacked a central supply organisation, so contractors simply pushed as many supplies forward as possible, cruelly exposing the army's inability to organise distribution from the railheads. The army had to live off the (fortunately rich) land, and during the siege of Paris in the winter of 1870–71 the Prussians had to suspend most military operations for two months to look for provisions.

During the campaign itself the destruction of a single viaduct at Fontenoy-sur-Moselle, which carried all the German military traffic, could have halted the Prussian advance if it had happened a month earlier – a month during which the Germans had captured Mezières, which provided them with an alternative route. During the winter of 1870–71 French saboteurs ensured that a whole army corps had to be employed guarding the lines, and the Prussians had to build a loop line round a tunnel at Nanteuil-sur-Marne when six mines exploded by *francs-tireurs* filled it with 4,000 cubic yards of sand.

After 1870 railways proved a tarnished weapon. In their campaign against the Turks in 1876 the Russians had forgotten that their own gauge was wider than that used on the winding lines in the Ottoman Empire. It took them ten weeks of painful loading, offloading and reloading to transport their army over 425 miles of twisting and winding railway, twice the time it would have taken the soldiers to march directly the 250 miles between their frontier and their destination.

Twenty years later General Kitchener relied on railways in his campaign against the Mahdi in the Sudan. He – or rather his chief engineer, Percy Girouard – had shown that lines could be built at high speed in an emergency, even through the desert, provided only that there was no enemy interference. But one young war correspondent, had understood the railways' potential problems. 'Victory,' wrote Winston Churchill, 'is the beautiful, bright-coloured flower. Transport is the stem without which it could never have blossomed. Yet even the military student, in his zeal to master the fascinating combinations of the actual combat, often forgets the far more intricate complications of supply.'

Kitchener's great rival, Lord Roberts, had not grasped the lesson which the Prussians ought to have learnt in 1870–1871, that the 'intricate complications of supply' included the ease with which saboteurs can force a theoretically superior, theoretically triumphant army onto the defensive. In the Boer War of 1899–1902 railways enabled the British to pursue their opponents far into the interior, but, in the words of Thomas Pakenham,[6] 'the troops still went hungry when they stepped far from the railway: and the repairs to the railway could not keep up with the pace of an ox.' Lord Roberts had ridiculed the idea of building an additional railway line to increase the capacity on the three hundred miles of single-track, narrow-gauge railway on which the British troops in the Orange Free State relied for all their supplies. The Boers naturally exploited the British weakness with a special Irish Brigade dedicated to wrecking the line – and ensuring that much of the army's strength was dissipated in manning hundreds of hot, lonely, often ineffective blockhouses guarding it.

No General Staff was less prepared than the Russian, its eastern army entirely dependent on the Trans-Siberian railway. When war broke out against the Japanese in 1904 the line consisted of 5,000 miles of single-track railway with two crucial gaps, one where a tunnel was incomplete, the other round Lake Baikal where the line was a mere sketch on the drawing-board.* It took their troops under General Kuropatkin six weeks to reach the Sea of Japan – weeks longer than the sea voyage from Russia's Black Sea ports. The delay was a godsend to the Japanese, who emphasised Russian problems by cutting the railway line behind the wretched general.

The Russians had not fully learnt the lessons of railway vulnerability in 1904. Ten years later the Prussians seemed determined to ignore the equally obvious problem of railway inflexibility. In 1870 their timetable system had worked perfectly. As Michael Howard puts it in *The Franco-Prussian War*: 'Railway timetables were drawn up, so that every unit knew the exact day and hour that it would leave its barracks and reach its concentration area. Mobilisation and deployment would follow one another in a single smooth and exactly calculated operation.'

---

* In the winter the troops could march over the ice on Lake Baikal, in the summer they could use ferry-boats, but in spring and autumn the lake was impassable.

In 1914 mobilisation had become deployment, eliminating the historic interval between the two, used by diplomats through the ages as a breathing-space to make one last effort for peace. This didn't matter in 1870, but legend has it that the compression proved fatal in 1914 when the system had been refined to be able to operate on an even larger scale. The demands on the system, and the men operating it, were enormous – hence the saying 'The best brains produced by the War College went into the railway section and ended up in lunatic asylums.'

In theory the inflexibility increased with the size of the armies being mobilised – in 1914 they amounted to forty German Army corps. According to Barbara Tuchman, in *August, 1914*, each one required '170 railway carriages for officers, 965 for infantry, 2960 for cavalry, 1915 for artillery and supply wagons, 6010 in all, grouped in 140 trains with an equal number for their supplies. From the moment the order was given, everything was to move at fixed times according to a schedule precise down to the number of train axles that would pass over a given bridge within a given time.'

The classical account of the outbreak of war, best expounded by A. J. P. Taylor, is that 'the decision for mobilisation which the German General Staff made and which Bethmann endorsed on 29th July was a decision for a general European war.' The theory is based on the apparent facts: when the Kaiser repented of his decision to mobilise, he was told by his chief of staff, the nephew of the great von Moltke, that it was too late, that the machine was irreversible, had become an organisational Frankenstein.

But Moltke was being unfair to the capacity of his own machine. His staff had prepared an alternative: for the French frontier to be held by a lightly-manned defensive wall, while the main weight of the army was hurled at the Russians. Such a deployment would at least have given the diplomats time to talk, a breathing space which, they claimed in retrospect, they were all eager to exploit. In the tragic event even the finest railway organisation in history could not cope with Moltke's inflexibility (based on his sensitivity to the charge that he did not measure up to his uncle's stature), combined with the Kaiser's fickle emotionalism.

August, 1914, was the last time that railways played a major part in strategic thinking. By 1939 motorised road transport had largely replaced the railway as the primary instrument. Railways became merely part of the logistical train: the 'intendance' had returned to the subordinate role to which Napoleon had consigned it. However, in World War II they remained crucial for transporting supplies and troops – it is now clear that had the Allies concentrated their bombing raids on the German railway system the war would have ended months earlier than it did. Moreover it was only the willingness of the Swiss to allow German supply trains through their Alpine tunnels which enabled German armies to continue to fight in Italy until April, 1945 and it was only the efficiency of the German railway system which enabled the Holocaust to proceed with its killing efficiency.

A mere three years later the Berlin airlift proved that the railways were no longer indispensable. Stalin belonged to the railway age and assumed that Berlin would be starved into submission within a few weeks after its rail links had been cut. But the rules had changed, as the Berlin airlift showed so dramatically.

The Great (Railway) Game

Russian interest in Afghanistan dates back more than a century before their invasion in 1979. In the last thirty years of the nineteenth century their involvement, real or imaginary, became an obsession with the British in India. The rivalry, aptly nick-named 'The Great Game', was played in the romantic setting of the high Himalayas and railways became the major symbol of Russian expansionist intentions.

The first proposal for a line along the old caravan route from Orenburg to Tashkent was made as early as 1874, only a few years after the Russians had completed their control of Turkestan. Their plans were delayed when a native revolt gave priority to the building of the Trans-Caspian railway to Kizyl Arvat, a line which soon seemed rather useless. It had not helped pacify the region and was nowhere near the agriculturally richer areas of Soviet Central

Asia. Nevertheless in 1885 the Russians started to extend it eastward to Merv, an oasis they had captured the previous year.

The seizure of Merv, and above all the new line, led to an outbreak of paranoid frenzy in British India. 'No longer the prudent auxiliary to a single campaign,' wrote Lord Curzon, the archetypal Imperialist, 'it became the mark of a definite policy, imperial in its quality and dimensions. Till then the Russians had regarded the line as an isolated and limited undertaking, rather than part of a great design. It now emerged as a warning to England and a warning to Asia . . . the flame of diplomatic protest blazed fiercely forth in England but, after a momentary combustion, was as usual extinguished by a flood of excuses from the inexhaustible reservoir on the Neva' – the river on which stood Saint Petersburg, then the Russian capital.

The devilish Russkies paused a mere six weeks after reaching Merv before pressing on towards the Afghan frontier. The line included a hundred-mile stretch over the Kara Kum desert, whose shifting sands simply swept away the tracks, which, finally, had to be built entirely on an embankment. Only regular water trains could relieve the permanent shortage of water, and herds of camels derailed the odd train or two.

To the British the line was no laughing matter. Immediately the Russians had completed their line to Merv the normally parsimonious, normally dilatory British Imperial government promptly built a railway to Chaman, within a few hundred yards of the Afghan frontier, complete with enough stores to complete the tracks a further forty miles inside Afghanistan to Kandahar. The project was so secret that it was code-named 'the Henrai Road improvement scheme'. It was later renamed more prosaically the Sind-Peshia State Railway.

Ten years later the Russians started to build from Samarkand to Tashkent, and by 1898 they had completed a through railway line stretching over a thousand miles. The line remained an empty symbol of Russian imperialism. In the event it was never used for a major military exercise. And when the Russians finally did invade Afghanistan, a hundred years after The Great Game had begun, they relied on road and air transport.

The Carriage at Compiègne

During the First World War Marshal Foch housed himself and his staff in three coaches formerly used to transport passengers on the Orient Express and other luxury trains. Towards the end of the war he ordered another, Number 2419, to be equipped as an office. In November, 1918, it was commandeered by Foch's chief of Staff, General Weygand, and in the forest of Compiègne outside Paris it became the setting for the signature of the Armistice on 11th November, which ended the war.

Number 2419 became the ultimate symbol to Germany of their country's defeat, and Adolf Hitler ensured that France's surrender in June, 1940, would be signed in the same carriage on the same spot which had witnessed Germany's humiliation twenty-two years earlier. The symbolism still remained, however. The Germans stored carriage 2419, apparently safe from Allied bombing, in the little town of Ohrdruf, in Thuringia during the Second World War. But they were not going to allow it to be the setting of a second German humiliation. Just before the Americans arrived, a special detachment of SS troops blew it up.

The General

When Buster Keaton was asked why his famous film, *The General*, looked so much more authentic than *Gone with the Wind*, he replied, simply and truthfully, 'Well, they went to a novel for their story. We went to history.'

The Reverend William Pittenger, formerly of the 2nd Ohio Volunteers, called his own account of the episode *The Locomotive Chase in Georgia.** He recounted how twenty-four Union soldiers under one James J. Andrews infiltrated the Confederate lines and very nearly managed to cut all the rail links between Chatanooga and the south and east.

* Reproduced by D. A. Botkin in *A Treasury of Railroad Folklore*. When Walt Disney filmed the story, thirty years after Keaton, he called it *The Great Locomotive Chase*.

Only twenty of the twenty-four turned up at the rendezvous which, as Pittenger pointed out, emphasised the foolhardiness of the whole venture:

> The railroad was found to be crowded with trains, and many soldiers were among the passengers. Then the station – Big Shanty – at which the capture was to be effected had recently been made a Confederate camp ... To succeed in our enterprise it would be necessary first to capture the engine in a guarded camp, with soldiers standing around as spectators, and then to run it from 100 to 200 miles through the enemy's country, and to deceive or overpower all trains that should be met – a large contract for twenty men!

They rode as passengers for a mere eight miles, then:

> When we stopped, the conductor, engineer, and many of the passengers hurried to breakfast, leaving the train unguarded. Now was the moment of action! Ascertaining that there was nothing to prevent a rapid start, Andrews, our two engineers, Brown and Knight, and the fireman, hurried forward, uncoupling a section of the train consisting of three empty baggage or box cars, the locomotive and tender. The engineer and fireman sprang into the cab of the engine while Andrews, with hand on the rail and foot on the step, waited to see that the remainder of the band had gained entrance into the rear box car. This seemed difficult and slow, although it really consumed but a few seconds.

While a sentinel a few feet away stood aghast, 'Andrews, with a nod to his engineer, stepped on board. The valve was pulled wide open and for a moment the wheels of "The General" slipped around ineffectively; then, with a bound that jerked the soldiers in the box car from their feet, the little train darted away, leaving the camp and the station in the wildest uproar of confusion.'

Andrews had a copy of the timetable for the single track line, according to which they would encounter only two trains.

Unfortunately the operation had been delayed a day. On the original date 'every train had been on time, the day dry, and the road in perfect order. Now the road was in disorder, every train far behind time, and two "extras" were approaching us.'

At first all went well. They stopped for wood and water – Andrews coolly telling all and sundry that the train was a special carrying vitally needed supplies of gunpowder. At Etowah station they found an ancient engine, the 'Yonah', with steam up. They did not have time to disable it, so it was requisitioned by two pursuers, the train's conductor, W. A. Fuller, and Anthony Murphy, foreman of the Atlanta workshops, who had started the pursuit in a handcar.

The Union soldiers were averaging over a mile a minute in 'The General', giving the time to break a rail and thus stop the 'Yonah'. Undeterred, Fuller and Murphy commandeered another train. They were too close to allow Andrews and his men time to break any more rails, or to destroy the first of the key bridges on the line:

> We broke out the end of our last box car and dropped cross-ties on the track as we ran, thus checking their progress and getting far enough ahead to take in wood and water at two separate stations. Several times we almost lifted a rail, but each time the coming of the Confederates, within rifle range, compelled us to desist and speed on. Our worst hindrance was the rain. The previous day had been clear, with a high wind, and on such a day fire would have been easily and tremendously effective. But today a bridge could be burned only with abundance of fuel and careful nursing.

The Union men could not shake off Fuller and Murphy, who were merely jolted even when they ran over a rail skilfully dropped on the track on a blind bend. Fuller had managed to send a message to Chatanooga, which set off a panic among inhabitants unaware that the Union soldiers were desperately short of wood and water:

The side and end boards of the last car were torn into shreds, all available fuel was piled upon it, and blazing brands were brought back from the engine. By the time we approached a long covered bridge the fire in the car was fairly started. We uncoupled it in the middle of the bridge, and with painful suspense awaited the issue.

Alas, before the bridge had caught alight the pursuers were upon them, driving the burning car before them to the next side-track. At this Andrews's nerve finally gave way and he ordered his men to jump and try and save themselves. Most were caught, and seven hanged as spies. The others escaped by attacking their guards, but six of the fourteen were recaptured – though they were repatriated in an exchange of prisoners less than a year later.

Keaton took as his hero the Confederate engineer, Murphy, whom he renamed Johnnie Gray, and he gave Johnnie, not the Unionists, the 'General'. Gray loved the engine almost as much as his beloved Annabelle Lee, who had spurned him because of his supposed cowardice, not realising that locomotive engineers were too important to be allowed to enlist.

Keaton used contemporary wood-burning locomotives, and every possible railway gag, some not far from the real life chase. He used logs thrown at him by his pursuers as fuel; the trains race each other on parallel tracks and then rejoin the main line, with the pursuer emerging ahead of the train it was pursuing. After the pursuers had finally collapsed into a river Johnnie walks off into the sunset arm in arm with his beloved Annabelle.

XI

THE GREAT RAILWAY RENAISSANCE

Over the past thirty years railways throughout the world have made an extraordinary comeback. Yet in the three decades after 1945 it had been assumed that their decline – and eventual disappearance – was inevitable, a typical piece of misleading techno-forecasting. Even though they have retained their role in history as the true revolutionaries of mechanical transport, with the petrol engine and the jet aircraft merely representing evolutionary developments, the renaissance is surprising, for in an age obsessed with technical progress railways look increasingly old hat. Steel wheels still run on steel rails, which are still mostly 1435 mm apart and that most modern form of rail traction, the electric motor, first appeared well over a century ago. Yet 'steel on steel' retains its biggest single advantage, that it has a lower coefficient of friction than any other form of contact and therefore requires less effort, less energy than, say a rubber tyre on a road.

Today the words of Louis Armand, greatest of 20th century railwaymen, ring truer than ever. When asked why he wanted to electrify France's main railway lines at a time in the 1960s when it was assumed that cars buses and lorries would take over the role played by railways he replied simply 'when everyone has a car they will return to the railways'. Indeed, as soon as car ownership became the norm people could make a rational judgment as to the worth of the railways. Their advantages have increased as travel by car has become less and less attractive, hampered by a lack of road capacity, higher petrol prices, an increased concern for the environment – as well as cleaner, faster trains. Moreover the younger generation seems less keen on driving than its car-obsessed parents. So throughout the world

– apart from the United States – railways are again recognised as an essential element in any society whose members are aspiring to a civilised life, resulting in ever-more ambitious plans for countries' railway systems.

In fact, despite the seemingly unstoppable rise of motorised transport, only a minority of the tracks were lost, and those were mostly little-used rural routes. In Britain, a sentimental country, the attempts by Dr Richard Beeching as chairman of British Rail to make a logical distinction between commercially viable routes and those which could be justified only on social grounds made him a hate figure for those who love railways for their own sake not for their utility. Fortunately few architecturally important stations, apart from Penn Station in New York and Euston in London (together with its heavy, ugly but much-lamented Doric Arch), succumbed to the wreckers' ball though many suffered from neglect.

The only major exception to the retreat suffered by the railways in the thirty or forty years after 1945 was in China. When Mao Tse Tung came to power in 1949 the country's railway system was a mere 14,000 km – excluding Mongolia where the Japanese occupiers had built several thousand more miles. Most of the lines had been built before 1911 by the Europeans who had dominated the country, and as a result railways had been indissolubly associated with their imperial attitudes. Mao instituted a massive programme which resulted in an eight-fold expansion within forty years, starting with two what might be called 'imperial' lines from the coast to areas in the west threatened with revolts against Beijing's supremacy. These were followed by an enormously impressive line into the mountainous south west of the country and, more recently, a stupendous line up to the Tibetan plateau, 11,000 feet high.

The massive expansion has been accompanied by an equally staggering increase in the speed of the trains. Because the Chinese had plenty of coal and virtually no oil they continued building steam locomotives until the 1980s and the last steam train service survived into the 21st century. But as electrification spread speeds rose from a maximum of 120kph to 200kph and that was before they embarked on the most ambitious programme of high-speed lines in the world. As so often the Chinese called in foreign businesses, learnt from them, and thus became steadily more independent. Although the programme was temporarily halted in 2011 because a major accident revealed the depth of corruption and incompetence in the Ministry of Railways they can now boast some 10,000km of high speed lines, more than the rest of the world put together, including the longest single route, 2,300km long, from Beijing to Gungzhou.

For the biggest single contribution to the return of rail as a viable competitor not only to the motorcar but also to air travel has been increasing speed, not only on existing routes but also on the many new high-speed lines the world over from France to South Korea. Not only are the speeds up to 200mph, nearly double that available on historic lines. The pioneers, the Shinkansen in Japan and the Trains Grande Vitesse – the French and now international name for these trains – were those rarest of phenomena, a major step forward which employed proven technology and were pioneering efforts which made a profit from day one. The first Shinkansen between Tokyo and Osaka was designed to demonstrate the extent to which Japan had recovered from the war in time for the opening of the Tokyo Olympics in 1964. Unfortunately the line's pioneering engineer had underestimated the cost of a route that involved 3,000 bridges and 67 tunnels. As a result of the overspend he was frozen out, not even invited to the opening. The TGV, which went into service in the early 1980s was a result not only of French attempts to keep up with the Japanese but also of the vast increase in petrol prices resulting from the first oil crisis of 1973.

The French example set off a pan-European race to provide high-speed travel. The Germans are trying a mix of new and old tracks even on such major routes as that from Berlin to Munich – partly because the ferocity and effectiveness of the country's green lobby makes it both time-consuming and expensive to build new lines. After several decades of effort – the Apennines have always proved a notoriously difficult obstacle for tunnelers – the Italians have finally completed their major line north from Naples through Rome, Florence and Bologna to Milan while the

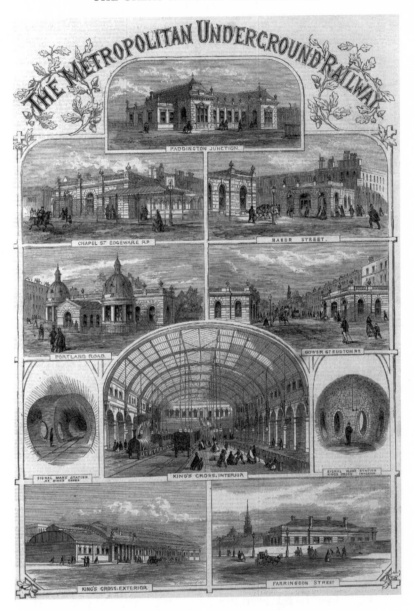

Celebrating the world first underground railway.

Spanish have proved the most ambitious of all, planning to ensure that nine tenths of the population will soon be within 50km of a high-speed station. Unhappily European countries –

or rather their rail operators – remain firmly nationalistic. As a result national prejudice ensures that the much-vaunted international route network sponsored by the EEC has largely proved to be a non-starter with only three out of 14 schemes completed. Outside Europe the efforts can be even more ambitious. The Kenyans are trying to jump generations of speed, while they used to say 'if you're in a hurry you take a bus not a train' they are planning to build a line which will reduce travel time from Mombasa to Nairobi from 13 to 3 hours. But throughout the world the growth of traffic on lines old and new has been emphasised by the abandonment of the old tradition of a select few especially fast trains in favour of regular fast services.

The TGV network was predicated on the belief that trains could compete with travel by air only for journeys of up to three hours – though even this limit gave rail the advantage for journeys of up to 450 miles. But the sheer ease of train travel, the ability to use computers – and increasingly wifi – on trains, and the airports' obsession with irritating, time-absorbing security has added another hour to the time, allowing for competition between cities over 500 miles apart – even when some of the route is travelled on older, slower tracks. The same applies to them, until recently a great many planes flew between London and Manchester, a mere 200 miles away. But the arrival of a reliable two-hour rail service has greatly reduced the number of flights – as has the Eurostar service from London to Paris and Brussels.

Another happy sign of the renaissance of the railway has been the involvement of major architects, most notably Salvatore Calatrava whose most breathtaking achievement has been the new station in Lisbon. But perhaps the greatest achievement has been not a new station but the rebirth of Saint Pancras station in London in which 700 Victorian iron columns now support the trains destined to travel to the Continent.

Significantly it was Mrs Thatcher, who hated everything to do with railways – and didn't much like the Europeans – who gave the go-ahead to a rail tunnel under the English Channel, a major engineering triumph finally opened in 1994 after 190 years of hesitation – and repeated doses of hysterical xenophobia – on the part of the British. But the Chunnel is not alone, three new tunnels are being dug under the Alps including a 57-kilometre wonder under the Saint Gotthard Pass. Like the Chunnel this will serve for both passengers and freight.

In general, however, rail freight is now largely confined to journeys of less than several hundred miles, often dealing purely with the transport of raw materials. Nevertheless the discovery of new deposits of minerals has led to some impressive new lines, like that in Western Australia from Mildara to transport iron ore to the Pacific – the Australians have also completed a north–south railway from Adelaide to Darwin through thousands of miles of scrub and desert. Similarly in the mid-West of the United States a new line was built to exploit the Powder River coal deposits in Wyoming. This was a sign of the way that although passenger rail travel – apart from sedate tourist trains – is almost completely confined to the 'North East Corridor' from Washington to New York and Boston, freight has surged ahead after the passage in 1979 of the Staggers Act which freed the railways from the often ridiculous restrictions imposed decades earlier when they had a monopoly of long-distance travel. So successful and profitable have they been that in 2010 Warren Buffett, that most thorough of investors, bought one of the biggest groups, the Burlington Northern Santa Fe network.

But perhaps the most astonishing change of attitudes to railways has occurred in Britain. In the words of Will Hutton, starting in the 1960s 'some talented managers starting with the much-reviled Richard Beeching' had 'managed to pull an under-invested service up by its bootstraps over thirty years' after which it had become one of the most efficient railway systems in Europe even though it received a mere £9 per head of financial support every year from the government as opposed to £21 in France and £33 in Italy. The situation darkened after privatisation in the 1990s which split British Rail into over ninety companies for the sake of spurious 'competition' but today state investment in the industry has soared and has been spared any of the cuts imposed by the coalition on virtually all other government activities.

Much of the investment has been on improving London's rail

transport system. For the single most dramatic development of rail travel in the 20th century, at a rate that looks like accelerating in the 21st, has been in urban travel in the world's growing number of major metropolises during a period when the – ever-increasing – population of the whole world seems to be concentrating into ever larger conurbations. The effects of rail transport on the growth of cities is hopelessly underestimated because it is divided into so many categories, from trams and light rail running along city streets, through metro systems to 'overground' lines running within the metropolises. But they are all railways combining the two key elements in the definition of the term 'steel wheel running on steel rail', generally with a 1435mm gauge. Typically London has one of the world's longest networks of both sub-surface and deep subway lines, an ever-increasing 'London Overground' system, a driverless network serving the city's former docklands and a single, but lengthy, tramway. Under construction there is Crossrail, an ambitious route half in new tunnels and taking in existing suburban routes at both ends, an even-longer imitation of the RER which was built through Paris thirty years ago.

If in the 19th century railways were above all means of transport between towns and cities in the 20th the major growth was within the urban environment. Indeed within a few years after 1900 railways had shown that they were capable of yet another revolution. This has ensured that the world's major cities could continue to thrive and expand seemingly almost without limit, a revolution as fundamental and important as that achieved by any of their overground brethren since the creation of 'mega-cities' was one of the fundamental developments of the 20th century and one that shows no sign of slowing down during the 21st. As William Barclay Parsons, the engineering genius who built the first New York subway put it 'We have no means of foretelling the ultimate fate of a modern city or assigning a limit to its growth.'

The key to this massive new role was the underground railway. The first was of course the steam-powered Metropolitan in London in 1863 that by the end of the century had expanded to form a circle round the heart of London. This was a one-off, which, until the arrival of electric power involved travel in tunnels in which only the inhabitants of London, permanently subject to the city's fogs and its universal coal smoke, could be expected to survive. But at the time only a tenth of the city's 600,000 workers 'commuted' by train, though that was far more than in New York or Paris. The only other truly urban railways were experiments, notably in Chicago and New York, with elevated railways that were clearly undesirable blots on the urban landscape.

City railways underground only exploded on the scene in a few years after 1900, simultaneously in New York Paris and London, the three exemplars of a modern city. But after the examples set by the Big Three the idea spread fast – by 1914 more than a dozen cities including Boston, Glasgow and Budapest had introduced metros of a sort. Tunnelling was no longer by hand but largely mechanical thanks to use of a circular shield at the point of tunnelling. The first had been invented by Marc Brunel, father of Isambard Kingdom Brunel, who had used it to dig the world's first sub-aqueous tunnel under the Thames, a task which took nearly twenty years. By the end of the century two engineers, Peter Barlow and James Henry Greathead had developed a more sophisticated machine, first used to dig another subway under the Thames.

By the 1890s short stretches of underground railway had been tunnelled under the Thames south from the City of London but the subsequent rapid world-wide growth was due to two Americans Charles Tyson Yerkes and Frank Sprague. Yerkes, a dubious 'public utilities' entrepreneur, monopolised the electric traction companies running the elevated railways in Chicago but had fled, first to New York and then to London where he combined all the struggling underground railway companies – the first of which, the City and South London had been completed in 1890 – built a power station and was responsible for the first stretches of London's four major historic deep level lines, the Central, Piccadilly, Northern and Bakerloo, fortunately dying before he could exploit the passengers and the shareholders! These lines form the heart of their present network, were all operating before the outbreak of World War One. Unfortunately the tunnels were narrow and to this day the carriages have been smaller than those in other systems. It was Sprague, a former colleague of Thomas Edison who developed 'differential motors' which provided every carriage in a train with its own source of power which could be controlled by a single driver, thus obviating the need for locomotives and allowed trains to reverse without any problems at the end of the line.

In France the situation was complicated by the historic rivalry between Paris and the rest of the country that had culminated in the massacre of thousands of Parisians by soldiers from the national government in 1871 after the Franco-Prussian war. This hostility ensured that the tracks on the Paris Metro were laid to a different gauge to the country's main line system. It was designed and built as a whole covering only the city itself and ignoring the much-despised suburbs (the banlieues) until after 1945. It was dug by a cut and cover system improved by the great engineer responsible, the one-armed Fulgence Bienvenue, who also managed to lower the shell of entire stations into the muddy banks of the Seine.

In New York after many delays a Rapid Transit Commission was appointed in 1894 and on May 24th 1900 the first spadeful was dug in a ceremony that involved fireworks consuming 100,000 tons of dynamite. The first contract, to build a line up the whole of the west side of Manhattan went to a brilliant contractor John B McDonald and to Parsons who foresaw correctly that 'The instant that this line is finished there will arise a demand for other lines'. Both in Paris and New York the entrances to the stations were delightfully decorated iron work – in Paris the variation of Art Nouveau was even called Style Metro – unhappily all New York's iron work 'kiosks' have disappeared and only a few have been preserved in Paris.

In the 1930s the Soviet Union boasted many of the largest investment projects of that unhappy decade. The biggest was the Moscow Metro. Work began in 1931 but progress was only possible when 'grouting', a chemical process, was developed for hardening the subsoil which was sometimes like a limestone sponge so that a tunnel could be driven through it. In charge was Stalin's toughest henchman Lazar Kaganovitch but the project was completed thanks to a young peasant Nikita Khrushchev, who had shown his capacity for effective slave-driving in completing the Moscow-Volga canal in his native Ukraine. He relied on imported tunnelling shields which he drove at speeds totally incompatible with safety – sometimes whole shifts of workers were crushed to death or drowned. Even so when the first line was opened in May 1935 it was six months late on the absurd timetable demanded by Stalin. As Benson Brobrick remarks* 'The Moscow Metro was a many-splendored thing. In the stations' spacious vestibules and along their lofty vaulted halls lights flashed and coruscated from carved crystal chandeliers of a magnificence not likely to be encountered in the capitalist world outside the mansions of the Vanderbilts and Astors.' By 1943 70,000 square metres of marble had been installed in the Metro's first 22 stations. There were mosaics, frescos, friezes, bas-reliefs, statues and stained glass windows aplenty celebrating past triumphs and more recent Soviet achievements.

By 1940 there were still only nineteen metro systems in the world but two decades after the war there were sixty six. Since then the number of cites involved has increased dramatically. By the end of the century barely a single major city outside the United States lacked some form of subway/metro/tube with no fewer than 190 systems in 54 countries from Armenia to North Korea. Today dozens more systems are being built – or at least being planned with twelve in China alone – and that's not counting the overgrounds and the tramways! Which all goes to show that steel wheel on steel rail is still alive, flourishing – and innovative – as it approaches to within a decade of its 200th anniversary.

* *Labyrinths of Iron* Newsweek Books 1981

ACKNOWLEDGMENTS

I was first given the chance to write about railways at any length in the summer of 1985 when Andrew Knight, the editor of *The Economist*, and Gordon Lee, the Surveys Editor, encouraged me to write a long survey called 'Return Train', analysing the railways' comeback. I was particularly grateful for their backing since my findings challenged the paper's previous ideas on the subject.

But the ideas I generated would not have been transformed into a full-length book without my agent Robert Ducas, who provided the ideal mixture of encouragement, support and discipline: Chris Holifield, then the editorial director of The Bodley Head, who forced me to think through my originally rather vague ideas into something approaching cohesion; and her successor, Jill Black, who deployed the same mixture of tact, firmness, professionalism and charm in wrestling with my sprawling manuscript. Peter Dyer designed a superb jacket which expressed my ideas far more imaginatively than I could have done, and Sarah Heneghan managed to find some splendid photographs in a ridiculously short time.

All my friends seemed to know more about the subject than I did, a superiority which I welcomed, partly because it was often true, but also because it showed that I was writing about an interesting subject. The actual research was carried out in a few key libraries: those model institutions the Library of Congress and the London Library as well as the Bodleian and the British Libraries, where the devoted staffs were clearly struggling with inadequate resources.

N.F.
Oxford, Talmont, Holloway

BIBLIOGRAPHY

The number of books I could have consulted is virtually limitless. In this note I have confined myself to the more important sources. I have divided them into the general historical works whose authors appreciated the railways' importance and more specialist 'railway works', mostly by authors who showed some understanding of the world beyond the footplate. I have omitted works quoted directly in the notes.

GENERAL HISTORIES

Blainey, Geoffrey, *The Tyranny of Distance* (Melbourne 1962)

Carr, Raymond, *Spain 1808–1939* (Oxford 1966)

Carosso, Vincent, *Investment Banking in America* (Boston 1970)

Les Chemins de Fer Suisses après un siècle (Bern 1949–67)

Giedion, Siegfried, *Mechanization Takes Command* (New York 1948)

Gross, Nahum, *Austro-Hungary in the world economy* (Jerusalem)

Henderson, W. O., *The State and the Industrial Revolution in Prussia* (London 1958)

Hobsbawm, Eric, *The Age of Capital 1848–1878* (London 1975)

——*The Age of Empire* (London 1987)

Klingender, Francis D., *Art & the Industrial Revolution* (London 1968)

Landes, David S., *The Unbound Prometheus* (Cambridge 1969)

Macartney, C. A., *The Hapsburg Empire 1790–1918* (London 1969)

Marx, Leo, *The Machine in the Garden; Technology and the Pastoral Ideal in America* (New York 1964)

Mumford, Lewis, *Technics & Civilisation* (London 1934)

——*The Culture of Cities* (London 1938)

——*The City in History* (London 1961)

Poppino, Rollie E., *Brazil, the Land and the People* (New York 1973)

Price, Roger, *The Modernisation of Rural France* (London 1983)

Scobie, James R., *Revolution on the Pampas* (Austin, Texas 1964)

——*Argentina, A City and a Nation* (Oxford 1971)

Stern, Fritz, *Gold and Iron* (London 1977)

Weber, Eugen, *Peasants into Frenchmen* (London 1977)

Woodruff, William, *The Impact of Western Man* (London 1966)

A HANDFUL OF SPECIFICALLY RAILWAY BOOKS WERE PARTICULARLY HELPFUL:

Baroli, Marc, *Le Train dans la Littérature Française* (Paris 1969)

Berton, Pierre, *The Impossible Railway* (New York 1972)

——*The Promised Land, Settling the West 1896–1914* (Toronto 1984)

Coleman, Terry, *The Railway Navvies* (London 1965)

Holbrook, Stewart H., *The Story of American Railroads* (New York 1947)

Huenemann, R. W., *The Dragon & the Iron Horse, the Economics of Railroads in China 1876–1937* (Cambridge, Mass. 1984)

Kellett, John R., *The Impact of Railways on Victorian Cities* (London 1969)

Klein, Maury, *History of the Louisville & Nashville Railroad* (New York 1972)

——*The Life and Legend of Jay Gould* (Baltimore 1986)

——*Union Pacific* (Baltimore 1987)

Miller, Charles, *Lunatic Express* (London 1971)

Richards, Jeffry & Mackenzie, John M., *The Railway Station, a Social* History (Oxford 1986)

Robbins, Michael, *The Railway Age* (London 1962)

Schievelbusch, Wolfgang, *The Railway Journey, The Industrialization of Time and Space in the 19th century* (Berkeley 1969)

Simmons, Jack, *The Railway in Town and Country 1830–1914* (Newton Abbot 1986)

Stover, John F., *Life & Decline of the American Railroad* (Oxford 1970)

Theroux, Paul, *The Great Patagonian Express* (London 1980)

——*Riding the Iron Rooster* (London 1988)

Tupper, Harmon, *To the Great Ocean* (London 1965)

Ward, James A., *Railroads and the Character of America 1820–1887* (Knoxville, Tenn. 1986)

Westwood, J. N., *A History of Russian Railways* (London 1964)

Williams, John Hoyt, *A Great and Shining Road* (New York 1988)

OTHER GENERAL RAILWAY BOOKS

Andrews, Cyril B., *The Railway Age* (London 1937)

Arnautovic, Dragomir, *Histoire des Chemins de Fer Yugoslaves* (Paris 1937)

Bagwell, Philip, *The Transport Revolution from 1770* (London 1974)

Berghaus, Erwin, *The History of Railways* (London 1964)

Blanchard, Marcel, *Geographie des Chemins de Fer* (Paris 1942)

Botkin, B. A. & Harlow, Alvin F., *A Treasury of Railroad Folklore* (New York 1953)

Caron, François, *Histoire de l'exploitation d'un grand réseau* (Paris 1973)

Carr, Samuel, *The Poetry of Railways* (London 1978)

Chandler, Alfred, *The Visible Hand* (Cambridge, Mass. 1977)

Clark, W. H., *The Story of Inland Transportation* (Boston 1939)

Cochran, Thomas, *Railroad Leaders, 1845–1890* (Cambridge, Mass. 1953)

Cohen, Norm, *Long Steel Rail, the railroad in American folklore* (Urbana, Illinois, 1981)

Currie, A. W., *Economy of Canadian transportation* (Toronto 1954)

——*Economic Geography of Canada* (Toronto 1945)

Dmitriev-Mamonov, *Guide to the Great Siberian Railway* (1900, reprinted Newton Abbot 1971)

Far, André de la, *Les chemins de fer dans la vie des hommes* (Paris 1972)

Fawcett, Brian, *Railways of the Andes* (London 1963)

Hopkins, Kenneth, *The Poetry of Railways* (London 1966)

Kalla-Bishop, P. M., *Italian Railways* (Newton Abbot 1971)

——*Hungarian Railways* (Newton Abbot 1973)

Kennedy, Ludovic, *A Book of Railway Journeys* (London 1981)

Kirkland, Edward, *Men, Cities & Transportation* (New York 1948)

——*Business in the Gilded Age* (Madison, Wisc. 1952)

Lamalle, Ulysse, *Histoire des Chemins de Fer Belges* (Brussels 1943)

BIBLIOGRAPHY

Legg, Stuart, *The Railway Book* (London 1952)

Lewis, Oscar, *The Big Four* (New York 1938)

Middlemas, R. K., *The Master Builders* (London 1963)

O'Dell, Charles, *Railways and Geography* (London 1956)

Overton, Richard, *Burlington West* (Cambridge, Mass. 1941)

Parry, Albert, *Whistler's Father* (New York 1939)

Perpillou, M., *Géographie de la Circulation* (Paris 1953)

Peyret, Henri, *Les Chemins de Fer en France et dans le monde* (Paris 1949)

Sandstrom, Gosta, *The History of Tunnelling* (London 1963)

Taylor, George R., *The Transportation Revolution 1815–1860* (New York 1951)

Vallance, H. A., *The railway enthusiast's bedside book* (London 1966)

Van Onselen, Lennox, *Head of Steel* (Cape Town 1962)

Walker, Charles, *Thomas Brassey, Railway builder* (London 1969)

Wheeler, Keith, *The Railroaders* (New York 1973)

Wright, M. C., (ed.), *China in Revolution* (New Haven 1968)

Yat-Sen, Sun, *The International Development of China*, 1922

NOTES

INTRODUCTION

1. *Victorian Studies*, Vol. 13, No. 1, September 1969
2. *The Age of Empire*
3. *The Old Patagonian Express*
4. *Civil Engineering and Architecture Journal.* My thanks to Judith Pearsall of the OED, who drew my attention to this article and to the article by Kurt Moller.

I THE FIRST IMPACT

1. L. T. C. Rolt, *George and Robert Stephenson*, (London 1960). See also the same author's *Isambard Kingdom Brunel* (London 1957) and *Victorian Engineering* (London 1970), a most impressive trio.
2. John Rowland, *George Stephenson, creator of Britain's railways* (London 1954)
3. Samuel Smiles, *Lives of the Engineers*, (London 1862)
4. op. cit. See also Asa Briggs, *Victorian Cities*, (London 1943)
5. John Francis, *A History of the English Railway*, (London 1851).
6. *Great British Stations*
7. *Railway Station Architecture*
8. M. C. Reed, *Investment in Railways in Britain*, (Oxford 1975)
9. Quoted by H. G. Lewin, *The Railway Mania and its aftermath*, (London 1936)
10. Richard S. Lambert, *The Railway King*, (London 1934)
11. Quoted by Lewin op. cit.
12. Francis op. cit.
13. *The Transportation Revolution, 1815–1860*
14. *The Age of Capital*
15. On William James, see the *Railway Magazine* Volume V, 1900

II THE HOPES AND FEARS OF ALL THE YEARS

1. *The Great Railway Bazaar*
2. *The Organisation Man*

403

3. *The Dickens World*

4. Nicholas Wood, *A Practical Treatise on Rail-Roads*, (London 1832)

5. *Mr Facey Romford's Hounds*

6. *Lives of the Engineers*, op. cit.

7. Letter to Lady Grey, February 1841

8. Quoted by Wolfgang Schievelbusch, *The Railway Journey*

9. Alan Trachtenberg in his introduction to Schievelbusch

10. Quoted by Schievelbusch, op. cit.

11. H. Perkin, *Age of the Railway*, (London 1971)

12. *Riding the Iron Rooster*

13. In his paper, 'La Dernière Mode', 1874

14. *Le Train dans la Littérature Française*

15. *For such a comparison see Peter Gay, The Bourgeois Experience, Victoria to Freud*, Vol. ii, p. 320 (Oxford 1986)

16. *Riding the Iron Rooster*

17. *Charles Dickens, Resurrectionist*

18. I owe this reference to Professor Marilyn Butler

19. See Marc Baroli op. cit., and Peter Gay, *The Tender Passion*

20. Louis Armand, 'Le Chemin de fer dans l'Art' (Introduction to Catalogue of 1956 exhibition in Geneva)

21. Gareth Rees, *Early Railway Prints*, (Oxford 1980)

22. John Rewald, *The History of Impressionism*, (London 1973)

23. C. Hamilton Ellis, *Railway Art*, (London 1977)

24. *Prose Works of William Wordsworth* vol. iii

25. Christopher Taylor, *Portrait of Windermere*, (London 1983)

26. *Ruskin, Works*, ed. E. T. Cook and Alexander Wedderburn

27. R. S. Joby, *The Railway Builders*, (Newton Abbot 1983)

28. Florence Emily Hardy, *The Early Life of Thomas Hardy*, (London 1928)

III RAILPOLITIK

1. Ms Antonia Byatt kindly referred me to the entry in Michelet's Journal

2. Quoted by Henri Pirenne, *Histoire de Belgique*, vol. vi

3. Klaus Harder, *Environmental Factors of Early Railroads*, (New York 1981)

4. Fritz Stern, *Gold and Iron*

5. Quoted in *Les Chemins de Fer Suisses après un siècle*

6. E. Bonjour, H. S. Offler & G. R. Potter, *A Short History of Switzerland*, (Oxford 1952)

7. See David Landes, *Bankers and Pashas*, (London 1956)

8. Sir Arnold Wilson, *Persia*, (London 1932)

9. William Fleming, *Regional*

development and transportation in Argentina, (London 1987)

10. George P. T. Glazebrook, *A History of Transportation in Canada*, (Toronto 1938)

11. Quoted in G. R. Stevens, *Canadian National Railways*, (Toronto 1960)

12. A. W. Currie, *The Grand Trunk Railway of Canada*, (Toronto 1957)

13. Quoted by G. R. Stevens op. cit.

14. *Railroads and the Character of America 1820–1887*, also the source of the quotes in the following paragraph

15. Quoted by Leo Marx, *The Machine in the Garden*

16. See Eugen Weber, *Peasants into Frenchmen*

17. Klaus Harder, op. cit.

18. Clive Trebilcock, *The Industrialisation of the Continental Powers*, (London 1981)

19. Paul Wallace Gates, *The Illinois Central and its Colonisation work*, (Cambridge, Mass. 1934)

20. Pierre Berton, *The Promised Land*

21. Geoffrey Alderman, *The Railway Interest*, (Leicester 1963)

22. G. R. Stevens op. cit.

23. Quoted in Alfred Chandler, *Railroads, the nation's first big business*, (New York 1965)

24. Gabriel Kolko, *Railroads and Regulation*, (Princeton 1965)

See also:
Haney, L. H., *A Congressional History of Railways in the United States*, (Madison, Wisc. 1910)
Nelson, James C., *Railroad Transportation & Public Policy*, (Washington 1959)
Newcomb, R. *The work of the ICC*, (New York 1981)

25. Jean Autin, *Les Frères Pereire* (Paris 1984)

26. *History of the Louisville & Nashville Railroad.*
See also:
Hood, Fred, *Kentucky, Its history and heritage*, (St Louis 1978)

27. James Marshall, *Santa Fe, The Railroad that built an Empire*

28. *The Making of the President, 1968*
See also:
Bouvier, J., *La 'grande crise' des compagnies ferroviares Suisses*, (Annales, Paris 1956)
Buck, Solon Justus, *The Granger Movement*, (Cambridge, Mass. 1913)
Miller, George H., *Railroads and the Granger Laws*, (Madison, Wisc. 1971)
Parris, H., *Government and the Railways in 19th-century Britain*, (London 1965)
Starr, John W., *Lincoln & the Railroads*, (New York 1927)

Stryker, Lloyd Paul, *Andrew Johnson*, (New York 1929)

IV CAPITALISM, CAPITALISTS – AND CONTRACTORS

1. 'Railway Morals and Railway Policy', *Edinburgh Review*, 1854
2. Quoted by Lawrence Popplewell, *Bournemouth Railway History: an exposure of Victorian engineering fraud*, (Sherborne 1974)
3. *Edinburgh Review*, op. cit.
4. Berton, *The Promised Land*, op. cit.
5. Berton op. cit.
6. *Louisville & Nashville Railroad*, op. cit.
7. *Railroads and the Character of America*, op. cit.
8. Quoted by Marshall, op. cit.
9. Sir Henry Peto, *Sir Samuel Morton Peto*, (Private 1893)
10. Dorothy Adler, *British Investment in American Railways*, (Charlottesville, Va. 1976)
11. Edward Chase Kirkland, *Charles Francis Adams; the Patrician at Bay*, (Cambridge, Mass. 1965)

V THE ECONOMY OF RAIL

1. *Journal of Economic History*, 1974
2. R. W. Fogel, *Railroads and American Economic Growth*, (Baltimore 1964)
3. *Journal of Transport History*, March 1983
4. Stanley Libergott, *The Americans, an Economic Record*, (New York 1984)
5. *The Age of Capital*
6. Patrick O'Brien, *The New Economic History of Railways*, (London 1977)
7. Peter Lyaschenko, *History of the National Economy of Russia*, (New York 1949)
8. Libergott op. cit.
9. Lionel Wiener, *Les Chemins de Fer Coloniaux en Afrique*, (Brussels 1930)
10. Currie op. cit.
11. Bruce Mazlish, *The Railroad and the Space Program, An Exploration in Historical Analogy*, (Cambridge, Mass. 1965)
12. *Transactions of the Illinois Department of Agriculture*, quoted by Libergott, op. cit.
13. Quoted by R. W. Huenemann, *The Dragon & The Iron Horse*
14. John Moody, *The Railroad Builders*, (New Haven 1920)
15. R. S. Joby, *The Railway Builders*, op. cit.
16. Rayner Fremdling, 'Railroads & German Economic Growth', *Journal of Economic History*, vol. 37, 1977
17. Richard Graham, *Britain and the onset of modernization in Brazil 1850–1914*, (Cambridge 1968)

18. Fleming op. cit.
19. *A History of Russian Railways*, op. cit.
20. George Lynch, quoted by Donald Treadgold, *The Great Siberian Migration*, (Princeton 1937)
21. Gates op. cit.
22. Albert Fishlow, *American Railroads and the ante-bellum economy*, (Cambridge, Mass. 1965). Fishlow's name is often bracketed with that of R. Fogel, but Professor Fishlow's judgments are far more balanced.
23. James B. Hedges, *The federal land subsidy policy of Canada* (Cambridge, Mass. 1934)
See also:
Beard, Henry, *The Railways and the US Land Office*, (New York 1889)
Henry, Robert S., 'The railroad grant legend' (*Mississippi Valley History Review*, vol. 32, Sep., 1945)
24. A. S. Morton, *History of Prairie Settlement*, (Toronto 1938)
25. Quoted by Dee Brown, *Hear that Lonesome Whistle Blow*, (London 1977)
26. *Peasants into Frenchmen*
27. Quoted in Maury Klein, *History of the Louisville & Nashville Railroad*
28. Rayner Fremdling, *Journal of*
Economic History, Vol. 37, September 1977
29. Quoted in G. R. Hawke, *Railways and Economic Growth in England 1840–1870*, (Oxford 1970)
30. Rondo Cameron, *France and the Economic Development of Europe*, (Princeton 1961)
31. *Railroads, the nation's first big business*, op. cit.
32. Richard Perren, *The Meat Trade in Britain 1840–1914*, (London 1978)
33. Emilio Viotto da Costa, *The Brazilian Empire*, (Chicago 1986)
34. Fleming op. cit.
See also:
Blanchard, Marcel, *Essais historiques sur les premiers chemins de fer Languedociens*, (Montpellier 1935)
Henderson, W. O., *The Industrial Revolution on the Continent*, (London 1961)
Jackman, W. T., *The Development of Transport in Modern England*, (Cambridge 1916)
Metzer, Jacob, *Railroad Development and Market Integration*, (Chicago 1973)
O'Brien, Patrick, *Railways and the development of Western Europe*, (London 1983)
Pounds, Norman, *The Ruhr*, (London 1952)

Reed, M. C., *Railways in the Victorian Economy*, (Newton Abbot 1969)

VI IMPERIAL RAILWAYS

1. *The Age of Capital*
2. Quoted by Graham, op. cit.
3. Bell, Horace, *Railway policy in India*, (London 1894)
4. See Antonio Gomez Mendoza in his 1981 Oxford PhD thesis, 'Railways and Spanish Economic Growth in the late 19th century'
5. See Fritz Stern, *Gold and Iron*, op. cit.
6. See Popplewell, op. cit.
7. See Adler, op. cit.
8. *The Railway Revolution in Mexico*
9. Delmer Ross, *Visionaries & Swindlers*, (Mobile, Ala. 1975)
10. H. S. Ferns, *Britain & Argentina in the 19th century*, (Oxford 1960)
11. Stacy May and Galo Plaza, *The United Fruit Company in Latin America*, (New York 1958)
12. Delmer Ross, *Rails across Costa Rica*, (Mobile, Ala. 1976)
13. *The Dragon* and *The Iron Horse*, op. cit.
14. According to Herbert Feis, *Europe, the world's banker* (New York 1931), the British accounted for a quarter of the total.
15. Ferns op. cit.
16. Watts Stewart, *Henry Meiggs, Yankee Pissarro*, (New York 1946)
17. Charles David Kepner, Jnr, *The Banana Empire; a case study of economic imperialism*, (New York 1973)
    See also:
    John Keith Hatch, *Minor C. Keith, Pioneer of the American Tropics*, (Private, Mckean, Virginia 1963)
18. Compagnie Générale pour l'Exploitation des Chemins de Fer de Turquie d'Europe.
    See also:
    Kurt Grunwald, *Turkenhirsch*, (Jerusalem 1966)
    A. du Velay, *Essai sur l'histoire financière de la Turquie*, (Paris 1903)
19. *Ferdinand de Lesseps, a biographical study*
20. George Kennan (not the diplomat), *E. H. Harriman* (Boston 1922)
21. Delmer Ross, *Visionaries* and *Swindlers*, op. cit.
22. E. M. Earle, *The Great Powers & the Bagdad Railway*, (London 1923)
    See also:
    Chereadame, A., *Le chemin de fer de Bagdad*, (Paris 1903)
23. Earle op. cit.
    See also:
    Baur, J. C., *La mise en valeur de*

l'AOF Ferroviare
Decharme, Pierre, *Les chemins de fer dans les Colonies Allemandes*, (Paris 1903)
Maignan, André, *L'achèvement du Transindochinois*, (Paris 1935)
On international financial markets see also:
Bouvier, Jean, *Le Krach de l'Union Générale*, (Paris 1960)
Gille, Bertrand, *La banque en France au 19e*, (Geneva 1908)
——*Les investissements Français en Italie*, (Turin 1970)
Hidy, Muriel, *George Peabody, merchant and financier* (New York 1978)
Jackson, W. T., *The Enterprising Scot*, (Edinburgh 1968)
Jenks, Leland, *The migration of British capital to 1875*
Kindleberger, Charles A., *Financial History of Western Europe*, (London 1984)
Levy-Leboyer, M., (ed.), *La Position Internationale de la France*, (Paris 1977)
Myers, Margaret G., *Paris as a Financial Centre*, (London 1936)
Ziegler, Philip, *The Sixth Great Power*, (London 1988)

VII THE ARMIES OF STEAM – AND THEIR BATTLEFIELDS

1. Quoted by W. Stewart, op. cit.
2. Gosta Sandstrom, *A History of Tunnelling*
3. Frederick Talbott, *The Railway Conquest of the World*, (London 1911)
4. Joseph Schott, *Rails across Panama*, (Indianapolis 1967)
5. Pierre Berton, *The Impossible Railway*, op. cit.
6. For a full description, see John Hoyt Williams, *A Great and Shining Road*
7. Harmon Tupper, *To The Great Ocean*
8. Williams op. cit.
9. A. J. Purkis, *The Politics, Capital and Labour of Railway Building in Cape Colony*
10. G. R. Stevens, *Canadian National Railways*
11. Quoted by Terry Coleman, *The Railway Navvies*
12. Quoted by John Keith Hatch, *Minor C. Keith*, op. cit.
13. Lennox van Osselen, *Head of Steel*
14. Stewart Holbrook, *The Story of American Railroads*
15. Sandstrom op. cit.
16. Schott op. cit.
17. Frank Mckenna, *The Railway Workers 1840–1970*, (London 1980)
18. *Railways in the Andes*
19. Walter Licht, *Working for the Railroad*, (Princeton 1983)
20. Yaqub Karkar, *Railway Development in the Ottoman Empire*, (New York 1972)

21. J. N. Westwood, *Railways of India*

22. Quoted in Richards & Mackenzie, *The Railway Station, A Social History*

23. Stewart Holbrook, *The Story of American Railroads*

24. O. S. Nock, *Historic Railway Disasters*, (London 1966)

25. François Caron, *Histoire de l'Exploitation d'un Grand Réseau*

26. Richards & Mackenzie, op. cit.

27. J. N. Westwood, *A History of Russian Railways*

28. Samuel O. Dunn, *Government Ownership of Railways*, (New York 1913)

29. Robert Bruce, *1877 Year of Violence*, (New York 1959)

30. Henry Reichman, *Railwaymen and Revolution*, (Berkeley 1987)

31. B. A. Botkin and Alvin Harlow, *A Treasury of American Folklore* See also:
Brooke, David, *The Railway Navvy*, (Newton Abbot 1983)
Kingsford, Peter, *Victorian Railwaymen*, (London 1970)
Schneider, Ascario, *Railways through the Mountains of Europe*, (London 1967)

VIII SOCIETY ON THE MOVE

1. J. A. R. Pimlott, *The Englishman's Holiday*, (London 1947)

2. Quoted in *Lost Pleasures of the Great Trains*

3. Albert Parry, *Whistler's Father*

4. Everett Lloyd, *Law West of the Pecos; the story of Judge Roy Bean*

5. Quoted by Charles Wilson, *First with the News*, (London 1985)

6. Jean Mister, *La Librairie Hachette de 1826 à nos jours*, (Paris 1964)

7. Report of Captain Tyler, Parliamentary Papers

8. Holbrook op. cit.

9. R. Whitbread, *The Railway Policeman*, (London 1961)

10. For a full analysis of the psycho-pathological consequences of railway disasters, see Schievelbusch, op. cit., pp. 134–145

11. *Long Steel Rail – the Railroad in American Folksong*

12. Tom Parkinson and Charles Philip Fox, *The Circus Moves by Rail*

13. Jean-Claude Toutain, *La consommation alimentaire en France de 1789–1964*, (Geneva 1971)

14. Westwood op. cit.

15. Eleuthere Eléfteriades, *Les Chemins de Fer en Syrie et au Liban*, (Beirut 1944)

16. Jack Simmons, *Railways in Town and Country*

17. *They Broke the Prairie*

18. Edmund Swinglehurst, *The*

Romantic Journey, (London 1974)

19. C. R. Fay, *Palace of Industry – a study of the Great Exhibition and its fruits*, (Cambridge 1951)

20. John K. Walton, *The English Seaside Resort, a social history*, (Leicester 1983)

21. 'Winter and Spring on the Shore of the Mediterranean', quoted by P. Howarth, *When the Riviera was Ours*, (London 1977)

22. Howarth op. cit.

23. Raymond Carr, *English Fox Hunting*, (London 1976)

24. Quoted in Stuart Legg, *The Railway Book*

25. Quoted in Jean Autin, *Les Frères Pereire*

26. David Leon Chandler, *Henry Flagler*
    See also:
    Annales, *Food & Drink in history*, (Paris 1970)
    Barker, T. C., *Our Changing Fare*, (London 1966)
    Barsley, Michael, *Orient Express*, (London 1966)
    Bartky, Ian B., 'The invention of Railroad Time' (Railroad History no 148, spring 1983)
    Billet, B., *Lourdes, Documents authentiques*, (Paris 1966)
    Cookridge, E. H., *Orient Express*, (London 1979)
    Cummings, R. O., *The American and his food*, (New York 1941)

——*The American Ice Harvests*, (Berkeley 1949)

Dron, Jean-Paul, *Essai sur la sensibilité alimentaire à Paris*, (Paris 1962)

Forster, E. & R., *European diet from pre-industrial to modern times*, (New York 1973)

Morgan, Bryan, *Express Journey*, (London 1964)

Musgrave, Clifford, *Life in Brighton*, (Eastbourne 1981)

Sutton, Felix, *Master of Ballyhoo*, (New York 1968)

Tannahill, Reay, *Food in History*, (St Albans 1975)

Waller, George, *Saratoga*, (Englewood Cliffs 1966)

IX RAILWAY IN TOWN AND CITY

1. R. N. Taaffe, *Rail Transportation and the economic development of Soviet Central Asia*, (Chicago 1960)

2. Weber, *Peasants into Frenchmen*, op. cit.

3. See Popplewell, *Bournemouth Railway History*, op. cit.

4. A. W. Currie, *The Grand Trunk Railway of Canada*

5. Charles Glaab, *Kansas City and the railroads*, (Madison, Wisc. 1962)

6. Harold M. Mayer and R. C. Wade, *Chicago; the growth of a metropolis*, (Chicago 1969)

7. Quoted by J. M. Russell in *Atlanta, 1837–1890*

8. Berton, *The Promised Land*, op. cit.

9. Paul Theroux, *Riding the Iron Rooster*, op. cit.

10. Marshall, *Santa Fe, the railroad that built an Empire*, op. cit.

11. Quoted by Christian Barman, *An Introduction to Railway Architecture*, (London 1950)

12. See particularly Richards and Mackenzie, op. cit.

13. Carroll Meeks, *The Railway Station, an architectural history*, (New Haven 1957)
    See also:
    Biddle, Gordon, *Great Railway Stations of Britain*, (Newton Abbot 1986)
    Hartscough, Mildred, 'Transportation & the Twin Cities', (*Minnesota Historical Bulletin*, Sep. 1926)
    Thompson, F. M. L., *The rise of suburbia*, (Leicester 1982)

X WAR ON THE RAILS

1. Albert Parry, *Whistler's Father*

2. Dennis Showalter, *Railroads and Rifles*, (Hamden 1976)

3. Martin Van Crefeld, *Supplying war, logistics from Wallenstein to Patton*, (Cambridge 1977) – a most stimulating book

4. Thomas Weber, *The Northern Railroads during the Civil War*, (New York 1952)

5. Quoted by William McElwee, *The Art of War: Waterloo to Mons*, (London 1974)

6. Thomas Pakenham, *The Boer War*
   See also:
   Curzon, George Nathaniel, *Russia in Central Asia*, (London 1889)
   Liddell Hart, Basil, *Sherman, soldier, realist, American*, (New York 1929)
   Mcpherson, James M., *Battle Cry of Freedom*, (Oxford 1988)
   Nevins, Allan, *The War for the Union*, (New York 1959)
   Turner, George Edgar, *Victory rode the rails*, (Indianapolis 1953)

INDEX